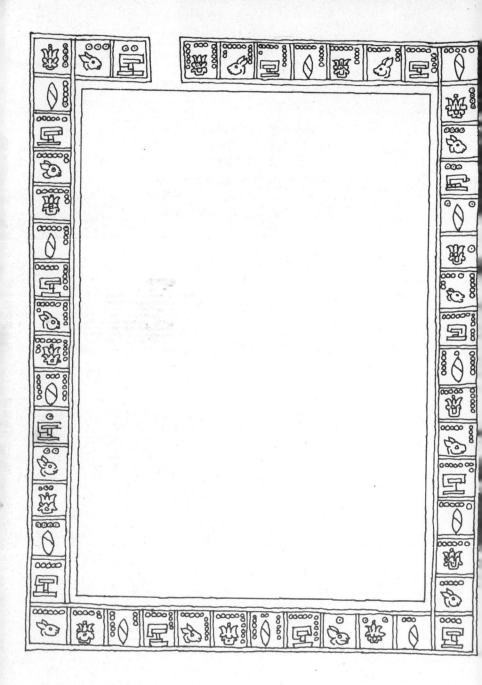

THE AZTECS

A HISTORY

NIGEL DAVIES

University of Oklahoma Press : Norman and London

By Nigel Davies

Los Señoríos Independientes del Imperio Azteca

Los Mexica: Primeros Pasos Hacia el Imperio

The Toltecs: Until the Fall of Tula

The Toltec Heritage: From the Fall of Tula
Until the Rise of Tenochtitlán

The Aztecs: A History

Extracts from THE BERNAL DIAZ CHRONICLES translated
and edited by Albert Idell, New York 1956 are reprinted by permission of the Barthold Fles Literary Agency.

Library of Congress Cataloging in Publication Data

Davies, Nigel, 1920-
  The Aztecs, a history.

    Reprint of the ed. published by Macmillan, Lon-
  don.
  Bibliography: p.
  Includes index.
    1. Aztecs—History.   I. Title.
  F1219.D276   1980   972'.01   80-12141
  ISBN: 0-8061-1691-9

Copyright © 1973 by Nigel Davies.
First published 1973 by Macmillan London Ltd.
All rights reserved.
First published 1980 by the University of Oklahoma Press,
Publishing Division of the University, Norman;
second printing, 1982; third printing, 1986;
fourth printing, 1989.

5   6   7   8   9   10   11   12   13   14   15   16   17   18   19

To
Fanny Vernon

CONTENTS

ILLUSTRATIONS

All photographs are by Sonya de la Rozière.

Following page 34:

The Mexica leaving Azatlan, from the *Codex Boturini*.

A Spanish depiction of the journey of the Mexica, from Herrera's *History*.

The Foundation of Tenochtitlan, from the *Codex Mendoza*.

The goddess Coatlicue (*Museo Nacional de Antropología*, Mexico City).

The Tepozteco.

Ehécatl, god of wind (*Museo Nacional de Antropología*).

The Quetzalcoatl Pyramid.

Coyolxauhqui, sister of Huitzilopochtli (*Museo Nacional de Antropología*).

The Pyramid of Tenayuca; the wall of serpents.

Tenayuca, closeup of a serpent.

Acamapichtli.

Moctezuma I receives the crown from Nezahualcóyotl.

A seated Macehual (*Museo Nacional de Antropología*).

The glyph of Ahuítzotl, the great conqueror (*Museo Nacional de Antropología*).

Macuilxóchitl, god of music (*Museo Nacional de Antropología*).

A Spanish view of Tenochtitlan, from *The History of the Conquest of Mexico by the Spaniards*, Antonio de Solis.

Following page 232:

Tlatelolco, with the pyramid in the foreground.

A closeup of part of Tízoc's Stone (*Museo Nacional de Antropología*).

Malinalco—a jaguar.

Conversation between a jaguar and an eagle (*Museo Nacional de Antropología*).

A model of the main temple (*Museo Nacional de Antropología*).

A view of Tenochtitlan (*Museo Nacional de Antropología*).
Plan of Tenochtitlan, traditionally attributed to Cortés.
Scenes of Aztec life (*Codex Mendoza*).
The Spaniards approach the coast (*Codex Durán*).
The Butchery of Cholula (*Lienzo de Tlaxcala*).
The meeting between Moctezuma II and Cortés (*Lienzo de Tlaxcala*).
The Spaniards leave the city (*Codex Durán*).
The 'Aperriamento'.

LINE ILLUSTRATIONS

Nos. 1, 3, 4, 6, 7, 8, 9, redrawn by Sally Clare

MAPS

ACKNOWLEDGMENTS

I would like to express my gratitude to all those who have helped me in the preparation of this book, and in particular to the late Dr. Paul Kirchhoff, Professor Wigberto Jiménez Moreno, Professor Alfredo Lopez Austin, and Mrs. Thelma Sullivan. I owe a special debt to Sonya de la Rozière whose photographs adorn the book.

INTRODUCTION

THIS BOOK IS intended to give the history in broad terms of a remarkable people who, like their Peruvian contemporaries the Incas, rose to prominence only in the last period before the Spanish conquest.

It is a dramatic story, concerning a rather wretched little group of late immigrants into the Valley of Mexico, who finally, after many mishaps, settled on two tiny islands in the lagoon and then proceeded to overcome all their proud neighbours. In a matter of decades they extended their city until it was larger than any in Europe, and their empire until it reached the shores of the two oceans.

When I first visited Mexico many years ago, like so many others I was astonished at the wealth, beauty and variety of the monuments that bore silent witness to its great pre-hispanic past. It seemed to me quite extraordinary that people at that time entirely separated from the remainder of mankind should have created civilizations that rivalled those of the Old World, with which I was already acquainted.

I became even more enthralled by the fact that, at least for the more recent of these ceremonial centres, historical records existed as detailed and personal as for many of the ruins of other and more familiar regions. Moreover, it was intensely revealing to find that, although these people were as remote from contemporary Europe and Asia as if they had lived upon the moon, in thought and deed they were not so totally different.

In the course of subsequent studies and investigations, what struck me most forcibly was the yawning gulf which divided the visitor to Mexico from any contact with the known history of the region, simply because this was not made available in any accessible form. It is, of course, true that the works of certain chroniclers can be bought, and some are even translated into English. They tend, however, to seem diffuse and even tedious without the help of additional knowledge, only to be acquired in libraries that specialize in such matters.

On the one hand, therefore, streams of visitors will devote endless time and effort to reaching far-off archaeological sites, without even being aware that, directly or indirectly, they can be related to history, in the normal sense of the word. Moreover, I have continually found during my life in Mexico that people who are not strictly speaking professionals, but who have become deeply interested and well informed as to other aspects of ancient Mexican culture, such as art or architecture, will not even have heard of the existence of, say, the Tepanecs, an important and historic people; these, as we shall see, taught the Aztecs the art of empire-building!

Much has, in fact, been written about the Aztecs, or Mexica; but such studies principally concern their religious and social organization. In addition, such aspects as trade, war, arms, mode of dress, and even eating and drinking habits have received due attention.

Little, however, has been published in recent times on their political history – that is to say, on the deeds that were done – and on the men, whether heroes or villains, who performed them. It is this gap which I wish to try to fill in the present book.

At a time when Mexico is assuming an increasingly prominent place in the modern world, and when the general interest in pre-Columbian peoples is daily growing, it would appear to be a worthwhile task to present a historical picture of what actually happened in the last centuries before the coming of the Spaniards, when the existing cultures suffered a sudden eclipse, such as had never befallen any other civilization.

In reality, the time of the Aztec Empire, and perhaps the century which preceded its formation, constitutes the only part of ancient Mexican history for which detailed information as to events and personalities is available.

It is, of course, true that the science of modern archaeology has revealed or confirmed the existence of other higher civilizations in Mexico long before the Aztecs – starting with the Olmecs in the first millennium B.C. and ending with the Toltecs around the tenth and eleventh centuries A.D. – who did form large spheres of cultural and possibly military influence. However, owing to lack of written records, the exact extent and nature of their sway is hard to determine. Even our knowledge of Toltec history is mainly limited to their period of decline and fall. Accordingly, among the dominant peoples of Mexico it is only about the last, the Aztecs, that a true history, in the accepted sense of the word, can be written.

In ancient Mexico, however, changes came about very slowly. As in Mesopotamia, empire succeeded empire, and the Aztec period should simply be regarded as the last act in a long drama. In many respects they were imitators rather than initiators. Just as many Toltec practices can now be traced back to previous civilizations, so also much that is often considered as typically Aztec really derives from these Toltecs. And in many respects the Toltec and Aztec cultures themselves are only variations on a theme already established in the first centuries of our era in the vast metropolis of Teotihuacan, whose awe-inspiring monuments still survive near the city of Mexico, and whose cultural influence stretched into distant Guatemala, which even the Aztecs barely penetrated.

The actual term 'Aztec' is apt to confuse. Originally in their own language there existed the terms *Azteca* or *Aztlaneca* – the name deriving from their traditional place of origin, Aztlan. They were subsequently renamed by the fiat of their patron god, and became known as *Mexica* (pronounced 'Mesheeka'); from this appellation comes the modern 'Mexican' and 'Mexico'.

When the Spaniards arrived, the people concerned do not appear to have referred to themselves as 'Aztecs', and earlier chroniclers do not usually employ this term. It was not until the eighteenth century that the term 'Aztec' was brought into more frequent use by the historian Clavijero; in particular, he wrote of the 'Aztec Empire', and as such it has subsequently come to be known.

The term 'Aztec' has really become an indispensable convention, for want of a better one. This is because the term 'Mexica' or 'Mexican' is the name of only one of several peoples who conquered the Empire. The latter is best, therefore, referred to as 'Aztec', in accordance with the established custom.

As regards the Mexica, who were in fact the backbone of the Empire, it is preferable, at the risk of appearing pedantic, to describe them as 'Mexica' rather than as 'Mexicans'. This latter, or hispanized, version is confusing, since the term has subsequently come to embrace all the inhabitants of modern Mexico, relatively few of whom are, strictly speaking, descended from the original Mexica.

It may be helpful to add a few words on the available sources of information, fortunately rich and abundant. Broadly speaking, they are of two kinds: the first consists of the pictorial records known as codices, painted on native paper and folding like screens. Codices relating to historical events in the Valley of Mexico are relatively few in number, and are themselves post-conquest copies of original manuscripts.

The second category is formed by books written in roman script after the Conquest, either in Spanish or in the native Nahuatl, widely used in central Mexico. Such material, based both on previous codices and on oral traditions, is full and varied: in this respect, we are deeply indebted to the early Spanish friars and their Indian pupils.

But, excellent as these written sources are, the information which they provide is often contradictory and hard to unravel. Since this work is intended for the general reader, I have tried to generalize and simplify as far as is humanly possible what is really a complex piece of political history. In certain aspects, such as the complicated questions of chronology, the results of previous investigations have been condensed for the purpose of this book. Readers who wish to pursue the subject further will find the bibliography and notes useful.

Naturally, in addition to the written sources, for certain parts of our story some archaeological evidence is of assistance. However, the Spaniards tended to destroy as works of the devil the ceremonial centres still functioning at the time of their arrival; many of their own churches and monasteries, such as Santiago de Tlatelolco, were built of the very stones of the former pyramids, and on approximately the same sites. Accordingly, many of the surviving monuments which are visible today are very much older than the Aztec period. It demands an effort of imagination on the part of the modern visitor to realize that he is separated from the time of the Aztecs by fewer centuries than those which divide the latter from some of the greatest vestiges of the Mexican past.

The emphasis of this book is on the last period before the Conquest. It will give me the greatest satisfaction if it can serve to place this period in its historical perspective and perhaps, if only to a modest degree, add to our general understanding of the peoples of ancient Mexico.

N.D.

A CHRONOLOGY
OF PRINCIPAL
EVENTS

THE DIFFICULTIES ENCOUNTERED in arriving at an exact chronology are considerable. Most of the later dates are reasonably certain, but some of the earliest ones are much less sure, and what seems the most probable figure has been given, in the light of the author's own investigations and those of others.

A.D.

1111	The Mexica leave Aztlan
1163	New Fire celebration by the Mexica in Coatepec
1168	Final fall of the Toltec capital of Tula
1215	New Fire celebration by the Mexica in Apaxco
1267	New Fire celebration by the Mexica in Tecpayocan
1299	The Mexica reach Chapultepec
1319	The Mexica expelled from Chapultepec
1343	The Mexica escape from Culhuacan
1345	Foundation of Tenochtitlan
1358	Foundation of Tlatelolco
1371	Accession of Tezozómoc of Azcapotzalco
1372	Accession of Acamapichtli of Tenochtitlan and Cuacua-pitzahuac of Tlatelolco
1375	Commencement of Tepanec–Mexica hostilities against Chalco
1391	Death of Acamapichtli
1395	Xaltocan war
1398	Mexica expedition against Cuauhtinchan
1402	Birth of Nezahualcóyotl
1403	Mexica celebrate New Fire ceremony in Tenochtitlan

1407	Death of Cuacuapitzahuac of Tlatelolco, succession Tlacateotl
1409	Accession of Ixtlilxóchitl of Texcoco
1414–18	Tepanec–Mexica war against Texcoco
1417	Death of Huitzilíhuitl of Tenochtitlan, accession of Chimalpopoca
1418	Death of Ixtlilxóchitl of Texcoco
1426	Deaths of Tezozómoc of Azcapotzalco, Chimalpopoca of Tenochtitlan and Tlacateotl of Tlatelolco Accession of Maxtla, Itzcóatl and Cuauhtlatoa
1428	Defeat of Tepanecs of Azcapotzalco by the Mexica, Texcocans, etc.
1431	Reconquest of Texcoco by Nezahualcóyotl
1440	Death of Itzcóatl, accession of Moctezuma I
1446–50	Renewed hostilities against Chalco
1450–4	The great famine
1455	Celebration of the New Fire ceremony in Tenochtitlan
1458	Coixtlahuaca campaign
1461–2	Cotaxtla campaign
1465	Final defeat of Chalco
1468	Death of Moctezuma I, accession of Axayácatl
1472	Death of Nezahualcóyotl, accession of Nezahualpilli in Texcoco
1473	Defeat of Tlatelolco Death of Moquihuix
1474	Toluca campaign
1478	Tarascan campaign
1481	Death of Axayácatl, accession of Tízoc
1486	Death of Tízoc, accession of Ahuítzotl Ahuítzotl's Matlazinca campaign
1487	Huaxtec war, taking of Xiuhcoac
1488–9	Campaigns in the region of Oaxaca
1491–5	Subjection of the coast of Guerrero from Acapulco to Zacatula
1494–5	Further campaigns in Oaxaca
1496	Conquest of the Isthmus region of Tehuantepec
1499–1500	Soconusco campaign
1500	The flooding of Tenochtitlan

1502   Death of Ahuítzotl, accession of Moctezuma II
1503   Taking of Achiotla
1504   Outbreak of war against Tlaxcala
        Quetzaltepec and Tototepec campaign
1505–6 Capture of Yanhuitlan and Zozollan
1507   New Fire ceremony in Tenochtitlan
1508–13 Aztec campaigns against Huexotzingo
1511   Taking of Tlaxiaco
        Spaniards occupy Cuba
1515   Death of Nezahualpilli of Texcoco, succession of
        Cacama
        Renewed war against Tlaxcala. The Huexotzingans
        take refuge in Tenochtitlan
1517   Hernandez de Cordoba leads expedition to the coast of
        Mexico
1518   Aztec occupation of Huexotzingo ended. Huexotzingo
        again becomes ally of Tlaxcala
        Juan de Grijalva leads expedition to Mexico
1519   10 February: Hernán Cortés embarks for Mexico
        8 November: Cortés enters Tenochtitlan
1520   27 June: Death of Moctezuma II; succeeded first by
        Cuitláhuac, then, after a short reign, by Cuauhtemoc
        30 June: La Noche Triste. Cortés abandons Tenochtitlan
1521   28 April: Final siege of Tenochtitlan begins
        13 August: Fall of Tenochtitlan. Capture of Cuauhtemoc

THE AZTECS

CHAPTER ONE

THE LONG MIGRATION

WITH THEIR WORLD in ruins and their gods departed, the Aztecs who survived the Spanish Conquest sought consolation in the glories of their past. To the once-proud conquerors, now poor underlings, no traditions were more hallowed than those of their early wanderings, when, once before, they had been hard-pressed and humble, and yet had survived. Nearly a century after the Conquest, a prince of the royal blood, called Tezozómoc, wrote his version of these early happenings:

And in the year 1609 I, Don Hernando de Alvarado Tezozómoc, who am a grandson of the person who was the great king, Moteuczoma [Moctezuma] the Younger, and who am descended from his nóble daughter, from the body of the princess, my most loved mother, Doña Francisca de Moteuczoma, whose husband was Don Diego de Alvarado Huanitzin, my most revered father, a man of noble birth; these are they who engendered me, and in all truth I am their son. . . . . What they [the ancient nobles] stated and affirmed in their writings all occurred, all is true, and contains no lie; they only set it down without invention and without falsehood.

And also for this reason I, Don Hernando de Alvarado Tezozómoc, certify and affirm the story of these elders, for it is not only from the mouths of just a few that the account comes which I now give; what is related I attribute to those already named, to those same elders who put it in order; I keep my trust by my own resolve; from their well-loved lips I learnt what the revered kings and nobles told who lived then, and whose doings I recount, and whom may our Lord God pardon.*

The Mexicans, or Mexica, are not unique in the obscurity of their early myths and legends. Such ambiguities, however, make this part of their story harder to relate.

The events of the early Mexica migration, as told in codices and chronicles, have long been the object of critical studies. The first of these, made in the eighteenth century, tended towards a literal interpretation of the original accounts, partly symbolical or mythical in nature.† The Mexicans were thus credited with the most remote origins, both in space and time.

Following a more critical approach by nineteenth-century historians, such as Orozco y Berra, scholars then went to the opposite extreme, interpreting the tale of the migration as being nothing but mere myth. The original Mexican home of Aztlan, an island surrounded by water, was for them nothing more than a reflection of

---

* References in the text are fulfilled in the Notes and References on pp. 308–347, indicated by the page-number of the text and the last word of the passage concerned. Source-references are indicated by an asterisk. An obelisk (†) indicates an explanatory note.

the situation of the great capital which they later founded in the Valley of Mexico.†

Students of the subject were thus left to wonder whether the Mexican homeland was to be sought in Mexico City itself or nearly 2000 miles away, in distant California, mentioned in certain early texts. However, more recent reappraisals have sought to draw a balance, finding in the old legends a certain ring of truth. Whether they concern ancient Greeks or ancient Mexicans, such sagas are often linked with actual happenings and with real people.

The first crucial question regarding Mexican antecedents naturally concerns their place of origin. Curiosity on this point was not confined to post-hispanic times; the great Aztec emperor Moctezuma I wished that those who had remained behind in their traditional home of Aztlan might share in the dazzling triumphs of his empire – at that moment, in about 1450, reaching the summit of its power.

He accordingly sent for as many magicians as could be mustered, and sixty in all were found. Furnished with sumptuous gifts of mantles, precious stones and feathers, they set forth and reached a place reputed to be the birthplace of their god, Huitzilopochtli. Here they found a demon who turned them into birds and monstrous beasts. Thus transformed, they took wing towards a remote destination. Having resumed human form, they found themselves among kinsmen, who arrived in canoes and asked them in their own language who they were and whence they came.*

They were then taken to a very old man who was himself related to their deity; he asked them who were now the priests of the god. In reply he was naturally given the names of men of whom he had never heard, including the Emperor Moctezuma himself, who had sent them thither.

The same old man promised to take them to the mother of their god Huitzilopochtli. They encountered various adventures on the way, including immersion in treacherous quicksand, from which the dotard rescued them with one finger. He proceeded to scold them severely for their wanton habits and luxurious ways since they had become great and powerful, far removed from the spartan life which they had left behind them in Aztlan. They finally came into the presence of the mother of Huitzilopochtli, now a very ancient hag, so hideous that she resembled something straight from hell. They told her the story of the spectacular creation of the Aztec Empire by her son's chosen people: 'Know that the four previous kings [before Moctezuma I] lived a life of hunger, poverty and labour, and paid tribute to other provinces; but now the city is prosperous and free, and has opened up and secured for itself the ways of the coast and of all the earth. Mexico is now lady and princess, and queen of all the cities, which now obey her commands.' * The magicians gave her the magnificent presents which they had brought; she, seemingly unimpressed, replied that she herself was poor and miserable. Instead of wondering at their dazzling accomplishments, she prophesied only doom: the Mexica in their turn would one day be overthrown, as they had overthrown others. With these fell tidings, the sorcerers returned to the Emperor Moctezuma.

Now, while later investigators may tend to eschew the aid of magic, the problem has none the less attracted their attention, and displayed their divergences. Padre Durán, writing in the late sixteenth century, tells how he consulted elders, who gave different opinions as to Mexican origins. Some said that they had emerged from springs of water, others from caves, and yet others maintained that they were the offspring of the gods. He mentions that many native records were burnt by the first friars as works of the devil; consequently it was impossible to know the whole truth. Such a conclusion holds good today.*

The learned padre then hazards his own guess as to Mexican Indian origins, suggesting that they came from the lost tribes of Israel. His theory tended to become widespread and to die hard. He produces curious arguments to support his view; quoting from the Prophet Hosea, he tells how God, as punishment for their sins, condemned ten tribes to be perpetually cowardly and pusillanimous. Since the Indians had allowed themselves to be conquered by Cortés and a mere 300 men, they had displayed precisely these characteristics; thus, *ipso facto*, they must be the lost tribes! For the same chronicler, certain of their religious rites, such as sacrifices made on mountain peaks, or in caves, ritual cannibalism, or the offering of children, also described in the Bible, confirmed the connection. (He perhaps does the Israelites an injustice in suggesting that they shared the ancient Mexican propensity towards ritual consumption of human flesh, though his comments on infant offerings are more correct – possibly these innocents fared better as victims of the Mexican Rain God than when 'passed through the fire' to propitiate Moloch.)

Even today, differences have persisted as to Mexican origins and as to the location of Aztlan. Some placed it as far off as the southern United States, others as near as the Valley of Mexico itself; certain writers have insisted that it never existed at all. Some have also favoured the coast of the Gulf of Mexico as a point of departure.†

Most modern observers, however, following more closely the established traditions as expressed in the chronicles, agree in focusing their attentions in a north-westerly direction. The question still remains: how far distant from the Valley of Mexico should Aztlan be sought? Any answer to that question must be linked to the whole problem of the cultural development of the Mexica. If, as would appear, they possessed a modicum of civilization when they reached their ultimate habitat, they could hardly have been living in the remotest wilds. If, on the contrary, they were mere nomads on their arrival, the reverse would be true, and their place of origin should be sought farther afield, beyond the pale of Middle American civilization.

The sources which tell most about the Mexica route agree that, after leaving Aztlan, the first places visited were called Seven Caves (Chicomoztoc) and Curved Mountain (Culhuacan).† The question of the whereabouts of Aztlan and these two localities can only be studied as a whole; the three are mentioned together by practically every source, but often as being synonymous rather than separate – for instance, 'Aztlan-Chicomoztoc' or 'Aztlan-Culhuacan'. If they were thus not one single place, this at least implies that they were to be sought in the same area.

Aztlan itself is described simply as being surrounded by water; the Mexica lived there as fishermen, making great use of boats.* As to what we know of the Seven Caves:

And there in Quinehuayan, the rock is called Chicomoztoc, which has holes on seven sides; and from there came forth the Mexicans, carrying their women, when they came out of Chicomoztoc by pairs; that was a fearsome place, for there abounded the countless wild beasts established in the area: bears, tigers, pumas, serpents; and it is full of thorns, of

5

sweet agave, and of pastures; and being thus very far-off, no one still knew later where it was.†

Aztlan is specifically the place of origin of the Aztecs or Mexica, but the Seven Caves are of legendary importance not only for this tribe, but also for those countless others who came to the Valley of Mexico before them – according to the traditional accounts, each had originally emerged from the Seven Caves.* In this way it was the mythical place of departure for the whole mass of migrants who descended on the Valley of Mexico in the mid-twelfth century, after the collapse of the Toltec Empire and may perhaps be regarded as a general place of assembly as much as a Mexica starting-point.

Curved Mountain, or Culhuacan, the third locality mentioned in connection with these early wanderings, is also of deep significance as its Toltec connections represent the great cultural traditions of the past. The city of the same name in the Valley of Mexico was later to play a great part in the history of the Mexica, as the connecting link between them and the former Toltec Empire.†

As to the actual location of these places, so closely interrelated, there exist two principal modern viewpoints. Firstly, Doctor Paul Kirchhoff considers that the original Culhuacan is to be identified with San Isidro Culiacán, some 170 miles north-west of Mexico City, and beyond the modern town of Queretaro. The Seven Caves would lie not far to the east of this, and Aztlan a little to the west (see page 9).*

Secondly, Professor Wigberto Jiménez Moreno, while agreeing that the Seven Caves lay to the north-west, thinks that they were located nearer at hand, some sixty miles distant from Mexico City.† He, however, places Aztlan much farther away, in a lagoon called Mexcaltitlan on the coast of the modern state of Nayarit, far to the north-west. In the midst of this is an island, which corresponds closely with codex pictures of the original Aztlan as an inhabited place, surrounded on all sides by water. There is still a place called Aztatlan near by, which would have been situated within the original lagoon, now reduced in size. However, notwithstanding the remarkable coincidences as to name and geography offered by this far-off site, it might appear more logical to seek for the starting-point of the Mexica – and for a collecting-place for the other migrant tribes – nearer to their final home. For one thing the standard of culture of

6

many of them was fairly high when they first arrived in the Valley of Mexico.†

Accordingly, while there is now a wider acceptance of the notion that the general place of mustering, the Seven Caves, was relatively near to the City of Mexico in a north-westerly direction, the two leading viewpoints are still at variance as to the location of Aztlan, whence the Mexica themselves set forth. The question therefore remains to be answered: was Aztlan situated on the far-off north-west coast, or was it also relatively near to the Valley of Mexico? This raises the question of whether there were, perhaps, two Aztlans.

The closer one studies Mexican origins the more one feels that although the Mexica were distinct from other tribes one is not dealing with the migrations of one homogeneous tribe, and that two main groups, quite different in nature, had joined forces. The early Mexica tended to present two distinct sides to their nature, contrasting the civilized and the nomad. In the records they are sometimes depicted as semi-savages, clad in skins; sometimes they are written of as erecting stone buildings. It is thus very possible that the original Aztec clans were later joined by three others, of a lower cultural level, coming from much farther afield.*

The presence of two types of migrant is strongly suggested by the order of the god Huitzilopochtli to his chosen people to change their name from Aztec to Mexica, or Mexicans (this latter name probably derives from the Nahuatl word *meztli*, meaning 'moon').†

According to what the ancients tell, when the Aztecs came from Aztlan, they were not yet called Mexicans, but were still called Aztecs, and it was after what we have already told that they took this name and were called Mexicans. According to this version, it was Huitzilopochtli who gave them this name.

Then he immediately changed the name of the Aztecs and said to them: 'Now you shall not call yourselves Aztecs any more, now you are Mexicans.' Then, when they took the name of Mexicans, he painted their ears, and also gave them the arrow, the bow and the little net, and thus the Mexicans shot with arrows very well at what they saw on high.*

This presentation of bows and arrows reinforces the notion of the joining of two groups, one nomad and one more civilized. The bow and arrow were *par excellence* the nomad weapons, whereas the javelin-thrower (*atlatl*) was characteristic of the more civilized peoples.

Possibly, therefore, the different opinions as to the location of Aztlan are not totally irreconcilable. It seems likely that the more cultured half of the whole tribe had already lived for some time within the bounds of the ancient Toltec civilization even if they originally had come from farther afield. Their early habitat, Aztlan, was very possibly not too remote from the area of the Seven Caves, the place of muster, nor from the Valley of Mexico (the central valley in which Mexico City now stands) itself. For instance, the island of Janitzio on Lake Patzcuaro corresponds to the usual description of Aztlan as a confined space, surrounded by water.

These people – already semi-civilized – were probably joined by another group, more nomad in nature and arriving at this time from much farther away, perhaps the distant north-west. But names repeat themselves frequently throughout Mexico, and such nomad newcomers to the group perhaps also came to conceive of their original and more distant home as 'Aztlan'. There may well therefore have existed more than one Aztlan. Accordingly, it is probably a fruitless task to go much farther in pinpointing the exact whereabouts of the place. The name is not only legendary, making it hard to fix in space or time; it must equally be appreciated that Aztlan is as much a concept as a place. After all, the future Tenochtitlan was to be in effect another Aztlan, a centre of population by lagoon waters – though it was never to be given that name.

The Mexica probably set out on their migration in about A.D. IIII. It was to be a long journey before they finally settled in 1345.† The original migrants were poor and few in number; they proceeded under the guidance of four priest-rulers, or *teomamas* – meaning literally 'bearers of the god':

They had an idol called Huizilopochtli, who was borne by four guardians who served him; to these he spoke very secretly of the events of their route and journey, telling them of all that was to happen. And this idol was held in such awe and reverence that no one else but they dared to approach or touch it. And it was kept in an ark of reeds, and up to this

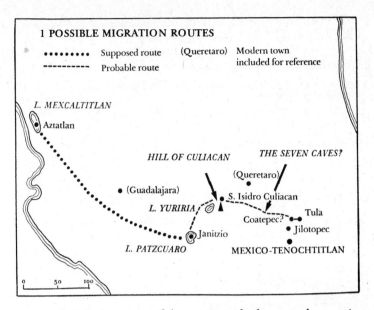

1 POSSIBLE MIGRATION ROUTES

·········· Supposed route   (Queretaro) Modern town
---------- Probable route   included for reference

L. MEXCALTITLAN

Aztatlan

HILL OF CULIACAN   *THE SEVEN CAVES?*

(Queretaro)

(Guadalajara)   S. Isidro Culiacan

L. YURIRIA   Tula
                   Coatepec?
          Janitzio   Jilotopec

L. PATZCUARO   MEXICO-TENOCHTITLAN

0   50   100

very day there is not one of these natives who knows or has seen its form. And the priests held it up as a god, preaching to their peoples the laws that they had to follow and observe, and the ceremonies and rites which should accompany their offerings. And this they did in every place where they set up their camp, after the manner of the Children of Israel during all the time when they wandered in the desert.*

The chroniclers' accounts of these happenings are visibly coloured by their familiarity with the Old Testament. The information given by pictorial codices is of necessity more cryptic, though they name more of the places visited.

At the outset the Mexica were divided into seven clans called *calpulli*, and they led the typical life of a wandering tribe:

Thus for considerable time the Mexicans wandered through Chichimec [nomad] territory; when they established themselves in a good place, they remained for some twenty years; when they were well off, they settled in the place for two, three, four, five, ten or fifteen years, when they were not well off they settled for some twenty or forty days (they set out for Cuextecatl-Ichocayan and for Coatl-Icamac); everywhere

9

they gave names to the land; for food and sustenance they ate meat, beans, amaranth, chia, chiles and tomatoes.

Where they stayed long enough they built temples, and erected the dwelling place of their god, Huitzilopochtli. . . .*

At longer halts on their journey they not only constructed temples, but at times even a court for the ritual ball-game which formed an integral part of ancient Mexican culture.* They used stone, and at a later stage even made simple fortifications. They usually sowed maize, sometimes harvesting the crop, and sometimes leaving before it had reached maturity,* and they adopted the seemingly heartless custom of abandoning their old people at suitable stopping-places. But a journey undertaken on foot over the arid and mountainous country of this region must have been arduous, and there was probably no alternative.

The wanderers at times suffered hardship, going hungry, thirsty and almost naked. But they consoled themselves with hopes of better times that lay ahead, and their god was lavish in future promises to his chosen people:

. . . because we shall proceed to establish ourselves and settle down, and we shall conquer all peoples of the universe; and I tell you in all truth that I will make you lords and kings of all that is in the world; and when you become rulers, you shall there have countless and infinite numbers of vassals, who will pay tribute to you and shall give you innumerable and most fine precious stones, gold, quetzal feathers, emeralds, coral, amethyst, and you shall dress most finely in these; you shall also have many kinds of feathers, the blue cotinga, the red flamingo, the tzinitzian, all the beautiful feathers, and multicoloured caco and cotton; and all this you shall see, since this is in truth my task, and for this have I been sent here.*

All this was told them by their priests, who learnt of it in dreams sent by the god.

In addition to rather haphazard agriculture, the Mexica wanderers lived by hunting. Their original lagoon habitat abounded in aquatic fauna, but on leaving Aztlan they came to depend more on land animals such as deer, rabbits, birds and even snakes.* Since they only grew crops periodically, their diet must have been mainly meat.

Neither their way of living nor their social organization was thus purely primitive. The predominance of the four priest-rulers implies the existence of a certain hierarchy – perhaps of a rudimentary class-structure. It should be added that even at this stage they spoke Nahuatl, the language of the more civilized peoples of central Mexico; moreover, they knew the use of the ritual calendar of ancient Mexico, with its sacred cycle of fifty-two years. They had even been initiated into the arts of human sacrifice.

Certain accounts rightly stress the more nomadic characteristics of the Mexica at this time. Our general picture, however, is of a migrant group, few in numbers, poor and ill-provided, but not altogether uncivilized. By virtue of their building, social organization, agriculture, language and religion, they are far removed from the nomads, some of whom had preceded them into the Valley of Mexico. The latter are invariably depicted as dressed in skins, dwelling in caves and worshipping rudimentary gods. Above all, unlike the Mexica, they did not practise agriculture.* Thus, the Mexica definitely come within the pale of Middle American civilization, though possibly situated at the farthest extreme of its cultural spectrum.

The Toltec Empire, whose glories the Mexica would one day emulate, was in a state of incipient dissolution at the time when they set forth from Aztlan. Such convulsions may even have occasioned their departure. The Empire, whose apogee lasted from the mid-tenth to the mid-twelfth century, had been the ruling power in the region through which the Mexica were now passing. There exist many doubts as to the actual area which the Toltec physically controlled; however, their culture and influence were spread throughout the length and breadth of Middle America, stretching even as far as Chichen Itza in the Yucatan peninsula. The famous remains of Chichen, in fact, reproduce on a more grandiose scale many of the main features of the Toltec capital of Tula, and are rich in representations of Quetzalcoatl, the Plumed Serpent, the great deity of the Toltecs.

Tula finally fell towards the middle of the twelfth century, for reasons probably connected with barbarian incursions from the north. The Toltec collapse, like the Roman, left a power vacuum, and their empire was thereafter nostalgically revered as the upholder of stability and civilization. Those accustomed to the world as they had ordered it were left dazed by the Toltec fall. Suddenly their legendary priest-ruler departed, to disappear in the east:

> And when these things had happened, Quetzalcoatl was now troubled and saddened and thereupon was minded that he should go – that he should abandon his city of Tula.
> Thereupon he made ready. It is said that he had everything burned – his house of gold, his house of coral; and still other works of art, the marvellous and costly things, all of these he buried, he hid there in treacherous places: either within the mountains or in the canyons.
> And, moreover, the cacao trees he changed into mesquites. And all the birds of precious feather – the quetzal, the blue cotinga, the red spoonbill – all these he sent away beforehand. Taking the road before him, they went away to Anahuac.*

It was into the fluid situation created by this great débâcle that the Mexica were to step – actually visiting the abandoned and desolate capital of Tula long before reaching their final destination. They themselves belonged to the outer fringes of Toltec civilization, rather than to the nomads who partly contributed to its doom, and may even have served as Toltec mercenaries. This is not to suggest that, at this moment, the Mexica were either important or prosperous. They were still a group of poor wanderers, who had so far developed a propensity to cause trouble to their neighbours but little else.

Of the events of the first fifty-two-year calendar-period, between the departure of the Mexica from Aztlan and from the initial place of muster at the Seven Caves, and continuing till their arrival in the vicinity of Tula, about forty miles to the north-west of Mexico City, we have little knowledge. After gathering at the Seven Caves, 'they lost themselves in the mountains, the woods and the place of crags, and just as their fancy pleases, the Mexica wander'.* So reads the brief text in Nahuatl appended to the illustration of their wanderings depicted in the Codex Azcatitlan. Such events as occur are told in a context more magico-religious than political. They mostly concern the relationship of the tribe with their god Huitzilopochtli, and are recounted by chronicles plainly well versed in the Old Testament. As to the places visited *en route*, the two main sources tend to differ.† They occasionally fought battles with their neighbours, and even took prisoners, whom they would sacrifice. A picture has also survived of the four bearers of the god sacrificing women in the early stages of the migration.*

The migrants at this point clearly suffered from certain dissensions. The first incident of its kind occurred when the Mexica settled under a certain tree, which then split in two. This was interpreted as a terrible omen; the god Huitzilopochtli told his priests that, as a consequence, part of the tribe must separate from the remainder. Only the most virtuous were to be his chosen few; they were to proceed on their way, leaving the rest behind. This was the first break away from the main body; others were to follow.

A further one occurred almost at the outset, also implying some kind of religious schism. The god Huitzilopochtli had a sister who became a sorceress, using charms and incantations to gain special authority over animals, and particularly over such dangerous pests as snakes, scorpions, centipedes and deadly spiders. These, at her behest, would bite anyone opposed to her wishes.

Huizilopochtli, unwilling to countenance unorthodox opposition to his rule, instructed his people simply to abandon her in the night, together with her adherents:

> Thus forsaken, she wept bitter tears. When the sister of Huitzilopochtli, Malinalxoch, awoke after they left her sleeping, she stood up, wept, and said to her supporters: 'O my fathers! Whither shall we go, since certainly my elder brother Huitzilopochtli has left us by stealth. Whither will the villain have gone? Let us search for the land to which we must go, since everywhere there are peoples already established.'*

Once again, the dissenters were banished from the tribe. They made their way to a place called Malinalco; we shall hear more of them later, when they try to rejoin the main body of the Mexica, already established in the Valley of Mexico. Huitzilopochtli now again lectured his people, reminding them that it was only by virtue of their courage that he would lead them to greatness, and not through the mere use of magic: 'Because your god says that he did not come to cast spells upon the nations or to bewitch them, nor to bring them to your service by such means, but only by their spirit and the valour of their hearts and arms; by such ways does he think to make his name great, and to lift the Mexican nation to the clouds. . . .'*

The main body journeyed onwards and reached a place called Coatepec (Hill of the Serpent), which is usually described as being near Tula. Here they celebrated the first New Fire of the migration, marking the beginning of a fresh fifty-two-year cycle in the ritual calendar of ancient Mexico. It was not until the fifth New Fire, centuries later, that they were established in their promised land; thus, in terms of time, most of their journey from Aztlan still remained before them. However, as far as distance was concerned, at Coatepec they now stood only some forty miles from their final home, but the road thither was to be circuitous. It was therefore more of a wandering than a migration on a fixed course.

The main event in Coatepec was the birth, or rather the rebirth, of the god Huitzilopochtli, probably marking the final assumption of authority by his adherents. The story is told by Fray Bernardino de Sahagún, perhaps the greatest of all the Spanish chroniclers. Writing between 1548 and 1585, he transcribed into the original Nahuatl and also into a Spanish version all that he learnt from a great body of informants. Every aspect of pre-hispanic life is covered, including detailed accounts of all known fauna and flora. His third book relates the origin of the gods, and begins with what happened in Coatepec, which he himself states to be near Tula. Here lived a devout woman named Coatlicue ('Skirt of Serpents'), who was the mother of 400 sons. One day, she was sweeping in the temple on the Hill: 'And once, as she swept feathers, as it were, a ball of feathers descended upon her. Then Coatlicue snatched it up and placed it in her bosom. And when she had swept, when she came to take the feather ball which she had placed in her bosom, she found nothing. Thereupon Coatlicue conceived.'*

Her 400 sons were not overjoyed by the prospect of a happy event, so miraculously inspired. On the contrary, they adopted an attitude of righteous indignation against their seemingly wanton mother. Her single daughter even advised them to kill her before her shame became known: 'And their sister, Coyolxauhqui, said to them: "My elder brothers, she hath affronted us; we must slay our mother,

14

the wicked one who is already with child. Who is the cause of what is in her womb?"'*

However, one of the 400 played traitor, and told of their plans to Huitzilopochtli, still in his mother's womb. Thus forewarned, he made it his business to be forearmed. On birth, he emerged equipped with shield and buckler, and brandishing the famous Serpent of Fire (Xiuhcoatl), symbolic thereafter as the weapon of the god. The 400 brothers also prepared for war: 'They were in war array, which was distributed among them; all put in place their paper array, their paper crowns, their nettles [sic], painted paper streamers, and they bound bells to the calves of their legs. The bells were called *oyoalli*. And their darts had barbed points.'*

But Huizilopochtli ignited his Serpent of Fire: 'With it he pierced Coyolxauhqui, and then quickly struck off her head. It came to rest there on the slope of Coatepetl [Coatepec]. And her body went falling below; it went crashing into pieces; in various places her arms, her legs, her body kept falling.'* In the National Museum of Anthropology in Mexico City there is a magnificent statue of this goddess in decapitated form – not as a fragmented head, as is sometimes thought. Huitzilopochtli then completed his task by routing his 400 brothers; only a very few escaped.

His arm, the Serpent of Fire, became a sacred relic. When the Aztec capital was in desperate straits, as a last resource a lone warrior was sent against the Spaniards, armed with the hallowed weapon. This time it was of no avail.

In Coatepec, Huitzilopochtli, now in truth supreme deity among the Mexica, gave orders through his priests that a near-by river should be dammed:

> Once the dam was made, the water flowed and spread over all the plain, forming a great lagoon; this they surrounded with willows, poplars and sabines; it became filled with cuperus and reed-mace; it began to be stocked with every kind of fish upon earth. Marine birds came, such as ducks, geese, herons, widgeons, with which the whole surface was covered, as well as with many other kinds of fowl, which the lagoon of Mexico today maintains and feeds.*

In other words the Mexica were seeking to reproduce the conditions of their former home, Aztlan, as well as those of their future island capital.

Coatepec thus magically transformed into a kind of paradise, the Mexica lived most contentedly, devoting much time to the pleasures of song and dance. Such were the delights of the place that voices were raised to suggest that they should settle there for ever. This, however, did not at all suit Huitzilopochtli; his chosen ones had as yet been insufficiently tried and he became irate:

> In anger the god replied to the priests and said: Who are they who thus wish to set aside my resolutions and place objections in their way? Are they perchance mightier than I? Tell them that before tomorrow I will take my vengeance of them, that they may not dare to give opinions on what I have determined and for which I was sent, and that all may know that only me shall they obey.*

The rebellious leaders were found dead the next morning, with their hearts cut out, as in the most usual form of human sacrifice. The watchful god now told his people to destroy the dams and let the river resume its former course. With the lagoon waters released, the reedlands began to dry, as well as the reed-mace and the trees and all the freshness; the fish and frogs started to die as well as all the other reptiles engendered by the water, and which these people used for their nourishment; the marine birds began to go away and leave the place as dry and sombre as it had been before.*

Quite apart from the information thus provided on their route and their life, such stories are of great symbolic significance. Much is implied both as to the composition of the the group, and as to its beliefs.

Once the two original and disparate elements had joined forces, one semi-civilized and one nomad, it is natural to assume that the Mexica proceeded on their way as a single composite body. But the truth was less simple, and it seems that during the long migration smaller groups joined the main nucleus from time to time; equally others fell away. The first incident of this kind, which I have already mentioned, involved the splitting of the tree, when Huitzilopochtli divided his faithful adherents from the remainder. The second episode involved the abandonment of the god's sister and accounts emphasize that her supporters were also left behind. The third division took place in Coatepec; it clearly took the form of an uprising against the established leaders, again with the involvement of a sister of the god.

16

It seems likely that the first story of separation refers to dissensions between supporters of Huitzilopochtli and those of other gods, at a time when the former was not fully established as the supreme deity. On the other hand, the two subsequent incidents, both affecting so-called sisters of Huitzilopochtli, probably represent differences between clans, each led by followers of the god himself – or even clashes between different factions within the god's own personal clan, with which he was always to be specially associated.† What emerged from such conflicts was a more homogeneous group, among whom Huitzilopochtli's own clan came to dominate the remainder; this clan in its turn was controlled from now on by an inner ring of the god's priests and devotees.

The true origins of Huitzilopochtli, the special god of the Mexica, whose cult bestowed upon them the status of a chosen people, are obscure. The orthodox accounts depict him as the presiding deity of the whole tribe from the very start, though each of the seven clans had its own patron god. Like Jehovah, Huitzilopochtli guides his people, through the medium of his priests, leading them on to the promised land, exacting in return the virtues of courage and obedience. But, in studying ancient Mexican history, one often discovers that a situation prevailing at a much later date is projected backwards in time. If a certain deity predominates at the end of a long migration, the chronicles assume that the same god was paramount at the outset. Huitzilopochtli is described as in command right from the start; yet, his 'birth' in Coatepec is described as if he had not existed before the Mexica arrived there. An element of contradiction is clearly present. It would therefore seem much more likely that the original leader called Huitzilopochtli was not a god but a mortal who had died. Mention is made in more than one source of a human leader of that name; one may thus suppose that a hero of early times became first a legend, then a deity. In fact, it was nothing new for a human leader to bear the name of a god.†

The unique cult of the god Huitzilopochtli was probably consolidated by his 'birth' in Coatepec. But it was really more the case of a god being promoted, rather than created. The name Huitzilopochtli derives from a combination of 'humming bird' (*huitzilin*) and the word for both 'left' and 'south' (*opochtli*), and can best be interpreted as 'the humming bird of the south'. The humming bird itself is a symbol of the greatest antiquity in Mexico. This tender little creature was intimately linked with human sacrifice, occasionally even depicted with his beak boring out the blood of the victim.* He was also associated with rain, since he makes his appearance in the rainy season.† Moreover, Huitzilopochtli's birth in Coatepec is in more than one sense a rebirth. It not only marks the assumption of supremacy by his supporters over the whole Mexica tribe; in addition his very nature was transformed. He virtually discards his prosaic existence as a mere fisherman's god or an undistinguished earth-deity, to become instead the glittering Lord of the Daylight Sky.

The usual interpretation of this rebirth is that his sister and 400 brothers symbolize the Moon and Stars; in routing them, Huitzilopochtli personifies the action of the sun at the beginning of his daily course.* In his new and spectacular role as Lord of the Daylight Sky, he is associated with the colour blue, and with the south.† The humming-bird element in his name represents the fallen warriors, who, in the guise of this bird, were believed to accompany the risen sun on his daily journey. He thus equally becomes the god of war, embodying the Mexica will to conquer.†

Huitzilopochtli is therefore, like his chosen people, a combination of the old and new, of the sedentary settler and the nomad invader. Both concepts are fundamental to an understanding of the Mexica themselves. In the main, as an incarnation of the fiery orb, it is the dynamic element in the god which was to predominate; for the Mexica, the older and more pacific gods now yield precedence to their militant patron deity, with his imperious insistence on war and strife, whose victims provide his daily nourishment of blood and fill his paradise with slain warriors, ready to accompany him on his celestial journey.

On leaving Coatepec, traditionally in the year 1168, the Mexica proceeded to Tula itself, by then in a state of utter desolation. The Toltecs themselves were now fleeing from their stricken capital, though it would not appear that the Mexica played much part in its destruction. Their stay in Tula itself was brief; thereafter they resumed their wanderings, and accounts vary as to the places actually visited as they entered the Valley of Mexico, the plain ringed by

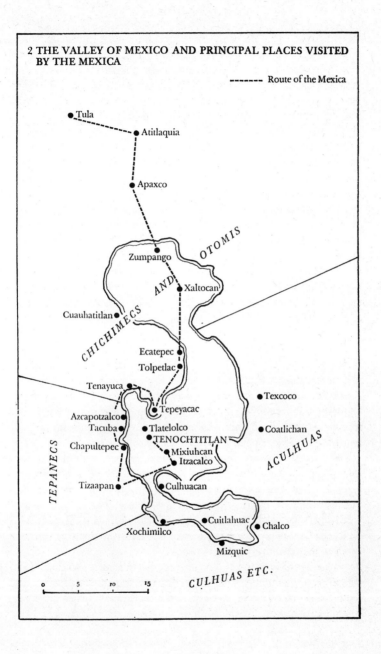

2 THE VALLEY OF MEXICO AND PRINCIPAL PLACES VISITED BY THE MEXICA

------- Route of the Mexica

mountains where they were finally to settle.† One important place where they sojourned was Xaltocan. This city was then situated in the midst of a lagoon of the same name and must have accordingly seemed like home to the Mexica. At the same time it was one of the leading powers of the Valley of Mexico, and capital of an extensive region, stretching some distance to the north-east.*

The Mexica were now beginning to come into contact with the leading peoples of the Valley; however, though this part of their journey lasted for nearly a century, information on their life is not plentiful; it must be assumed to have continued in unaltered form as they went from one city to another, and as each generation succeeded the one that went before. The small tribe continued to move from place to place, hunting and fishing, sowing and reaping, as the circumstances permitted, and if their stay anywhere was prolonged, building a temple to the god Huitzilopochtli.

The Mexica were now only a few miles distant from their final home, even if many tribulations still lay before them, and the scene which confronted them as they approached was naturally very different from that which meets the eye of the modern visitor.

The Valley of Mexico itself constitutes the heart of the whole central part of Mexico, and lies midway between the two seas, at an altitude of over 7000 feet. By definition, it is not a valley but a basin, since it lacks any natural outlet. Measuring some 60 miles from north to south, and 40 miles from east to west, it covers a fertile area of about 2500 square miles. It is ringed by a kind of giant horseshoe of mountains on the east, south and west sides; of these the most impressive are the snow-capped volcanoes to the south-east.

The benign climate of the region has often been described as an eternal spring, for great extremes of temperature are unknown. In the winter season, frosts do occur in the early morning, but are quickly dispelled by the warming rays of the sun. In the hotter weather of April and May, which precedes the four months of rains, the thermometer may rise to the mid-eighties at noon; but at such an altitude the nights are always cool.

Nowadays, the general aspect of the Valley is arid and dusty for part of the year, owing to the drying-up and subsequent drainage of the greater part of the former great lakes or lagoons, which covered much of its surface. At the time of the Conquest and before, they numbered five, and were fed by springs and short streams from the surrounding mountains. These would still have been heavily wooded when the Mexica appeared on the scene, though deforestation had already taken its toll before the arrival of the Spaniards, as each successive civilization cut down its quota of trees.

Another major difference that would strike the visitor of today, if he could miraculously be transported back into the pre-hispanic past, would be the absence of the ordinary domestic beasts, the horse, donkey, pig and goat, that have since become so much part of the landscape. Ancient America possessed no flocks and herds, like those of the Mongols and other nomads of the Old World, and before Cortés only the turkey and dog were present to serve the needs of man (together with the llama and the guinea-pig in parts of South America). Wild life was, of course, more abundant than today, particularly on and around the lagoons. The vegetation, too, was different. The two principal types of tree that now predominate in the Valley are the Pepper Tree and the Eucalyptus. Whereas the latter was naturally a late arrival from Australia, the former originated in Peru, not Mexico, as its Spanish name (*pirul*) implies. But, whereas in Mexico many things change rapidly, others remain much as they were. Not only were there adobe houses little different from some of those in villages of today, but the principal crop, then as now, was maize. Nowadays it tends to be grown more on the lower ground, whereas formerly, when the plough was unknown and the only available instrument was the *coa* or planting-stick, it was easier to sow on the slopes of the hills and mountains, where the coating of grass and weeds was less thick. Then as now, moreover, the peasant diet was based on the combination of three plants – maize, beans and squash – that have been predominant in Mexican agriculture since time immemorial.

The Valley at this time, in the twelfth century, would already have been studded with villages, and even cities, though none approached the proportions of the capital which the new arrivals were one day to build. The Mexica themselves, having left Xaltocan, stopped at a further series of resting-places, and then came to Tenayuca. This had become the capital of the nomad Chichimecs, who had occupied the Valley of Mexico after the fall of the Toltecs, and who had formed an 'empire' of their own, which reached its height from about 1200 to 1250. These people, originally depicted as mere cave-dwellers, dressed in skins, soon intermarried with the survivors of the civilized Toltec world and adopted more sedentary ways. Like so many places famous in the annals of Mexico history, Tenayuca ('the place where walls are made') is now an undistinguished outer suburb of Mexico City. However, unlike others, it can at least boast of substantial archaeological remains; apart from its imposing pyramid, with its many superimpositions, the ruins of Tenayuca are distinguished for their wall of serpents, such as was later to be constructed round the great Temple in the Mexica capital.

When the Mexica arrived at Chapultepec, a little before A.D. 1300, the situation might perhaps be compared with that of Italy, say a century after the fall of Rome.* The Valley had been invaded by a series of tribes, some of which, like the more advanced of the Goths, had previously resided within the confines of empire, and had adopted relatively civilized ways. Others, however, were semi-barbarous, though equally disposed to learn the ways of their former masters. The principal cultural centre was still Culhuacan, not to be confused with the legendary Old Culhuacan, where the Mexica started their journey. The name Culhua probably derives from the Nahuatl word *colli*, or 'grand father', denoting people with forefathers, that is to say of high descent. Culhuacan, was *par excellence* the surviving Toltec city of the region, and memories of the Toltecs still tended to be treasured as those of a golden age. But Culhuacan also persisted as an important political entity; like Ravenna after the fall of Rome, it represented a renewal of Toltec civilization, as much as a survival. In such disturbed times, it was Culhuacan that upheld the principle of legitimacy and continuity.

However, by the time the Mexica arrived upon the Valley scene, it was no longer dominated either by these surviving Toltecs or by the nomad invaders, whose tenure of power had been brief. The lead had since then been assumed by later arrivals, boasting of a fairly high level of culture, having already largely adopted Toltec ways.†
Accounts, perhaps apocryphal, suggest that the nomad ruler gave lands to these newcomers, and married them to his daughters, just as his own followers on their arrival had taken Toltec royal wives.*
Of the various invading groups, two were outstanding in import-

ance. One of these, the Acolhua, went to settle in the region of Texcoco, along the eastern shore of the lagoon (see page 19).† The main centre of the tribe was originally Coatlichan, now a village, until recently renowned for the huge monolithic statue which was found there. After being hewn out from the rock to which it was still attached, the enormous block of stone was taken to Mexico City and now stands at the entrance to the National Museum of Anthropology. It is popularly known as 'Tlaloc', the Rain God; however, since it sports a skirt, it may rather represent his sister, the Water Goddess.

The second people of great significance among those who preceded the Mexica into the area were the Tepanecs.† They settled more to the west of the lagoon, and their principal city was Azcapotzalco ('place of the ant-heaps'), now also a mere suburb of Mexico City. Like many others, it was not founded by its most recent occupants, the Tepanecs, but could boast of a long tradition, going back nearly a thousand years more.† The historical importance of these Tepanecs cannot be over-emphasized. They were to dominate the Mexica during their early years in their final home; it was under their tutelage that the latter were to be transformed from an impoverished tribe into a nascent great power. The Aztecs were to build on these foundations; it was more from the short-lived Tepanec Empire, rather than from the Toltecs, that they were to learn the art of empire-building.

In the Valley of Mexico and the surrounding region then, no single master ruled, since the Acolhua and the Tepanecs were only beginning to emerge as the super-powers of the region, facing each other across the lagoon. Politics presented a scene of almost Balkan complexity and flux, and we find few fixed bonds of friendship, but rather a kaleidoscope of fleeting combinations among petty rulers.

To add to the complexity of the situation, one encounters a multiplicity of princelings, often apparently ruling simultaneously over the same city. They are constantly referred to by Spanish chroniclers as *reyes* or 'kings'; but this European concept cannot be readily applied to the monarchies of Mexico: frequently the title of ruler is partly elective in nature and, equally, rule tends to be pluralized, with more than one lord for each people. But, notwithstanding such apparent confusions, these communities enjoyed a common culture;

they had in the main been subjects of the fallen Toltec realm, and as such they shared the same cultural heritage. Part of this was formed by their religious beliefs; while each people tended to have a special or patron deity, the general pantheon was common to all, including the Mexica themselves.

This comprised a vast concourse of gods and goddesses, one or more of whom presided over every aspect of human life (see pages 306–7). Two of the most important and ancient gods were the Rain God (Tlaloc), who actually came to share the main temple in Tenochtitlan with Huitzilopochtli, and the Plumed Serpent (Quetzalcoatl), who performed a variety of important functions, having bestowed on man the sciences of agriculture and writing; he was also the god of the morning and evening star and of the wind.† Having left Tula at its moment of disaster, he was reportedly expected to return one day from the east, and did – in the person of Hernán Cortés.

Almost as significant were certain goddesses, such as Coatlicue, a kind of earth goddess and the mother of Huitzilopochtli, and the Goddess of Love (Tlazolteotl); to this deity each man had once to make confession, towards the end of his life. She was also the goddess of excrement – the confession of evil things symbolizing the act of pouring out verbal filth. Love was naturally associated with the moon and the Goddess of Love was also connected through the rabbit with the many gods of *pulque*, the sacred drink. These were often referred to as the Four Hundred Rabbits, because it was the rabbit who had discovered the *pulque* when he nibbled at the agave plant, from whose juice the precious liquid was derived. The connection between the rabbit and the moon came from the shadows on its surface, in which the Mexicans discerned the likeness of this animal.

As in many religions, there also existed a divine pair of creator-gods, known as Two Lord (Ometecuhtli) and Two Lady (Omecihuatl), who resided in solitary state in the thirteenth Heaven, called Two Place (Omeyocan). But, as sometimes occurs, notwithstanding lip-service paid to this venerable couple, they had been rather forced into the background by more gaudy deities. Their existence merely serves to underline the ancient Mexican passion for duality. Among the Aztecs we later find two principal priests, two merchant leaders and, in many city-states, two monarchs.

24

Moreover, two is not the only divine number. Four is of great moment; we shall constantly be finding examples of missions carried out by four ambassadors and ceremonies conducted by four priests. The number five is also of significance; there are four cardinal points, but five directions, if the centre is included as well, a concept equally familiar to the Chinese. Another similarity to Chinese thinking is that the cardinal points are identified with specific colours.

The sacred 260-day calendar formed an integral part of Mexican religion, linking all the peoples of what is best known as Middle American civilization (see below, page 29). From its place in this calendar, each day would thus be named after one of twenty signs, preceded by a numeral, running from one to thirteen. Each child was given as part of his full name that of the numeral and day-sign of his birth; according to whether this was propitious or the reverse, his own fate would be good, bad or indifferent. For instance, Seven Rain was good, and those born on that day would be merciful, pitying and compassionate. The following day, Eight Flower, was equally propitious; but infants had to be quickly bathed and baptized, lest any part of the ceremony fall upon the succeeding day, Nine Crocodile, described as perverse and full of vice. Anyone named after Nine Crocodile would be exclusively dedicated to evil; one of his lesser faults would be a propensity towards slander and rumour-mongering; so incapable would he be of taking care of himself that he would be destined to appear dressed only in rags and tatters.*

Bad days tended to outnumber the good in such an inexorable system. However, protection could sometimes be sought from remorseless fate by the very simple device of postponing bathing and baptism, by arrangement with the priest, until the child could be named after a better day.

Of the many migrant tribes, the Mexica were the last to arrive, and probably the least welcome. Somewhat reputed for savagery, they were to be numbered among the less civilized inhabitants of the Valley of Mexico, although they spoke Nahuatl and practised agriculture.†

They finally settled in Chapultepec ('Hill of the Locust') at the end of the thirteenth century. They had not yet reached their promised land, but it lay literally within sight of this hill. The years spent in this place are an important period in the history of the Mexica. On their arrival, they were still principally governed by their priest-rulers, the four Bearers of the God, who had ordered their wanderings. The latter now continued to rule the tribe, supposedly inspired by dreams and visions sent by Huitzilopochtli. He was not slow in warning them against the temptation to settle down, telling them that before long they would be expelled:

> To these bearers of the idol, called priests, he spoke: My fathers, look to that which has to come about, wait and you shall see, for I know all this, that which will happen and come to pass. Prepare and make ready, and observe well that we are not to tarry much here, and that we shall go on a little farther, to a place where we shall stay, sojourn and settle; meanwhile let it be sung that two kinds of people will very soon come upon us.*

Meanwhile they should await events, and he would in due time tell them what to do.*

Parallel to these priest-rulers, the clans had their own individual chiefs. The number of such clans had by now risen from the original seven to a figure of fifteen or twenty. Their leaders are sometimes referred to as 'captains', indicating a certain military role. Since each clan had its own patron god, they also possessed a religious significance. The phrase 'military democracy' has sometimes been employed to describe the government of the Mexica at this time. But it was in reality more theocratic than democratic. Neither democracy on the one hand nor kings by divine right on the other have exact parallels in ancient Mexico.

For the first part of their stay in Chapultepec, the religious leaders thus held effective sway. Probably because of external pressures, the government later devolved upon a single leader, named Huitzilíhuitl ('Humming Bird Feather'). In their present abode, hemmed in by greedy neighbours, collective leadership was eventually found wanting. In actual fact, however, plural rule was more in conformity with local traditions, and many neighbouring peoples continued to possess two, four or more rulers.

The Mexica, in choosing a single leader, were opting for a system more prevalent among the nomads, and other peoples of non-Nahua origin.† Nonetheless, as far as they were concerned, it was an important step forward; plural kingship had obvious disadvantages, particularly for a people nursing ambitions to conquer others. The new office of single leader evolved largely from the power of the priest-rulers, but also in part from the original Huitzilopochtli, the human chief, later revered as a god.* In fact, this new development may even mark the final establishment of his undisputed sway as principal deity.

Chapultepec was a former Toltec stronghold, and it was here that the last Toltec ruler, a poor refugee, had hanged himself.* Some Toltecs still clung to the locality, but they were few in numbers and had no ruler of their own.* Chapultepec never lost its importance in Mexican history; on this hill the Aztec emperors had their portraits engraved upon the rock; here the Emperor Maximilian made his residence, and here, in 1847, the naval cadets made their heroic last stand. As any visitor to the hill can see today, it has a commanding view over the city of Mexico and dominates the surrounding country. Appropriately, the castle of Chapultepec, situated in a fine park of the same name, is now the National Museum of History.

The Mexica, still an insignificant tribe, were in no position to make their mark in local politics. They had no friends and were definitely cast for the role of vassals and menials. As landless latecomers, they held a situation that was modest in the extreme; it is perhaps a mystery how they were ever permitted to occupy such a strategic site. In spite of their wretchedness, however, the Mexica were not slow to make a nuisance of themselves and to offend their neighbours by their antics:

> The Mexicans settled in this place of Chapultepec, and although it is true that they arrived tired, afflicted and in disarray, after the long journey which they had performed, nevertheless they did not cease to multiply, and increase in number, after the fashion of the Sons of Israel in Egypt under King Pharaoh. And their neighbours, when they saw the growth in their numbers, began to be troubled, and to make war upon them, with the intention of destroying them, that their name might be no longer known upon the face of the earth, and that their kind might not establish itself there.*

Faced with such threats, they proceeded to fortify themselves as best they could.*

The Mexica were attacked and expelled from Chapultepec on two separate occasions. The first assault occurred in about 1315.* It was occasioned by the arrival of Copil, the son of Huitzilopochtli's malevolent sister, who, it will be recalled, had been previously abandoned on the instructions of her divine brother:

> The Mexicans were then surrounded by innumerable peoples, of whom no one showed goodwill towards them, and awaited their future misfortunes; at that time the witch whom they had abandoned [Malinalxochitl], and who called herself sister of their god had a son called Copil, of mature age. To him his mother had revealed the injury that Huitzilopochtli had inflicted upon her. Copil was most grieved and angered at this and promised his mother to avenge the ill treatment she had suffered as best he could. Then, when Copil received the news that the Mexican warrior stood on the Hill of Chapultepec, he began to contrive with all the nations to destroy and kill that generation of Mexica, branding them as pernicious, bellicose, tyrannical, and of bad and perverse ways, as he well knew.*

Copil succeeded in his machinations, and the Mexica were defeated and driven from their home. He himself, however, was slain; his heart was cut out and was cast on to that very spot in the lagoon where the Mexica were to make their final abode.

> After he had killed him, Huitzilopochtli began to run with the heart of Copil. The Bearer of the God, Cuauhtlequetzqui, came to meet him and said: 'You have endured much travail, O priest!' The former replied: 'O Cuauhtlequetzqui, come, I have here the heart of the villain Copil, whom I went to kill; run and bear it among the rushes and reeds, to the spot where you shall see a rock on which Quetzalcoatl rested when he departed hence; of his seats, one is red and the other black; there you shall stand when you cast away Copil's heart.'*

The Mexica succeeded in returning to Chapultepec, but they were hard pressed and their second stay was brief. It was during this sojourn that they chose a single ruler, Huitzilíhuitl, to command their defence. A few years later, in 1319, a new war was unleashed on them by a powerful combination. Doubts exist as to the prime movers of the grand coalition; it would seem, however, likely that the Tepanecs took the lead. As long as a kind of balance of power in the area had been maintained, the Mexica presence might have been tolerated in Chapultepec. However, as the Tepanecs' strength grew, they must have coveted this strategic position, so near to their own capital. No doubt they found ready allies eager to quell the upstart Mexica.†

A fierce battle took place behind Chapultepec and a further massacre ensued, after the Mexica had taken refuge in the lagoon.

The unfortunate ruler of the Mexica was sacrificed in Culhuacan, as behoved a war-prisoner. The main body of refugees found themselves in a pitiful condition, lacking even clothing. They eventually found their way to Culhuacan, where they threw themselves upon the mercy of the lords of that place. While the main body of fugitives had managed to cling together, some degree of dispersion inevitably took place, and certain Mexica, including many women, fled to neighbouring cities.*

The surviving pictorial records provide illustrations bearing cogent witness to this tragic fate. The actual events took place 200 years before the Conquest, but were faithfully recorded for posterity.† The first, the Codex Boturini, shows Chapultepec, depicted as a hill with a locust perched on top. By its side are pieces of wood, symbolizing the kindling of the New Fire at the beginning of a fifty-two-year cycle. Throughout ancient Mexico two calendars were used: firstly the sacred or ritual round of 260 days, divided into 20 'weeks' of 13 days; and secondly the ordinary year of 18 periods of 20 days with 5 supplementary days, to make a total of 365 days.† The Mexicans further counted their time in 'sheafs', consisting of 52 years of 365 days. Their system of designating these can best be described by reference to a pack of cards. It is as if we called our years 'One of Spades', 'Two of Hearts', 'Three of Diamonds', 'Four of Clubs', 'Five of Spades', 'Six of Hearts', and so on. The resulting combination of thirteen possible numbers with four possible names or suits [the Mexican years were named 'House', 'Rabbit', 'Reed' and 'Flint'] gives us a total of fifty-two different designations for the years, after which the cycle starts again. In Mexico, the new cycle always started with the year Two Reed, and its beginning was a fateful occasion.†

Below the drawing of Chapultepec with the symbol of the New Fire ceremony, the same codex shows people of the Mexica tribe weeping copiously.† Farther to the right we see the unfortunate ruler, Huitzilíhuitl, and his daughter in the presence of one of the lords of Culhuacan. All three are identifiable by the name-glyphs above their heads, and the ruler and his daughter are shown being dragged by the hair, the conventional manner of illustrating war-prisoners. The second source, the Codez Azcatitlan, depicts an even more dramatic scene. In the top left corner we see the installation of Huitzilíhuitl as ruler; below this is the glyph of Chapultepec followed by a drawing of the lagoon, full of tall reeds. Within it, the Mexica are seen struggling against their foes.† Farther to the right, the ruler and other Mexica are being carried off as captives by the same peoples. Above is a picture of a warrior being sacrificed by the removal of his heart. The relevant year-signs are placed beside the drawings.

The Mexica came to Culhuacan as wretched suppliants. Their humiliation was so complete that they even felt forced to present to their new masters the treasured banner and cloak of Huitzilopochtli, as a sign of utter submission. Notwithstanding their present disarray, the arrival of this sorry band placed their hosts in something of a quandary; two of the four rulers tended to favour them, but a fierce argument ensued in their council as to how to treat the intruders. They decided to play safe, adopting an attitude of strict reserve. The Mexica were accordingly invited to establish themselves in Tizaapan, some six miles to the west of Culhuacan, near the present site of the National University of Mexico; it was far enough for them to be out of the way, but not so distant that a watchful eye could not be kept upon their activities. Moreover, they were dispatched to Tizaapan on the firm assumption that no one could conceivably prosper in such a wasteland of volcanic rock, infested with snakes and other dangerous reptiles. But, to the astonishment of their masters, they not only survived, but actually thrived:

> Then Huitzilopochtli said to the Mexicans: 'O my fathers! ask Cox-coxtli [one of the rulers of Culhuacan] where we have to go'; where-upon they asked Coxcoxtli and said to him: 'Whither in truth have we to go, O Lord and King? For we know full well that the place is yours; help us by the grant of a little land whither we may take ourselves!' Then Coxcoxtli answered them and said: 'It is well.'
> Forthwith Coxcoxtli summoned his co-rulers, the Culhua, and said

to them: 'Whither shall they go?' The rulers responded: 'O Lord O King, let them go and stay there beside the mountains here in Tizaapan': and forthwith they went and left them there, to settle in Tizaapan. And those who had left them there, informed the King, saying: 'O Lord, O King, we indeed went to leave the Mexicans in Tizaapan' and Coxcoxtli said to them: 'It is good, for they are no true people, but great villains, and perhaps they will perish there, eaten by the serpents, since many dwell in that place.'

But the Mexicans were much pleased when they saw the snakes, and they cooked and roasted them all, and ate them. And then Coxcoxtli recalled and spoke to the Culhuas: 'O Culhuas, go and see those whom you left, for perhaps they are dead.' And they said to him: 'It is well, O lord; we will go and see them!' And when they went there, they saw that they were making fire and smoke, and they said to them: 'Have you suffered O Mexicans? we have only come to see you, greet you and enquire how you are faring!' And immediately they answered: 'You have done us a favour and we are content.' And the Culhua said: 'It is well, now we will go.' They went straight to the palace, and informed Coxcoxtli, telling him: 'O Lord, O King! We went to see them, they have finished with the serpents and eaten them all.' Then Coxcoxtli said: 'See what rascals they are; have no dealings and do not speak to them.'*

In such adverse situations as these, the Mexica would display a degree of courage and endurance which distinguished them from their neighbours. Far from yielding to adversity, they were spurred to renewed efforts. Determined to survive in such inhospitable surroundings, they not only devoured the pests but settled down to cultivate the fields and construct their temples and dwellings. Their nomad instincts had not entirely left them, and thus helped to make a virtue out of necessity. They succeeded in living, as they were accustomed, by a combination of agriculture and hunting, presumably adding to their menu forms of wild life more appetizing than the snakes. In Tizaapan, after their recent disasters under a sole leader, collective rule was restored, and the government again devolved upon four priest-rulers.* Tenoch is mentioned as the foremost of these, and he continued as such until well after the foundation of the new capital.*

The powers of resistance of the Mexica impressed the rulers of Culhuacan. According to another version of the events related above, it was suggested that, if anyone could survive under such conditions, they must enjoy a special divine protection. According to one of the envoys sent to spy upon them: 'Already I told you that this people is specially favoured by the god; they are bad people and of evil ways; leave them in peace, do them no harm, since as long as they are not provoked, they will stay quiet. From that moment on, the Mexicans began to enter Culhuacan and trade and deal freely, and to become related one to another, treating each other like brothers and kinsmen.'* This interbreeding is an important event in Mexica history and transformed their status by linking them with the oldest and most civilized of the peoples of the Valley of Mexico. No longer rude parvenus or intruding nomads, now become the 'Culhua Mexica', it was they who were to be the upholders of hallowed traditions, and who styled themselves the heirs by marriage of Culhuacan, and thus of the Toltec Empire and of the Toltec rulers.

Soon the Mexica were engaged on their masters' behalf in a war with the near-by people of Xochimilco. Culhuacan, in danger of defeat at the hands of this enemy, requested help from the Mexica. The latter naturally pressed for the provision of adequate arms, but were told that they would have to provide their own. Huitzilopochtli as usual stepped into the breach and instructed them to make shields out of reeds and lances from staves.* Thus armed, they joined forces with the Culhua, themselves well equipped, and proceeded to battle partly in canoes and partly along the lake shore. The arrival of the Mexica saved the day, and with their home-made equipment they routed the enemy; they were ordered to take no prisoners:

'O Mexica, do you now know what order I [the Culhua ruler] give you? That none of those who must go may take prisoners. Only shall we maim them, tearing their ears from one side of their head.' And thus they did. Whoever took one, two or three captives, took away so many ears. When they had arrived, they informed the rulers of Culhuacan and piled the ears before them, and counted exactly how many prisoners they had made.*

The Mexica, elated by their triumph, now began to put on airs and don fine clothes. The Culhua, far from being overjoyed at their escape, took fright at the military prowess of their vassals. One of the rulers of Culhuacan who had always favoured them gave warning that if they did not escape immediately they faced annihilation.*

Another story, yet more gruesome than the tale of the prisoners' ears, is told of their mode of departure. Huitzilopochtli, whose blessings were seldom those of a tranquil life, spoke to his people:

> We must needs seek a woman, who shall be called 'the woman of discord', and she shall be named my mother or grandmother in the place where we shall go and dwell. Because this is not the place where we are to make our home and habitation; this is not the seat which I have promised you: it lies behind us, and it must needs be that our way of leaving our present abode shall not be in peace, but with war and the death of many. Let us begin to raise our arms, bows and arrows, shields and swords, and make the world know the valour of our persons.*

Thus provoked by their god, they went to one of the rulers of Culhuacan and asked that he should give them his daughter as their sovereign and as the wife of their god. He granted their request, and the princess was duly carried off to Tizaapan. Notwithstanding her beauty, so striking that she was likened to a precious necklace, she was promptly killed and flayed, and a priest donned her skin.

Thereupon they invited her father, Achitometl, to partake in the festivities in honour of the new 'goddess', who was now to become the wife of Huitzilopochtli. He arrived, accompanied by numerous princes and nobles, and loaded with gifts. Meanwhile the priest dressed in the princess' skin had placed himself in the sanctuary, beside the god's image. Achitometl, as yet unsuspecting, entered the dimly lit chamber:

> He took the rubber, the incense, the flowers, the tobacco, and the food, and placed them before the fictitious god, the flayed one, in whose honour he decapitated quails: and after this, as he offered incense, he lit the censer and recognized the skin of his maiden daughter, and was struck with horror. He immediately cried out to his fellow princes and vassals, saying: 'Who are ye, O Culhua? Do you not see that they have flayed my daughter? These villains will not stay here. Let us kill and destroy them, and may they perish on the spot!' Immediately fighting broke out as a result and Huizilopochtli said to his fathers: 'I know well; go from here calmly and cautiously.'*

This story may have an apocryphal ring, like so many in the early history of the Mexica. Regardless of this, they had clearly outstayed their welcome and had become so sure of themselves as to commit acts of overt provocation against their former masters. The tale itself hardly shows the more attractive side of their character. However, it cannot be said too often that they were only the last of a long line of devotees of the Flayed God; like many deities, he was originally a god of vegetation, the donning and shedding of human skins symbolizing the waxing and waning of the seasons.† This god may lack an Old World equivalent; however, one has only to recall the unhappy fate of Marsyas, Apollo's presumptuous rival, to appreciate that the practice of human flaying in itself was not confined to the New World.

This drawing from the *Codex Boturini* shows the Mexica leaving their home on the island of Aztlán in the year One Flint and arriving at the hill of Culiacan (curved mountain).

A highly imaginative Spanish depiction of the journey
of the Mexica.

The foundation of Tenochtitlan—from the *Codex
Mendoza*. In the centre the eagle alights on a cactus,
surrounded by the ten Mexica leaders.

The goddess Coatlicue (she of the skirt of serpents), the mother of Huitzilopochtli.

The temple on the hillside overlooking Tepoztlan, known as the Tepozteco.

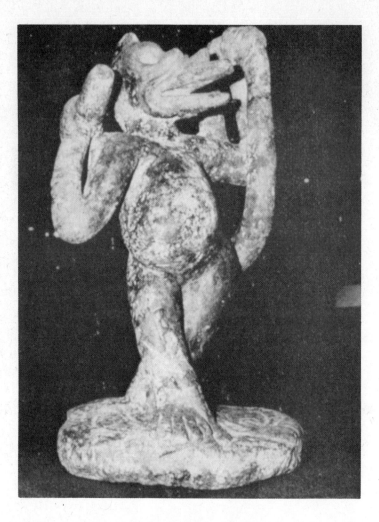

A monkey, wearing the facial duckbill mask of Quetzal-coatl, in his avocation as Ehécatl, god of wind. This is probably one of the finest pieces to be discovered during the tunnelling for the Metro in Mexico City.

The Quetzalcoatl Pyramid, which can today be seen in the Pino Suarez Metro station in Mexico City.

Coyolxauhqui, sister of Huitzilopochtli.

The Pyramid of Tenayuca; the wall of serpents.

Close-up of a serpent.

The first ruler of Tenochtitlan, Acamapichtli, as seen by Padré Durán. His glyph of a handful of reeds is on the left.

Moctezuma I receives the crown from Nezahualcóyotl.

A seated Macehual, or peasant.

The glyph of Ahuítzotl, the great conqueror. The animal is a small mythical creature, having a hand like a man's. It lived in the water, and when it killed, would eat only the eyes and nails of its victims.

Macuilxóchitl, god of music, emerging from a tortoise.

A Spanish view of Tenochtitlan, from *The History of the Conquest of Mexico by the Spaniards,* Antonio de Solis.

CHAPTER TWO

EARLY RULERS

HARD PRESSED BY THE angry rulers of Culhuacan, the Mexica
sought the protection of the lagoon:

Finding themselves so harassed, and with their women and children
crying out loudly, they started to shoot off so many javelins – which
are a kind of harpoon, in which they have great confidence – that the
people of Culhuacan, after suffering many wounds, began to withdraw.
As a result, the Mexicans could make headway and retreat towards
Iztapalapa, and they went on to a place called Acatzintlan, where they

threw themselves into the water and made themselves rafts with those same javelins and shields, together with coarse grass; as the water was fordable, they could pass the women and children onto these. And after they had crossed over to the other side, they took shelter among the reeds and rushes, where they passed the night in great anguish and sore affliction, with their women and children still crying and begging that they should be left to die there, as they could bear no more travails.*

However, the god Huitzilopochtli spoke to his priests and enjoined them to console his people in their suffering: 'The priests spoke with the people, and consoled them as best they could, and thus all that day was spent in drying their clothes, as well as their shields and arms, and in erecting a bath, where they bathed in their accustomed fashion, and which they call *temazcalli*. And this is the place which they afterwards called Mexicatzinco.'*

They finally reached a point about a mile to the south-east of where the great square of Tenochtitlan was to be situated. The place, at that time one of many a reed-covered islet, came to be called San Pablo; there still exists a church and square of that name.† Here Huitzilopochtli appeared to one of his priests and told him that the heart of his nephew Copil, previously killed by the Mexica, had been cast away near by: 'Know well that this heart fell upon a stone, and from this a cactus plant grew, so large and beautiful that an eagle lives in it, and dwells above it, and eats the most beautiful and brightly coloured birds; there he stretches his large and lovely wings and takes in the warmth of the sun and the freshness of the morning.'* They should proceed to this place the next day, and they would find the cactus, and all around the gaudy plumes of the birds that the eagle had devoured; 'To this place where you find the cactus plant, with the eagle perched upon it, I give the name of Tenochtitlan.'* The name signifies 'place of the Cactus' (*Tenochtli*) – or more precisely 'place of the fruit of the cactus'.

So, the following morning, the Mexica saw the plant, with the great eagle upon it, bowing his noble head as they approached. They prostrated themselves, as if before a divine being; they were overcome with joy, for at last they knew that they had reached their final destination and that their centuries of wandering were at an end. Filled with wonder, they proceeded to found their city; their first thought was to build a shrine to their guiding deity, Huitzilopochtli. They cut sods from the reed-covered earth, and made a little platform, on which they constructed a modest straw-covered oratory.* The date of this foundation is a key one in Mexican history. Tradition places it in the year Two House, usually taken to be the equivalent of A.D. 1325. However, it seems probably more correct to assume that the event really occurred in A.D. 1345.†

The foundation legend tells little of the march of events, but is nevertheless significant. The eagle is, of course, symbolic of the sun, and therefore connected with Huitzilopochtli himself; the hearts of his sacrificial victims were – as will be seen – placed in the Eagle Vessel (cuauhxicalli). The cactus fruit (tenochtli) both for its red hue and for its shape represents those very human hearts which the sun, or eagle, devoured. The cactus, moreover, has some further significance as denoting that this uninviting little island was at least habitable. It was, however, small and marshy, and at that time only a few miles in circumference. But, in Mexican thinking, symbolism is ever apparent. In this respect, not only is the eagle significant, but even the very reeds surrounding the place. Tollan (today called Tula) had been the capital of the Toltec Empire; now, Tollan means literally 'place of rushes', but the name Tollan had come to signify to the Toltecs simply 'the Great City'. Thus Tenochtitlan, being also in effect the City Among the Rushes, was therefore also Tollan, and would become the new Great City, and would equally one day rule the world. As their god told them: 'Here we will make ourselves lords of all these people, of their possessions, their sons and daughters; here they must serve us and pay us tribute; in this place shall the famous city be built that is destined to be the queen and lady of all the others – where we will one day receive all the kings and lords, and where they will have to come in homage, as to the supreme capital.'*

But there was method in the apparent madness of their deity; evidently reasons more practical had also dictated the choice of site. The Mexican promised land flowed with neither milk nor honey, but the prospects were less bleak than the chroniclers are apt to imply. In the first place, this island and those near by were probably not virgin territory; they may well have contained small settlements of Toltecs – the latter had certainly occupied many sites on the surrounding mainland.† Unconsciously perhaps, the priests of Huitzilopochtli had made an ideal choice. In the first place, the material advantages were considerable: birds and fishes positively abounded, and conditions for plant cultivation proved to be excellent. As space was restricted every available square inch was exploited to the full by means of the *chinampa* system of growing crops. This consists of platforms, constructed of layers of mud and aquatic plants, and held in place by walls of basketwork, to form small patches of land, intersected by canals. *Chinampas* can still be seen today in the Xochimilco area, whose nursery gardens serve the city of Mexico.

The new site also enjoyed the advantages of water communications with the cities which studded the lagoon shore, an incomparable asset in a land without pack animals or wheeled vehicles. Overland transport had always presented a major problem in ancient Mexico, particularly if any city outgrew the normal size. When all other loads had to be borne on the human back, the canoe was the most efficient carrier.

But the greatest merit of the cities' location lay in the strategic protection which the lagoon afforded, and this was the first settlement which the Mexica never had to abandon. Their muddy little islands afforded many of the blessings which had also paved the way to greatness of that other lagoon people, the Venetians. Moreover, in their aquatic milieu, the Mexica were reverting to their traditional lacustrine pattern of life established in their original home of Aztlan. On the other hand, they were to be plagued by certain shortcomings. Food, both animal and vegetable, was abundant, but raw materials were scarce. They were thus exposed to the threatening presence of their larger neighbours, on whom they were entirely dependent for wood and stone. Map 2 illustrates the proximity of these; the Valley of Mexico at this time constitutes a world in miniature, and the new Tenochtitlan was only a few miles distant from several major cities.

After its foundation, Tenochtitlan was divided into four districts, a symbolic form of subdivision respected since most ancient times.† These in their turn contained smaller sub-districts, each with its own god and temple, in accordance with the number of clans, or *calpulli*; their number had by now risen from the original seven to fifteen, or perhaps twenty, which were grouped together into the four districts.† At this time, the available land was probably held principally by the communal *calpulli* organization, a situation later to be considerably modified.

The outstanding event of early days was the founding of the sister-city of Tlatelolco, probably in 1358, or thirteen years after Tenochtitlan. The name Tlatelolco derives from the word *tlatelli*, meaning 'a built-up mound of earth'. The island on which it was founded was probably about the same size as Tenochtitlan, and each was ringed by even more minute islets of mud, all gradually to be joined together to form the great metropolis of Tenochtitlan-Tlatelolco, linked by causeways to the surrounding mainland.

The migration to Tlatelolco was apparently occasioned by disagreements over land distribution. Clearly the Mexica felt themselves cramped on one tiny island, and, with another one near by, colonization was a natural step. The two cities, at the same time close associates and keen rivals, developed on somewhat different lines; Tenochtitlan took the lead in war, while Tlatelolco was to become paramount in commerce.† Nevertheless, notwithstanding certain antagonisms, they complemented each other, and the contribution of the merchants of Tlatelolco to the future triumphs of the Mexica cannot be overstressed. Tlatelolco assumed a significant role from the very start, and during their early history it may well have been the more important of the two cities. Archaeological evidence – mainly from pottery finds – indeed suggests that Tlatelolco in particular may have existed for some time before the official date of its foundation.*

Equally, the principal surviving structure of the Great Pyramid of Tlatelolco (fragments of no less than eleven subsequent superstructures can still be seen today) bears a striking resemblance to the equivalent edifice of the Pyramid of Tenayuca, which should be dated to nearer 1250 than 1350.* It is possibly from this place that such early settlers might have come.

Between the official founding of the cities, probably in 1345 and 1358, and the accession of their ruling dynasties, a considerable period elapsed, of which we know relatively little. It would have been normal for such small fry to have recognized the suzerainty of a more powerful neighbour and to have become its tributaries. Theirs was, however, a borderline territory, situated on the frontiers of three powers: 'When they erected their oratory, it was still small, for they were in an alien land, when they came to establish themselves between the reeds and rushes. From where should they obtain stone or wood? For they were in the territory of the Tepanecs of Azcapotzalco, and also of the Acolhua, and equally on the border of the land of Culhuacan – and for this they suffered greatly.' *

Some of the Mexican leaders were in favour of submitting to the Tepanecs, in return for the supplies of wood and stone which they so badly needed. Finally, however, it was decided not to give formal allegiance to any one power, but to trade their abundant lagoon products in near-by markets:

> After they had all joined together in council, to some it appeared best that they should humbly present themselves to the people of Azcapotzalco and the other Tepanecs, of Tacuba and Coyoacan, and that they should offer them their friendship and submission with the aim of requesting stone and wood for the construction of their city; but the remainder were of the opposite opinion, saying that the Tepanecs had no respect for them, and that they ran the risk of being badly received, insulted and ill-treated; accordingly, the best course was that on market days they should go out to the villages and cities situated round the lagoon and that they and their women should take fish, frogs, all kinds of marine reptiles and all the birds that frequent the lagoon. By selling these, they should buy stone and wood for the construction of their city, and this should be done freely and without doing homage or submitting to anyone, since it was their god who had given them this place.*

At this time Tenochtitlan was still led by Tenoch, who had already played a prominent part during the captivity in Culhuacan. His authority even approached that of the future ruling dynasty. The Codex Mendoza actually depicts him with the little blue tongue or speech-glyph emerging from his mouth, which always characterized the later ruler or *tlatoani* (the word *tlatoani* means literally 'he who speaks'). He is depicted by the Codex as surrounded by ten other leaders, though other sources speak of the existence of four or thirteen leaders at the time.*

During these early years they were mainly absorbed in the task of building and consolidation, albeit on a modest scale. The initial hardships of the settlement are not to be underrated. To construct the elaborate, though highly productive system of *chinampa* cultivation was a backbreaking task, in addition to the erection of the city. In Tenochtitlan, the Mexica were presented with a refuge, and a challenge. The situation, obscure in detail, is dramatic in its essence; the Mexica, though still poor and despised, lacking raw materials and initially with little cultivation, had at last found a home of their own, after endless searchings for the promised land. In these modest settlements of fisher-folk lay the nucleus of the imperial city, at which Cortés and his men were to marvel barely two centuries later as outrivalling all that they had known in Europe.

Tenoch had died some twenty-five years after the founding of the city. It was then decided, probably in 1372,† not to elect another priest-ruler of pure Mexican stock, but to seek the added prestige of a royal dynasty of wider antecedents and connections.

In many ways it was natural that they should look towards Culhuacan for this purpose. Not only was the latter revered as the heir of Toltec civilization; in addition, the Mexica had enjoyed close connections with Culhuacan ever since their captivity. Accordingly, they addressed themselves to the ruler of this place:

> Great Lord, we the Mexicans, your servants and vassals, shut in as we are among the reeds and rushes, alone and unprotected by any nation, directed only by our god to the place where we now are, which lies within the jurisdiction of Azcapotzalco, of your kingdom, and of Texcoco. In view of this, since you have permitted us to stay there, it would not be just that we should remain without a chief or lord, who might command and guide us, and show us how we are to live; who might free us and defend and protect us from our enemies.
>
> For this reason we come to you, knowing that among your people there are sons of our blood, related to yours, brought forth from our bodies and yours. And among those of your blood and ours we have learnt that there exists a son of Opichiztahuatzin, whose name is Acamapichtli. He is also the son of your daughter, called Atotoztli. We beg that you give him to us as our lord, so that we may maintain him as is fitting, since he is of the lineage of the Mexicans and of the kings and lords of Culhuacan.†

Acamapichtli (meaning 'handful of reeds') was thus chosen. Most other accounts of the event also state that he was the son of a Mexican nobleman and a princess of Culhuacan. This city in fact possessed four reigning dynasties; that from which the new ruler stemmed had close ties also with Coatlichan, the main centre of the Acolhua, second only to the Tepanecs among the peoples of the Valley of Mexico. Acamapichtli was actually living in Coatlichan at the moment when the Mexica came and sought him as their ruler.*

He thus represented an ideal choice; while, as will later be seen, Tlatelolco was to be governed by a son of the Tepanec ruler, Tenochtitlan chose a prince who partly originated from the Toltec centre of Culhuacan, but who was also connected with the powerful Acolhua. In this manner the Mexica had managed to associate themselves with all the great names of the region. This whole inter-locking system of dynastic ties is perhaps reminiscent of nineteenth-century Europe, when newly established nations, such as the liberated Balkan states, sought monarchs from leading ruling families, to whom they could look for patronage and protection.

So far, only Acamapichtli has been mentioned, but of almost equal importance is his wife, Ilancueitl. Her situation *vis-à-vis* her husband is confusing; she was also from Culhuacan and of royal descent. She is usually stated simply to have been Acamapichtli's wife, though she was older than he and bore him no sons. According, however, to certain versions, she was really his mother, or even both his mother and his wife at the same time.* According to one story, she was so ashamed at her inability to bear children that she resorted to a strange ruse to hide her ignominy: 'The king, seeing her sadness, and because he loved and cherished her dearly, consoled her as best he could. And she, observing that the king was so fond of her, begged him as a favour that, since the Lord of Creation had deprived her of the blessings of offspring, and that the people might lose their bad impres-sion of her as a barren woman, he might concede that, when sons were born of his other wives, she might press them to her breast, and might take to her bed in feigned childbirth, and thus those who came to see her might congratulate her on the delivery and the new son.'* According to one account, Ilancueitl was the real ruler at the outset, Acamapichtli playing the part of a kind of prince consort – or perhaps enjoying a situation more comparable to that of William III of England, as a co-ruler who subsequently reigned in his own right, after the death of his spouse.*

The origins of the Tlatelolco dynasty are not in doubt. The founder, who ascended the throne at the same time as Acamapichtli, bears the rather formidable name of Cuacuapitzahuac, meaning 'Pointed Horn'. He was the son of Tezozómoc, the great Tepanec monarch. He acceded after a delegation from Tlatelolco had visited his father, humbly to seek a ruler. He was not allowed to live in Tlatelolco for a year, while a worthy residence was constructed for him. From his new subjects he collected tribute, which he in turn delivered to his father Tezozómoc.*

The marriages of Acamapichtli, and the resulting offspring, are important politically and socially. Both he and his successors, apart from their first or legitimate consort, also possessed an ample number of secondary wives, whose children could succeed in the absence of descendants from the principal spouse. Acamapichtli married up to twenty other wives – probably the daughters of each clan-leader.* It is usually suggested that the nobility were all descended from his numerous progeny. It would appear, however, that these constituted a new aristocracy, since some kind of older ruling class must have existed. As we have already seen, the Mexica were far from primitive; when they reached the Valley of Mexico their social organization had already passed beyond a merely tribal condition.†

It is difficult to form an exact judgement of how the first rulers governed, since information on the subject is meagre. Most of what is known of the office of *tlatoani* derives from the last reigns before the Conquest. The inner council of four, as well as the larger consultative body, the Tlatocan, were probably officially established some sixty years later, after the Aztec rise to power.* However, they surely existed in less well-defined form at this earlier period, and the system of government was thus based on an elected monarch, advised by counsellors chosen from a small ruling class.

Apart from other restrictions on the powers of the early rulers, the significance of the ancient clan, or *calpulli* organization should not be underestimated. Probably totemic in origin, with the foundation of Tenochtitlan the clans became in effect territorial units, grouped together into the four larger districts of the city. In addition to holding the land, they provided the basis for the raising of army units, and the clan-leader was also a military captain. They also possessed a certain religious importance, and each had a god and temple of its own.

43

Little is known about internal affairs under Acamapichtli except that he reigned peacefully, building up the city and constructing houses, *chinampas* and canals.* Life, indeed, cannot have differed so greatly from that of those humble fishermen who had set out from Aztlan over 200 years before. Their more glorious achievements still lay in the future.

Humdrum tasks, such as the preparing of the land and the building of the capital, receive rather scant mention in the surviving records. Of diplomacy and war, within this micro-world, somewhat more is told. At the time of the foundation of Tenochtitlan, power in the surrounding areas was mainly shared by three lakeside cities and peoples: the Tepanec capital of Azcapotzalco to the north-west of the lagoon; Coatlichan, the chief city of the Acolhua, to the east; and Culhuacan to the south. At about the time when Acamapichtli acceded to his throne, a new phenomenon was arising – the emergence of one of these peoples, the Tepanecs, as a kind of super-power, intent upon swallowing up its neighbours one by one.

The Tepanec Empire was created by one man, Tezozómoc of Azcapotzalco, and was brought into being as much by diplomatic skill as by military prowess. Tezozómoc's very longevity – he reigned for over half a century – gave him ample opportunities to display his talents and to expand his realm. He developed a Machiavellian skill in dividing his enemies, and in using others to further his ends. Inevitably in such schemes, future victims would play a prominent if unwitting part in overcoming the enemy of the moment. It was Tezozómoc who was the true preceptor of the Mexica in their advance to power; his rare and ruthless genius served to form the empire which his Mexica vassals later managed to seize from his successor and then expand. Tezozómoc had already overthrown Tenayuca and Culhuacan, with the help of his Mexica vassals, and Texcoco, now emerging as the leading city of the Acolhua, was the only power left in the immediate vicinity which could even hope to stand up to him.

The Tepanecs, in aiming at supreme power, were placing themselves on a different level to any people since the Toltecs.† Before the death of Tezozómoc, the Tepanec domains, which provided the hard core round which the Aztecs were to build a greater empire,

44

included almost all the Valley of Mexico; they also dominated considerable territories beyond, in the Valley of Toluca, to the northwest, and in the Valley of Morelos to the south, as well as an extensive region to the north-east.† In the acquisition of empire, Tezozómoc went out to further the interests of his own dynasty. Quite apart from creating the throne of Tlatelolco for one of his sons, he liked to secure his other conquests by replacing vanquished rulers by his own relatives.* Like the later Aztec Empire, that of the Tepanecs was basically a tribute-gathering organization and accounts exist of what was taken from the Mexica and from other peoples. The two Mexica rulers were therefore at that time simply Tepanec tributaries like many of their neighbours.

Moreover, in the reign of Acamapichtli, their lot was a hard one, owing to the onerous levies imposed. To humiliate his vassals, Tezozómoc began to make preposterous demands. Firstly he requested that, apart from the usual tribute consisting of fish, frogs and greens, the Mexica should provide fully grown willows and other trees, as well as a raft planted with every kind of vegetable. They began to weep and lament at such impositions. However, Huitzilopochtli consoled them, saying through the mouth of one of his priests that he would make everything easy. And to be sure: 'Thus they found easily the willows, which they took to Azcapotzalco and planted in the place commanded by the ruler and they brought the raft upon the water, all sown with maize with ripe ears, chile, tomatoes, amaranth, beans, gourds and roses.'*

To test his tributaries yet further, Tezozómoc now demanded on pain of death that they should again produce such a raft, but that this time they should add a duck and a heron, in the act of hatching their eggs. Once more, their god came to the rescue and provided what was required. 'And once the raft had been made, and sown with every kind of vegetable, there appeared among them a duck sitting on her eggs, and likewise a heron; they took it to Tezozómoc in Azcapotzalco, and at their god's bidding added a gift of some large cakes, made of coloured worms of the lagoon, which are called *ezcahuitli*.'†

Various sources list 'conquests' made by the Mexica during the reigns of their first rulers. Since, however, they themselves at this stage were Tepanec tributaries, it is logical to suppose that such places, if conquered, became subject to the Tepanecs rather than to their underlings. These early Mexican conquests, if such they are to be called, may be divided into two categories: on the one hand, those made ostensibly under direct Tepanec leadership, and on the other those described as if they were separate Mexican expeditions. That they should have been permitted by the Tepanecs to fight some campaigns of a more or less independent nature is not altogether surprising. In the heyday of the Aztec Empire, references occur to wars initiated by tributaries, without any apparent intervention on the part of the central power. It is, therefore, perfectly conceivable that the Mexica, within the general framework of the Tepanec *Weltpolitik*, should have been occasionally permitted to fight battles on their own – even if the fruits of victory accrued partly to their masters.

In addition to Acamapichtli's conquests of settlements in the Xochimilco region, a short distance to the south-east of Tenochtitlan, an expedition is mentioned against Cuernavaca, a considerable distance farther to the south, and therefore perhaps a rather ambitious objective for the Mexica at this early stage in their career of conquest.† In the Xochimilco area, the Mexica were operating among people with whom they enjoyed close ethnic ties; possibly the Tepanecs felt that they were well fitted to deal with those with whom they had so much in common.* But apart from such successes, attributed by Mexican sources to the Mexica themselves, others are listed, mainly in the Valley of Toluca, and covering a fairly large area to the north-west; they occur in the latter part of Acamapichtli's reign. This was in effect the land of origin of the Tepanecs, and it may therefore be assumed that its conquest was very much a Tepanec affair, in which the Mexican tributaries would have played an auxiliary role.†

One further war needs to be mentioned in connection with Acamapichtli – though it was no conquest. The bitter conflict with the Chalca to the south-east of the lagoon probably started in 1375, or three years after his accession. It was only to end in final victory two generations afterwards. A bewildering medley of tribes and rulers went to compose the confederation of Chalco-Amecameca.† The accounts of Chimalpain, the chronicler *par excellence* of that region, suggest that Chalco must have enjoyed a long tradition as a powerful, much respected and closely knit state. At the start of the conflict, it still seems to have possessed some kind of 'empire' of its own.* For the first ten years, until about 1385, the war was fought mainly by the Tepanecs themselves. In the early stages, it was a fairly gentlemanly affair, prisoners being returned, rather than sacrificed according to custom.* After 1385, however, the struggle grew increasingly ferocious. The Mexica were now playing an increasingly important part in hostilities, though it was not until the reign of Acamapichtli's successor that it was to become a predominantly Mexican commitment.

Acamapichtli died, probably in 1391, after a reign of some nineteen years.† He had consolidated the infant Mexican state. He had not only played an important part in the building of the city and the formation of its institutions; in addition, he had instituted in a modest way that career of conquest that was later to become a flood.

The dying monarch had addressed the nobles at considerable length as to the future: 'And thus, when he was about to die, he called together all the leaders and made them a long and careful address, commending into their hands the affairs of state, as well as his wives and children. He did not, however, designate any one as heir, but said that the nation should elect as ruler one of these, or some other, according to their wishes. He wished to leave them free in this matter, and ended by expressing deep regret that he had not been able to set the city free from servitude and tribute to Azcapotzalco.'*

As a result, an elective council was held, for the purpose of choosing a ruler. Like others that were to follow later on, it took place behind closed doors, and the right of the people as a whole to ratify the choice was reduced to a pure formality. The significant point was the establishment of the principle that the fittest of the royal princes should be chosen. In this as in other respects, the Mexican state was to be a meritocracy; the office of ruler or *tlatoani* thus differed fundamentally from contemporary European monarchies, based upon succession by primogeniture.

On this occasion, it appears that the leaders of the four main divisions into which the city had been divided played the foremost

47

part in the selection of a ruler. The prince chosen was Acamapichtli's son, Huitzilíhuitl ('Humming Bird Feather'). In the long addresses always made to the new monarch, he was reminded of his duties to his people, as well as of his religious role, as the likeness on earth of Huitzilopochtli: 'Valiant young man, our king and lord: do not be dismayed or lose heart on account of the new charge that has been laid upon you in that you should protect the land and water of your new kingdom, which is surrounded by rough reeds, rushes and canes, and where we live under the protection of our god, Huitzilopochtli, whose likeness you represent.... Do not think that you are chosen in order to rest, but to work; you know well the poverty and want that attended your father's reign, and which he bore with great patience and courage.'*

Huitzilíhuitl certainly improved the lot of his people, and his success was due, at least in part, to his successful marriages. Following the death of his first wife, a Tacuban princess, it was decided to seek a royal bride from the family of Tezozómoc. The Mexicans went to the great ruler to make their request, bringing gifts of fish and frogs, and addressed themselves in most humble fashion to their overlord.* Their plea was granted and Huitzilíhuitl was permitted to marry a granddaughter of the Tepanec ruler. This union was to have the most significant consequences. Not only was the ruler of Tlatelolco himself a son of Tezozómoc, but the dynasty of Tenochtitlan was now also to be counted among his close relations. From this moment on, the Mexicans began to assume a special position among his many vassals.

In internal affairs Huitzilíhuitl was thus able to pursue a more forward-looking policy than his predecessor, adding to the city and its temples, and paying the greatest attention to the ordering of religious ceremonies: 'He ruled and governed with much peace and assurance, and was much loved by his lords and by all the common people. He began to make laws and regulations for the state, especially as far as the cult of the gods was concerned, which was something over which all the lords and kings showed a special zeal, since they considered themselves to be their living representatives, and thought that whatever honour was done to the gods was also done to themselves.'*

Huitzilíhuitl was a monarch who was clearly out to increase the importance of his realm. But it was still a small one, and he had to proceed with caution: 'And with this feigned humility which he showed towards his neighbours, he arranged his affairs so well that his city was filled and increased by people from neighbouring towns. . . .'*

A certain change of status is discernible, and economic advances were certainly facilitated by Huitzilíhuitl's marriage into the Tepanec royal family and the Mexicans' enhanced standing with their overlords. Following the birth of a son and heir, half-Tepanec, we are told that the nobles and court of Azcapotzalco actually came to Tenochtitlan, bearing lavish gifts from their sovereign: 'And when the Mexicans went away, in their wake also came all the lords of Azcapotzalco, Tacuba, and Coyoacan, bearing the best presents that they could bring, after their usual fashion. . . .'* Later on, Tezozómoc actually sent ambassadors to Tenochtitlan announcing that he desired so greatly that his Mexican vassals prosper that, except for the natural products of the lagoon, such as fish and frogs, they would be required to pay no more tribute.* Such gestures suggest that the Mexica were now beginning to be wooed as associates, rather than oppressed as vassals. The significance of these concessions was sufficient to arouse strong opposition within Tezozómoc's own ruling council.*

Huitzilíhuitl's Tepanec wife died when their only child Chimalpopoca was nine years old. While retaining his good standing with his masters, he succeeded in making a second principal marriage of almost equal significance, since it furthered Mexican expansion towards the warmer and lower regions to the south, and thus brought in its train added economic progress. In the reign of Huitzilíhuitl, military campaigns in the Cuernavaca region, where cotton and other sub-tropical luxuries abounded, provided the Mexica, used to dressing in rough maguey fibre, with their first cotton clothes.* The romantic circumstances surrounding the ruler's second principal marriage with a Cuernavacan princess should not obscure the fact that it was basically achieved by force of arms.†

The ruler of Cuernavaca was also famed as a sorcerer, and he made use of his talents to protect his lovely daughter from the embraces of adventurous suitors. He called on all the spiders and centipedes to guard her, as well as on an army of bats and scorpions. And, just in case such a force was not sufficient to protect her, she was closeted within the palace, the gates of which were defended by immense wild beasts. The numerous offers of marriage presented by neighbouring princes were rejected out of hand. As the result of a dream, Huitzilíhuitl decided to make a bid to marry the princess. He accordingly sent ambassadors to her father, who dismissed his suit, adding that in the wretched lagoon-township of Tenochtitlan his daughter would be deprived of the dainty dishes and the abundance of cotton clothes to which she was accustomed – something which was probably only too true at the time. Prompted by a second dream, Huitzilíhuitl made an arrow that was beautifully painted, and placed a fine precious stone inside. Thus armed, he proceeded to the confines of the land of Cuernavaca, and aimed his weapon so that it landed in the courtyard where the princess lay cloistered:

> King Huitzilíhuitl did thus, and went to the borders of Cuernavaca, and immediately shot his arrow, using the shaft that was very well painted and admirably made, in the inside of which was placed the' previously mentioned precious stone, which shone most dazzlingly. The arrow fell in the middle of the patio where the lady Miahuaxihuitl lay cloistered.
>
> When the shaft fell in the middle of the patio, and the lady Miahuaxihuitl saw it fall from the sky, as has been indicated, she straightway took it in her hand, and marvelled as she eyed and observed its varied colours, such as no other arrow possessed. She immediately broke it in the middle, and saw the precious stone that shone so beautifully.*

She then took out the jewel. To test its consistency she put it between her teeth and inadvertently swallowed it. Legend has it that as a result she conceived a child, who was to grow up to be Moctezuma I, the greatest of Aztec emperors.*

While he was able to score certain victories on his own account, Huitzilíhuitl was naturally obliged to partake in the campaigns of the Tepanecs. With his conquests in the Valley of Mexico and the subjection of the Valley of Toluca to the north-west, Tezozómoc had already absorbed many of the surrounding peoples. Two potential rivals remained: Xaltocan and Texcoco. The war against the latter began, strictly speaking, in Huitzilíhuitl's reign, but was not concluded until after his death, and its story can therefore be more conveniently told in connection with his successor. It was not unnatural that Xaltocan should be chosen as Tezozómoc's next victim. Its power was visibly declining, whereas that of Texcoco was rising. It had previously been a powerful state: Don Pablo Nazareo de Xaltocan, legitimate descendant of the rulers of that place, in his famous and rather pathetic letter to Philip II in 1566, lays claim to perpetual dominion over a vast territory to the north and north-east of Xaltocan, which he claimed as having belonged to his ancestors.*

Accounts of the actual war are brief, and merely relate that Xaltocan was destroyed in 1395, and that the ruler and some of his followers escaped northwards, while others went to Tlaxcala.† While the war was mainly a Tepanec affair, it had great significance for the Mexica; as a reward for their services they acquired lands formerly belonging to Xaltocan. This was a momentous step forward, for not only was their rising status confirmed, but they acquired what they most lacked – additional land to cultivate.*

During this reign, the Mexican–Tepanec forces also initiated an ambitious drive in the direction of the coast of the Gulf of Mexico. It was from this Tierra Caliente, or warm coastal land, that they were eventually to obtain the precious stones and gaudy feathers with which the nobles and warriors loved to adorn themselves.

In 1398, an expedition was undertaken which resulted in the capture of Cuauhtinchan, lying to the south-east, beyond the modern city of Puebla de los Angeles. At first sight such an expedition might seem over-ambitious, and it has been argued that it took place at a much later date. But, in the first place, Cuauhtinchan is not so much farther afield than Cuernavaca; in the second, it lies near Cholula, then still a great trading centre, as well as a holy city. The merchants of Tlatelolco would surely by this time have begun to trade with their counterparts in Cholula, exchanging their own products for those of the Gulf Coast. It therefore seems natural that it was chiefly Tlatelolco that was involved in the execution of this campaign.†

One other conflict still requires mention: the interminable struggle against the intrepid people of Chalco. Under Huitzilíhuitl, the Mexica appear to have borne the brunt, and little is heard of Tepanec intervention except, rather curiously, on the side of Chalco. During the early part of the reign, little is told of the war, but it was subsequently resumed in all its fury, and in 1406 Chalco suffered a serious setback.* It was, however, a ding-dong struggle, and two years later they appear to have made a remarkable recovery.* In 1411, the Mexica actually took Chalco, and the chief among its many rulers was forced to flee, while the victors installed others, who were favourable towards themselves. Their triumph was short-lived, since its very extent startled various neighbours, whom they were not yet powerful enough to defy. A combination of powers was assembled, which forced them to give way. The most remarkable thing about this coalition was that it included the Tepanecs of Azcapotzalco.*

Huitzilíhuitl died in 1415 or 1416, and was succeeded by his son Chimalpopoca, meaning 'Smoking Shield':†

Chimalpopoca, grandson of Tezozómoc and a young man of eighteen years, was elected by the common consent of the whole Mexican community; and the city rejoiced at the election. The boy was placed upon his throne and given the royal insignia; the diadem was placed upon his head, he was anointed with the divine unction, as they call it, a shield was placed in his left hand, and in the other a club armed with obsidian blades, such as they were wont to use. He was equipped with certain arms, in conformity with the god whose likeness it was intended to impersonate, as a sign that he promised to defend his city and die for it.*

Information on the internal affairs of Tenochtitlan during the reign of Chimalpopoca is no more plentiful than for those of his two predecessors. Economic progress certainly continued; the aged Tezozómoc had a great affection for his grandson, and this led to a further relaxation in the Tepanec demands for tribute. Living conditions gradually improved, and people no longer lived in huts, but built themselves houses of stone.

But such advances brought the usual troubles in their wake. Pollution problems arose at an early stage in Mexican history, affecting the waters of the lagoon, and it became necessary to seek alternative supplies. Leading Mexicans addressed themselves to the ruler: 'Dear son and grandson, to your fathers and grandfathers it seems fitting that you should send for the water from Chapultepec that flows into this lake from all sides; this is necessary for you and for your people, because our water is becoming foul.'*

A request to that effect was made by Chimalpopoca to Tezozómoc, and was readily granted. Later, however, when the Mexica asked in addition for the necessary raw materials for an aqueduct, a storm arose within the Tepanec council. The question caused a commotion, and certain leading Tepanecs, already ill-disposed towards the Mexica, stirred up feeling among the populace of their capital. Tezozómoc was so distressed at this turn of events that, according to one version, it actually caused his death, in 1426.* The improvement in conditions was not confined to Tenochtitlan. In this growing Mexican prosperity, the merchants of Tlatelolco certainly played a leading part; at this time, they first began to trade in their market feathers and precious stones, those status symbols of the nobility.*

By this time, therefore, it is possible to envisage Tenochtitlan and Tlatelolco as very different from the first modest settlements on two muddy little islands, built of straw and reeds, and whose scanty inhabitants dressed in rough maguey fibre. By now, the two cities had begun to take shape; they could boast of impressive ceremonial centres, and houses of stone, inhabited by dignitaries clothed in fine cotton and adorned with gaudy plumes, the produce of an active external commerce. The soil had been fully tamed, and formed into the richly cultivated *chinampas* intersected with countless canals.

Towards the end of their first twenty years at Tenochtitlan the Mexican armies had already conducted distant campaigns under the aegis of the Tepanecs – as far as the region of Cuernavaca, and beyond the modern city of Puebla.

In Chimalpopoca's reign, the most significant military operation is the war against Texcoco, started in 1414, while Huitzilíhuitl still ruled, and continued by his son.†

From this point on, Texcoco is of crucial importance in the history of the Mexica, first as adversary, and later as leading partner. Texcoco, until about the year 1400, was not the principal city of the region inhabited by the Acolhua.† It had, however, already existed for several centuries, having been founded in Toltec times.*

It was then re-established by the descendants of the nomad Chichimecs who invaded the Valley of Mexico after the fall of the

Toltec Empire. It was Quinatzin, their third ruler, who transferred his capital to Texcoco, and thus became the first Chichimec 'emperor' to rule from this place. But in point of fact the 'empire' of the Chichimecs had ceased to be a reality by this time, and Quinatzin's domain hardly stretched beyond the confines of Texcoco, which had not yet assumed its leading role among its neighbours.

But, under Quinatzin and his successors, great cultural changes took place. In the first place, Nahuatl, that symbol of civilization, was adopted, and became the official language.* Moreover, the arrival of important groups of immigrants furthered this process. Already in the reign of Quinatzin people described as of Toltec descent had arrived from the region of Oaxaca to the south.* Possibly from these the Texcocans learnt the goldsmiths' art, as well as the painting of manuscripts, both of which flourished in Oaxaca. Under the cultural stimulus of such outside influences Texcoco, from being the capital of the nomads, came to be considered as the 'Athens of America'.

These first immigrants were followed by others; these are also described in general terms as belonging to the 'Toltec' family – that is to say, speakers of Nahuatl.* In point of fact, they may have been more closely akin to the Mexica than to any other group.† As such, they would account for the close spiritual bonds that subsequently united Tenochtitlan and Texcoco – in particular the shared cult of Huitzilopochtli and the presence in both capitals of a great temple, jointly dedicated to his cult and to that of the Rain God.*

But, during the decades when Texcoco was rising to a position of importance, the wily Tezozómoc was achieving a dominating position for the Tepanecs in the Valley of Mexico, and in certain regions far beyond. It clearly irked him that one people should elude his grasp – and thus the two powers, albeit of rather unequal strength – the Tepanecs and the Acolhua – were left facing each other across the lagoon.

Quinatzin's successor as ruler of Texcoco did not himself seek to challenge the growing power of the Tepanecs; he seemed to prefer to reach a *modus vivendi* with Tezozómoc, neither claiming the controversial title of 'Lord of the Chichimecs', nor challenging him in war.† The accession of his son, Ixtlilxóchitl, in 1409, transformed the situation. He was bold and forthright, and little disposed to play second fiddle to Tezozómoc. Not only did he firmly assume the leadership of the Acolhua, but actually challenged Tezozómoc, by asserting his right to be called 'Lord of the Chichimecs' or 'Emperor'. The latter naturally rejected this impudent claim, and matters were made worse by Ixtlilxóchitl's rejection of one of Tezozómoc's daughters as his legitimate spouse; instead, he married the sister of Chimalpopoca of Tenochtitlan, a union that was to have the most far-reaching consequences.

Tezozómoc was not slow to move in response to this provocation. He resolved to suppress the upstart and make the Acolhua province his own. He first summoned to his presence his loyal lieges, the two Mexican monarchs; he insisted that on no account would he recognize Ixtlilxóchitl's assumed title, and inveighed against his haughtiness and presumption. On the contrary, he himself would be 'emperor', and, as his grandchildren, the Mexican rulers would be the twin mainstays of his throne; together, the three would rule the earth.* In addition, he reminded his visitors that he was the paymaster or relative of the rulers of several of the Acolhua cities, and could count on their support against their legitimate overlord, Ixtlilxóchitl of Texcoco.

Tezozómoc's tirade is exceedingly significant. It firstly underlines the enhanced status of the Mexica, now well on the way to becoming allies rather than servants of the Tepanecs. It further stresses the deep divisions prevailing among the Acolhua, whose loyalty to Ixtlilxóchitl was uncertain. Tezozómoc, who knew no rival in the art of splitting and undermining his opponents, triumphed as much through his devious diplomacy as by the might of his armies. As a preliminary to his designs against Texcoco, Tezozómoc made a typical gesture in 1410.

Then, some days after Tezozómoc's meeting and council, he sent his messengers to Ixtlilxóchitl, and dispatched much cotton as if in a gesture of friendship, saying that he particularly requested that the latter might be good enough to command his vassals that they should make very fine mantles of the cotton, as they knew how to do in that city at that time, because he had need of them. . . . And when Tezozómoc saw that Ixtlilxóchitl had instructed his vassals to make the mantles, and had sent them to him promptly, he understood that it would be easy to force Ixtlilxóchitl to submit to his domination.*

Although the request was phrased in the diplomatic language of the times, and so presented as if a mere favour were expected, in fact it was intended, and understood, as a token of submission.

Tezozómoc then went further:

> He sent a second time more cotton than the first, announcing simultaneously that he had received the mantles and that they were very remarkable as made by his vassals, and that he requested that he would be kind enough to have more made from the cotton that he was now sending. Ixtlilxóchitl received this message, and as the amount of cotton was very large, and he realized that he could not deal with it all in his city, he called together some subject rulers and ordered them to divide the cotton among their vassals, that they might make very fine mantles for Tezozómoc, as he had commanded should be done.*

Tezozómoc then proceeded to dispatch yet greater quantities of cotton. The limit, however, had been reached; Ixtlilxóchitl, unwilling to develop any further this unremunerative textile industry, at last refused, saying that this time he would keep the cotton and use it to make armour; he addressed his subjects as follows:

> He [Tezozómoc] must think that we are mere women, or that our vassals make the mantles from fear. It is not just you should have to do this, for you well know that I am the legitimate ruler of all the earth. Take the cotton and make the arms that you may need and since they will not acknowledge me, you will swear allegiance to me as your King and Universal Lord, and after that, we will dominate them by force of arms.*

He proceeded now to muster his forces, and summoned to his presence his allies, those few Acolhua cities which remained loyal, having resisted the blandishments of Tezozómoc.† And finally, in 1414, Ixtlilxóchitl took the fateful step of having himself sworn in as 'Universal Monarch'. Only the rulers of his two most stalwart allies were present at the ceremony. As a supreme act of defiance, he sent to Tezozómoc, announcing that he would pardon the latter's past misdemeanours, if only he would pay homage to the newly anointed Lord of All the Earth.

The story of the war can be told fairly briefly. Tezozómoc first assembled a powerful army, reinforced by contingents of the Mexica and other associates and subjects. He then, in 1415, mounted a frontal attack which, after some initial successes, was repulsed.† Ixtlilxóchitl then made a major counter-move. He first marched north-eastwards and captured Otumba, which had recently declared for Tezozómoc; he then moved north-westwards and fought a big battle near Tula. He then wheeled southwards, and after a series of successful engagements arrived at the gates of Azcapotzalco, the Tepanec capital, which he besieged for several months.†

Tezozómoc, now hard-pressed, decided that attack was the best method of defence. After a vigorous diplomatic offensive, to wean away Chalco and Otumba from their alliance with his enemies, he made a counter-thrust in the form of a pincer movement early in 1418. He cunningly pretended that it was to be concentrated to the north of Texcoco; this was only a feint, and his main objective lay to the south, towards Huexotla.

Texcocan records insist that this attack was repulsed.* Such a contention, however, would appear doubtful, since shortly afterwards Texcoco was abandoned by its ruler. As part of his deception plan, before this event, Tezozómoc reportedly went so far as to pretend that he would actually recognize Ixtlilxóchitl as 'emperor', if he would personally come to meet him at an appointed rendezvous. The latter, suspecting an ambush, sent one of his sons, who was duly taken for the ruler himself, caught and flayed, and his skin stretched out on a near-by rock.

At all events, Ixtlilxóchitl was forced to flee from Texcoco; already in desperate straits, he was then set upon by his former friends, the people of Chalco and Otumba, and killed after a valiant struggle.

And then King Ixtlilxóchitl donned his arms and went towards a place called Topanohuayan, by a stream which descends from the mountains; he was accompanied by a few vassals and loyal friends and by his son, Prince Nezahualcóyotl, whom he told to hide, that the royal line might not end with him. And the Prince, to please his father, climbed a tree called a Capulin, covered with thick foliage, which stood just by a hillock in the vicinity, and from this point he watched all that happened to his unfortunate father, although he longed to die for him.

And as Ixtlilxóchitl arrived near to the stream that passed by some cliffs, those of Otumba arrived on one side, and those of Chalco on the other, and they asked him with appearances of deep respect if they might do him some service – for they pretended that they wished to help him and celebrate with him. Ixtlilxóchitl replied that he did not require this – and that they might do with him as they wished, as he well knew that they were traitors and servants of Tezozómoc.*

Ixtlilxóchitl was then killed and his slayers took away his arms and insignia and gave them to Tezozómoc. One faithful follower then came and gathered up his body, adorned it with fresh insignia, and burned it according to custom.

The harsh conditions imposed on the defeated Texcocans were to have important consequences; like certain more recent peace-settlements, they sowed the seeds for subsequent wars of revenge. Tezozómoc took much for himself but gave the actual city of Texcoco to the Mexica. The latter had to pay over part of their share of tribute to the Tepanec monarch, who thus received the lion's share for himself.†

The unfortunate Texcocans subsequently made a pathetic protest against such exactions; they sent a deputation to Tezozómoc, lamenting that, owing to the depredations of war, they could not meet his demands. First a Texcocan of Toltec descent spoke up, saying that they simply did not possess the precious stones, gold and silver that they were expected to produce; as a result of war, they had not even been able to sow their fields. Then a Chichimec, representing the other half of the Texcocan nation, declared that such luxuries were simply unknown to his people. His forebears had not even possessed clothing and had covered their nudity with deerskin. If their rulers had worn crowns, they were made of foliage.*

The grant of Texcoco to the Mexica as tributary, together with previous assignments of land, marks a major step forward. Now they themselves were tribute-gatherers as well as tributaries; they thus occupied already a kind of intermediate position in the regional hierarchy. They may have been still subordinate to the Tepanecs, but they were now elevated far above their original status as mere under-lings, forced to beg for small favours from their mighty overlords.

Of perhaps yet greater significance are the suggestions in certain historical sources of the possibility of open dissensions between the two powers before the great clash in 1428. It is often suggested that the Mexica were humble satellites of the Tepanecs until this date: however, it would seem more probable that they were getting out of control before the final war.† Tepanec support for Chalco against the Mexica has already been mentioned. Chalco, the bitter foe of Tenochtitlan, continued to be in favour with the Tepanecs, had helped to eliminate their foe, Ixtlilxóchitl, and was actually rewarded for its part in this war.* This did not deter the Mexica from continuing their hostilities against Chalco during Chimalpopoca's reign.* Thus a curious state of affairs persisted whereby the Tepanecs tended to favour Chalco, and the Mexica, their tributaries, waged war against them.

Tezozómoc died in 1426, and his funeral was celebrated with elaborate rites, such as later attended the passing of the Aztec rulers, of whom in his day he was the true counterpart:

Before this [the arrival of the guests], as he died, they washed the body very well, and dried it out with clover water and other sweet-smelling things, in order that the body might take on their perfume. And then they dressed it in the royal robes and the jewels of gold and precious stones, just as Tezozómoc had dressed on feast days and for public business. They then cut certain locks from the top of his head as a memorial of the ruler, and put emeralds in his mouth. The body was then shrouded on top of this with seventeen royal mantles, all very fine and costly, and sewn with many pearls, and after that they stitched on to it another very fine robe on which was portrayed very naturalistically the God Tezcatlipoca; thereupon they put it on a mat in a seated position, and placed a very lifelike turquoise mask on the face, made according to the features of the dead man. This was only done if the defunct was monarch of all the earth; on other kings they placed a mask of gold.*

The funeral procession was most impressive:

By the side [of the body] went Maxtla [the next ruler], leading with a baton in his hand and his hair unfastened, and wearing the clothes and insignia that was customary on such occasions; in the same fashion the others came with their batons, Moctezuma, the first of that name, following directly behind Maxtla, then in third place came Tayauh and lastly Teyolcocoyhua, king of Acolman. . . .

Behind these came countless other dignitaries and then:

> Many lords and ambassadors from different places, and many knights who had been vassals, all wearing many pendants and feathers and jewels that had belonged to the king, together with shields and swords, bows and arrows, clubs and spears. They all went singing a ballad of his death, his doings and triumphs, and the kings, lords and ambassadors, bearing their batons and insignia, all went weeping for the defunct. Also there followed certain slaves and servants of the king, all very well dressed, to be sacrificed and die with their lord, although at that time they were not so numerous as on later occasions.*

As Tezozómoc's long life was ebbing, profound dissensions had already appeared among his subjects. One cause of disagreement was the treatment of the Mexica. It has even been stated that this burning question led to a state of virtual civil war.* It would seem, in fact, that the ephemeral Tepanec Empire was beginning to dissolve as Tezozómoc's end drew near. It had been the creation of one man, and could not easily survive his passing.

The aged monarch had chosen as his heir his son Tayauh, but, in the prevailing state of discord, the throne was usurped by another son, Maxtla, who had already declared his dislike of the Mexica. One of his first moves was to reimpose a heavy tribute upon them.

Chimalpopoca of Tenochtitlan and Tlacateotl of Tlatelolco, faithful to the wishes of the dying Tezozómoc, made the fatal mistake of choosing the losing side and espoused the cause of Tayauh, the legitimate heir. Chimalpopoca conferred with the latter and advised him to kill his usurping brother. He proposed to Tayauh a simple method: he should have a palace built and invite his brother to a feast to celebrate its completion; at the banquet, Maxtla would be strangled by a rope disguised as a garland of flowers. Unfortunately, he was overheard by a dwarf in the service of Maxtla, who ran to his master to report the conversation. Tayauh was then stupid enough to allow himself to be eliminated by the self-same ruse which had been proposed to him for use against his brother.*

Chimalpopoca was not to be let off lightly for this unwise intervention. Maxtla sent to Tenochtitlan and had him unceremoniously put into a cage and thereafter killed. He then went on to dispose of Tlacateotl of Tlatelolco, who had managed to escape with all his treasures. However, Maxtla's henchmen overtook him, and his over-burdened canoe was sunk in the middle of the Lake of Texcoco.* According to another variant of the same story, Chimalpopoca decided to commit suicide when he learnt of his impending doom.* He first dressed in the full attire of Huitzilopochtli, performed a ritual dance, and offered himself to the priests for sacrifice. At that moment, Maxtla's contingent of Tepanecs arrived upon the scene, put Chimalpopoca into his cage, and carried him off, still dressed in the regalia of the god – surely a most unsuitable attire for such cramped conditions.

According to a quite different account of events, it was Chimalpopoca's successor, Itzcóatl, and his supporters who – disliking appeasement of the Tepanecs – instigated Tepanecs of Tacuba, basically hostile to Maxtla, to kill Chimalpopoca.* This story certainly has a ring of truth. It is hard to see why Maxtla should want to take the extreme step of killing Chimalpopoca, and then stand idly by while a much less pliant successor was elected in his place.

Subsequent events clearly illustrate that a version which suggests that Chimalpopoca was eliminated on account of his subservience to Maxtla – and that this was done at the behest of those who wanted to take a stronger line – is more likely to be accurate.

CHAPTER THREE

THE OBSIDIAN
SERPENT

ITZCÓATL ACCEDED TO the throne in 1426, following the
demise of the luckless Chimalpopoca. His assumption of power
hardly bears the stamp of a routine succession. If not an actual
revolution, dramatic changes followed, both internal and external.

The name Itzcóatl means 'Serpent of Obsidian': he was to live up
to it. To the Mexicans, this hard black volcanic glass was the counterpart of iron in contemporary Europe. Apart from its many domes-

62

tic uses, it provided the cutting edge to the warrior's club and the sharp head to the bowman's arrow.† But, in the trial of strength that was to come, subtle minds were as much required as keen blades. The Obsidian Serpent was aptly named.

Itzcóatl as ruler was ably seconded by two outstanding leaders – to such an extent that his government is sometimes described as a triumvirate. The first was Moctezuma Ilhuicamina, who was to succeed him on the throne; the second was the latter's younger brother, Tlacaélel. He assumed the key title of Woman Snake, or Cihuacóatl; this office was henceforth, under Tlacaélel and his descendants, to assume an importance second only to that of *tlatoani*.†

Under this new government, Mexica policy, of late so submissive to the Tepanec interest, was reversed. The Tepanecs were not slow to perceive the change of course; they soon recognized the inflexible disposition of the new ruler, little content to govern his realm as a mere vassal, subservient to the whim of the Tepanec tyrant, Maxtla. They accordingly blockaded Tenochtitlan, posting guards on the approaches to the city. At the same time, they put their own people on a war footing, aware that open hostilities were approaching.†

Events were to prove their appreciation of the situation to be correct. On Itzcóatl's accession, a speaker gave the usual homily on the duties of the *tlatoani* to the gods and his obligation to protect the helpless and the aged:

> Have you perchance to let fall and destroy the state? Are you to let slip from your shoulders the load which has been placed upon them? Shall you allow the old people, the orphans and the widows to perish? . . . The City of Mexico Tenochtitlan rejoices and exults under your protection; she felt as a widow, but now her spouse and consort has been resuscitated, to come back to her and give her sustenance. My son, have no fear for the burden of toil, and do not be sad, but remember that the god, whose form and likeness you represent, will favour and succour you.*

The orators on this occasion, not content with conventional phrases, advocated a generally warlike policy. Such harangues, however, tended to backfire, since they created alarm within the ranks of the common people and despondency among certain of their leaders: 'But the common people, seeing the valour and strength of the Tepanecs, were afraid; holding victory to be unattainable, they sought to deter the ruler and the other leaders, giving vent to great cowardice and weakness, tears and tremors, and caused dismay to the king and to the lords.'*

It was even proposed that the image of Huitzilopochtli should be delivered into the custody of the Tepanec ruler, as a sign of submission. A heated discussion ensued, and the new Woman Snake, Tlacaélel, roused at such humiliating appeasement, spoke up: 'What is this proposition, O Mexicans? What are you doing? You are out of your minds; be patient and calm, and let us take further counsel on this matter. Is there such cowardice among you that you have to go and mingle with those of Azcapotzalco?'*

The ruler himself now spoke; he decreed that it would be a betrayal to submit to the Tepanecs; instead, he would send a deputation to Azcapotzalco. At first no one dared to volunteer; finally Tlacaélel himself offered to undertake the dangerous mission – few notions of diplomatic immunity prevailed in ancient Mexico, and an ambassador's role was hazardous. On this occasion, Itzcóatl actually promised to take care of Tlacaélel's family, if he did not return.

Tlacaélel accordingly made his way to Azcapotzalco, persuading the Tepanec guards to let him through their barriers. The ruler, Maxtla, expressed astonishment that he should have arrived unharmed. Tlacaélel replied in a vein of rather feigned humility, begging that the tyrant should have pity on their old people and children, and spare them the horrors of war. The latter replied that, while he himself was well disposed towards them, his people now harboured such feelings of hostility against the Mexica that he must first take counsel; Tlacaélel should return another day for his reply.

On his second visit to the Tepanec capital, the ruler spoke as follows: 'My son Tlacaélel, what will you that I should reply? Although I am king, those of my realm desire and wish to make war upon you. What can I do against them? Because if I show any disposition to counter them, I risk my own life and that of all my children; they are angry and enraged against yourselves and demand that you should be destroyed.'* Tlacaélel accordingly anointed the ruler's body, as if he were a dead man, placed feathers upon his head, and put a shield in one hand and a club in the other, thus making a formal declaration of war. This time-honoured ritual was normally to be repeated whenever the Mexica initiated hostilities. Though not specifically mentioned on this occasion, it was usual to let pass three periods of twenty days, involving a further series of visits and ceremonies, before the start of actual warfare. In the final analysis, the outcome was decided by the gods, and success depended upon their favour – not to be secured by surprise attacks or unorthodox tactics, but by the strictest conformity to their prescribed rites.

After this formal declaration, Tlacaélel's return journey was even more perilous; the Tepanec ruler rather considerately suggested that he should leave the palace by a hole in the wall, to escape his own irate subjects.* He finally got safely home, after extricating himself from a band of infuriated Tepanecs.

At this point, with war imminent, the people of Tenochtitlan reportedly took deeper fright; many even wanted to flee the city. Another heated discussion arose among the leaders, the faint-hearted making the usual appeals to spare the women and children, to pity the aged and defenceless. It was an argument in which the young and adventurous were pitted against the old and timid. The lords – that is to say, the nobles – seconded by the warriors, wanted war; the commoners preferred peace.

Tlacaélel made his customary appeal for courage, and finally a most singular bargain was struck. The lords agreed: 'If we are unsuccessful in our undertaking, we will place ourselves in your hands that our bodies may sustain you, and you may thus take your vengeance and devour us in dirty and broken pots.' The people in their turn replied: 'And thus we pledge ourselves, if you should succeed in your undertaking, to serve you and pay tribute, and be your labourers and build your houses, and to serve you as our true lords.'*

Foremost in statecraft as in war, the two brothers Moctezuma and Tlacaélel are invariably depicted as playing a leading role in events. The more orthodox accounts at times even convey the surprising impression that Itzcóatl was little more than a weakling, only

induced to stand up and fight by the indomitable Tlacaélel. Moctezuma also, the next ruler, is sometimes depicted as a mere pawn in
his brother's hands. In fact, starting with Itzcóatl, a whole series of
five rulers, over a period of some sixty years, are often made to appear
like the Merovingian monarchs of France, manipulated like puppets
by this all-powerful mayor of the palace, Tlacaélel.

However, other chroniclers, such as Torquemada, go to the
opposite extreme, and simply deny that Tlacaélel ever existed, maintaining that he was really one and the same person as Moctezuma.*
Other accounts mention him only briefly, or not at all.

Certain modern commentators, true to the first of these opposing
versions, have tended to see in Tlacaélel's office of Cihuacóatl, or
Woman Snake, a counterpart to that of the ruler, implying a kind
of dual government, as existed in certain other cities; some even
write of Tlacaélel as the true founder of the Aztec Empire. This is
probably an exaggeration. Itzcóatl was forty-six when he ascended
the throne,* and was unquestionably a senior commander and a
brave man. Equally, his successor, Moctezuma, was an outstanding
ruler. Suggestions of Tlacaélel's predominance over men of such
calibre may have stemmed from the records of Tlacaélel's own descendants; it was not uncommon for later chroniclers to extol the
pre-eminence of their own ancestors.†

On the other hand, in view of all the available details of the life
and genealogy of the great Woman Snake, it appears equally incorrect to take the opposed view and deny his existence altogether.
It would seem most probable that Tlacaélel did exist as a historic
personage; as such, he played an outstanding part in events that were
to follow, a service for which he was for ever honoured. The reign
of his brother, Moctezuma, offered ample scope for statesmanship
and military talent, and Tlacaélel continued to play a distinguished
though not exclusive role in guiding the destinies of the new empire.
He even survived, as will later be seen, into the reign of Moctezuma's successor.

It is now necessary to retrace our steps, to a point some nine years
previous, well before the death of Tezozómoc. At this stage, two
quite separate stories have to be told: the one refers to the Mexica,
and the other to the Texcocans. Their courses may run parallel, but

their stories are still distinct, and do not become merged until later – at the point where the two peoples combined to fight the Tepanecs.

Until they actually joined forces, it is unavoidable to treat separately the actions of the Texcocans and their young ruler Nezahualcóyotl on the one hand, and those of the Mexica on the other.

Nezahualcóyotl, in 1418, was the boy who had perched in a tree, a helpless witness to the butchering of his father by the Tepanecs' henchmen. After the Texcocan war, his kingdom had been divided between the Tepanecs and the Mexica. He therefore had little cause to love the latter.

Nezahualcóyotl was an outstanding historical figure; it is not, therefore, surprising that his early life as a fugitive came to be told as a kind of saga, unique in the annals of ancient Mexico, and handed down by word of mouth and in pictorial records from one generation to another.†

After the death of his father, the young prince, accompanied by his brother and by his loyal follower Coyohua, followed a tortuous route, as they fled from the Tepanecs. They eventually reached the lands of their friends that lay beyond the great volcanoes, the Tlaxcalans and Huexotzingans.

Some four years later in 1422, through the intervention of Nezahualcóyotl's aunt (his mother was a Mexica princess), he was permitted to live in Tenochtitlan, but was confined within the bounds of the city, on pain of death.* During these formative years of his life, he was to be most closely associated with Itzcóatl, not yet ruler, but already a leading figure. In spite of bitter memories of former wrongs, Nezahualcóyotl probably emerged from this period in Tenochtitlan almost as much Mexica in outlook as Texcocan. It was a measure of his greatness as a man that he was able to bury past differences and unite with his former persecutors, in order to recover his lost kingdom.

Nezahualcóyotl now captured his first prisoners, under the guidance of Coyohua – an important step in the life of a young warrior: 'Meanwhile Nezahualcóyotl lived and grew, and as he reached manhood he took prisoners with the aid of others; on the second occasion this occurred in Zacatlan. Then he came to Tenochtitlan; he dared to come and he duly arrived.' He then visited Tezozómoc, to deliver to him his captives: 'O Xollotl, my lord, O

Tezozómoc, a fatherless orphan enters your presence to make his offering.'† However much he yearned for revenge, it was necessary for him to seek the goodwill of the Tepanec ruler.

His wooing of Tezozómoc was so successful that in 1424 he was finally permitted to return to Texcoco and establish himself there. However, only some smaller palaces were returned to him, and he enjoyed no sovereign power.* Moreover, he was not to be left in peace for long. Tezozómoc had now grown very old and capricious:

> The tyrant Tezozómoc was the most cruel man who ever lived, proud, warlike and domineering. And he was so old, according to what appears in the histories, and to what elderly princes have told me, that they carried him about like a child swathed in feathers and soft skins; they always took him out into the sun to warm him up, and at night he slept between two great braziers, and he never withdrew from their glow because he lacked natural heat. And he was very temperate in his eating and drinking and for this reason he lived so long.*

It was not long before the aged monarch had second thoughts about Nezahualcóyotl. He sent for his companion Coyohua, and told him that he had had a most sinister dream:

> Listen, Coyohua, it is for this that they came to fetch you. I dreamed another thing that was truly evil: that an eagle came upon me; that a tiger came upon me; that a wolf came upon me; that a snake came upon me, huge, brightly coloured and very venomous. Coyohua, may it not be that Nezahualcóyotl destroys me; may it not be that he seeks out his father Ixtlilxóchitl and his uncle Cihuacuecuénotl; may it not be that he himself resumes the war against my sons, lords and princes?*

To ward off the peril, Tezozómoc tried to persuade Coyohua to kill his master. Evidently he did not wish to appear openly responsible for his death, and dropped gentle hints that perhaps the young prince should succumb to an accident: 'Coyohua, let his companions play with him; perhaps they will pass by a river somewhere and they might kick and push him; accidentally he might fall into the water. Or they could play together on a rooftop.'*

Coyohua went back to Nezahualcóyotl and told him what had

occurred. Tezozómoc summoned Coyohua once more to his presence, and offered him lavish presents of land if he would kill his master. He told the ruler that he could never do this; he would have to call Nezahualcóyotl and do the deed himself. Shortly after this, the prince did go to Azcapotzalco, but Tezozómoc was already dead, and he came to attend his funeral. He managed to escape death on this occasion, since the new Tepanec ruler, Maxtla, considered it sacrilegious to commit murder during the funeral rites of his father.*

Following Tezozómoc's funeral Maxtla was not slow to implement his father's last injunctions regarding Nezahualcóyotl. He first appointed a bastard brother of the latter as ruler of Texcoco.* He then adopted that well-tried ruse, and his half-brother invited Nezahualcóyotl to a banquet, in order to kill him. Not surprisingly, the intended victim was forewarned, and a young man of low extraction, carefully instructed to dress and behave as the prince, was sent in his place and duly assassinated. The messengers deputed to take his head to Maxtla, as proof of death, were to have a nasty shock:

He [Nezahualcóyotl] was meanwhile on the lookout. As soon as he knew of the death of the man who had been his representative, he embarked for the city of Mexico to congratulate his uncle Itzcóatl on his recent election as ruler. And at dawn he arrived at his palace and entered; shortly after, Maxtla's messengers arrived with the boy's head, to inform of the death of Nezahualcóyotl. The envoys, seeing him alive and well with his uncle, were astonished and petrified. He told them not to weary themselves with efforts to kill him, because the almighty and powerful deity had made him immortal.*

Indeed, so miraculous were Nezahualcóyotl's many escapes from the jaws of death during this troubled period of his existence that stories of his charmed life became a legend: 'And thus, many old natives would say that Nezahualcóyotl was descended from the principal gods of the earth, and thus they held him to be immortal, and they were not wrong in saying that he was procreated by the gods, because Tezcatlipoca and Huitzilopochtli, the greatest of all, were his ancestors. . . .'*

From Tenochtitlan, he now returned to Texcoco, and Maxtla

again sent after him to have him killed. He welcomed the latter's henchmen with garlands of flowers. When they declared that they had come to play with him the ritual ball-game, he invited them first to dine, and feasted them lavishly. To reassure them during their banquet, he first sat upon his throne, where they could all see him. At a well-chosen moment, however, he made his getaway through an escape-hole prepared by Coyohua, and once more fled his native city.*

Maxtla, infuriated by this latest deception, was now determined to track down his prey dead or alive, and there was no limit to the rewards he was prepared to offer for the purpose. If his captor were a bachelor, he would receive a noble and beautiful wife and lands of his own, regardless of his social standing. If on the other hand he was already married, he would be given numerous slaves in place of a wife.*

After further adventures, such as are apt to befall fugitive princes (like Charles II, he had already once sought safety in a tree), he once again took refuge in the lands to the east of the volcanoes; he himself had wished to stay in Texcoco, but his trusted advisers warned that his forces were not yet sufficient to resist the tyrant.

As he fled towards safety, he tried to persuade his followers to return to their homes:

> Go back to your houses and do not seek to die for me. Do not for my sake fall into disfavour with the tyrant, and thus lose your homes and lands. Quauhtlehuantzin and Tzontecochatzin and all the others replied that they only desired to follow him and die where he died. On hearing this, Nezahualcóyotl was deeply moved, and began to weep, together with all those who accompanied him.*

It was sunset when they finally crossed the mountains, and the rich valley of Puebla came into view, already obscured by the shadow of the great peaks, which now lay behind them to the west. Nezahualcóyotl's first thought was to tell the rulers' envoys, sent to greet him, that they should instead kill him and claim the ransom. However, they insisted that he was now on friendly soil, and that they would do all that lay in their power to further his cause.*

In the year 1428, Nezahualcóyotl of Texcoco was again a victim of Tepanec persecution, and once more a refugee beyond the mountains. Itzcóatl of Tenochtitlan, his uncle, was equally in conflict with the new Tepanec ruler, and already virtually besieged in his own capital. The inevitable outcome was the alliance of the Tepanecs' two major victims, the Mexica and the Texcocans.

Both parties were henceforth united in common enmity to their oppressor, Maxtla. The Mexica were now governed by a dynamic régime, eager to throw off the yoke of servitude. Nezahualcóyotl, though militarily weak, was most firm in his resolve to wrest his ancestral possessions from the hands of his enemies.

It was perhaps Tepanec weakness more than their opponents' strength which caused the war. The conflict was partly triggered off by their dissensions, beginning even before the death of the ageing Tezozómoc. Sharp disagreements had previously arisen over the manner of treating the Mexica. These rifts were so deep that they apparently degenerated into a kind of civil war.*

The divisions were clearly accentuated by the controversial usurpation of Maxtla, a man of violent disposition, with a talent for making enemies and losing friends. Personalities played a considerable part in the final outcome, and that of Maxtla was unfortunate by all accounts. He may have begun to lose control of the situation, even before the outbreak of hostilities. He went out of his way to provoke the Mexica; in particular he complained that they had previously been relieved of tribute, and pressed new demands for payment upon them. He clearly resented their enhanced status of recent years, and sought to reduce them once more to their former servitude.

His conduct contrasted sharply with that of his father, Tezozómoc, who was a pastmaster in playing off one opponent against another, and who would never have antagonized the Mexica and the Texcocans at the same time. Had he been succeeded by a son of like calibre, the Tepanec Empire might have continued to expand, and future historians would have had very little to say about the Mexica.

But, faced by Maxtla's provocation, the Mexica and the Texcocans automatically came together, and the first stage was accomplished in the formation of the Triple Alliance of Tenochtitlan, Texcoco and Tacuba. At this point, it was more strictly a dual alliance, since the part played by the dissident Tepanecs of Tacuba remained ill-defined.

It was unlikely that the Mexica, aided only by Nezahualcóyotl's limited forces, could prove a match for the Tepanecs. It was therefore vital to secure the allegiance of the peoples of the Puebla–Tlaxcala Valley to the east. Since Tezozómoc had eliminated all rivals in the Valley of Mexico, there were no other major powers within striking distance. Accordingly, the attitude of Tlaxcala and Huexotzingo was likely to prove decisive; any combination capable of defeating the Tepanecs would probably have to include them.

Of the two, Tlaxcala is the better known to us, simply from the part which it played in the Spanish Conquest. However, until about fifty years before that event, the major power of the region was not Tlaxcala but Huexotzingo to the south of it. In 1428 the latter was still in the process of forging for itself a small independent empire, after a succession of forceful rulers had succeeded in subduing a number of neighbouring cities.*

Nezahualcóyotl was himself at this very moment in Huexotzingo, after his recent escape from Texcoco. He was, therefore, ideally situated to secure the allegiance of that city; moreover, a traditional friendship seems to have prevailed between his own dynasty and the Huexotzingans. This did not deter the Tepanec ruler from also sending a delegation to woo Huexotzingo (no mention is made of Tlaxcala, though they also went to Chalco). They bore costly gifts of jewels, arms and insignia.*

They were followed by a delegation from Tenochtitlan, complaining bitterly of the iniquities of the Tepanecs. An embassy also arrived from Cuauhtitlan, recently defeated and cruelly treated by Maxtla, who had gone to the extreme of planting the city market with agaves, and transferring the important centre for slave-dealing to Azcapotzalco, where it remained until the Conquest.* The latter brought modest presents, which was all that they could afford. As a result, they were considered as of little consequence, and were imprisoned, with a view to being put to death – a reminder that the favours of the Huexotzingans were not to be had for the asking. Even Tlatelolco, as well as Tenochtitlan, sent its own delegation; complaining that the Tepanecs had actually boasted of the number of rulers whom they had killed.*

The representatives of Tenochtitlan were led by Moctezuma, the ruler's nephew. Like the Tepanec delegation, he first went to Chalco, accompanied by a brother of Nezahualcóyotl. But the people of Chalco so hated the Mexica that they would not hear of an alliance, and imprisoned Moctezuma. However, like Nezahualcóyotl, he seemed to enjoy a charmed life; he managed to escape and made his way to Huexotzingo. It was thus that the greatest of Aztec emperors avoided an ignominious and premature end in a wooden cage in Chalco; he was later to prove the most implacable enemy of that place.

In Huexotzingo itself, the issue between the rival contenders for favour still lay in the balance. The delegates pleaded their respective causes; finally, however, those of Cuauhtitlan – the paltry nature of their gifts now apparently forgotten – were released from their impending doom and brought out of captivity to testify. So terrible was their tale of Tepanec excesses that the envoys of the latter were taken out and publicly killed in front of the statue of the local patron deity. They were then cut to pieces with obsidian knives, and thus became the first casualties of the war.*

As a result of Nezahualcóyotl's appeals to Huexotzingo and Tlaxcala, they first helped him to reoccupy his own domains, before rallying to the assistance of the beleaguered Mexica.* This was only the first step in a slow process of reconquest; it was not until three years later, in 1431, that Nezahualcóyotl was to regain full control of his possessions.

In 1428 he returned to his native province, backed by these allied forces. Nezahualcóyotl, in a lightning thrust, himself entered Texcoco, while his friends occupied the neighbouring centres of population.* Maxtla was so alarmed by his success that he made new efforts to appease Nezahualcóyotl's subjects.†

Many accounts survive of the decisive happenings that now follow. In this instance the Texcocan version seems to attain a greater measure of truth; the official Mexica sources pretend that it was they who fought the war single-handed; neither Nezahualcóyotl nor the Huexotzingans are even mentioned, and any account which totally omits such important elements has to be treated with caution.†

With Texcoco subdued, the combined forces of Nezahualcóyotl and his friends proceeded to answer the appeals of the Mexica who were being besieged by Maxtla in Tenochtitlan. They embarked in

their canoes in order to attack Azcapotzalco, the
which lay on the opposite side of the lagoon to 1
reached the lake-shore in front of the city, th
fortified. Maxtla was by this time so alarmed that
the siege of Tenochtitlan and retreated to his own
    The first move against Azcapotzalco was now ma
jointly commanded by Nezahualcóyotl and the rulei
zingo; they approached from the north.† Nezahualoyo
the order to his men to leave aside their fine feathers a
stones, and to go into battle clad only in white cotton m
was a most unorthodox instruction, and caused dismay a ung the
troops; in particular it irked them to be outshone by the Mexica, who
were not disposed to forgo their accustomed sartorial display. Neza-
hualcoyotl, however, always diplomat as well as warrior, addressed
them as follows:

> I feel happy and amused to see you among such an array, brilliant
> with every colour; it seems as if I was in a garden filled with a variety
> of flowers, and in which you, the fragrant blossoms of the jasmine,
> with no more adornment than a simple whiteness, are supreme among
> the blooms. External decorations do not increase the valour of those
> who sport them, but that of the enemy, whose greed drives him to
> victory, to obtain the spoil.*

Such an attitude to finery was hardly usual in ancient Mexico, and
it may rather be a measure of the straits to which Texcoco had been
reduced that its levies were not possessed of any.
    While Nezahualcóyotl was making his southward advance, by a
prearranged signal the main forces of the Mexica made a frontal
attack against the eastern defences of the enemy citadel. This assault,
however, met the strongest resistance:

> Here occurred the hardest fight, the Mexica rolled back the enemy
> in their initial advance, and made them withdraw a fair distance,
> capturing a wide and deep ditch constructed near a place called
> Petlacalco. . . . However, the enemy turned against the Mexica with
> such fury, that they drove them back over the captured trench, and
> forced them to retire to the shore of the lagoon.*

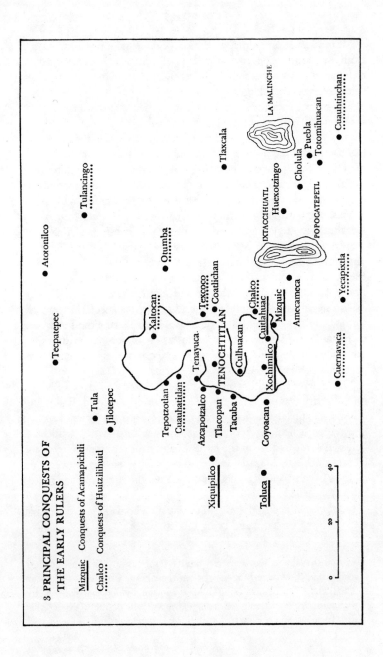

3 PRINCIPAL CONQUESTS OF
THE EARLY RULERS

Mizquic   Conquests of Acamapichtli
Chalco   Conquests of Huitzilihuid
....

Xiquipilco

Toluca

Tepotzotlan
Cuauhatitlan

Azcapotzalco
Tlacopan
Tacuba

Coyoacan

Tenayuca.
TENOCHTITLAN

Culhuacan
Xochimilco

Xaltocan
....

Texcoco
Coatichan

Cuitlahuac
Chalco
....

Mizquic

Amecameca

Cuernavaca
....

Yecapixtla

Teepatepec

Tula
Jilotepec

Atotonilco

Otumba
....

Tulancingo
....

Tlaxcala

IXTACCIHUATL
POPOCATEPETL

Huexotzingo
Cholula
Puebla
Totomihuacan

LA MALINCHE

Cuauhtinchan
....

0   20   40

Meanwhile Moctezuma, on the left of these main forces, advanced from the south, and took the Tepanec city of Tacuba, without encountering much resistance; although it was well fortified, the ruler favoured the Allies.*

The main Mexica forces now renewed their assault on the eastern defences of Azcapotzalco. They stormed the outer defence line from which they had previously been ejected, and the Tepanecs fell back on their principal fortifications, consisting in a ring of earthworks surrounding the whole city. Night was now falling, and the Allied generals decided that the defences were so formidable that they must invest the city, rather than risk further losses by direct attacks. For this purpose, they divided their forces into four parts: Nezahualcóyotl swung round to occupy the western sector – the most dangerous, since behind him lay the heartland of the Tepanec domains, from whence he could be taken in the rear – while the Mexica forces under Tlacaélel, Itzcóatl and Moctezuma blockaded Azcapotzalco from the north, east and south respectively.

The siege lasted for several months; the Tepanecs made many sorties, while the besiegers in their turn tried to take the inner ring of forts. The fighting was inconclusive, with substantial losses on both sides; those of the defenders were the more serious, since they could not be made good by reinforcements.

The Tepanec situation grew desperate after 114 days of siege, since the city was starving and their forces sadly depleted. Following a pressing appeal for help, a relieving force from other Tepanec cities approached Azcapotzalco from the north-west, while the besieged made a sortie in the same direction. After a fierce fight, the Tepanec general, Mazatl, was felled by a blow on the head from a club; as in most Mexican battles this settled the issue, and the rest of the army turned and fled.*

It only remained to drag forth the tyrant Maxtla from his place of refuge in a steam bath, and bring him to justice:

And as Nezahualcóyotl entered the city, the leaders of Azcapotzalco, seeing that they were lost, sought out their king, who went to hide in a *temazcal* which stood behind a garden, and which is a bath. With many insults, they dragged him before Nezahualcóyotl, saying that they brought him, in order that the Prince might do as he wished with him. They added that, had it not been for Maxtla and his forebears, who had always been inclined towards tyranny, the state would not have suffered such wars and casualties. They said this and much else to Nezahualcóyotl, who now had a great scaffold constructed in the square, on which he sentenced the culprit and killed him by his own hand; he cut out his heart and scattered his blood in the four directions. He then ordered that full honours should be paid to the body, and that it should be buried with all the solemnity pertaining to a great lord.†

In thus overthrowing the power of the Tepanecs, the Mexica and their allies had performed a feat that was remarkable, if not astonishing. Naturally it was partly the fault of the Tepanecs themselves; the Mexica and Texcocans were subsequently to consolidate and expand this self-same empire – but on sounder lines. The latter almost invariably restored and protected vanquished local rulers; the Tepanecs on the other hand, in order to satisfy their own dynastic ambitions, overthrew the princes and oppressed their subjects.

One city, in ancient Mexico, could not long pursue a policy of domination, unless it could augment its resources by the addition of reliable allies and vassals. To defeat Azcapotzalco had been a collective triumph; it was in this respect that Nezahualcóyotl excelled; his greatest feat had been to enlist the support of Huexotzingo and its neighbours, without which the mighty Tepanecs could never have overcome. He was thus the principal architect of victory – a remarkable feat for a king still deprived of his kingdom and a general without large forces of his own.

The Huexotzingans and their friends no doubt believed that they were simply redressing the balance of power, too favourable to the Tepanecs. They were later to discover their great mistake; as will become clear, they were setting up the Mexica as a far more hideous scourge for their own backs.

For it was the latter who were the true beneficiaries of the victory, and who deserved their full share of the credit. If Nezahualcóyotl had been the architect of victory, the main instrument was the military genius of the Mexica. This was not fashioned overnight, as some would suggest, after an argument between nobles and commoners on the eve of war; their army had been forged as a powerful weapon of offence over half a century of increasing achievement –

admittedly under the Tepanec aegis, but as vassals growing ever more powerful and independent.

Great successes usually come about through the full use of opportunities, and in this the Mexica showed their talent. In the ever-changing kaleidoscope of Middle American politics, with its shifting pattern of alliances and its constant betrayals, it was they who doggedly pursued a consistent line, as the chosen few of Huitzilopochtli. They always made use of any available friends to achieve their own ends and it was they who came out supreme. It had been a great feat to crush their masters; with the Tepanecs once defeated, the world of ancient Mexico lay at their feet.

We have already described the singular 'bargain' whereby the privileges of the nobles would be enhanced or virtually eliminated, depending on the outcome of the war. Before their victory over the Tepanecs the Mexica, as their principal underlings, had acquired the use of some extra land. Such territory was, however, limited in comparison with the vast domains which they had so suddenly won. Whichever class or group controlled these would equally dominate the Mexican state.

The actual distribution could hardly have been more inequitable from the point of view of the toiling masses. Indeed, the rather apocryphal story of the bargain may well have been inserted into the official record to provide some justification for such disparate rewards to the few and to the many. By all accounts, the major share went to the nobility and warriors, and very little indeed to the clan organizations. Tlacaélel and Moctezuma between them took about as much land as went to the clans, each of which received a limited acreage for the upkeep of their temples.†

Private holdings of land had probably existed previously, apart from those controlled by the ruler himself – but on a relatively modest scale. Now, however, the conquest of the Tepanec and other territories radically altered the balance; the proportion that was individually occupied increased out of all proportion.

This private tenure was of two kinds: the first consisted of lands owned outright by a small and privileged class of nobles – the *pillis* or princes, of whom at least a fair proportion descended from the ruling dynasty. These were farmed by serfs, who were tied to the soil.†

Apart from such established private properties, a further major share of the total was, at least in theory, at the ruler's disposal – in the form of land held by leading warriors on a kind of life tenure. This was a recognized method of rewarding distinguished service; however, the occupation tended to become hereditary, if a suitable heir was available, and could win his spurs on the field of battle.†

In addition to such holdings of an individual nature, the state itself controlled various categories of land, dedicated to the upkeep of the palace and its officials (the equivalent of a modern government), to the maintenance of the temples, and to the expenses of war. Large tracts, of course, belonged to the ruler himself.

Last but not least came the communal lands (*calpulalli*). Even if their proportion of the total had been reduced, their extent was considerable. The freemen who farmed them (*macehuales*), formed the backbone of the nation and furnished the rank and file of the armies. These tribal lands were inalienable, and a family would enjoy hereditary usufruct of its parcel, which was only redistributed if the user died without heirs. Tribute was paid to the ruler on such holdings.

The organization of the soil, thus established, formed the basis on which the Mexican state reposed. It was not merely the chief source of wealth, as in the ancient kingdoms of the Old World; there was really no other form of durable property. The principal means of exchange – cacao beans and small mantles – were no lasting substitute for a metal currency. Admittedly, small axe-shaped copper sheets and gold dust in quills were also used for monetary purposes in parts of Mexico; however, hoarding of these does not seem to have occurred on a large scale.

Land-holding thus provides the key to the social order; by taking the lion's share of the broad acres of the newly conquered, the ruler and nobles assured for themselves a firm basis of economic power, independent of the communal organizations. They were thus free to pursue their dreams of further conquest, unfettered by the fears or inhibitions of the masses. Whatever its original structure, the Mexican state was now in essence a tightly controlled oligarchy.

At the top of the social pyramid was the ruler (*tlatoani*). He was always chosen from the same family and was usually a son or brother of his predecessor. He was advised in the first place by a council of four, from the ranks of which his successor was normally chosen.* These four councillors additionally played a major part in the choice of a new ruler, though elders and warriors, as well as the allied rulers of Texcoco and Tacuba, also took part, in order to give added ceremony to the occasion. The key council of four members probably came into formal existence at the time of Itzcóatl.* Supreme power was thus very much concentrated in the hands of the royal family, to which the four councillors, as eligible to succeed to the throne, naturally belonged. There also existed a larger council, called the Tlatocan, variously described as having from twelve to twenty members; in addition, there was a war council to advise on military matters.

Thus, as an elective monarch, assisted by different bodies, the *tlatoani* was not absolute. However, his personal power tended to increase, owing to a gradual process of centralization, culminating in the reign of Moctezuma I. In a state dedicated to conquest, the ruler must receive huge quantities of tribute, and his power will automatically be augmented at the expense of his subjects.

Next below the *tlatoani* in the social order, at one remove, stood the hereditary nobility, restricted in numbers, and perhaps mainly of royal descent. They were well endowed with land, but not on the vast scale of their European counterparts. Service to the state was obligatory, and they were expected to participate actively in war, to justify the retention of their privileged position.

In addition to this select few, a much larger upper, or leading, class existed – the distinguished warriors – based chiefly on meritorious service; in principle, they enjoyed their rank and land for their own lifetime. Often, however, such privileges tended to pass from father to son.

Equally to be taken into account were the priests. They formed an important and numerous caste – an intellectual élite more to be classed with the rulers than the ruled. In some respects they are hardly to be distinguished from the nobility, for the ruler himself was of priestly rank. They also went to war and took captives. The distinction between priests and warriors is not an absolute one. They performed the important additional task of educating the upper classes in the privileged schools (*calmecac*). The rest of the population went to what was virtually a college for military training (*tepoch-calli*), which existed in each clan.

A smaller, but significant, group was the officials and judges; from the accounts of Sahagún and others, it can be seen that in Tenochtitlan justice was meted out to rich and poor alike with severe impartiality. In addition to other special classes, there existed the merchants, whose position will later be discussed in more detail. They constituted a group apart, and enjoyed many privileges, such as their own law courts.

Below these favoured sectors stood the common people. Of these, the most important category was the freemen (*macehuales*), who formed the basis of the clan organization. The relative lowliness of their situation was defined by rigorous sumptuary laws; only the upper classes were permitted to wear cotton clothes or to drink cocoa. The elaborate attire, the fine jewels and sumptuous food of the nobles were taboo for the people; the latter were unceremoniously killed if they dared to indulge in such luxuries.

Next as a group came the serfs, bound to the nobles' hereditary lands. And last of all were the slaves. The institution was less highly developed than in the Old World, partly because prisoners of war were usually sacrificed. People lost their freedom chiefly as a consequence of certain crimes, or of unpaid debts; men could voluntarily sell themselves into slavery, and equally could be redeemed by a stipulated payment. Slaves were mainly used in domestic service, and as carriers in the absence of pack animals. Unlike their Old World counterparts, their children were not automatically born into the same condition.*

Thus, by the reign of Itzcóatl, the Mexican state had developed elaborate institutions, fully comparable in their sophistication to those of the ancient monarchies of the Old World. Basically, the Mexican polity was a meritocracy, the ruler being supported by appointed functionaries as well as hereditary nobles. In theory, at least, such a situation continued to prevail. However, it was a state in evolution; like others in the Old World and elsewhere it became increasingly centralized, reaching its culmination in the years before the Spanish Conquest.

At the same time, while the system of government was moving towards a greater degree of absolutism and privilege, it was still far from attaining that degree of social stratification that prevailed in contemporary Europe. The nobles owned only part of the land, and freemen could still attain high office. Marriage between freemen and nobles was even permitted. Equally, members of the ruling class could lose their status if their sons proved unworthy. For the privileged Mexicans, life was rigorous rather than relaxed, and probably the insistence on self-denial and service goes far to account for their triumphs. The Mexican upper hierarchy seems to have been imbued with an ideal of dedication to the state that recalls the early Romans, and that made for a notable singleness of purpose. The vanquished Tepanecs had foundered upon the rock of discord, while the Mexica invariably presented a united front; and on the whole their oligarchical constitution was to work admirably.

The Triple Alliance that would jointly rule the Aztec Empire was formally constituted only after victory: the Aztec domains were, initially at least, neither solely conquered nor controlled by Tenochtitlan. To mark the final establishment of the alliance, Itzcóatl adopted the title of 'Ruler of the Culhua' (from whom the Mexica, of course, claimed their descent); Nezahualcóyotl became 'Ruler of the Acolhua', and the *señor* of Tacuba was styled 'Ruler of the Tepanecs'. The latter played a somewhat secondary role in the councils of the alliance, but it was nevertheless significant to include a leading city of the defeated adversary. From now on it becomes appropriate to make more frequent use of the term 'Aztec' – as the best way of describing the forces of an empire that was not solely either Mexica or Texcocan.

After the triumph of 1428, Itzcóatl continued to reign for a further twelve years. Nezahualcóyotl, though a leading member of the victorious team, was not yet master in his own house; even according to Texcocan sources, he remained in Tenochtitlan for three years after victory was attained, before he could win back his own kingdom.* Notwithstanding his role in an overwhelmingly successful war, he had much difficulty with his own subjects, many of whom had long since displayed pro-Tepanec sentiments. Now at last, with the help of his partner Itzcóatl, he managed to come to terms with the various subject rulers of his province, and agreed to restore them to their thrones.* He immediately began to rebuild Texcoco, and Itzcóatl helped in the task by providing artisans.*

The latter years of Itzcóatl's reign were to witness the conquest of the remaining principalities of the Valley of Mexico; these included several Tepanec centres, which inevitably fell a prey to the Mexicans, once their leader had been overthrown. They made the fatal mistake of allowing themselves to be swallowed up one by one.

The Tepanec city of Coyoacan was the first to be attacked, and the war began on the pretext that Mexican women had been molested and robbed. On this occasion a final but futile attempt was made to unite the potential victims of the Aztecs into a coalition, and to plan a joint defence. A conference took place in Chalco, but it soon became clear that no agreement could be reached to help Coyoacan.†

Perhaps those present were mindful of the wise words of Nezahualcóyotl, who had also been approached and had declared that the Mexica were invincible because the god Huitzilopochtli was always at their side.* At all events, the policy of divide and rule continued to prevail.

There followed a curious incident in the war against Coyoacan. The rulers of the city invited the Mexica to a banquet. Itzcóatl himself did not attend, but other leaders accepted their bidding, including his nephew Tlacaélel. To their utter astonishment, they were ordered to don women's clothes and dance before the assembled Tepanecs. Thus arrayed, they returned and presented themselves before Itzcóatl, telling him how they had been mocked.*

An even odder form of retaliation was devised, equally disconcerting, if less insulting:

And they did thus: they took a large quantity of cakes made of *ezcahuite* – which are the red worms which grow in the mud of the lagoon and which are a special delicacy of the Mexicans – and threw them on to a fire, together with ducks, fish, frogs etcetera. And so great was the smoke which arose, that it entered the streets of Coyoacan, and made women miscarry from sheer desire to eat what the Mexicans were cooking, while children pined away, clamouring for these delicacies.*

Subsequently, battle was joined; it was an even fight, until the Mexicans turned the tide by a surprise flank attack. They thus won the day, but feeling ran high; some of the inhabitants fled to other cities rather than face subjection to the Aztec yoke. However, Coyoacan continued to be a place of importance and later served as

Cortés' provisional capital, while the new city of Mexico was being built.

As in the previous case of Azcapotzalco, the conquered lands were distributed in most unequal proportions, the common people again receiving but a meagre share. Even communal lands of Coyoacan were taken; it was perhaps an act of policy to soak the poor, but permit the nobles to retain their holdings in order to ensure their future loyalty to the Empire.*

After Coyoacan, it was the turn of Xochimilco, whose people as we have already seen enjoyed a degree of kinship with the Mexica. However, as often happens in such cases, a long tradition of rivalry persisted, dating back to the days when the Mexica, during their captivity, had cut off the ears of the people of Xochimilco and accumulated them in baskets, as an offering to their masters.

This time, another pretext was chosen to pick a quarrel, the Mexica sending to request wood and stone from Xochimilco, with which to build a temple. This was a customary manner of demanding token submission, and the request was refused. The people of Xochimilco still ruled an important and rich territory and had a large army.* However, they adopted a defensive strategy, shutting themselves in behind their barricades; once these were stormed, they promptly surrendered. It is clear that on this occasion the Mexica were determined to remain on good terms with the vanquished; the troops were not permitted to pillage or even to enter the city. Itzcóatl showed special favour to the ruler of Xochimilco, allowing him to eat in his presence.* His subjects, however, had to pay for the war, and the victors took some lands. It was at this time that the great causeway was commenced, linking Coyoacan with Tenochtitlan across the lagoon. Labour from Xochimilco was used for the purpose.* This constituted one of the three great arteries by which the Spaniards were later to assault the city.

A similar attack was now made on Cuitláhuac.* In this case a new pretext was found; the Mexica made the unusual demand that maidens from noble families should come and dance in Tenochtitlan at the feast of Huitzilopochtli. The request was, of course, indignantly rejected by the ruler: 'Mexicans, do you know what you are saying? Are my daughters, sisters and relations, and those of the lords of Cuitláhuac mere toys or buffoons of your god, that they must sing and dance before him? Tell your lord Itzcóatl that I do not hold in such low regard the girls of my city, even the most humble, that I may send them at his behest, to act as jesters to his god.'*

Cuitláhuac lay in the midst of the lagoon, and a combined military and naval operation had to be undertaken, involving the use of fleets of canoes. The Mexica levies must have formed a most impressive sight as they set forth upon the water:

And when the canoes arrived, all the men of the army embarked, and passed an arm of the lagoon, which had no causeway nor other means of passing, and was fairly deep. And thus, as the Mexican army crossed and jumped out on to the land of Cuitláhuac, the people of that place came out against them, all in canoes and very well arrayed with their rich and colourful insignia, the canoes themselves being adorned with shields and richly hued feathers with which the oarsmen were covered. And the fighting men were all very well armed and bedecked with feathers, white, red, yellow, blue, green, black, and every colour, all with different plumes on their heads and backs; round their necks they wore many jewels of gold, set with stones, as well as bracelets of brilliant gold; and above their feet, anklets of gold, to complete the arms which they wore from head to foot.*

Shortly after the successful conclusion of this campaign, Itzcóatl died, in 1440, after also reconquering Cuernavaca and neighbouring cities.† In addition, he is reported to have taken Tula, as well as certain places in the northern part of the modern state of Guerrero, though he did not campaign in this direction as far as the Pacific coast.†

The emphasis, however, in Itzcóatl's reign had been placed mainly on the consolidation of the Valley of Mexico and contiguous areas – acquisitions which paved the way to the more far-reaching conquests of his successor. He had undoubtedly proved to be a notable ruler; his master stroke had been the overthrow of the Tepanecs and the formation of the Triple Alliance. Of importance also during his reign had been the consolidation of the Mexican state and of the machinery of government, as an essential preliminary to further advances.

CHAPTER FOUR

MOCTEZUMA I
THE EMPIRE
TAKES SHAPE

Following the death of Itzcóatl in 1440, Tlacaélel, continuing in his role as leading minister of state, made an unusually stirring speech:

Now the light that illuminated you is extinguished, the voice at whose sound all this kingdom moved is still, and the mirror in which all men saw themselves is darkened. Thus, illustrious warriors, it is not fitting that this kingdom be left in obscurity; may another sun rise to give it light. . . . Who does it seem to you to be best fitted to follow in the footsteps of our dead king? Who will preserve for us what he has won.*

Following this discourse, after due deliberation, Moctezuma was elected as ruler. He is usually known as Moctezuma I, or Moctezuma the Elder, to distinguish him from Moctezuma II, who ruled when the Spaniards arrived. He also bore the additional name of Ilhuicamina, 'the archer of the skies'.† The name Moctezuma means 'the angry one'. He was already one of the four inner councillors, from whose ranks the ruler now had to be chosen.* As nephew of the deceased monarch and as son of a previous ruler, he was in the direct line of succession.† As can be seen from the genealogical table on page 305, it was a fairly common practice for the throne to pass from one brother to another, and only subsequently back to the son of the elder brother.

It will be recalled that the mother of Moctezuma was the daughter of the ruler of Cuernavaca, who had been wooed by Moctezuma's father in such romantic fashion – by shooting an arrow containing a precious stone into the courtyard where the princess lay, protected from all suitors by a jealous father; the princess had swallowed the stone, thus conceiving the child that was to be Moctezuma I. It is easy to imagine how deep must have been his attachment to the region of Cuernavaca, from whence his mother came; it was near by, at Oaxtepec, that he was one day to build his famous gardens, of which some traces can still be seen. Even today, those who live in the chillier and more rarefied atmosphere of Mexico City still flock at weekends to the balmier lands beyond the mountains, where, as one descends, the rich vegetation bears witness to another and gentler climate, at an altitude intermediate between the high plateau and the hot lands bordering the tropical sea. Nowadays Cuernavaca is only a little more than one hour's drive from Mexico City, but in ancient times the journey entailed a long walk over rugged pathways, rising to 10,000 feet, before descending to the plain surrounding the city.

Moctezuma was the ruler who was to break out of the limited territory surrounding the Valley of Mexico, and initiate the great

Aztec career of conquest that was to take their armies to the shores of the two oceans and eventually as far as the present border of Guatemala. During the elaborate ceremonies of his coronation, this truly great ruler perhaps already dreamt of conquests in the 'Tierra Caliente', or hot land, that lay beyond his mother-land of Cuernavaca, already conquered by his predecessors. For such tasks Moctezuma was singularly well fitted, since he had already played a leading part as commander in the overthrow of the Tepanec overlords, together with his brother Tlacaélel, who was to continue in this reign to act as the principal counsellor of the ruler. When he acceded to the throne, Moctezuma was a mature man of well over forty, and enjoyed a great reputation both as soldier and statesman.

While the descriptions that survive are less complete than for subsequent occasions, it is clear that the ceremonies which followed Moctezuma's election were much more splendid than for previous coronations, in conformity with the enhanced riches and power of the Mexica.* The new ruler was taken forthwith to the temple of Huitzilopochtli, where he was clothed with the royal robes. He then performed austere acts of autosacrifice, piercing his ears and thighs with pointed ocelot and ram bones.

Many days and nights were occupied with feasting and dancing, attended by numerous neighbouring rulers, who gave presents to the new monarch, as well as abundant gifts of clothing to the poor of the city. Conspicuous among those offering gifts and making speeches was Nezahualcóyotl of Texcoco; according to most accounts, the rulers of the Triple Alliance had the right of giving formal consent to each other's election once this had taken place.

It was customary for a new ruler, when first elected, to conduct a military campaign to show his fitness for the principal task for which he had been chosen – that of making war.*

On this occasion, the Chalca were to be the chosen victims.† They were still unconquered by the Aztecs, though their territory lay not very many miles to the south-east of Tenochtitlan, between the edge of the great lagoon and the snow-covered peaks of the volcanoes (see page 160). Since the early days, when they had played a leading part in the routing of the Mexica in Chapultepec, a traditional enmity had existed between the two peoples. Already in 1376, in the first years of the Mexica monarchy, a long and desperate war against Chalco had begun, still in effect unconcluded at the accession of Moctezuma; the Chalca had foolishly stood aside in 1428 when the Mexica and their allies overthrew their Tepanec masters. It was, however, to be expected that once the various peoples surrounding the Valley of Mexico had been absorbed into the new empire this ancient and powerful state, which had already inflicted so much damage on the Mexica and defied them for so long, would stand high upon their list of victims.

It is not surprising that Chalco was among the last of their immediate neighbours to be subdued. Now a mere village, surrounded by fertile land and enjoying a special reputation as a producer of cheese and cream, it was in those far-off times not just another city-state, but the head of a powerful confederation. Its chief partner was Amecameca† – a town enjoying a unique geographical situation, at the foot of the two volcanoes which tower over the town, which is still known for its colourful market.

In all, the confederation possessed no less than thirteen rulers.* Thus, because of its relatively greater extent and manpower, Chalco could put larger armies into the field and offer tougher resistance to the Aztecs than any other near-by state. Moctezuma himself knew Chalco and the Chalca well, and was not likely to underestimate their strength. Not only had he been imprisoned there just before the Tepanec war and been lucky to escape with his life, he had also visited Chalco in 1439, a year before his accession, ostensibly to cultivate their friendship.*

The war itself started in a not unusual fashion. One of Moctezuma's first concerns on his accession was to plan the building of a vastly more sumptuous edifice to replace the older and more modest temple of Huitzilopochtli. He began by sending messengers to all his vassals, instructing them to provide stone and wood. At the same time, he sent a seemingly innocuous request to Chalco, saying that he lacked the very large blocks of stone needed to make statues to adorn the new temple; he would deem it a favour if the Chalca could help to provide these. The customary four messengers were sent, and were received by two rulers of Chalco. The latter gave them an equivocal answer, saying that they could not oblige their freemen to do the work involved, and that in any case they would have to consult their two colleagues. When the same messengers returned for a final reply, they were told that, rather than yield to their request, the Chalca preferred war. Moctezuma and Tlacaélel there-upon decided to send an expedition of well-armed scouts to the boundaries of Chalca territory. Two valiant captains were chosen, and told to take careful note of any frontier posts or defences which they saw. These scouts actually found the Chalca forces drawn up and preparing for war; they were so numerous that they covered the whole plain. Matters had meanwhile come to a head between the Chalca and Moctezuma's Texcocan allies. They had actually captured two sons of Nezahualcóyotl; these they proceeded to kill, and their dried bodies were used as candelabra in the ruler's palace.

These preliminary moves probably took place in 1444.† The Mexica now made their usual preparations for war, but of a special intensity on this occasion, mobilizing every man and boy capable of bearing arms. The extra effort may have been partly due to an apparent absence of forces from vassal states. The Mexica actually found it necessary to send back observers to watch for signs of disloyalty in Xochimilco and other subject cities, and it is quite probable that they could not be relied upon to fight the Chalca, with whom they had many ties. Naturally, however, the Chalca war was jointly conducted by the three members of the Triple Alliance, and Texcoco played a prominent part in operations.

Eventually, when the army of the Aztecs was drawn up and ready for battle, Tlacaélel gave one of his accustomed exhortations: 'Remember that those who stand opposite are not lions that will tear you to pieces, nor demons who will swallow you. Note well that they are men like yourselves, and that you hold in your hands the self-same arms that they bear.'* A hard-fought battle ensued, with heavy losses on both sides; it lasted all day, but the Chalca would not yield. By mutual agreement the fight was then resumed the following day, again with no decisive result. The Aztecs then decided on the adoption of different tactics; to wear the Chalca down, they would limit themselves to light skirmishing for five days, making a major attack on the sixth day. This proved highly successful, and the new assault carried all before it.

Then a curious episode occurred, typical of the ritual element always present in these wars. The Chalca, seeing themselves in dire straits, asked for a truce, saying that in five days they were to celebrate the great feast of their god, Camaxtli.† They would prefer that the final battle should take place on that day, in order to have prisoners fresh from combat to sacrifice to their god on that occasion. Perhaps surprisingly, the Mexica agreed, Moctezuma vowing that, when completed, his temple too would be dedicated with Chalca blood. For this battle they then mobilized and armed even boys of twelve years; they were placed at the back of the army, to make the Chalca think that they were now opposed by an even greater force. As the Mexica charged, the Chalca called out that their women were waiting to cook them in hot chile. However, undismayed by this admonition, the Aztec forces again carried the day, and the Chalca withdrew, losing more ground. The Mexica took 500 prisoners, who were taken to Tenochtitlan and sacrificed.

By now a point had been reached in the long Chalca war, lasting in all twenty years, by which the Aztecs had already taken much territory, but had not yet captured the main bastions of the Chalca confederation. Then, at a moment when Chalco was weakened but by no means prostrate, a kind of truce was enforced by the great famine of 1451-4, of which we shall now come to speak, and which struck both foes with equal intensity. As will be seen later, the war came to be resumed after this, but by then the Aztec armies were partly dedicated to distant conquests, a fact which possibly postponed the final defeat of Chalco.

The first decade of Moctezuma's reign had now ended, marked at home by the beginning of the Great Temple, while abroad events had been dominated by the Chalca war, still continuing, though other military expeditions must surely have taken place as well. However, in 1450, a four-year period of famine began and the nascent Aztec Empire was afflicted by its greatest crisis until the arrival of the Spaniards. As a forerunner of trouble, there was a plague of locusts in 1446; the insects devoured all crops and caused a preliminary period of food shortage.* This was followed in 1449 by inundations; the level of the lagoon rose until it flooded the whole city. Moctezuma, not knowing what to do, summoned his wise friend Nezahualcóyotl of Texcoco, who enjoyed a reputation as

a master builder. On his advice, and with the help of other neighbouring rulers, a great embankment was constructed as a protection
against the waters, measuring nine miles in length and constructed
of large stone slabs, brought from a distance of twelve miles.
Moctezuma and Nezahualcóyotl initiated the task with their own
hands, thus setting an example for the other rulers and their subjects
to follow.* In 1450 there began a series of very bad harvests; work
had meanwhile continued on the Great Temple, but food began to be
so scarce that Moctezuma could give only one meal a day to the
conscripted workers from surrounding cities.† At the commencement of the trouble, there were sharp frosts, and a very heavy snow-
fall, not only on the surrounding peaks, but also in the city itself.†
Being such a rare occurrence, the effect was disproportionate, and
plants and even trees were destroyed, and many houses collapsed.*

This marked only the beginning of a long period of crisis. What
actually occurred is most clearly told by Fray Juan de Torquemada.
The frosts of the first year of famine came early, as sometimes occurs,
and destroyed the maize cobs, when they were still green and tender;
not a grain was harvested, and the disaster affected the surrounding
country, lying at the same altitude as Tenochtitlan. However, in
this year, there was no great suffering, as reserves had been carried
over from the previous one. In the following year, early frosts
again destroyed the maize, then as now the staple diet of the Mexican
peasant, and then as now mainly eaten in the form of flat, round
tortillas. In the succeeding year, the crops were affected by drought,
the other factor which can still adversely affect the harvest in Mexico,
particularly if the summer rains start unduly late in the season. As a
consequence of this further disaster, there was no seed to sow in the
fourth famine-year, and it was then that the great catastrophe
occurred.* The results were not confined to the immediate neighbourhood of Tenochtitlan, but were felt in Texcoco, Chalco, and in
places lying at a considerable distance.* Many actually died of hunger,
particularly the elderly. Even the younger people came to look as
if they were old, so parched and wrinkled did they become. Vul-
tures, seldom to be found at such altitudes, were everywhere to be
seen, scouring for corpses.

As might be expected, since the rainfall is more constant in this
region and no frosts occur, the lands bordering the Gulf of Mexico,

then known as Totonacapan, were not afflicted by the famine. And by this time the people of the high plateau were so desperate that they actually sold themselves as slaves to those of the coast, in exchange for maize. They presented a heart-rending spectacle, as they filed out of their native cities, their necks fastened with wooden yokes. Some who tried to escape died on the way, collapsing under their burdens. Long after that date, a Nahuatl-speaking population from Tenochtitlan and neighbouring cities was to be found in certain places in those regions.* Even today, Nahuatl is still spoken in part of the state of Veracruz, perhaps partly deriving from the migrations of that time.

One of the greatest tragedies that occurred was that children were actually sold in exchange for maize, with the rather curious provision that they could be redeemed for the same amount after the hunger ended. The price was 400 cobs of maize for a girl and 500 for a boy.*

The king and all the other lords wept and sent the people away, no longer able to bear their sorrowful complaints. The people also wept, and began to leave the city and go to different places where they thought that they could find relief, and where they knew that there were rich people. And there they sold their sons and daughters to the merchants and to the lords of the cities that could give them food. And they gave for a child a very small basket of maize to the mother or father; in return, they agreed to maintain the child for the duration of the famine, with the provision that if the parents wanted to ransom their offspring afterwards, they would have to pay for the food received.*

The truth is probably that the Aztec Empire was simply not organized to face a calamity of this magnitude. As will later be seen, it was at this stage more an alliance for tribute-gathering than an empire, lacking the meticulous organization and the highly elaborate storage-systems developed by the contemporary empire of the Inca in Peru.

Moctezuma in Tenochtitlan, as well as Nezahualcóyotl in Texcoco, did all they could to relieve the misery and to prevent their cities from becoming depopulated as a consequence. In the first years of the famine, scores of canoes brought maize to the city, which the ruler distributed to the poor in the form of large tortillas, a ration of one to each person. But supplies became increasingly hard to obtain, owing to the widespread nature of the famine, and to the fact that the Aztec Empire did not yet control the coastal lands, which were unaffected. Naturally the best possible use was made of fish and frogs and all the varied produce of the lagoon, but there was not enough of this to feed the people.

By the last year of the crisis, 1454, Moctezuma's reserves were exhausted, and it was then that the grim events occurred, described above. The ruler was forced to tell the people that they must simply fend for themselves and that he could do nothing more to help them: 'Till now, my sons, you have seen that I have done everything that was possible to preserve you, and that all supplies are now consumed. All that remains is to say that the Lord of the Heavens wills that each one of you should now seek his own remedy.'* After this the king, weeping bitter tears, dismissed his people.

In other words, the imperial system, such as it then existed, had virtually broken down, and Moctezuma was forced to admit it – a calamity which, as will become apparent, was to have far-reaching consequences.

In 1455 the rains at last fell in abundance, and prosperity returned to the land. The harvests were of record size, and the ears of corn ripened as never before.

In this year was celebrated the ceremony of the Binding of the Years, or the New Fire, which occurred every fifty-two years, to mark the beginning of the sacred calendric cycle.†

These last fifty-two years had witnessed tremendous achievements. The old cycle had begun in 1403, when the Aztecs, both Mexica and Texcocans, were still vassals of foreign overlords; when the cycle ended, they together controlled a great and growing empire, the like of which had not been seen since the time of their Toltec forebears.

However, this particular cycle, for all its glories, had ended in temporary disaster; it was, therefore, with relief, as well as with awe and wonder, that the citizens of Tenochtitlan, yellow and debilitated with hunger, greeted the new year Two Reed, which had followed the unlucky year One Rabbit. (The fifty-two-year cycle always began with the year Two Reed.) In their wanderings, after leaving Aztlan, the Mexica had celebrated the New Fire four times in different places; since the founding of Tenochtitlan, two more New Fires had been celebrated, always on a hill just by Culhuacan, now known as Cerro de la Estrella, or Hill of the Star. Some archaeological remains are still to be found there today. The ceremony of 1455 was, in fact, the last occasion on which the Binding of the Years was to take place before the Spaniards reached the New World. By the time of the next and last New Fire, in 1507, the Aztecs and Spaniards were already living side by side on the shores of the Caribbean, though still unknown to each other.

As Padre Sahagún relates, after the passing of the year One Rabbit, each of the four year-signs, Rabbit, Reed, House and Flint had reigned thirteen years, and the full fifty-two years had passed. When One Rabbit, the sign of the south, had fulfilled its task, it delivered its charge to Two Reed, the sign of the east.* Before the hour at which the old cycle was to end, fires were put out everywhere, and household statues of the gods were cast into the water, as well as pestles and hearth stones. The New Fire was awaited with anguish and dread, for, if the fire was not drawn, the sun would cease to shine and the world would perish – this fifth world known as 'Movement', which, as all knew, would one day come to an end. Women who were with child were treated with special precaution; they were confined indoors under guard and had to put on masks of agave leaves, as also did small children. It was believed that, if the fire was not drawn, the women would be changed into wild beasts and eat men (since, if the fire failed, the world was to end anyway, a more logical people might have regarded such precautions as superfluous!), and the children would be transformed into mice.

When the crucial moment came, at the hour when the cycle ended, the New Fire was drawn on the Hill of the Star, the priests operating the fire-drill on the breast of a well-born captive. As soon as the flame appeared, a priest slashed open the captive's breast, and cast his heart into the flame. In Sahagún's words: 'All remained facing, with neck craned, the summit of Uixachtecatl [the Nahuatl name for the Hill of the Star, meaning "Hill of the Prickly Bush"]. Everyone was apprehensive, waiting until, in time, the new fire might be drawn. And when a little flame came forth . . . it was seen from afar. Then all the people quickly cut their ears, and spattered the blood repeatedly towards the fire. Although a child still lay in the cradle, they also cut his ears, took his blood, and spattered it towards the fire.' Then fire priests, dressed as the different gods, rushed forth. They first rekindled the flame in the temple of Huitzilopochtli; they then lighted new fires in the houses of the priests, and it was then dispersed to the homes of the common people. This was followed by much rejoicing; quails were decapitated, and special amaranth seed-cakes, spread with honey, were eaten.

As was inevitable, especially among a people so given to superstitious practices, such a dire sequence of events as the great famine was attributed to the wrath of the gods. And for those who had already practised human sacrifice on an increasing scale for many centuries past what remedy could appear more appropriate than to quicken the tempo and offer up ever greater quantities of human hearts as food for the gods, in order that they in their turn should feed their mortal subjects? To supply this need, we are told that Moctezuma and Tlacaélel, conferring together in their usual fashion, decided that they should establish a system of perpetual war against the cities of the Valley of Puebla-Tlaxcala, beyond the great volcanoes, and in particular against Tlaxcala and Huexotzingo, in order that both sides should secure for themselves a permanent supply of victims for sacrifice.†

The intention was not to conquer these peoples, an achievement which would be self-defeating, since no further wars could then be fought with them. Instead, by mutual agreement, a battle would take place from time to time at an appointed place, and prisoners would be captured by each adversary for sacrifice upon their altars; their gods would thus be suitably appeased.* These ritual contests came to be known as Wars of Flowers. Not only would they offer the advantage of providing a constant source of victims near at hand, without recourse to distant wars, a further important consideration was that such prisoners from neighbouring states, sharing the same language and in most cases the same deities, were more acceptable to the gods themselves than barbarian captives from far afield.* Furthermore, such wars would provide an excellent training-ground for warriors.

To reinforce this decision, Moctezuma decreed that henceforth war was to be formally exalted to be the principal occupation of the Mexica; anyone who did not go to war, even the son of a ruler, would enjoy none of the privileges granted to nobles and to warriors: 'He shall not be permitted to wear cotton clothing, nor plumes, nor shall he be given roses, like other lords, nor perfume to sniff. He shall not drink cocoa, nor eat fine foods, and shall be regarded as a man of low estate and shall do the same work that they do, although he be of royal blood.'*

The complex problem of human sacrifice will be discussed in connection with the reign of Ahuitzotl, the greatest of sacrificers. In point of fact the chronicler's assertion that Moctezuma initiated the War of Flowers hardly tells the whole story. In spite of a certain degree of ferocity that had crept in of late, the long struggle against the Chalca clearly presented elements of a ritual war and is equally referred to with a certain frequency as a War of Flowers.† Contests known by this name also took place in other parts of ancient Mexico.* Equally, it would not be altogether accurate to assume that the struggles which now ensued between the Aztec Empire on the one hand, and Huexotzingo and Tlaxcala on the other were nothing but light-hearted ceremonial affairs. It may well be that on occasions wars were fought with these peoples mainly for the ritual purpose of obtaining victims for the gods, and were truly Wars of Flowers. It is also true that all other Mexican conflicts contained a strong element of ritual – that was one of their troubles when faced with total war on the part of the Spaniards. On the other hand, as will later become apparent, the wars against Tlaxcala were not all mere Wars of Flowers and they became increasingly ferocious in the years before the arrival of the Spaniards; the last Emperor, Moctezuma II, is several times reported as being reduced to tears by the casualties inflicted on his armies by the Tlaxcalans.

In two respects, however, the wars which began at this time do indeed constitute a new departure. In the first place, they marked the beginning of a period of continuous hostility and warfare with the peoples of the Puebla-Tlaxcala Valley, first mainly with Huexotzingo, and later Tlaxcala. These were in part occasioned by the Aztec *Drang nach Osten*, which resulted in the conquest of the coastal regions, and the consequent encirclement of Tlaxcala and its neighbours. Secondly, the steps taken by Moctezuma at this time inaugurated an era of human sacrifices on a much greater scale, amounting to mass offerings, as opposed to individual sacrifice, which had already been practised in Middle America in the fairly remote past, as well as in many other parts of the world. In itself this mass immolation was a stimulus to greater wars of conquest, since Tlaxcala and its neighbours could not be depended upon to produce all the necessary victims.

Though the first decade of Moctezuma's reign was mainly a period of consolidation, his empire had already begun to extend its bounds in more limited form before the great expansion, which began in 1458.

It can be seen from Map 4 that, apart from the major gains to the east and south-east, the Empire was also enlarged during Moctezuma's reign to include such places as Atotonilco to the north and Chilapa to the south. It is also quite probable that, well before the main drive to the sea-coast, towns lying in that direction had already been absorbed. These lay in an area for which Nezahualcóyotl and his Texcocans were at least partly responsible.†

Such achievements were of a less spectacular character; it might indeed be the case that Moctezuma, unlike that other great Aztec conqueror Ahuítzotl, was by nature more organizer than soldier, and that the urge to conquer was stimulated by other events, at a time when he himself was too old to lead his armies – however much in his youth he might have dreamt of attaining personal glory in distant wars. At all events, the great campaigns only took place in his latter years – a situation with few parallels among that small class of rulers who were virtual founders of extensive empires. His comparatively slow start in the career of conquest may have been in part due to preoccupations over the Chalca war, but is hardly explained by this alone; in any case the Chalca war still continued while the other conquests were achieved.

In 1450 the Aztec Empire was already extensive by the standards of the times, controlling most of its neighbours, as well as important lands beyond. It probably already exceeded the domain of the Tepanecs, the greatest that men could still remember. In the normal course of events, it is not inconceivable that the Aztecs might have confined themselves to further conquests of a more limited nature. However, if there was one decisive happening to alter this course, it was the great famine. In 1454 the Empire had been brought to its knees – and a race of conquerors driven to the humiliation of bartering away its children in return for supplies of maize from the unsubjected peoples of the coast. It is hardly, therefore, to be wondered at that Moctezuma's greatest campaigns were directed towards the plains of the Gulf Coast, rather than to the much drier lands of the Pacific, only conquered a generation later. After their experiences in the famine, the Aztecs must have hankered after these well-watered lands to the east.

Mexico is a land of great climatic variation, but in the whole country there is no contrast so marked as may still be encountered on the road to Veracruz. From an arid and infertile plain, the traveller descends precipitously towards the town of Orizaba, one of the first of the area to be conquered by Moctezuma. Almost in a matter of minutes the vegetation is transformed, and even the smell of the air and the song of the birds is different; from a stony waste, the land assumes a verdant hue reminiscent of parts of England, were it not for the tropical vegetation, including many mango groves (unknown in ancient Mexico). To the Mexica this country, of which their merchants must have told fabulous tales, was truly a prize worth winning.

For a tribe that was the chosen of Huitzilopochtli, and for a people so god-fearing, action cannot spring solely from the search for material gain. Such considerations, however, played their part in the urge to conquer. They were faced with a double need: firstly, to be able in an emergency such as could always arise on the arid plain to be able to feed their people; secondly, to obtain the gaudy feathers, the rich jewels and the fine cloth, which were the perquisites of their nobility. These were at least status symbols, if not essentials, as being their marks of rank or the valour they had displayed in war. Strange as it might seem in more prosaic times, on a supply of such finery the social fabric literally depended.

Thus, in 1458, was mounted the first of a series of campaigns of far greater scope than any so far undertaken.† Moctezuma did not, as might have been logically expected, make his first big push towards the coast, but south-eastwards, in the direction of the modern state capital of Oaxaca.

The ostensible motive, as for so many Aztec campaigns of aggression, was provided by the killing of Mexica merchants as they came out of the market-place of Coixtlahuaca. This was one of the main cities of the Mixtecs, a people remarkable for having produced some of the earliest known codices of Middle America, as well as for their very fine gold work and pottery. The best examples of the former can today be seen in the museum of Oaxaca. Coixtlahuaca was an important commercial centre on the road to Oaxaca and to the south-east; that this campaign was undertaken first, before the drive to the Gulf Coast, illustrates the significance which the Aztecs attached to their trade with the Mixtec region and beyond. According to some accounts, the passage of their merchants farther south was actually blocked; this was something which they saw themselves forced to avenge, notwithstanding the hazards of fighting a distant and powerful enemy. Moreover, the advantages of imposing actual domination were considerable; Coixtlahuaca, if conquered, would provide a springboard for trade, and possibly for the conquest of the whole Mixtec region and of the lands that lay beyond. For Coixtlahuaca was not just another small city-state, like some that the Aztecs had conquered nearer home; it actually possessed a 'mini-empire' of its own, and was ruled by a remarkable monarch, Atonal, who himself, like the Aztecs, exacted tribute from a wide area of surrounding territory.†

At the start of the campaign, the usual muster of Mexica allies took place, but, in view of the distances involved, special emphasis was placed on logistics; such was the accumulation of tents and field equipment, as well as foodstuffs, that it almost seemed as if they were setting forth to found a city. The journey to their destination, on foot, and using porters in the absence of any kind of pack animal, was long and arduous. However, once completed, they mounted an attack of such fury that their powerful enemy was quickly routed, and their principal temple seized and burnt. (It was the burning of the adversaries' temple that set the formal seal on victory in all campaigns.) Weary from their long march and eager for vengeance, the Aztecs killed without pity. At this point, as on innumerable subsequent campaigns, the rulers of the conquered people came forth, undismayed by their defeat, and a bargain was eventually struck. By virtue of this they retained their thrones and continued to rule their people, but as Aztec tributaries, with the obligation to provide specified quantities of tribute every eighty days, according to the produce of their district. In this case, the rulers negotiating the treaty did not include Atonal among their number, since the Codex Mendoza shows a picture of him, strangled with a rope, beside his burned temple. Here, as in other places, an Aztec tribute-collector was appointed to the district, with a corresponding official in Tenochtitlan to ensure the arrival of the tribute. The task of this local tax-gatherer was not to act as governor of the province, but more as a kind of imperial agent, to ensure payment of the amounts stipulated.

Then, once the pact had been made, the Aztec leaders and nobles were lavishly entertained and loaded with rich presents, in addition to the tribute exacted, which in the case of Coixtlahuaca included large capes, loads of chile, cotton, salt and various types of dye-stuffs. After the feasting, the victorious army then departed on its return journey, accompanied by long sad columns of prisoners. These were the 'children of the sun', destined for sacrifice. However, at the end of their journey, their outward appearance was not so tragic as might have been expected; as they arrived in Tenochtitlan, they actually danced and sang, having been given the sacred *pulque* to drink, as a solace to their woes.† They were then received with special ceremony by the elders of the city, as men dedicated to the gods. Thereafter, they filed before the great image of Huitzil-opochtli, touching the soil and placing it in their mouths as a ritual gesture of submission; finally, they were taken to pay homage to the ruler, as the representative on earth of the god.

It should perhaps be added that, apart from this campaign, the chroniclers make mention of another in the time of Moctezuma I, actually involving the conquest of Oaxaca, farther to the south-east, and now capital of the region.* This is reported to have led to such a massacre of the inhabitants that the Mexica were forced to send colonists to replace the lost population. It may be assumed that some such campaign did take place, but it does not seem that it led to an actual conquest during the reign of Moctezuma.†

Having finally disposed of the powerful kingdom of Atonal, the time was at last ripe for the push towards the coast of the Gulf of Mexico – to those fertile Totonac lands where some Mexica had gone as slaves during the famine, and of which they were now determined to become the masters so that famine might never occur again. Moctezuma first sent ambassadors to Cempoala, that lies north of the modern Veracruz, and where Cortés was to sojourn some sixty years later, in company of the Fat Chieftain – substantial archaeological remains are to be found there today, including a pyramid surmounted by two temples, typical of Aztec constructions. As usual, the demands were seemingly modest: some large sea-snails and other shells, that were needed for religious rites, and in order to satisfy Moctezuma's curiosity as to their nature. Again in this instance, the attack was directed not merely at a single city, but against something more like a confederation. Cempoala belonged to the province of Cotaxtla, from which, as can be seen on Map 4, it lies many miles distant. Ambassadors also went to Orizaba, which belonged to the same grouping of cities. Some leading Tlaxcalans were at that moment visiting this province; as a result of their offers of help, Moctezuma's messengers were ambushed in Orizaba, before they ever reached the coast. A few escaped to tell of what had happened.

After the usual muster of forces, including, of course, the other members of the Triple Alliance, the armies set forth.† For supplies they relied mainly on places on their route, which were threatened with destruction if the inhabitants did not provide these. As a consequence, villages where they passed became deserted; so afraid were the people, that they shut themselves securely in their houses and hid away their stocks of maize and chile, and their dogs and turkeys – the only domestic animals which existed at the time.† The first battle took place against the people of Orizaba, and they went on to defeat the combined forces of the other cities. The Tlaxcalans merely sent good wishes in answer to appeals for help – they were evidently prepared to fight to the last Totonac to avenge themselves of the Mexica.† They would have perhaps been better advised to join forces with the Totonacs, since the Aztec occupation of the coast led to their complete encirclement; as a result, when the Spaniards arrived, they found Tlaxcala deprived of products essential for their economy. The Totonacs themselves had put up quite a stiff fight, and at one time the Aztecs even contemplated retreat. It was the ruler of Tlatelolco, whose merchants played so prominent a part in trade with this region, who rallied the allied forces, saying that if the rest retreated he would stay and fight alone.* As a result of their victory, a large area, including a number of prosperous towns on or near the coast, was added to the Aztec domains. The leaders were taken to Cotaxtla, the capital of the federation, and royally feasted. The usual arrangements for payment of tribute were made, and an official left behind to supervise their fulfilment. However, notwithstanding the presence in their midst of Moctezuma's tax-gatherer, the people of Cotaxtla soon thought better of their acceptance of such a burden upon their economy; in this they were spurred on by the Tlaxcalans, who reproached them for being so ready to pay. The chiefs whom the Aztecs had left in control proved ready listeners to this kind of advice, and killed Moctezuma's representative; instead of the tribute, they gave presents to the Tlaxcalans.

The Mexica sent special ambassadors, for whom an unusual death was prepared. They were shut in a room by the door of which a load of chile was placed and ignited, emitting fumes that suffocated the envoys. To complete their mockery, the corpses were then stuffed with straw and clothed with sumptuous robes, and much food was set before them. The Totonacs prostrated themselves before these figures, addressing them as lords, and asking obsequiously why they did not eat.* When Moctezuma heard of this, his fury knew no bounds: 'It is my resolve that the people of Cotaxtla shall be utterly destroyed, and that no memory of them shall remain.'* However, his words of wrath were not to be taken too literally; he added a few revealing sentences, expressing his innermost thoughts – evidently directed more towards extracting tribute than vengeance. He added that Cotaxtla would now have to provide mantles twice the length of those supplied before; if previously they had furnished spotted skins of beasts, they would now have to be of pure white; they would even have to provide live serpents as tribute – something they could hardly accomplish if they had been obliterated. Moctezuma ended by instructing his captains to cease to kill, and accept surrender, if their enemies laid down their arms.

The Aztec armies were again victorious, and many enemies were killed; then something curious happened, almost unique in the annals of their conquests. We are told that the common people came forth and denounced their rulers, insisting that they themselves had done the Mexica no harm. They then went and found two of these leaders hiding in a cave and handed them over. The Mexica then caused new chiefs to be chosen and, having imposed double tribute, departed. This was to include such items as very richly worked mantles, as clothing for lords and rulers, as well as war dresses trimmed with rich feathers, and labrets of crystal with blue smalt, mounted in gold.†

Once in Tenochtitlan, there was some discussion as to how to treat these deposed rulers. Moctezuma hesitated to sentence them, 'because they were lords, and made in the likeness of the gods'.* It might offend the gods and amount to sacrilege if they were killed. It was only at the insistence of the remorseless Tlacaélel that they were put to the sword and then flayed. This step, however, was not at all in conformity with the usual Aztec practice. Normally they relied heavily on the monarchical principle and the links between royalty and deity in order to maintain their sway over conquered peoples. It was not at all usual to foment any kind of popular uprising against local chiefs, which might perhaps have had repercussions nearer home. Moreover, the Mexica rulers appear to have regarded those of other peoples as in the same category as themselves, and to kill them amounted to regicide, if not sacrilege.

Another unusual feature of this campaign was that the prisoners were not sacrificed. Whether this was decided upon as a gesture to the common people, who had turned against their masters, or whether they were not considered worthy of the gods, we are not told. Instead, the captives were distributed to the nobles, Tlacaélel taking a generous share for himself.*

The next great campaign took the Mexica armies even farther afield. Beyond the conquered territory of the Gulf Coast, and somewhat farther to the north, lay the territory of the Huaxtecs. These people were related to the Maya, and possessed an ancient tradition and culture of their own. They even dressed in a distinctive manner, and are always depicted in the codices as wearing conical hats, also a distinguishing mark of the Flayed God, Xipe Totec, who had originated probably among the Huaxtecs, and who was specially venerated by them. As on many other occasions, the reasons were partly commercial. The principal cities of the region, Xiuhcoac and Tuxpan, were important market-towns, where the people congregated for this purpose every twenty days.* Perhaps resenting competition from intruders, they killed visiting Mexica merchants, throwing them off a high cliff.

The Aztec armies raised for this expedition first passed through Tulancingo, now a loyal bastion, previously conquered by the Texcocans. Here they were given copious supplies and were regaled with such delicacies as maize cakes stuffed with quails.*

Victory in this war was achieved by the simple device of an ambush, offering an early example of the use of camouflage in war. Two thousand knights covered with straw were posted on the flank of the enemy line of advance. The Huaxtecs came forward, with painted faces, and gaudily attired in feathers and adorned with jewels; whereupon these knights took them in the flank, and a massacre ensued. After the usual banqueting and bargaining, the Aztecs departed with their train of captives, whose hands were tied behind their backs and necks made fast with wooden collars. (Although this was a victory, at this stage it was probably not a conquest in the full sense – these lands were probably too distant to be absorbed as yet into the Aztec domains, which had recently expanded with such astounding rapidity. Further battles were to ensue before they were to be finally subdued by Moctezuma's successors.†)

At the end of this campaign, which was to serve as a preface for others in the same direction, Moctezuma solemnly reaffirmed the Aztec will to conquer, enjoining his people to sharpen their swords for further far-off battles: 'Mexicans and brave knights of all my provinces. I wish you to have no illusions that our wars are at an end. We must continue to march onwards.'*

The unfortunate prisoners arrived in Tenochtitlan at a moment hardly auspicious for their own welfare. The date of the feast of the Flaying of Men was drawing near; it was to be a special occasion this year, owing to the availability of so many captives. The rulers of neighbouring states were invited, and fine gifts bestowed on them. This feast was dedicated to the Flayed God, Xipe Totec, the special deity of the Huaxtecs; by sacrificing them to their own deity, the Mexica were indeed repaying them in their own coin. The sacrifices involved were of a very special nature; the prisoners were first dressed in the conventional manner for sacrificial victims, their faces whitened with chalk, feathers placed upon their heads, and with darker colouring round their lips. Each prisoner was then taken in turn by the presiding priest, and tied with a rope to a large, flat and round stone. He was given as arms a shield and a kind of wooden club, with no blade, but covered instead with feathers; he was also provided with four wooden balls, made of a light wood, as missiles. Finally, to rouse his spirits, he was given a drink of the sacred *pulque* in a gourd; he raised this four times as an offering to the gods before drinking it.

The gladiators who were to be his adversaries came out one by one. They consisted of four knights dressed as eagles and ocelots, the orders to which they belonged. They also were armed with wooden clubs, but these had blades made of hard obsidian. Each in turn was to attack the prisoner; normally, of course, he succumbed to the first gladiator, and was promptly sacrificed, his heart being dedicated to the god. In the extraordinarily rare event of his being victorious against all four gladiators, a fifth warrior was sent against him, who was left-handed, and who wounded him in the arm which bore his club. After the gladiatorial sacrifice, the priests flayed the victims, and wore their skins as part of the ritual of the feast of Xipe for the next twenty days.

In this peculiar form of gladiatorial sacrifice, as in others, the original captor of the prisoner played a very special role. After the sacrifice, the captor took the blood of the victim into a green bowl with a feathered rim. He then visited all the shrines, omitting none, and placed the blood upon the lips of the stone images, using a hollow cane for the purpose, as if giving them nourishment. The captor might not participate in the ritual eating of the flesh of the prisoner; so special was their relationship that he would have regarded this as eating his own flesh. For when he had taken the captive he had said, 'He is as my beloved son'; and the captive had said, 'He is as my beloved father.' * Such concepts, so alien to the thinking of other peoples, even of the ancient world, serve as a good example of the complexities of the question of human sacrifice, which we shall come to discuss later.

Moctezuma's last great campaign, in 1466, was directed against Tepeaca and neighbouring cities. This lay much nearer to Tenochtitlan than did the places recently conquered, being situated to the south of the borders of Tlaxcala. However, as a glance at Map 4 will show, it was strategically placed on the Aztec military and trade routes to the south and south-east.† Probably, therefore, these places had been conquered before, and this campaign was more in the nature of a punitive expedition, following a revolt – as so often occurred in the rather loose-knit Aztec Empire.

Hostilities started in a particularly brutal fashion; the Mexica merchants were not merely killed, but actually thrown to the wild beasts.* The usual embassy of four was sent, but on this occasion there was to be no parleying; Moctezuma simply sent shield, sword and feathers as a ritual declaration of war without any further ado. The fact that no resistance was offered adds to the impression that the campaign was undertaken more as a punishment than as an original conquest. The people of Tepeaca and three neighbouring towns, thinking discretion to be the better part of valour, simply agreed to pay tribute and to include Huitzilopochtli in their pantheon.† The rulers repaired to Tenochtitlan to pay their homage, and the special charge which Tlacaélel laid upon them underlines the importance of this southern trade: 'I order you that, since you are situated on such an important highway, you shall pay special attention to ensure that of all who pass, whether foreigner or native born, none shall be ill-treated nor robbed, nor molested in any way, but that in all your territory you shall take special care to protect the merchants who go to trade in Xoconochco and Guatemala and in all the land, because it is these who enrich and ennoble the earth and give to eat to the poor and to all peoples.'*

To sum up, perhaps seldom until the British came to India was the acquisition of empire so much interlinked with questions of trade and commerce. As Tlacaélel points out, these merchants were already blazing a trail as far as Guatemala, a thousand miles away. With the Mexica, it was not so much a question of trade following the flag as the reverse. As will be later seen, they were destined to conquer the distant province of Xoconochco, on the Guatemalan border, even if they never took Guatemala itself.

By the end of Moctezuma's reign, the Empire had already taken definite shape, though many far-off provinces were still to be subdued. At this point, therefore, it is timely to ask: What kind of empire was it, and how was it ruled?

We have already discussed the government of Tenochtitlan and Tlatelolco, where the general pattern was established by previous rulers. But as the burden of empire began to make itself felt changes in the central government were inevitable, further consolidating the power of the monarch and the ruling classes – a tendency already perceptible under Moctezuma's immediate predecessor. In the New World, as in the Old, acquisition of empire led to greater concentration of power and privilege; both military honours and the spoils of war were the perquisites of the few rather than the many. The distinction between ruler, nobility and common people grew ever sharper. Moctezuma, the great *tlatoani*, assumed the remote dignity of an eastern potentate; he would only appear before the multitude on rare occasions, that the unworthy might not gaze upon his sacred countenance. Only the ruler and his *alter ego*, Tlacaélel, might wear shoes in the palace precinct; others must enter barefoot, though a favoured few, specially distinguished in war, were privileged to wear sandals in the monarch's presence, but of the simplest kind, unadorned with gold. Moctezuma himself wore different jewels every day, together with the gaudiest plumes and the finest robes; he must have presented a dazzling spectacle as he held council, seated upon his throne, the lower part of which was formed by the skin of a jaguar, with small mirrors inserted in the eyes and teeth, giving the impression that the animal was still alive. Stringent sumptuary laws were enforced, rivalling those of an oriental court. For Moctezuma's subjects, the use of jewels, feathers and even cotton clothing was governed by meticulous regulations depending on birth and distinction in war. Different styles of dress were to be established for the ruler's counsellors, the nobles, the different grades of warriors and for the people. Death was the penalty for any of the latter who wore cotton clothing, or whose mantle reached to his ankles. If such a one had the temerity to appear in a long mantle, his legs would be examined; if he bore no war wounds, alone considered to justify a garment of such length, he was instantly killed.

And thus, when they found someone [a plebian] who was wearing a mantle longer than what was established by regulation, they examined his legs, to see if he had any sign of a wound received in war. And if they did not find any, they killed him: if on the other hand they found a wound, they allowed him a longer robe to hide the scar, received in the legs as a valiant warrior.*

Privileges were in part hereditary, and in part granted for valour in war. Birth and bravery were the two hallmarks of distinction, and considerable differences prevailed between the two. The more splendid finery, such as gold bracelets, headdresses of gold with plumes attached, and the precious green stone – of deep religious significance, and the emblem of the gods – were reserved for the nobility.† The distinguished warriors could display simpler baubles, such as necklaces of bone or small shells, and were permitted to to wear eagle feathers on their heads; the common people on the other hand must content themselves with plain obsidian earplugs and with rabbit fur.†

It was ordained that only the great lords could use lip plugs, made of gold and precious stones, as well as nose plugs and earrings; no others should wear these, but the brave captains and courageous soldiers could wear lip plugs, nose plugs and earrings made of bone or wood, or of other baser materials, of no great value.*

It should be emphasized that Moctezuma's work as a lawgiver was by no means confined to court etiquette and sumptuary rules; he issued, in addition, a new legal code governing such general matters as education, religious practices and festivities, whilst not ignoring such detailed questions as the treatment of adulterers, who were to be stoned and then thrown into a river.* Drunkenness was another capital offence. This provision was applied even more strictly to nobles than to commoners; the former were to be killed for a first offence, while the latter were given a second chance before being delivered to the executioner.† The severity of the laws on such matters was to astonish the Spanish conquerors. Even certain kinds of theft were subject to the death penalty, though punishment of this crime was generally based on the notion of restitution; for instance, if anyone stole from a temple or private house, he became a slave in that place until he had doubly repaid the loss, once as compensation and once as a fine.

Great attention was paid to correct behaviour on the part of the judges:

> And likewise the ruler chose and placed in office judges who were not noblemen. . . . Such as these the ruler gave office and chose as his judges – the wise, the able, the sage; who listened and spoke well; who were of good memory; who spoke not vainly nor lightly; who did not make friends without forethought nor were drunkards; who guarded their lineage with honour; who slept not overmuch, but rose early; who did nothing for friendship's or kinship's sake, nor for enmity. The ruler might condemn them to death; hence they performed their offices as judges righteously. For otherwise, these judges could find excuse for the wrongs they might do.*

Moctezuma's provisions for the government of Tenochtitlan, running parallel to those of Nezahualcóyotl in Texcoco, confirm tendencies previously apparent. What was perforce new was the need to provide for the governing of the expanded empire.

It has first to be emphasized that this was not an empire at all in the very strictest sense; the very word 'empire' conjures forth in the imagination a whole apparatus of provincial governors, and standing armies, to control the subject peoples. In reality, however, the Aztec realm was more an alliance between three powers for the purpose of collecting tribute – to be obtained by predatory expeditions. Continuity of payment was enforced by tax-gathering officials in key places; if their demands were not met, a further expedition was undertaken, dire punishment meted out and the exactions greatly increased. It was a case of remote control by threat of harsh reprisal, rather than direct government through proconsuls. Nearer to Tenochtitlan and Texcoco such methods were mainly effective, and a fairly tight hold was maintained. However, recurring rebellions in more remote parts suggest that fear of punishment did not always remove the temptation to revolt.

The existing rulers of conquered cities normally remained in undisputed control, subject only to payment of tribute. A number of these in turn had their own tributaries, ruling areas where Aztec control was thus even remoter.† It might, of course, be argued that other empires, and notably the British, made similar use of local potentates, and even of sub-potentates. The Aztecs, however, tended to keep such rulers on a rather loose rein, and they clearly enjoyed a large measure of autonomy. They were even free in certain instances to conduct their own campaigns against other peoples, both within and without the Empire.† Each retained his own fully developed institutions, and only in exceptional cases did the Aztecs impose direct or military rule, and even then more as a temporary expedient.† At the time of the Conquest, local rulers certainly existed everywhere; not only did the Spaniards on their marches encounter certain of them, but we have lists of rulers for that moment for most of the territory of the Empire.* Their persons were held to be in a certain sense inviolable; like the Mexica monarchs themselves, they were the representatives on earth of their own gods.† The Empire not only lacked local governors, as opposed to tax-gathering officials, but equally there is no concrete evidence of the presence of military garrisons of the central power stationed in the provinces, a normal accompaniment of empire in the Old World.†

As will be seen more clearly later, when methods of warfare are discussed, there was no Mexica standing army in the true sense, apart perhaps from the ruler's guard. In its place there existed a more limited class of knights and warriors, whose main calling was the profession of arms, but who could hardly by themselves have provided provincial garrisons. The Spaniards on their long march from the coast encountered no Aztec forces billeted in distant provinces; it was only after their retreat from Tenochtitlan that they met their armies in the field, clearly sent out from the capital and not locally stationed.† What they did, of course, find were the tax-gatherers; five of these duly appeared in Quiahuiztlan, bearing their curved staffs of office, but armed with no weapon more fearsome than an elaborate fly-whisk. Bernal Díaz, however, describes the place as a kind of fortress, situated on a hill; the Aztecs may at times have sent a force of their own there, but it was normally guarded by local levies, who were tributaries of the Empire.

Nevertheless, the fiscal control imposed upon such people was strict, and the presence of the tax-collectors feared; this is made clear by the fact that they dared to appear virtually unarmed. The quantities of tribute, the delivery of which they supervised, was truly vast.

III

At the time of the Spanish Conquest, endless trains of porters from far and wide bore to the capital on their bended backs an annual tribute that included no less than 52,000 tons of foodstuffs. An annual total of 123,400 cotton garments was delivered and, on a less utilitarian level, 33,680 bundles of feathers; at the lower end of the quantitative scale, ten turquoise masks were received annually and two live eagles. All items were carefully checked on arrival, as indeed must have been necessary to ensure that, for instance, ten turquoise masks did not get simply mislaid beneath the mounds of more general merchandise.*

It is, moreover, important to appreciate that this tribute in kind was only a part of what the provinces of empire contributed. In addition, services were exacted in many cases, in the form of labourers to build Moctezuma's pyramid and other buildings; as slaves both to work and to be sacrificed; and, particularly in frontier areas, supplies and auxiliaries were provided for war – such places were often exempted from tribute in kind in other forms.

One might well ask what purposes such huge quantities of tribute (by the time of Moctezuma I they must have been already considerable) could serve, particularly since such items as the cotton mantles were not permitted to the common people, let alone the feathers. It needs, however, to be borne in mind that, apart from providing for the ruler's large establishment, for the public administration and for the costs of war, the state regularly incurred huge outlays for ceremonial purposes, whether in the form of the elaborate religious festivals, or simply as lavish presents, invariably distributed to visiting rulers, to dazzle them with the might of the Mexica.

It might with justice be argued that, notwithstanding the apparent absence of such trappings of empire as provincial governors and garrisons, the Aztecs, like the Romans and others, continually faced certain dangers, both from within and without – requiring a greater display of force than could be provided by one city. It should be added that, for the Aztecs, the danger from within not only took the form of local revolts, but also derived from the independent territories lying within the bounds of empire, and which were never conquered, such as Tlaxcala; equally, as will be seen, powerful enemies lay without. It would have been virtually impossible for the Mexica alone, or even for the three city-states of the Triple Alliance, to dominate such a territory without some system of supplementary alliances. Arising from this need for additional manpower, in most of their campaigns, the Aztecs – that is to say, the members of the Triple Alliance – relied in considerable measure on levies drawn from near-by conquered peoples.† The texts frequently refer to the use in distant campaigns of the people of the Chinampa – that is to say, the area surrounding Xochimilco – as well as to the people of Chalco, once they had been conquered, and even to auxiliaries from the Valley of Toluca to the north-west, and from Cuernavaca to the south. It is, of course, true that these peoples paid tribute, and were therefore second-class citizens, compared with those of the three capitals of the Empire. But it has already been shown that the Aztecs tended to adopt a conciliatory attitude towards most near-by peoples, once conquered, in comparison with their more distant subjects. Until the Empire fell apart under Spanish attack, the former seem to have remained loyal. And, though they paid tribute, they were rewarded for their military aid, since on many occasions they partook of war booty.

The basic strength of the Empire rested, therefore, upon broader foundations than a mere combination of three cities. In effect, it could bring to bear on distant enemies the overwhelming strength of an area with possibly several million inhabitants at the time of the Conquest.* It was not only by virtue of ruthless resolve that the Aztecs overcame their enemies, but by the application of superior force.

In addition to the use of near-by subject peoples, certain more distant tributaries seem to have been rather especially favoured, and assisted the Aztec armies with supplies and auxiliaries against their neighbours. The Fat Chieftain went out of his way to bewail to Cortés their cleverness in finding some special friends and favourites among the conquered, who helped to control the remainder.* Among these favoured few must be considered such cities as Oaxaca, one of the few places which the Mexica actually colonized.† This city undoubtedly became a bastion of empire, as did Tehuantepec, yet farther to the south-east, on the isthmus which still bears its name; the ruler of this place was even given the daughter of the second Moctezuma in marriage.* Equally to be included in this

category were a number of frontier posts, which were cities protected by some fortifications, natural or artificial, rather than actual
garrisons or fortresses, and were normally guarded by local levies.*

It may thus be seen that, for control of an area so vast, in comparison with the available means of transport, the Aztecs relied on a
radiating system of allies and associates. At the centre of the circle,
of course, stood the Triple Alliance, as a close combination of the
three cities. Next in order came the circle of associated subjects in
the Valley of Mexico and near-by territories. At one remove farther
afield were the strongpoints throughout the Empire, based on peoples
who, perhaps out of mere enmity towards their neighbours, could
generally be counted upon as friends. The outermost circle consisted
of actual frontier posts, townships whose people did not pay tribute
in other forms, but only owed the obligation to provide for frontier
defence.* It must also be appreciated that between areas under their
control there must have been many a far-off hill or mountain valley
where the Aztec armies scarcely penetrated, and where, if their writ
ran at all, it was in remote fashion; such localities would, of course,
normally have paid tribute to a local subject ruler. The very nature
of the terrain, so unlike the flat and more confined spaces of the Nile
Valley or of Mesopotamia, militated against total control by the
central power.

The Empire was thus in many respects a far cry from certain of
those of the Old World, whose meticulous bureaucracies could
watch over the doings of the remotest of the king's subjects. It is,
however, worth remarking that this more loose-knit type of domain
did have its Old World counterparts; whereas earlier rulers of
Mesopotamia had built empires in the fullest sense of the word, with
a complete apparatus of provincial governors and garrisons, the
Assyrians of the ninth century B.C. really confined themselves to
raiding outlying territories and exacting tribute, such expeditions
taking place annually. It was only in the seventh century that the
Assyrians incorporated the territories thus dominated into a true
empire, ruled by the central government. The Aztecs on the whole
seem to have had more control than the earlier Assyrians, since they
secured more regular payments. They were not, however, to be
granted such a span of time, in order to tighten their grip, by new
methods.

It has been mentioned that the innermost Aztec circle consisted of the three cities of the Triple Alliance, among which Tacuba was a very junior partner. One important question, therefore, still remains to be asked: what respective parts did the two senior partners play in the ordering of empire?

It was perhaps a special feature of Middle American empires and civilizations that they tended to derive their strength not from one single nucleus, but often from the association of two or more peoples, not necessarily of equal strength and significance. What is not always clear is the respective role of each partner.

In this the Aztec Empire is no exception; as far as Texcoco is concerned, not only its greatest historian, himself a scion of the royal line, but also later writers, are such loyal partisans as to insist, not only that Texcoco was equal in all respects to Tenochtitlan, but even that it played the principal part in the earlier conquests.

In certain things, equality certainly did exist. In particular, by all accounts, the two cities were on the same footing concerning the quantity of tribute received, each getting two-fifths of the whole, while the junior partner, Tacuba, was allotted one-fifth.

Nevertheless, it is hard for an empire to serve two masters, and it should be borne in mind that quite apart from sources admittedly partial, less biased accounts insist that Tenochtitlan held the primacy in military matters, and even go so far as to suggest that in the councils of war Texcoco actually obeyed the dictates of the Mexica ruler.* And, to keep things in their true perspective, it must not be forgotten that it was the Mexica who installed Nezahualcóyotl in his Texcocan kingdom after their joint victory over the Tepanecs; even the Texcocan historian Ixtilxóchitl admits that this only took place four years after the war, and during the interval Nezahualcóyotl remained in Tenochtitlan. Only by virtue of Mexica arms could he eventually succeed in subduing his disloyal subjects.* Even in economic affairs, the same source, no Mexica partisan, implies a certain primacy on their part, by virtue of the fact that most of the imperial tribute was first sent to Tenochtitlan, not Texcoco, and from thence redistributed.* On the other hand, the Texcocans unquestionably controlled certain territories, including the region surrounding their city, and in addition a further stretch of lands to the north-east, around Tulancingo.* Equally, many accounts suggest that they drew tribute from a very much larger area, including parts of the coast of the Gulf of Mexico.† It must, however, be added that, whatever the original situation, Texcoco's sphere of influence was diminished as time went on, and its power greatly reduced.†

Regardless, therefore, of what territory the Texcocans administered on behalf of the Alliance, and notwithstanding their right to undertake certain military campaigns on their own, the Mexica held the final say in military matters; and in a state whose very being centred on the display of valour and the cult of conquest this was decisive in the final analysis, as events were indeed to prove.

Such considerations in no measure detract from the political significance of Texcoco nor from its cultural fame. That she enjoyed great renown as a centre of learning was in no small measure due to the genial personalities of Nezahualcóyotl and of his son and successor, Nezahualpilli. As a city ruled by a kind of universal genius, cast in the mould of the Italian Renaissance, Texcoco was perhaps more the Florence than the Athens of its epoch.

Like many a Renaissance prince, Nezahualcóyotl's public virtues plead forgiveness of his private failings, at moments of like proportion. For instance, he caused one of his sons to be arraigned before his judges, because he coveted his son's wife. After his acquittal, and saddened by this unfortunate affair, his eye lit upon the future bride of one of his subject rulers, as she waited upon him at table; when he first gazed upon her, all his melancholy departed – and no sense of fair play deterred him from arranging that the future husband should be killed by the Tlaxcalans in ritual fray; notwithstanding the existence of many other wives, he then married the princess, with elaborate ceremonies, attended among others by Moctezuma.

In spite of any such aberrations, Nezahualcóyotl was a remarkable ruler, his greatness residing not only in his fame as soldier and poet, but equally in his prowess as builder and lawgiver. It is hard for us to envisage the glories of Texcoco, since the modern town of that name covers the ruins of the old. It is, however, interesting to note that Ixtlilxóchitl, writing nearly a hundred years after the Conquest, actually saw his ruined palace, from which he observes that pilferers had robbed wooden supports, left at Nezahualcóyotl's command.* Nezahualcóyotl himself, a great poet as well as a master builder, knew that all that he constructed with such loving care would one day lie in ruins. In a poem he wrote:

> I, Nezahualcóyotl, ask myself
> If perchance we take root in the earth:
> We are not here for always,
> But only tarry for a short while.
> Though it be of jade it will be shattered,
> Though it be of gold it will break,
> Though it be of quetzal feathers it will come apart.
> Nothing lasts for ever on this earth,
> But is only here for a little.*

In its day, the palace was of almost Byzantine splendour; it had 300 rooms, and among its more notable features was the great council chamber, with its throne of gold, encrusted with turquoise. Here the monarch would hold court, attended by his more intimate councillors and by subject rulers – the government of Texcoco was not unlike that of Tenochtitlan, and its laws were of like severity. In addition, there were the halls of judgement, of great importance, as well as quarters for the royal guard. Last but not least were the rooms for controlling the vast quantities of tribute that fell to the share of Texcoco. The buildings, whose functional and administrative aspects recall the Cretan and Mycenaean palaces, occupied a large area, interspersed with courtyards and gardens, perhaps the most fantastic part of the whole complex. A special patio was set aside as a kind of university, where poets, philosophers and historians taught, and close by were the royal archives. The gardens contained many fountains and basins, together with a labyrinth and even a zoo. The latter housed many exotic beasts, but, if any species was not available in the flesh, then the gap was filled by a painted stone statue of the same animal.*

Nezahualcóyotl was especially famed for his gardens of recreation. We actually have a description of the large baths which he constructed, supplied by elaborate water-works, on a hill outside Texcoco, the vestiges of which today are still known as 'Nezahualcóyotl's Baths', and which can be reached from the modern city of Texcoco after a short drive and a moderate climb on foot.†

Of the gardens, the most original and pleasing formed the wood of Tetzcotzingo, for, apart from its large wall it had steps to ascend to the summit, partly made of mortar and partly hewn out of the rock; and to bring the water from its source to supply the fountains, basins, baths and pipes, used for watering the flowers and groves of this wood, it was necessary to build strong and high walls of stone from one hill to another on an incredible scale, thus forming a water channel which reached the highest part of the wood.*

It has already been related how Nezahualcóyotl helped Moctezuma to build his dike, and as a master builder the latter did not fall behind his Texcocan colleague. In the great domain that he was creating, monumental architecture was a necessary manifestation of the might of empire.

Moctezuma's first efforts were concentrated upon one major undertaking, his temple to Huitzilopochtli. For the purpose, quantities of materials were requisitioned and hordes of workers conscripted from subject neighbours; one can imagine the trains of canoes on the lagoon and the lines of porters on the causeways as they brought every kind of stone from far-off quarries to complete the work, which continued even during the great hunger. Our sources, perhaps to dramatize its significance, concentrate their attentions upon this one building, the temple of Huitzilopochtli. It cannot however, be conceived as standing in splendid isolation, like a single mountain peak. It must have been one of a series of buildings forming a grandiose ceremonial centre, such as the Spaniards were to find – and as had indeed existed in one form or another since time immemorial, wherever civilization had taken root in ancient Mexico. Until Moctezuma's day, one may envisage a Tenochtitlan of fairly modest proportions; inevitably, however, with the expansion of empire came the transformation of the capital; this led to the construction of a whole complex of temples, following the general plan of those which the Spaniards saw, even if, since Moctezuma, the size and number of the structures had increased.†

Most accounts insist that this ruler never completed his temple – it was to be officially inaugurated only in 1487, and the need to enlarge and complete serves his successors as a pretext for campaigns yet more distant and sacrifices yet more huge. However, mention is also made of this same temple as a complete building in Moctezuma's lifetime, all painted in bright colours, with 360 steps leading to the summit, where stood the idol of the god.* It, therefore, appears that little was lacking to finish the structure; nevertheless, in a sense, no ruler could ever complete a temple of this kind in its final form. Archaeological investigation invariably reveals, as layer upon layer is uncovered, not a symmetrical whole, but an untidy maze of alterations, reconstructions and additions.† One has only to walk over the ruins of the great temple of Tlatelolco – this was the pyramid that Cortés actually climbed – to observe that it was extended, and superpositions added, at least eleven times; the final pyramid covered a vast area, and is much bigger than the second, which is what we mainly see. Such major reconstructions must have taken place more frequently than each fifty-two-year calendar-cycle.

Whereas we are not told of the other structures which Moctezuma built, we do indeed have information concerning certain parts of his great temple, such as the stone for gladiatorial sacrifice which he inaugurated. In addition, he caused a great round monument to be carved, somewhat in the manner of the Stone of Tízoc, still to be seen in the National Museum in Mexico City. On its sides were finely carved reliefs, relating the conquests which he had made; the account correctly reminds us that such intricate carving was done with stone instruments.*

But, like Nezahualcóyotl, Moctezuma perhaps excelled most of all in the making of gardens, and it was these which helped to perpetuate his name. Just as, outside Texcoco, we can still visit Nezahualcóyotl's baths, so, at Oaxtepec, not far from his native Cuernavaca, the locality still exists that recalls the memory of Moctezuma and where he built his gardens. (It is still today a place of repose, and now houses an extensive rest-centre of the Mexican Social Security, which succeeds in making imaginative use of the exotic site.)

The great gnarled cypresses are still to be found along the side of the swift-flowing stream.† But little else remains, except one coiled serpent of stone near the stream, and a toad in the churchyard. However, the church itself is clearly built upon what was once a pyramid platform; it was incidentally under this very church that the Spanish priests were to bury the smashed statue of the god known as

'Two Rabbit', one of the many deities of the sacred drink *pulque*, and who was particularly venerated in this area. The conquerors greatly admired the gardens, even if they were less addicted to the god of *pulque*, who continued to have his following among the conquered. Bernal Díaz describes them as the most beautiful that he had ever seen; post-Conquest accounts tell of cultivation there of medicinal plants and herbs, for use in a hospital built specially near by.*

It was towards the end of his long reign that Moctezuma planned his gardens. In order to add to their magnificence, and give an air of lush beauty, elaborate works were undertaken to channel the water of near-by streams, to make basins, waterfalls and reservoirs. Around them were planted every kind of tree and flower brought from the hot lands of the coast.* The gardens could not, of course, be inaugurated without intricate religious ceremonies. The actual gardeners who had brought the plants from the coast fasted for eight days, piercing their ears in an act of auto-sacrifice, and anointing the plants with their blood. Using large quantities of ritual paper, rubber and incense, they made a great sacrifice to the God of Flowers, that the plants should all grow well and bear fruit. Somewhat to the disgust of the narrator, Padre Durán, these idolatrous prayers were amply ful-filled: 'And thus it was that, in order to deceive these people, and maintain them in a state of blindness in which some remain even today, our God permitted that for their great sins, none of the plants should die, but in the third year they produced flowers in abundance.' The account adds information to the effect that they even flowered better than in their own native habitat in the coastal regions.*

In 1465, as the reign drew to its close, there remained one task unfinished, before leaving an ordered realm in the hands of the prince to be chosen in Moctezuma's place – the final subjugation of Chalco.

After the end of the Great Hunger in 1455, the war had continued, possibly rather sporadically; in any case, Chalco was by this time probably sufficiently weakened as not to present a threat to the Aztecs when their armies were absent on distant wars in other parts – they had already previously occupied much territory of the people of Chalco, though not its principal cities. Even the great chronicler of Chalco, Chimalpain, writes of this latter part of the war as if their strength was already ebbing; he uses such phrases as 'Chalco still fought on', writing of the year 1458, and for 1463 'the war still continued'.*

But now the time was ripe for the final reckoning, after a struggle of some twenty years' duration, and Moctezuma had special reasons for wanting to witness the end. In one of the campaigns against Chalco, three of his brothers had been killed.* One of his first cousins had also been captured; rather than sacrifice him, the Chalca wanted to make him their ruler. Disdaining such favoured treatment, he offered instead a fine example of Aztec fortitude, addressing his fellow-prisoners as follows: 'Know well, my brothers, that the Chalca want me for their lord and king; this I would readily be, if they offered liberty to you all. But failing this, I must die like you, since I did not come here to reign, but to fight and to die as a man.'†

He was finally sacrificed at the great feast of the Fire God.* This ceremony was perhaps the nearest Mexican approach to the European maypole, though with rather more sinister undertones. A very high pole was set up and the youths and maidens danced around it. But the Aztec prince was more fortunate than other victims on this occasion. Instead of being burned in honour of the Fire God, he simply climbed the pole, danced and sang on the small platform erected at the top, and threw himself down to the ground, where his body was smashed to pieces.

In 1464 it was apparent that the war was nearing its end. In this year the Mexica actually succeeded in storming a hill overlooking Amecameca, the second city of the Confederation (nowadays this is known as the Sacromonte, since it houses an important shrine). Two Chalco rulers were killed in the fray.* There was then a lull in the fighting until the following year. By this time, the Mexica were resolved to do or die, and never return to their homes till Chalco had been overthrown. They even built huts in the plain facing Chalco, determined to remain there until the final victory. Now, at last, the omens favoured them, and even the owls screeched of bleeding hearts and bloodstained throats, referring, of course, to the people of Chalco.* Dispirited by such auguries, and certain that the end was near, three sons of one of the Chalco rulers preferred to join the winning side, making a timely decision to betray their cause.

Guided by these royal traitors, the Mexica penetrated the Chalca defences and their army was routed. Many stragglers were actually driven up the pass between the two volcanoes, now known as 'Paso de Cortés', from the passage of the Conquistador. Some Chalca, including many women, fled to safety by this route over the mountains; the Mexica, anxious to conciliate rather than kill, persuaded them to return. The people of Chalco now declared that they had fought to the last, to the utmost of their ability, and were now resigned to total submission, offering their lands as well as tribute. The Mexica, moved by their tears and entreaties, acted towards them with consideration. Tlacaélel addressed them thus: 'Brothers, until now we never met with people who could stand up to us like yourselves. Thus it is just, since we are equals in valour, that you should have equal honour.'* They were then granted the honours of war, and the emblems due to brave warriors were bestowed upon them. The rulers were apparently not thus honoured, and Chalco was subjected for some time to military government.

This story illustrates a major facet of Aztec policy towards the conquered, faithfully respected by Moctezuma. Once near neighbours had been conquered, they were to be treated in a comparatively conciliatory manner, that they might become loyal subjects and useful auxiliaries.

After the campaign was over, the Mexica returned home to pay homage to their dead, following for the purpose the peculiar rites prescribed for such occasions. Finding it difficult to mourn fitly without some image of the departed before their eyes, they made wooden mortuary bundles, complete with faces, adding to these eyes, nose and mouth. They marked these faces with chalk, as being symbolic of death by sacrifice; they put feathered devices on their backs and brightly coloured mantles on their bodies, attaching shields and clubs to their sides.

The relatives then danced before these strange figures to the sound of the music of drums and of instruments made of bone. After four days of this celebration, the pinewood bundles, known as 'lords of pinewood', were burnt. The family of the dead warrior then fasted for eighty days, eating only one meal a day. They abstained from washing their faces, which became so filthy after eighty days, as the dirt and dust mingled with their tears, that they looked like demons.*

Moctezuma knew that his life was drawing to its close, and that his work was done. Accordingly, with his end in mind, he sent out messengers to his farthest dominions with orders to seek out the best carvers and sculptors that they could find. They were ordered to carve two statues, one of Moctezuma and one of Tlacaélel, out of the living rock on the hill of Chapultepec, where the Mexica had first settled on their arrival in the Valley of Mexico. These memorial figures of the two brothers were carved so skilfully and with such speed that Moctezuma himself was astonished. This final task completed, he spent his last days ordering the arrangement of his gardens in Oaxtepec.

By any standard it had been an outstanding reign and Moctezuma might rank among the great empire-builders of history – even though his creation was to come to a swift and tragic ending. He had known tribulations as well as triumphs, particularly the famine. He had overcome them all, but at a price – the increasing tempo of conquest and the mounting toll of sacrifice. As so often happens, victories created their own problems and the chosen people of Huitzilopochtli were now the prisoners of their own successes. The demands of their gods for yet more victims, and of the state for greater spoils and grander ceremonies combined to make of conquest a necessity.

It is not impossible that such a situation did not altogether conform to Moctezuma's own designs and character, but even the greatest of rulers are not always master of the events which they inspire.

CHAPTER FIVE

A NEW ERA

MOCTEZUMA DIED IN 1468.† After the elaborate funeral-rites, his remains were buried within the precincts of his own palace, in the very place where Hernán Cortés later built his residence, in the new city of Mexico.* His death marked the end of an epoch, and in the inner councils of Tenochtitlan the problem of the succession loomed large: in spite of numerous natural offspring, Moctezuma left no legitimate sons.† As the leaders assembled, all eyes were fixed on Tlacaélel. He first spoke in praise of the late ruler:

Already you know of the death of my brother, who, like one who carries a burden for a certain time, has borne the brunt of the lordship of Mexico till the end of his days, fulfilling his duty like a slave subject to his masters' orders, protecting and defending all things which concern the realm. The same fate awaits me one day, and all who stand here, for life's joys, pleasures and contents are only lent to us and last but a little while. You see already that all my brothers have ended their days, and I alone remain.*

Having thus spoken, he wept copiously.

As might have been expected, by common accord, Tlacaélel was pressed to ascend his brother's throne. He, however, replied: 'What greater dominion can I have than what I hold and have already held ?'* He was too old to begin to reign: if they could not themselves pick a fitting successor, they should call for the rulers of Texcoco and Tacuba, normally consulted on such occasions. The latter were accordingly summoned, and a long discussion followed behind closed doors. As the final outcome, Nezahualcóyotl pointed a fateful finger towards a young prince named Axayácatl (meaning 'Face of Water'): he was accordingly seated on the royal throne, and dressed in the resplendent insignia of the *tlatoani*. As was the custom, his first obligation was to listen to a series of lengthy addresses – after which all present gave him magnificent gifts.

Axayácatl was about nineteen years old.* He was the son of a prince named Tezozomoctzin, and thus grandson of Moctezuma's predecessor.† Not only was the new ruler young and untried: at the outset, though he was later to prove himself, some doubted his capacities. His elder brothers, in particular, moved by jealousy, spoke disparagingly, suggesting that the only prisoners he could secure would be those purchased as slaves.† The electors, however, a small but experienced body, knew better. Tlacaélel himself had numerous progeny, and could surely have obtained the succession for one of his own sons. The election of Axayácatl, whose father belonged to another branch of the royal family, in itself stressed the elective nature of the monarchy. It is not inconceivable that Tlacaélel and Nezahualcóyotl furthered the choice of a raw youth, easy to control. Apparently, however, Tlacaélel died early in the new reign, thus enjoying for but a brief span the legendary prestige attaching to the only survivor of Moctezuma I's generation.†

Accordingly, at this point, we must take our leave of this venerable soldier-statesman. His continued existence seems improbable, notwithstanding certain chronicles which insist that he survived another quarter-century, treating Axayácatl and his two successors as insubordinate puppets, and living till the ripe old age of 120 years. It was perhaps better for Tlacaélel not to witness the last years of Axayácatl, and the reign of his successor, when the Mexica were to suffer such ignominious defeats, unknown in his heyday.

In 1472 Nezahualcóyotl, the only survivor of that great triumvirate which had created the Empire, also breathed his last. In the words of a poem attributed to his own pen:

> Just as a painting
> Our outlines will be dimmed,
> Just as a flower
> We shall become desiccated. . . .

> Ponder on this,
> Eagle and Tiger knights,
> Though you were carved in jade,
> Though you were made of gold,
> You also will go thither
> To the abode of the fleshless.
> We must all vanish,
> None may remain.*

The late ruler at least did not lack progeny, leaving sixty sons and fifty-seven daughters, descended from his forty wives. However, like Moctezuma, he had few legitimate heirs, and the throne accordingly passed to his son Nezahualpilli, aged only seven years – in Texcoco, the system of primogeniture was more firmly established, and the throne would pass to a son, rather than to a brother or cousin. Nezahualcóyotl, before dying, charged his three principal natural sons to protect and obey the infant Nezahualpilli, making the eldest regent and foster-father of the boy.*

Hardly were the funeral rites over, however, before these three began to plot against the legitimate heir, with the intention of supplanting him. Axayácatl and the ruler of Tacuba rushed to the rescue of Nezahualpilli, bearing him to the safety of Tenochtitlan (they had, of course, been party to his election, as was customary among the rulers of the Triple Alliance). This intervention on the part of Tenochtitlan, to protect the infant heir of Texcoco, suggests a growing Mexica influence in Texcocan affairs, even if Nezahualpilli himself came to enjoy a position of authority within the alliance, as a genial statesman.

The young Nezahualpilli was set upon a sumptuous throne and crowned as ruler of Texcoco; the ceremonies apparently took place in Tenochtitlan – also a point of some significance. The three disloyal brothers were 'saddened', but went unpunished.* They were even rewarded for their misdemeanours with palaces and provinces. Axayácatl himself spent some time in Texcoco, compelled personally to watch over the kingdom and its ruler's greedy relatives.

Axayácatl must have been struck with dread when Nezahualcóyotl pointed his gnarled finger, thus elevating him to the throne of the world and the seat of Huitzilopochtli; he was succeeding to a position occupied for forty-two years, or as long as men could remember, by two august monarchs: both were famed for valour and renown even before they ruled; between them they had transformed a modest heritage into a mighty realm. Axayácatl himself was deeply conscious of the legacy of the departed great ones, as these verses, attributed to the young ruler, clearly testify.

> People never cease to take their leave,
> All depart,
> The Princes, the Lords and the Nobles
> Will leave us as orphans.
> Rejoice not, my lords,
> Perchance may any one return?
> May any come back
> From the abode of the fleshless?
> Will they come back to tell us something,
> Moctezuma, Nezahualcóyotl, Totoquihuatzin?
> No, they will leave us as orphans,
> Be full of grief, O my lords.*

And now a mere fledgeling had received the awesome summons to fulfil the supreme imperial role, and to follow worthily in the footsteps of the founding fathers – for the *tlatoani* of Tenochtitlan, though no absolute monarch, was called upon to rule and to command.

However powerful his generals, however wise his counsellors, he was now set far above them. He, not they, wore the royal diadem and the blue robe of Huitzilopochtli; he alone was the successor of the king of Tula, the Plumed Serpent, soon to return – attired as a Spanish knight.

It was customary that a new ruler should conduct a campaign in the early days after his accession, to prove his valour. Axayácatl apparently undertook his first major expedition in 1470, to suppress a rebellion in the Cotaxtla region, to the south-east, already once conquered and reconquered by his great predecessor. This province was always intractable, and was to rebel again in the following reigns. Owing to the very nature of the Empire, lacking adequate regional organization to ensure central control, it often fell to the ruler's lot, before seeking new triumphs, to reassert his sway over areas previously conquered.†

But Axayácatl's greatest test of strength, or weakness, came only in 1473, when a dispute erupted between Tenochtitlan and her sister-city of Tlatelolco.† The latter was not merely a twin township, but an indispensable partner, on whose prowess Tenochtitlan, if not the whole Aztec realm, depended. Tlatelolco, perhaps the earlier of the two to develop, had fought many a campaign; above all, however, it was the commercial capital of the Empire and the site of its principal market.

Commerce, important in itself in any community, in the Aztec polity was inextricably linked with war. The Tlatelolco traders were blazing a trail into lands far beyond the present bounds of empire; it was consequently their forays which formed the basis of future conquest, apart from the wealth they offered. In very general terms, and leaving aside the role of Texcoco, the Empire was based upon the joint enterprise of the warriors of Tenochtitlan and the merchants of Tlatelolco (though we must not forget that Tlatelolco also had warriors, and Tenochtitlan traders). In spite of such interdependence, each was ruled by its own dynasty, installed a century ago, after the settling of the two cities by the Mexica tribes.

Since the ostensible origins of this quarrel are superficial, it may be fitting to seek deeper causes of discord. Of the two causes officially given, the more trivial may be first mentioned: certain Tlatelolcan maidens yielded to the blandishments of some youths of Tenochtitlan; after readily allowing themselves to be ravished, they went and complained to their fathers. Following this incident, hardly meriting a resort to arms, the Tlatelolcans prepared for war.*

The ruler of Tlatelolco, Moquihuix, had ascended his throne some years before Axayácatl; as the dispute gathered force, his advisers were quick to warn him that they could not hope to defeat their fellow Mexica of Tenochtitlan without the help of allies.* In his search for support, his success in the Valley of Mexico was limited; farther afield, his hopes of victory were discounted and his pleas ignored.† Meanwhile, Axayácatl also prepared for war, summoning his subjects and allies. In the main they proved loyal, in particular Texcoco. The adherence of the latter to his cause was crucial to the outcome.

Another rather more convincing reason is given for the falling-out between the two cities, taking the form of a personal dispute between their two rulers. Moquihuix of Tlatelolco had married the sister of Axayácatl, but he had long since wearied of a wife who had grown ugly, skinny, raddled and fleshless. In fact Moquihuix had conceived such a hatred for his legitimate spouse that he would take away the cotton clothing provided by her brother Axayácatl and give it to his concubines, leaving her with one tattered mantle. She was obliged to sleep in a corner by the wall, abandoned by her husband, who preferred the company of his other bedfellows, among whom some great beauties were to be found. Axayácatl, enraged by the treatment of his sister, was heard to remark that Moquihuix' concubines would bring destruction upon Tlatelolco. In addition, Moquihuix was nagged at by his wife; in this respect at least she showed prescience, begging him not to try conclusions with her brother and warning that such a venture would end in ruin. Moquihuix, however, turned a deaf ear to these entreaties, and continued with his plans, undismayed by evil omens: one day he visited the kitchens of his palace, and he was horrorstruck to see some birds dancing as if alive in the pot in which they were being boiled.*

Axayácatl's preparations were by now complete, and he made the following speech to the army leaders: 'Let not the fame and glory of such valiant men as yourselves be obscured, but guard and defend the realm and nation of Mexico. See where you have to fight: it is not so far distant and you will not have to cross fords, bridges, rivers, mountains nor deep ditches and defences, since Tlatelolco is near by and the way is flat.'* This must indeed have been a most comforting thought to his men, accustomed to the most arduous marches before reaching the scene of battle. In this instance their objective, the market-place of Tlatelolco, lay about one mile distant.

Axayácatl sent word to Moquihuix of his impending attack, together with the ritual feathers, sword and shield, reluctant to be accused of taking his enemy unawares – surprise attacks were occasionally employed against distant foes, but would have appeared ungentlemanly in a civil war among the Mexica. Then, after some preliminary fighting, he sent a second messenger to Moquihuix, whom the latter simply strangled. Axayácatl, still a very young man, had previously tended to display the more timid side of his nature, but now gave proof of the greatest vigour and courage, and personally led his forces to victory over the Tlatelolcans. The latter had evidently taken the offensive, and advanced towards Tenochtitlan, but Axayácatl made a counter-thrust, forcing them to retreat past a point now occupied by the fine Church of Santo Domingo, and pursuing them as far as Santa Ana, which also still exists, close to the main square of Tlatelolco. They were then besieged in the market itself.*

The Tlatelolcans, by now in desperate straits, proceeded to adopt the oddest of ruses; they dispatched squadrons of naked women against their enemies. They actually squeezed the milk from their bare breasts and sprinkled it over the opposing forces. To complete the effect, they were accompanied by another force, composed of a troop of young boys, also naked except for the feathers on their heads. Axayácatl, whose soldiers were apparently unnerved by these peculiar tactics, ordered that they should not be harmed, but simply made prisoners. Once this secret weapon had failed, Moquihuix saw that all was lost. Accompanied by his favourite dwarf, he mounted the steps of the main temple of Tlatelolco, fighting a brave rearguard action.* The forces of Axayácatl, however, stormed the pyramid, and threw him down from the top, together with the dwarf and many leading Tlatelolcans.

The elders came and sued for peace, promising to serve Axayácatl, who thereupon ordered that fighting should cease. The Tlatelolcans now declared that they were mere merchants, and could offer the fruits of their labours as tribute, in the form of the goods obtained from remote parts, including the luxuries deemed so necessary by rulers and warriors. Axayácatl accepted the offer but without losing sight of more pedestrian necessities, insisting that Tlatelolco should also provide biscuits and beans as wartime rations, as well as porters to convey them to the scene of battle. They must in future also furnish slaves for sacrifice and surrender much of their land; as a punishment, menial tasks, such as sweeping out the palaces of Tenochtitlan were imposed; as an additional humiliation, they would have no temple of their own dedicated to Huitzilopochtli.

Such provisions constitute an angry reaction against the act of civil war, and apparently they were not enforced for long, for Tlatelolco was a structural part of the Mexica community: their temple of Huitzilopochtli was certainly restored and functioning when visited by Cortés forty-six years later. But it was the end of Tlatelolco's independence; the dynasty disappeared and the city was henceforth ruled by a high-ranking official, acting as military governor.

Temporarily, however, Tlatelolco was harshly treated. At Axayácatl's command, the town was sacked, the victorious soldiers even robbing the kitchenware from the houses. Some Tlatelolcan women plunged into the lagoon for refuge, until the water reached to their necks. Axayácatl's soldiers, finding these women thus submerged, amused themselves by forcing them to make noises in imitation of ducks and other aquatic birds, in return for the privilege of being allowed to emerge from the water.

One may be willing to accept that a dynastic feud, exacerbated by the spurning of Axayácatl's sister, could have played its part in the quarrel between the two Mexica cities. It may also be the case that Moquihuix resented claims to supremacy on the part of Tenochtitlan, once the august Moctezuma had been succeeded by his own seemingly insignificant brother-in-law; however, such considerations are hardly sufficient in themselves to account for the sudden falling-out between close partners, so dependent on each other. The Mexica cities had always shown a remarkable political wisdom in their dealings both with one another and with their neighbours. A civil war within the Mexica family could easily rend asunder the whole fabric of empire, if their Triple Alliance partners and their subject peoples had taken different sides. Fortunately, almost all adhered to Tenochtitlan; the civil war was thus of short duration and its effects limited. One is, however, still left wondering why this war had to happen. A certain degree of rivalry had indeed persisted between the two cities, but until this fatal moment they had worked together, settling any differences by peaceful means. Tlatelolco, perhaps the more important in early days, had become the leading trading centre of Middle America, just as Tenochtitlan had risen to the rank of foremost military power. Moreover, Tlatelolcan armies had played their part in many campaigns, actually making their own conquests.

Tlatelolco's greatness as a commercial centre cannot be overstressed. Furthermore, the Tlatelolcans operated not as mere private traders, but were an integral cog in the state machine, paving the way to many a conquest. In fact, the military activities of their merchants may indirectly have cost the Tlatelolcans their independence. Even if Tenochtitlan and Tlatelolco had worked together as equal partners in political matters, some kind of joint military command was clearly indispensable. As conquests were made in parts even more remote from the capital, the need increased for spying and scouting by the merchants. Such activities could only bear fruit if the latters' activities were geared to military policy, directed primarily by Tenochtitlan.

As long as Moctezuma ruled in Tenochtitlan, it was perhaps not too hard for a man of vast prestige to exercise primacy in such a partnership. The Tlatelolcans were perhaps prepared to do Moctezuma's bidding in most instances; however, with the advent of a young and untried ruler in Tenochtitlan, this might have changed.

Owing, however, to the increasing military significance of the Tlatelolco merchants, now blazing a trail in advance of the armies towards distant Guatemala, their activities had become one aspect of a joint enterprise, part trade, part conquest. The need thus became more pressing to bring the two cities, still ruled by separate dynasties, under one control. In the long run the Empire required one ruler and one capital city; the war against Tlatelolco and the gradual decline in the status of Texcoco within the Alliance were part of the same process.

In view of the importance of commerce in all ancient Mexico, and not only among the Aztecs, some general comments are perhaps called for on the merchants of Tlatelolco and their neighbours. Of the great market of Tlatelolco, to be seen by the Spaniards forty-six years later, the Conquistador Bernal Díaz del Castillo gives us a wonderful description:

The chiefs who accompanied us showed us how each kind of merchandise was kept separate and had its place marked out. Let us start with the dealers in gold, silver and precious stones, feathers, cloth, and embroidered goods, and other merchandise in the form of men and women to be sold as slaves. There were as many here as the Negroes brought from Guinea by the Portuguese. Some were tied to long poles with collars around their necks so they couldn't escape, and others were left free. Then there were merchants who sold homespun clothing, cotton, and thread, and others who sold cacao, so that one could see every sort of goods that is to be found in all New Spain, set out the way it's done where I come from, Medina del Campo, during fair time. There were people who sold henequen cloth, as well as rope and shoes made from the same plant, and its cooked roots, which are very sweet, all in a special section of the market set aside for them. In another section they had skins of tigers, lions, deer, and other animals, some tanned and some not.*

Bernal Díaz goes on to describe the sellers of every kind of foodstuffs, turkeys and young dogs, as well as wild game and all sorts of vegetables and fruits. Like Cortés himself, he even noticed the many different kinds of honey which could be bought. After mentioning the sellers of tobacco, liquid amber, and herbs, among the countless variety of wares on display, he makes shrewd observations about the means of exchange employed by the merchants:

Then we went to the great cu [Temple], and as we approached its great courts there were many more merchants who sold gold in grains as it came from the mines. They put it in goose quills, and since the quills were white, the gold could be seen through them. They calculated how much so many blankets or gourds of cacao were worth, or slaves, or whatever else they traded, according to the length and thickness of the quills.*

133

Both Bernal Díaz and Cortés mention the close government control exercised over the market, though on this point Cortés is the more explicit:

There exists in this great square a large building like an audience hall, where ten or twelve persons are always seated and who act as judges and who give sentence on all cases and questions arising in this market, and who order punishment for those who break the law. And in the same square there are other people who continuously walk among the people, observing what is sold and the measures with which it is measured; and we saw one measure broken which was false.*

This great market is not visible today in its full extent. On the other hand Bernal Díaz also mentions certain courtyards of great size, which he saw before reaching the main temple and also in the area surrounding this edifice. As a result of excavations around the site of the temple of Tlatelolco, the visitor nowadays can still gain a remote idea of what these patios must have been like. In addition, he can see the approximate point from which the ruler of Tlatelolco was cast down to his destruction, though the actual pyramid now to be seen is prior to Moquihuix and would by then have been covered by many superpositions.

Of interest is the observant conquistador's mention of the means of exchange. The ancient Mexicans never evolved a single unit of exchange, and goods were therefore sold by a form of barter, using mainly cacao beans, as well as cotton mantles known as *quachtli*, and small flat T-shaped strips of copper. Quills filled with gold dust were also employed, though the chronicles, sharing the Spanish obsession for this metal, possibly over-emphasized its use as currency, at the expense of other items serving the same purpose and in terms of whose value all merchants, including slaves, were priced.

At the same time, it must be borne in mind that goods traded in the Tlatelolco market formed a limited part of the total activities of the merchant, whose operations are a unique feature of the Aztec world. Like so much else, this manner of doing business was not invented by the Mexica. The traders had probably not originated in the high plateau at all but in the coastal regions, where there is evidence of long-distance trading in obsidian in the second millennium B.C.; clearly, some kind of commerce existed between the Valley of

Mexico and the far-off regions of Guatemala in the early centuries of our era.† Moreover Cholula, one of the few cities with a continuous record of existence from early times until the Conquest, was long pre-eminent as a great trading centre. Probably the methods of those earlier traders were not so different. Since early times trade had existed as a unifying factor. As such, the traders probably tended to dictate the pattern of military conquests, rather than the reverse. From time to time, these highly itinerant merchants simply acquired new masters, the latest being the Aztecs.

Possibly, moreover, under the latter, the organization became more complex, and the merchants of Tlatelolco were certainly a hierarchized community, having two principal chiefs and being divided into a number of clearly defined categories and ranks.†

As previously explained, a very special feature of these merchants was their combining of trade and war. The ruler used them as a kind of secret service, to provide information on distant territories, as yet unconquered. Like other spies or reconnaissance parties, they usually travelled at night, visiting not only imperial provinces, but also regions described as 'enemy lands'. They learned the local languages and went disguised, concealing their place of origin; if discovered, they were often slain.* They faced conditions of the utmost austerity, living on dried tortillas and soggy maize.* On such expeditions, the merchants of Tlatelolco were accompanied not only by those of Tenochtitlan, but also of other neighbours, such as Chalco.

Apart from acting as spies and reporting to the ruler information gleaned in foreign parts, they sometimes even became involved in major military operations. On an expedition to the Pacific coast, south-east of the port of Acapulco, the Mexican export drive ran into fierce opposition, and the merchants were besieged for four years. They took their own prisoners in the fighting:

And when war came to pass there at Ayotlan, the merchants, the vanguard merchants, were besieged for four years. At that time, the city yielded; at that time they broke the rampart of eagle and ocelot warriors. And all the devices, the quetzal feather crest devices mentioned, all these the merchants assumed; in them they conquered, they completely vanquished the foe.

And when the ruler Ahuitzotzin heard that the distinguished merchants were besieged there, then aid was sent. The one who was sent was Moctezuma, who went serving as general. He had not at the time been installed as ruler.*

However, the efforts of the army commander and future sovereign, Moctezuma II, were superfluous. When the relief expedition reached them, the merchants had already won the war and addressed Moctezuma as follows: 'O our lord, thou hast tired thyself; thou hast suffered fatigue. No longer needest thou reach the place whither thou goest; for it is already the land of the master, the portent, Huitzilopochtli.'* It may be worth noting that the merchants, who at home dressed more simply, wore when fighting the full warriors' regalia; since it was their custom not to cut their hair during an expedition, we are told that on this occasion it was reaching to their loins when they returned home.

In spite of such forays, it would be a misconception to think of the merchants as mere warriors in disguise; they equally were vital to the economy, which probably depended on trade quite as much as on tribute; their activities are amply described by Padre Sahagún, who devoted a whole book to his native informants' descriptions of the Tlatelolco merchants. Much of his investigations were carried out in Tlatelolco itself and probably a few of those who described these expeditions had actually participated as young men. But equally, where trade itself was concerned, the merchants acted strictly under the aegis of the state, which shared the benefits. The ruler may have addressed them as his 'beloved uncles'; this, however, did not deter him, even after such ordeals, from relieving them of their luxury wares, such as turquoise mosaic shields, offering in return more modest trophies, such as bundles of rabbit-fur capes.*

On their major expeditions, the ruler would give them his own goods to trade.† On certain occasions he gave them 1600 cotton capes, presumably received by him as tribute; these, in themselves a form of currency, were in their turn exchanged by the traders for luxuries adapted to the special predilections of the sovereigns of places to be visited. Such goods remained the exclusive property of the ruler. At the same time, however, the traders took with them their own merchandise, including ornate articles of gold.* On reaching their destination, they would do business in the first place with local rulers, who offered the specialized produce of their own particular province or district. Owing to the problem of distance and transport, trade tended to base itself upon expensive items of small volume. As compensation for trading on the ruler's behalf, the merchants received important privileges; in certain provinces, only those acting under his protection might enter. They were thus in effect granted monopoly rights, often conceded only to the merchants of Tlatelolco and Tenochtitlan, and excluding those of neighbouring cities, who partook in their expeditions.

In addition to such operations beyond the boundaries of empire, they traded between the different imperial provinces, exchanging the status symbols of one area for those of another. They would thus proceed south-eastwards, towards Tochtepec, a principal centre where the Tlatelolcans had a protected base, with special hostels for their own merchants and for those of other cities. From thence, they would divide, some continuing eastwards along the coast, exchanging their goods for the famous green stones of the region, while others made their way towards the Guatemalan border; here the local balance of payments depended much on the sale of slaves.†

An odd situation thus prevailed whereby the Aztec ruler, not content with the avalanche of tribute which poured into Tenochtitlan, would use his merchants to sell the tribute of one subject province for the free produce of another. And, quite apart from the ruler's own property, the goods which the merchants themselves traded must also have been partly manufactured from raw materials obtained as tribute. Thus, by monopolistic commerce, the ruler multiplied his tribute, sometimes even imposing unfair terms of trade on conquered provinces, and selling them goods which they did not value. Long before the Europeans in Africa, the Aztecs discovered the advantages of supplying worthless baubles to the 'natives'.

The cities of Soconusco, near the Guatemalan border, were driven to oppose the Aztecs by force, weary of having their riches extracted each year in return for such dainties as cakes made from worms, cheeses of lagoon weeds, or simple toys and devices of little value, offered in return for much-prized cacao, gold, feathers and precious stones.* Thus the Aztec rulers, after imposing enormous tribute by armed force, took advantage of their military superiority to procure special conditions for their own traders; they thus exchanged these forced levies for even greater quantities of goods, for the ruler's own benefit.

The lives of the merchants, like all Mexicans, were governed by long-established forms of ritual. They had to await a lucky day, such as One Serpent or One Monkey, before setting forth on an expedition; equally, they could only come home on a day whose sign was propitious for the purpose. On their return they faced endless ceremonies in honour of the gods, including the merchants' own deity, and the interminable speeches of welcome from their own chiefs.† As a peculiar feature of their established customs, successful members of the fraternity were expected to give incredibly lavish banquets, entertaining the nobility, as well as their own colleagues.

Their whole way of life presented a strange mixture of feigned humility and lavish display. On the one hand, and as a symbolic form of humiliation, a chief merchant would accuse the returning traders of having simply stolen the merchandise which they had brought back. In addition, they were compelled to return to the house of a friend rather than to their own home, and unloaded their goods at night, actually pretending that these were not their property. When forced to fight, they wore full warriors' regalia, but at home they dressed in simpler attire. However rich, in daily life they avoided ostentation.

In contrast with this apparent modesty, they gave these sardana-palian feasts, at which one hundred turkeys and forty dogs might be consumed. We are told that the two were served together, with the dogs' meat underneath that of the turkey. The merchants were often referred to as 'Bathers of Slaves'; the central features of the religious ceremonies following the banquets was the sacrifice of slaves, who had previously been ritually bathed. These were bought in the local slave-market. Since they were expected to play their due part in the rites of their own sacrifice, their price varied accordingly, forty cotton capes being that for a slave skilled in dancing, and only thirty for one less talented.* After the gargantuan feasting, the priests would arrive and lead the slaves to the temple. Having been duly bathed, and soothed with a drink of the sacred *pulque*, they were slain; at times they were even submitted to a form of gladiatorial sacrifice. The host of the banquet, as a gruesome relic of the occasion, would keep for the rest of his life the accoutrements of the victim, including his hair, in a sacred box made of reeds.* It is an indication of the high status of the merchants that the sacrifice of their slaves was often allowed to coincide with the offering of war captives to Huitzilopochtli.

The merchants formed a community apart, in many respects highly privileged. They were allowed to own land, and some could even send their children to the special schools reserved for the children of the ruling classes. The second Moctezuma even treated them at times as noblemen, bidding them to sit at his side on important occasions. They were, moreover, the only community in the state to have their own law-courts. They differed from the normal concept of the merchant, not only because they were involved partly in state trading, quite apart from their military role, but also because the wealth acquired was devoted as much to banquets and display as to private accumulation. The reward for their great privations lay in riches used to impress through public display, rather than to hoard for personal comfort. This tendency reveals a distinctive attitude towards success and riches in ancient Mexico, common also to other classes of society, as will later be seen.

The merchants were certainly important, and it would seem that their status was increasing. It may be suspected that this trend gave rise to resentment on the part of the established ruling classes – hence their feigned humility and their tendency to hide their riches.

When the Aztecs overthrew the Tepanecs in 1428, they naturally incorporated most of the tributaries of the vanquished into their new-found empire. But, for reasons not altogether clear, the region of the Valley of Toluca – that is to say, the north-western part of the empire of the Tepanecs and their probable place of origin – became once more independent.*

A pretext for conquest, or reconquest, was offered in 1474 by a family quarrel between two local rulers.† War had broken out between Toluca and Tenancingo over the vital question as to who should pay tribute to whom (needless to say, they both ended as Aztec tributaries).

The ruler of Tenancingo appealed to Axayácatl for help, promising to become his loyal vassal. The latter was at this moment about to dedicate an important sacrificial stone, an inauguration that necessitated a good supply of prisoners to grace the ceremony. The ruler's visit was therefore opportune, and messengers were promptly dispatched to Toluca, with a request for pine and sandalwood, pleading an urgent need for these materials. The demand was rejected, on the grounds that the Tolucans had no such wood in their mountains. Even today, however, in an era of relative deforestation, the traveller from Mexico City to Toluca passes through dense pine-forests, and can readily observe that neither ruler really needed more pinewood, but only an excuse for war. Sandalwood also is still plentiful in the region of Toluca, and in its colourful market chairs and even spoons abound made of this material.

Axayácatl, in undertaking such an expedition, must have aimed to complete the conquest of the former Tepanec Empire and to dominate an area situated dangerously close to Tenochtitlan – Mexico City is only forty miles distant from Toluca by road. He possibly feared that the inhabitants might ally themselves with the Tarascans, a formidable power lying beyond Toluca, and now to become the mortal enemies of the Aztecs.

The usual preparations were made, including the mobilization of subject neighbours. Axayácatl and his army then set forth, following desperate new appeals for help from Tenancingo. The forces of the latter were to attack Toluca from the surrounding mountains, whilst the Aztecs advanced along the road leading towards the city. Mindful of the need for victims for his new stone, the ruler gave the strictest instructions that his troops were to capture rather than kill.

The Mexica themselves were placed in the van, occupying as usual the most dangerous position. Axayácatl still considered himself too young to address his veterans, and an orator harangued the troops, reminding them that their adversaries were not tigers or eagles, but only men.*

In spite of his youth, the ruler showed himself to be worthy of his forebears. He told his main body to retreat to the near bank of a river which they had already crossed, thus drawing on the enemy; he himself awaited them in ambush with part of his force, who covered themselves with earth and branches.

A serious snag, however, ensued: the enemy engaged in identical tactics, so popular in Mexican warfare. They too advanced, leaving a thousand men in hiding among the bushes and agave plants.*

With both protagonists now intent upon ambushing the other, no initial battle could ensue. However, the Mexica, as the more skilled in war, dissimulated the better, and finally the foe, provoked into an advance, was taken from either flank and from the rear.

Axayácatl himself rushed from his ambush and took several prisoners. The Aztec forces then pursued the enemy beyond the river and in their turn duly fell into their opponent's trap. The captain in command emerged from behind an agave plant and fell upon the unwary Axayácatl, wounding him in the thigh, and almost cutting through to the bone.† A hand-to-hand fight ensued between the two, until his captains came to the ruler's rescue; he ordered them to capture, not kill, his adversary, but the latter escaped. It was only by a hair's breadth that utter disaster was averted, and that the great *tlatoani* himself avoided death on the sacrificial stone.

Their cunning having been of no avail, the enemy forces were routed, the ruler of Toluca prostrating himself before the wounded Axayácatl, now borne in a litter. The lord of Tenancingo, as the cause of all the trouble, wept copiously and begged forgiveness. The future impost of tribute remained to be established; the Tolucans insisted that theirs was a poor country, offering no exotic tropical products, but only maize, beans, amaranth, as well as pine and sandalwood, to burn in the hearth at night.

There was great rejoicing at the young ruler's safe return to Tenochtitlan, after his escape from the jaws of death. Scouts were dispatched along the route to report on the arrival of the victors. Triumphal arches made of branches were erected, and the way was strewn with foliage from Chapultepec right up to the entrance into the city. As the army drew nearer, the priests sounded their drums, and the sound was so overpowering that none present could hear himself speak.* Bernal Díaz was to complain of the same deafening and continual roar during the last stages of the Spanish siege of the city.

Safely home, Axayácatl first paid his respects to Huitzilopochtli, giving thanks for his delivery and anointing the statue of the god with blood from his own thighs and ears. Once again, the unhappy prisoners were out of luck, since their arrival coincided with the feast of the Flayed God, with its accompanying gladiatorial sacrifices, as already described. The captives, dressed as usual in the attire of the god to whom they were offered, followed each other to the sacrificial stone; some preferred a quick death, not even resisting the gladiators sent against them – the Eagle and Ocelot Knights. Others vainly tried to prolong their wretched lives, fighting the fully armed knights with weapons made of wood and feathers.†

As usual, great efforts had been made to impress neighbouring peoples with Aztec splendour. On this occasion, invitations were extended to peoples from the coast of the Gulf of Mexico, not yet conquered at the time; these went accompanied by threat of war if not accepted – such was the Aztec insistence that their grim ceremonies should not go unappreciated.* These spectators at least suffered no discomfort, except perhaps a disquieting premonition that they might themselves one day serve as victims; they were placed in a special stand, decorated with flowers of every hue. They were seated upon soft and shining jaguar skins, and to protect them from the sun were given shades and fly-whisks of rich plumes.

It should perhaps be added that the cult of the Flayed God was not altogether unknown to the people of the Valley of Toluca themselves, at least in the period immediately preceding the Conquest. Not far away lies Malinalco, also conquered by Axayácatl, and where the principal temple is dedicated to the Eagle and Ocelot Knights, who performed the gladiatorial sacrifice. Part of a fresco was discovered, portraying warriors, one of whom is attached with a rope, such as was used for victims of this particular form of sacrifice.

It was apparently soon after this ceremony that another sacrificial stone was inaugurated, the famous Stone of the Sun. It first had to be taken to the top of the Temple of Huitzilopochtli – a somewhat arduous manœuvre in itself, since it weighed twenty-four tons. For its formal dedication, yet more prisoners were to be required.

This monolith, traditionally known as the Aztec Calendar Stone, today occupies a central position in the National Museum of Anthropology; for Mexico it is no longer a mere monument, but a national symbol. In 1790 it was dug up in the Main Square, together with other important sculptures, and for many years was placed against the west tower of the Cathedral. It remained there until, in 1885, General Porfirio Díaz, then President of Mexico, ordered its transfer to the original National Museum in Calle Moneda, whence it was moved to the new Museum of Anthropology in 1964.

The stone is important, not only for its aesthetic value, but because it symbolizes the Aztec cosmos. It is dedicated to Tonatiuh the Sun God, whose face is situated in the centre. On either side of this are claws which clutch human hearts, the food of the Sun God, himself closely identified with Huitzilopochtli. The face and claws are covered with ornaments of jade, the precious stone of the gods.†

Surrounding the face of the Sun God are reliefs in square panels, representing the four previous creations of the world; these in turn are surrounded by the glyphs of the twenty-days signs of the ceremonial calendar. The creation and destruction of four successive worlds – curiously reminiscent of the parallel Greek myth of four creations – is based on the ever-present Mexican principle of duality. In this instance, duality is conceived in the form of an eternal struggle between the Plumed Serpent (Quetzalcoatl), a basically beneficent god, though sometimes tempted into evil, and Smoking Mirror (Tezcatlipoca), the dark and all-powerful Lord of the Night Sky.*
The latter is a god greatly to be feared, but in some respects good as well as evil – a kind of creator-destructor, recalling perhaps Vishnu-Shiva of the Hindu pantheon.†

It was this perpetual struggle between the two gods that caused the destruction and creation of the four worlds or suns; these were successively destroyed by jaguars (symbolizing the earth), wind, rain (or in some versions by fire) and water. These elements, symbolized by their respective gods, are represented in the four panels which surround the figure of the Sun God, situated in the centre part of the Stone.† After the destruction of these four worlds, the men who had peopled them were successively transformed in turn into jaguars, monkeys, birds and fish. It might be worth noting that the four elements involved – earth, air, fire and water – are also basic to the beliefs of the peoples of east Asia.

It is, however, to the fifth sun that the stone is dedicated, that which lit the Aztec world. The whole configuration of the central part, including those elements already mentioned, is arranged to form the sign 'Four Movement' – that is to say, the glyph of the day on which the Fifth Sun was to end, as a result of earthquakes.

After the destruction of the Fourth Sun,

> It is told that when yet all was in darkness, when yet no sun had shone and no dawn had broken – it is said – the gods gathered themselves together and took counsel among themselves there in Teotihuacan [the great Pyramid site not far from Mexico City, that had flourished long before Aztec times]. They spoke; they said among themselves:
>
> 'Come hither. O gods! Who will carry the burden? Who will take it upon himself to be the sun, to bring the dawn?'
>
> And upon this, one of them who was there spoke: Tecuziztecatl presented himself. He said: 'O gods, I shall be the one.'
>
> And again the gods spoke: 'And who else?'
>
> Whereupon they looked around at one another. They pondered the matter. They said to one another: 'How may this be? How may we decide?'
>
> No one dared; no one else came forward. Everyone was afraid; they all drew back. There was present however a god called Nanauatzin, the little Syphilitic God. As he stood listening, the gods called to him and said: 'Thou shalt be the one.' He eagerly accepted the decision, saying: 'It is well O gods; you have been good to me.'*

Those chosen to become Sun and Moon then did penance for four days and four nights (as did also each Aztec ruler on his election). This rite they performed separately on two separate mounds. The latter became the great Pyramids and are today still known traditionally as the Pyramid of the Sun and the Pyramid of the Moon.*

Following this, the two gods were ritually dressed, and the remaining deities settled themselves around the great hearth, in which the two were to be immolated. The little Syphilitic God boldly cast himself into the flames, while his companion hesitated, and drew back four times, before finally taking the plunge. He was naturally the last of the two to emerge. 'Then one of the gods came out running. With a rabbit he came to wound in the face this Tecuziztecatl;

with it he darkened his face; he killed its brilliance. Thus doth it appear today.'* He thus became the moon, whose surface shadows reminded the ancient Mexicans of the rabbit.*

The gods who had thus emerged as Sun and Moon still remained motionless, and no dawn came. The solution was left to the Wind God: 'Thus it became the charge of Ehécatl, the wind, who arose and exerted himself fiercely and violently as he blew. At once he could move him [the Sun] who thereupon went his way. And when he had already followed his course, only the moon remained there. At the time when the sun came to enter the place where he set, then once more the moon moved.'*

This legend of the successive worlds and of their destruction, as symbolized in the central part of the Stone of the Sun, lies at the very basis of Aztec thought and action; in their philosophy, this world was not a once-and-for-all gift, but was equally doomed to destruction by the gods, who were cruel rather than beneficent. For the individual as for the whole universe, life was an ephemeral gift:

> As they say, we do not dwell in truth,
> Nor in truth did we come to tarry on earth.
> Oh, I must leave the gorgeous flowers,
> I must go down and seek what lies beyond!
> Oh, for a moment my heart grew weary: we are only granted
> The beautiful songs as but a loan.*

The Fifth World itself, in which the Aztecs lived, was a temporary concession, which the gods themselves would destroy if they were not amply nourished with sacrificial victims. To provide these was thus a bounden duty, not only to ensure the wellbeing of mankind, but also its survival. The Stone itself was as much a portent as a legend, portraying as its central motif not the Sun's birthday but its future day of doom. Through travail by the gods had this world been created; through sacrifice by man would it be maintained – but only for a while.

Life on this planet was thus imbued with the spirit of a duty to be done; they performed this, knowing that in doing so they could only postpone the awful hour of doom. Little did they guess that, for their empire, the days were already numbered.

Four years after the Tolucan campaign, another expedition was undertaken, aimed at further extension of the bounds of empire in the same direction. In the interval, another war had been waged, resulting in the conquest of Tuxpan, on the Gulf Coast, north of Veracruz. This area, the heartland of the Huaxtecs, was previously invaded by Moctezuma I, but not fully subdued.†

Beyond the Valley of Toluca, so recently absorbed, lay the land of the Tarascans, situated in what is now mainly the state of Michoacan, but stretching also into Queretaro and Guanajuato. Many Tarascan place-names still survive, notably those ending in *-aro*, such as Queretaro and Patzcuaro.†

Tarascan origins are unknown, but according to legend they arrived from the north-west at the same time as the Mexica, and tradition claims them as related tribes.† At all events, the Tarascans arrived relatively late upon the scene; like the Aztecs, they had formed a tripartite league of three cities, Patzcuaro, Tzintzuntzan, and Ihuatzio, all situated on the beautiful Lake of Patzcuaro, now deservedly a tourist attraction. Their government was not unlike that of the Aztecs; each centre had one ruler, whose role was religious as well as political, and who was supported by a whole apparatus of state officials and army commanders. Their principal deity was a kind of fire god, a cult not unexpected in a region of much volcanic activity.†

These Tarascans were brave, though a trifle uncouth; both men and women shaved their heads; they also depilated their bodies, using for this purpose metal pincers; those of the priests were made of gold. This detail is significant: the practical uses of metal, as opposed to mere ornaments, were more developed among the Tarascans than the Aztecs. In the long run this must have affected war potential, Aztec implements being made of mere stone or wood. Had the Spaniards arrived half a century later, it has been suggested, they might have encountered not the Aztecs but the Tarascans!

The latter, as the Aztecs were to discover for themselves, were formidable as warriors, whatever their aesthetic limitations. Their temples consisted of a curious kind of platform, surmounted by a series of round towers; such structures are known as *yacatas*, and a good example can today be seen at Tzintzuntzan, the principal of their centres.

As a preliminary move, the Aztecs took the town of Xiquipilco in 1478.† This in itself was a hard-fought campaign; many prisoners were taken and the enemy ruler was killed by Axayácatl. In such an act of reprisal, he ran counter to custom, whereby local potentates were conciliated, once victory was secured.†

It is not absolutely clear why Axayácatl decided to risk his luck against such a redoubtable foe; it may have been the recently subdued Tolucans who spurred him on. As a basic precept, the Aztecs believed in big battalions; this time, however, they were outnumbered from the start. We are told that their forces totalled 24,000, opposing 40,000 Tarascans. The latter, moreover, enjoyed interior lines of communication; this was no mere city-state, but a rival empire, fighting for its very life, and upon home ground.

Before hostilities began, the Tarascans sent emissaries, as usual numbering four, and who spoke Nahuatl. They sought to deter Axayácatl from invasion, addressing him as follows: 'Great Lord; what has brought you hither? To what cause was your coming due? Were you not happy in your own land? Who deceived you into journeying hither? Was it perchance the Matlatzinca, whom you destroyed not long ago? Look to what you do, Lord, for you have been most ill-advised.'†

Axayácatl, informed of the huge force which the enemy had mustered, apparently had second thoughts about the whole campaign. He was even prepared to call it off, but finally let himself be persuaded by his captains that the offensive must go forward.

After one day's battle, the enemies' fury was undiminished, and the Aztecs began to retreat. Their leaders, in consternation, held a council of war; their eyes, nose and mouth were so coated with grime and sweat that they were barely recognizable. Their spirits were low, and to bolster them they drank a potion called *yolatl*.†

The fighting was resumed the next day. The Aztec forces were divided as usual into separate contingents for each subject people; one after the other they were thrown against the Tarascans, to no avail. The latter captured many, including a close kinsman of Axayácatl, and one of his inner council of four.†

A discussion followed as to whether to abandon the struggle – something the invincible Empire had never before contemplated. The chief general insisted that it was simply useless to commit more troops to be sent as lambs to the slaughter: 'If you are still determined that we must all perish here, I will be the first to die, as the oldest among you. But if you feel that it is right that we should return, in order to reform our forces in Mexico-Tenochtitlan, then so let us do.'* He finally reminded them that the Chalco war had lasted for thirteen years; if they could live to fight another day, fresh opportunities to overcome this new enemy would arise.

The remnants of the army beat a hasty retreat, the Tarascans in hot pursuit, until they reached the safety of the mountains surrounding Toluca. In all, 20,000 had been lost, and only 200 of the actual Mexica contingent survived. Many of these were wounded.*

Axayácatl eventually reached the outskirts of Tenochtitlan with his pathetic little band, to be greeted with weeping and lamentation. To mark his return, ceremonies were performed as if to Huitzilopochtli, whose likeness the ruler personified. The high priest offered consolation, saying that he had fought bravely and that by the deaths of so many warriors he had given sustenance to the gods.*

But no honeyed words from the lips of sycophants could sweeten the bitter pill: the mighty Aztecs had suffered a crushing defeat. The anguish of the ruler was surely intense, at having proved unworthy of his forebears. And the fear must have persisted that such a humiliation would dissolve the loyalty of subjects – at the best of times apt to rebel against a control exercised mainly from afar, by threat of retaliation.

Moreover, the defeat left the Empire exposed to a powerful foe on its flank, and no major attempt was ever made to reverse the verdict. In the north-west, there now existed a frontier problem, such as the more pliant peoples to the east and south had never offered. Conquests were later undertaken to buttress the border, and frontier cities were even fortified, as a partial protection against the menace.

We know little of events following the Tarascan war, until Axayácatl's death in 1481, after a reign of twelve years. He was still a young man, in his early thirties. Possibly death was hastened by the rigours of his campaigns and by wounds received.

He had not been a great king, but at least a valiant one. As Map 4 shows, he expanded the empire in two principal directions: north-west, to take in the Valley of Toluca and adjacent areas; and north-east, to tighten his hold on the rich coastlands of the Gulf of Mexico; these were invaded but not fully subdued by Moctezuma I. In addition to the campaigns already described, he had also succeeded in extending his frontiers by making certain conquests to the south and south-east; thus, in almost every direction, the Aztecs controlled more territory at his death than when he ascended the throne.*

Like those of other rulers, his efforts had been partly against places like Cotaxtla, already once conquered, but which had rebelled against the heavy tribute. However, unlike his immediate forebears, he had also suffered a humiliating defeat. It says much for the resilience of the Mexica that they could survive this failure as well as those of his short-lived successor – finally redeemed by the military genius of the next ruler. By that time, Aztec stock had much declined among certain neighbouring cities, but the situation was still one which a forceful monarch could quickly restore. Moreover, however uncertain the loyalties of more remote provinces, the Aztecs had established a firm grip on the peoples of the Valley of Mexico and the surrounding country. Even in their hour of need, some of these at least were slow to join the bandwagon of the seemingly invincible Spaniards.

It was the duty of the Woman Snake (Cihuacóatl), still the second in the land, even after the passing of the great Tlacaélel, to announce the young ruler's death.† He first pronounced a long oration offering consolation to the leaders.† He then gave similar addresses to warriors and priests. Near-by rulers were also officially informed, being moved to bitter tears at the news.

Then followed a peculiar ceremony: the various rulers, each brought four slaves, two male and two female, sumptuously adorned as funeral offerings. These princes, each in turn, addressed the *tlatoani*'s remains, as if he were still alive, recalling above all his prowess and ardour in war. All those present were deeply moved.†

The ruler of Texcoco spoke first, as was his right: 'My son, most brave youth and excellent ruler, my Lord Axayácatl; this is the last occasion on which I may see your face. Now you have arrived at the place where you shall find your fathers and relatives, and enjoy the glory of the lord of creation, of the day and of the night, the air and the fire. I have brought this small gift, to help you to pass your time

pleasurably in that world.'* With these words, he placed the four
slaves and rich gifts before the body.

The king of the third member of the Alliance, Tacuba, waxed
even more eloquent, and the Mexica were astounded at the excellence of his rhetoric:

> My son, alone, defenceless and without consolation have you left the
> realm and city of Mexico, dependent only on the will of the Lord of
> Creation, this day or any other. Now you have laid down the burden
> for ever, and the people will no longer enjoy the defence and protection
> which they were wont to seek in you. You have already arrived at the
> place of the great lords, your kinsfolk and ancestors. Already you are
> resting in the shade of those dark meadows of the nine mouths of death
> and in the house lit by the splendour of the sun, where are also your
> forebears. May your body now repose, my son.*

Many other rulers, including those of the Cuernavaca region, then
presented their four slaves and their fine gifts, including of course
jewels, feathers, gold and cacao. They were followed by those of the
independent states such as Tlaxcala, often referred to as 'enemies',
who had come to pay their respects. The Woman Snake particularly
enjoined his subordinates to provide lavish hospitality for these
'enemies'; the Aztec craving to impress seemed to increase as the
Empire expanded.

The chief stewards ordered 600 turkeys, as well as much wild
game. The women of Xochimilco spent two whole days preparing
delicacies for the visitors, who marvelled at the largesse displayed
and at the rich gifts offered. That they should not prove unworthy
adversaries, the *señores* of unconquered cities received gifts of arms,
in addition to other presents.

A special building was now made ready, after these orations
addressed to the body of the dead ruler. In it was placed not the
actual body but a kind of mortuary bundle or likeness, made of
chips of sandalwood. This was dressed in a series of fantastic garments, representing the four principal gods. The first attire, of course,
consisted of the robes of Huitzilopochtli himself, and the second
represented those of Tlaloc, the Rain God; these were the two gods
whose shrine occupied the Great Temple. When dressed as the Rain
God, the figure was crowned with heron plumes, holding in one

hand a shield and in the other a staff shaped as lightning, characteristic of this deity. The third robe was of a god, whose name literally means 'the One who Drinks *Pulque* in the Night' and who is to be identified with the Flayed God.† The fourth god, whose robes were placed upon the image, was the Plumed Serpent (Quetzalcoatl), the deity who had once disappeared in the east, and for whom Cortés was at first taken. When thus arrayed, the mortuary bundle wore a tiger mask with a bird's bill, through which the deity, also god of wind, would blow to create turbulence.

Professional mourners now came forth, singing dirges before the sumptuously arrayed bundle. It was then offered food, including all kinds of maize cake, and jars of cacao. The principal lords filed past in due order, bearing flowers and sprinkling perfume over the figure representing their king. Next followed the slaves presented by the rulers, all regally clad. The jewel boxes of the defunct were then brought, and the slaves adorned with the gems which he had used. After this came his dwarfs and hunchbacks, also richly robed. The image was offered cups of *pulque* which were left for the singers to drink.†

It was finally taken out and burned in front of the statue of Huitzilopochtli, together with the actual body of the ruler.* As due preparation for the service of their master in the next world, the assembled hunchbacks and dwarfs were addressed as follows: 'My sons, may you happily reach your Lord Axayácatl in the other life, which awaits you with its rich gifts and with all the delights of the world; take care not to lose the things that belonged to your master, but bear them safely to him.'*

They then sounded Axayácatl's great drum, cut out the hearts of the dwarfs and hunchbacks, casting them into the eagle vessel.* The leading Mexica thanked the neighbouring rulers for attending their master's funeral. The guests then fasted for eighty days before returning to Tenochtitlan for the final ceremonies. None failed to reappear.

Following the death of Axayácatl, his elder brother Tízoc was elected to rule in his stead; like many *tlatoanis*, he had previously been one of the two principal generals, and had belonged to the ruler's inner council of four.

As to the qualities sought by the small committee of electors: 'They cast votes for all the princes who were sons of lords; men at arms; brave warriors, experienced in war, who shrank not from the enemy; who knew not wine – who were not drunkards, who became not stupefied; the prudent, able, wise; of sound and righteous rearing and upbringing; who spoke well and were obedient, benevolent, discreet, and intelligent.'* On other occasions the ruler selected had possessed such qualities in abundance. However, even the wisest can err, and this time the choice was unfortunate; as a consequence, an inglorious interlude in Mexica history ensued. Happily, its duration was short and Tízoc only reigned from 1481 to 1486.* In spite of his military rank, as a ruler he showed more proclivity to the practice of religion than to the art of war.†

Among the initial ceremonies, before Tízoc's actual coronation, was the ritual piercing of the nose, and the insertion of a delicately fashioned green emerald; he was equally adorned with earplugs of emerald and gold. He mounted a throne, decorated with eagle feathers and padded with jaguar skins, known as the Eagle and Jaguar Throne (the significance of the Eagle and Jaguar order of knights will be explained in the following chapter). Next, he followed the prescribed rites of auto-sacrifice, drawing votive blood from his ears and thighs with a pointed jaguar-bone, fitted with a handle of gold.

The ruler of Texcoco made the following speech:

> Most mighty lord and brave youth; you have inherited the royal seat, of very rich and fine feathers, and the hall of precious stones that the God Quetzalcoatl, the great Topiltzin, and the wonderful and glorious Huitzilopochtli have left behind them. This royal throne is only lent to you, and not for ever but for a short while only. The brave rulers who preceded you have exalted and extended this realm, more especially your grandfather Moctezuma, of high and revered memory, who, in his long life, raised it to a high pitch of glory such as it had never before attained.
>
> Therefore, my lord, take care not to be of faint heart. Look carefully to what you do. Take heed for the orphan and for the widow, for the aged who can work no longer, because these are the plumes, the eyelashes and the eyebrows of Huitzilopochtli. Most especially you must care for the eagles and tigers, those brave and valiant men, who act as a rampart of defence for you and for the realm, and who extend its

bounds by the shedding of their blood. With these words, my lord, I end my speech.*

Thereupon, according to the usual custom, followed many other addresses.

The words of Nezahualpilli of Texcoco may seem to us formal and tedious, like most of these Aztec homilies. They are, however, worth quoting, since they illustrate the Aztec concept of the righteous ruler, for whom reigning was a duty, not a right. Nezahualpilli first refers to the divine nature of the office – several rulers including Tízoc had previously been priests as well as soldiers. The *tlatoani* is the representative not only of Huitzilopochtli, but also of other gods and heroes of Toltec times, to which the Aztecs looked back as to a golden age.*

He is then reminded of the passing nature of his throne, being elected only for his lifetime, and of the glories of his forebears, whom he must emulate. He is next made aware of his dual calling, as protector of the toiling masses and master of the mighty warriors. The first role is most significant; throughout Aztec history we are conscious of the civic sense of the ruler and of his obligations towards ordinary citizens. In spite of the aura surrounding the *tlatoani*, his domains were no personal patrimony, enjoyed by divine right, but a charge to be held in trust. Whatever the faults of the system, the humbler classes throughout ancient Mexico always looked to rulers duty-bound to guard their rights, and to care for their needs, a safeguard entirely lacking when they were handed over to absentee Spanish landlords.

Notwithstanding the stirring speeches and the fine robes, the reign was not destined to open in a blaze of glory.

The formal coronation would have been incomplete unless accompanied by numerous offerings. It was a matter of custom and necessity that the new ruler should thus undertake a major campaign. This time the chosen victim was Metztitlan.† This region lay in the northern extremity of the Empire, as it then existed. It was later to be surrounded by Aztec territory, but remained one of those independent pockets, never fully conquered.† The local ruler possessed many subject towns and villages, and even at the time of the Conquest, after great Aztecs inroads, still controlled an extensive area.★ His subjects enjoyed a reputation as warriors; if they did not triumph on the first occasion, they would return to the fray day after day, until their foe was crushed.

On this particular occasion, no pretext was offered for war. The Aztec forces were mobilized, and proceeded to assemble on the northern marches of empire. Tízoc, who accompanied his army, then adopted a curious tactic, using only mercenaries from these northern provinces for the attack, while keeping the main Aztec forces in reserve. The defenders had been reinforced by Huaxtecs from the Gulf coast, old enemies of the Mexica, and still only partly conquered.★ The local levies, used as spearheads of the offensive, proved unequal to their task, and were forced to retire. The main army was then thrown into battle, the actual Mexica contingent bringing up the rear. Some of the hardest fighting was carried out by squadrons of boys of eighteen to twenty years old, doubtless interspersed, as usual, by seasoned warriors. They took forty prisoners and drove the enemy back over the river bordering his territory. But, in the course of this fighting, the Aztecs had lost 300 men, and thus for them the encounter was somewhat inglorious. At that point, the captains sounded the retreat, and the army withdrew. Apparently the faint-hearted Tízoc had already retired from the field of battle.★

The reception of the returning army, accompanied by its tiny band of prisoners, was a sad one. Notwithstanding their reduced numbers the full sacrificial ritual was followed, as part of the coronation ceremonies. These included a festive dance, in which 200 lords and knights participated – dressed in gorgeous attire provided by the monarch.★

By this time, Nezahualpilli of Texcoco was growing up. In spite of his accession at the tender age of seven he managed to survive and grew into a young man of talent, second only to his father in accomplishment. During his long rein, Texcoco remained, if not an equal, at least a partner of Tenochtitlan, rather than a mere vassal.

Nezahualpilli as a young man reputedly longed to distinguish himself as a warrior, and he succeeded in obtaining his baptism of fire at an early age. According to these accounts, every day seemed to him a thousand years, until he could prove himself on the battlefield.

He daily practised the use of arms and tried on his father's regalia which he had no right to wear in public; even rulers were not exempt from the laws limiting certain insignia exclusively to those who had taken prisoners. At this time, though hardly in later life, he practised austerity, and slept on the bare floor, covered in coarse blankets.*

Apparently, however, even at this early age, his show of military ardour may have been somewhat feigned, and his elder brothers actually upbraided him for not going to the wars. They even said that Texcoco had as ruler nothing but an effeminate boy, who delighted in wearing the jewels and finery which they had won in battle. Nezahualpilli replied to these taunts, saying that he regretted bitterly that he had been too young to fight before, but now he would participate in a campaign. In effect, he accompanied his army on an expedition to the Gulf Coast, taking among other places Orizaba. This city had been conquered before, but had evidently again rebelled against payment of tribute. During Tízoc's reign he also participated in other campaigns, particularly in the area between Texcoco and the Caribbean coast, where Texcocan influence was strong.

Early in life Nezahualpilli showed his talents as a master builder, reconstructing his father's temples and palaces and amplifying the great gardens and waterworks begun in the previous reign. The prodigal luxury of the royal household increased: in the course of a year the palace, including the countless officials, consumed 31,000 bushels of maize, 5000 bushels of chile, 8000 turkeys and 574,000 mantles.* Such quantities of produce derived mainly from tribute; even our Texcocan sources insist that this was originally divided up in Tenochtitlan, another indication of the primacy of the latter. Of what he received, Nezahualpilli, as a wise ruler, kept in reserve substantial amounts, as a precaution against bad harvests.

Nezahualpilli was also a great lover. He is reported to have had 2000 concubines, although only forty bore him children. By his legitimate wife, a niece of Tízoc, he had eleven offspring. But, like many a monarch, he preferred the company of concubines. His favourite was called the Lady of Tula – not because of her noble birth, for she was only a merchant's daughter. But she was so erudite that she was the equal in intellect of the ruler and his sages; she was

even an accomplished poetess. Such was her influence on Nezahualpilli, that he would grant all her wishes.†

Of Tízoc's activities towards the end of his reign, little is known.
Reportedly he preferred to seclude himself in his palace, showing
little interest in public affairs and even less in wars to enhance the
glory of the Mexica.*

It is fair to add that he also showed his talents as a builder, and
during his reign a major enlargement of the Great Temple was
initiated, only to be completed by his successor. Also, to commemor-
ate this ruler, we have the famous Stone of Tízoc. This magnificent
round monument depicts this ruler holding by the hair a series of
captives, symbolizing the conquered cities, each illustrated by its
respective glyph. Such a stone was also fashioned for Moctezuma I,
but only that of Tízoc survives.* We have an interesting description
of the monolith by the English traveller, William Bullock, who in
1822 found it interred in the cathedral square, about a hundred yards
from where the Stone of the Sun then rested. It was buried, with
only the upper surface exposed to view, apparently with the design
of leaving to the people's imagination the sanguinary nature of the
rites concerned.

I have seen the Indians themselves, as they pass, throw stones at it; and
once I saw a boy jump upon it, clench his fist, stamp with his foot, and
use other gesticulations of the greatest abhorrence. As I had been informed that the sides were covered with historical sculpture, I applied
to the clergy for the further permission of having the earth removed
from around it, which they not only granted, but moreover had it performed at their own expense. I took casts of the whole – it is twenty-
five feet in circumference, and consists of fifteen various groups of
figures representing the conquests of the warriors of Mexico over
different cities, the names of which are written over them. More information is to be acquired from these figures, respecting the gaudy
costumes of the ancient warriors, than can be obtained elsewhere.
During the time (and it occupied several days) the operation of taking
the casts was going on, the populace surrounded the place, and, although they behaved with great order and civility, would frequently
express their surprise as to the motives that could induce me to take so
much pains in copying these stones, and several wished to be informed

whether the English, whom they considered to be non-Christian, worshipped the same gods as the Mexicans did before their conversion.†

Attitudes to history change in time, and now the monument occupies a place of honour in the National Museum of Anthropology.

The stone indeed portrays certain conquests as having been made by Tízoc, and it appears that, notwithstanding his apparent faintheartedness, he took the field to suppress a rebellion in Toluca, already conquered by his brother. It is possible also that he made certain conquests in the states of Guerrero and Oaxaca.*

At all events, his performance failed to satisfy the standards expected from a Mexica sovereign, and his early death was thus timely, for reasons of state; it may even have been artificially hastened.* Torquemada supports suggestions that he was murdered, but introduces an element of magic, following the tendency in the annals of ancient Mexico to embroider fact with fancy. According to his version, the ruler of Ixtapalapa, for reasons unknown, wanted to kill Tízoc. Not trusting any of his own people to fulfil the task, he persuaded the ruler of Taxco to send some witches. Two or three were dispatched, who bewitched Tízoc as he was coming out of his palace. He returned bleeding copiously from the mouth, and died.*

The immediate causes of his death are not altogether clear; but in view of the godlike role of the *tlatoani*, and remembering the awe which Moctezuma II still inspired, even as a captive king, stories of Tízoc's assassination should possibly be treated with caution.

CHAPTER SIX

THE LION OF
ANAHUAC†

ON THE FOURTH day after Tízoc's death, in 1486, the Mexican leaders assembled to elect their new master.* The occasion was a grave one. After the early demise of the last ruler and the setbacks of recent years, the Atzec polity was unsettled, and subject peoples restive. Another mistaken choice could have brought irreparable disaster upon the Empire.

The obvious candidate was the younger brother of the two last rulers, following the tendency for the throne to pass from one brother to another, rather than from father to son. Some counsellors initially opposed such a step: 'They did not wish for this, because the greatness of Mexico required someone old and venerable, whom the nations would hold in awe, and whom they themselves would respect.'* These objections fortunately carried little weight, and Ahuítzotl, younger brother of Tízoc, was duly chosen.† He was still young at the time, but was soon to prove his mettle. The summons immediately went forth to celebrate the election, and the news spread to all corners of the Empire that the sun, once dimmed, had come to shine anew.*

And, in truth, during this reign the Aztec sun was to shine with a brilliance never surpassed, like a star whose light is intensified in spectacular fashion before it is suddenly and for ever dimmed. The electors, in making the most natural choice, had selected a giant among men. Tenochtitlan, and indeed the whole Empire, now possessed a monarch of a heroic stamp, who was to impose his will upon peoples living in remote lands, where only traders had so far penetrated, returning with fabulous tales.

The two great Aztec conquerors differed greatly. Moctezuma I, an older man, even at his accession, had not led his greatest campaigns in person. He was, however, a great administrator and organizer. Ahuítzotl on the other hand, inseparable from his armies, however remote the battle, gained distinction as a field commander of genius. If Moctezuma could be likened to a Julius Caesar, Ahuítzotl was by comparison an Alexander.

Like some of his predecessors, he was already one of the two army commanders when elected to the throne. He was a man whose character went to extremes; he was munificent to his friends and pitiless to his foes. His powers of leadership were outstanding and he always shared the hardships of his soldiers, spurring them by his example to superhuman feats. At times, however, he could be not merely cruel but ferocious. Not only did he increase the tempo of human sacrifice until it became a holocaust; in his dealings with subject rulers he could be peremptory, if not ruthless.

It fell to Nezahualpilli of Texcoco to address the new *tlatoani* on his election – telling him that, jointly with Huitzilopochtli, he would bear the burden of providing sustenance for his people.* Nezahualpilli

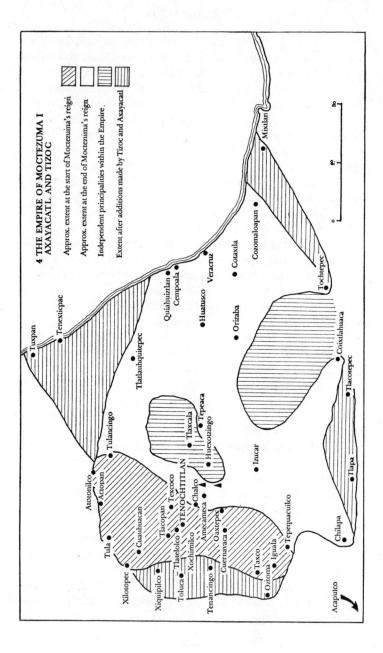

4 THE EMPIRE OF MOCTEZUMA I
AXAYACATL AND TIZOC

Approx. extent at the start of Moctezuma's reign

Approx. extent at the end of Moctezuma's reign

Independent principalities within the Empire.

Extent after additions made by Tizoc and Axayacatl

Tuxpan

Tenexticpac

Quiahuiztlan
Cempoala
Huatusco
Veracruz
Orizaba
Cotaxtla
Cozomaloapan

Tlatlauhquitepec

Tochtepec

Mixtlan

Tlaxcala
Tepeaca
Huexozingo

Coixtlahuaca

Tlacotepec

Tulancingo

Izucar

Tlapa

Atotonilco
Actopan

Tlacopan
Texcoco
TENOCHTITLAN
Chalco
Amecameca

Tula

Cuauhuacan

Tlalmanalco
Xochimilco

Oaxtepec
Cuernavaca

Tepequacuilco

Chilapa

Xilotepec

Xiquipilco
Toluca
Tenancingo

Taxco
Iguala
Oztoma

Acapulco

0   40   80

was at his best on such occasions, though, as will be seen, such ceremonies of state were more to his taste than the arduous campaigns of Ahuítzotl, in which he was expected to participate. The prescribed ritual was then followed, constituting the ruler's initiation, as opposed to his coronation, which took place later. This included the piercing of the nostrils, and the insertion of the special stone plug, the donning of the royal finery and the formal homage to Huitzilopochtli. Many tems of the royal regalia were turquoise in colour, including a mantle, made of a kind of netting and studded with jewels; this was the colour of the god himself, as Lord of the Southern Sky.† Among the many who came to pay their respects were the merchants; these, as previously explained, had attained a special position and prestige in society.

Ahuítzotl was not slow to conform to custom, and to initiate his first campaign, in order to obtain sacrificial victims for his formal coronation. This ruler, the future conqueror of a vast stretch of the Pacific littoral, and of lands bordering on distant Guatemala, chose a more limited objective for his initial operations – the rather arid region to the north-west of his capital, already once conquered. As frequently occurred, a new ruler had to reimpose his yoke on places previously subdued.†

He first overcame the resistance of Xiquipilco and of other towns of this neighbourhood.† After such successes, the army, perhaps grown unaccustomed to dynamic leadership, showed signs of battle fatigue; Ahuítzotl, however, forbade any soldier to abandon the expedition, on pain of death. He then proceeded to the conquest of the city of Chiapa (not to be confused with Chiapas, on the Guatemalan border, later to be subdued). A direct attack was made by the contingents of several subject peoples, while the Mexica themselves followed a path disclosed by local defectors, taking the city by surprise and storming the temple, which invariably served as a strongpoint in war, apart from its religious significance – the Spaniards were later to take frequent advantage of the protection offered by high pyramids. The victors slaughtered all the priests and burnt their dwelling-places. The enemy forces capitulated, many were made prisoner, and the city was sacked, as the normal reward for the soldiers.

The attack on the next place on the line of march, Xilotepec, became a rout. The troops were so sure of victory and so eager for spoils that they broke ranks, rushing forward like a horde of locusts devouring a field.* The enemy soon lost heart, and the huge army poured into the defenceless city. The citizens besought Ahuítzotl to hold back his soldiers; he sent his captains to stop the pillage, but they had to drag their troops from the houses by force, loaded with booty. Padre Durán wrily remarks that the scene recalled the sack of Rome, or the destruction sometimes wrought by the Spaniards themselves.*

The triumphant army returned to the capital, and, following the usual interminable speeches of welcome, the rulers of subject provinces went back to their own lands.

The day was now fixed for the *tlatoani*'s formal coronation.* As on all such occasions, efforts to attract the neighbouring peoples to the ceremony knew no bounds:

> The intentions of these Mexicans, in preparing a festival ... was to make known their king, and to ensure that their enemies, those of Tlaxcala, Huexotzingo, Cholula, and other cities of that province, as well as those of Michuacan and of Metztitlan, should be conscious of the greatness of Mexico and should be terrorized and filled with fear; and that they should know, by the prodigality and wealth of jewels and other presents, given away at the ceremonies, how great was the abundance of Mexico, its valour and its excellence. Finally, all was based on ostentation and vain glory, with the object of being feared, as the owners of all the riches of the earth and of its finest provinces. To this end they ordered these feasts and ceremonies so splendidly.*

This quotation casts a lurid light on an obsession lying at the very root of the Aztec will to conquer – not merely the urge to impress, but literally to strike terror, by display on a gargantuan scale.

Great preparations were set on foot for the occasion; carpenters and masons worked night and day to ensure that every building was well repaired and sprucely painted. Jewellers, goldsmiths and feather-workers toiled ceaselessly to prepare finery for the dancing and feasting. Even the garden-party element was not absent; those charged with flower arrangements made their special preparations – abundant floral decoration being indispensable for sacrificial ceremonies, whether for the temples where the rites took place, or the tribunes whence the spectators watched. On this occasion, determined efforts were made to attract the rulers of the yet unconquered territories. Channels of diplomacy were rather rudimentary, ambassadors travelling at the peril of their lives and considering themselves fortunate if not killed or kidnapped by frontier guards; they even went by night, using unfrequented mountain-tracks.*

The empire won by the great Moctezuma still dominated its subject peoples, and their presence could be counted upon. However, among those not yet subdued, its prestige had fallen to such depths under Tízoc that many rulers dared to reject the invitation – though to do so was tantamount to an insult, often taken to justify a punitive campaign. The rulers of Tlaxcala said that they could hold a feast at any time in their own city and at their own convenience; those of other cities of the region gave like replies.

Not surprisingly, the ruler of the triumphant Tarascans rejected the invitation out of hand, recalling the recent humiliation of the Aztecs: 'You must surely be demented; first you want war and then you seek peace; how could I feel secure, eating and drinking in your midst, after you have treated me as you did?'* The poor messengers, nonplussed, replied: 'Mighty Lord, there is a time set apart for hostilities, and a time to be dedicated to our neighbourly obligations, one to another. And thus says my lord and king, that, setting aside enmity and war . . . he begs you that as a kinsman and relative, you and your nobles may come to honour him in his coronation.'* That the people might not suspect a secret understanding at their expense, they could make their entry under cover of darkness. Their message was of no avail. The Tarascan ruler said that Ahuítzotl could be crowned where and when he liked; neither he nor any of his people would consent to be present.

In spite of the almost frantic exertions undertaken to secure a good attendance, the ruler of Cholula was one of the few 'free' princes to come, having been virtually bribed by the promise of lavish gifts. Special instructions were issued to stewards from subject provinces that nothing should be left undone to ensure his comfort.* After the guests had assembled, a thousand victims from recent wars were sacrificed. Endless ceremonies and ritual dances continued for four whole days, and four different types of songs were intoned, belonging to four distinct peoples.*

In a single day, gifts were distributed equivalent to the tribute received in Tenochtitlan in one whole year; some idea has already been given of the huge amounts that were received: for example, 33,000 handfuls of feathers were delivered annually.* It is as if the whole revenues of the British Empire, including all the jewels to be found in India, had been given away at the coronation of Edward VII; only a penchant for display of obsessive proportions could explain such largesse. This celebration was to set the tone for the reign of Ahuítzotl – a man who did nothing by halves.

Soon after this ceremony, the news broke that the whole Huaxtec province was up in arms. This, it will be recalled, had been partly conquered by Axayácatl. But Ahuítzotl was not a man to undertake such a campaign lightly, nor to endure its hardships unsupported; he therefore summoned all the other rulers and told them that it was his will that all should themselves take part in the war. On this occasion, everyone complied.*

The armies were rapidly mobilized, and Ahuítzotl ordered a forced march to the enemy borders, in order that a surprise attack could be mounted, leaving them no time to prepare their defence. Subject cities located on the line of march were detailed to provide the expedition with all necessary supplies and with additional complements of warriors. The *señor* of Huachinango himself joined the army, and invited Ahuítzotl to stay in his palace; the latter, however, replied: 'It is not fitting for a good king and a brave captain to leave his own encampment.'* Like the soldier-king that he was, he preferred to share all the discomforts of his troops; the subject ruler had to content himself with sending baskets of food and flowers to his master's tent.

Ahuítzotl then gave his usual address to the army, adding this time a salutary warning to the effect that those who did not fight with all their might would be deprived of rank and office; as a forceful commander, he sought to inspire both fear and affection in the men he led.

As a preface to operations against the principal enemy city, Xiuhcoac, a reconnaissance force numbering 1200 men entered the

fields surrounding the city and captured those who guarded them.†
Two hundred more scouts were then sent ahead, and once again that
infallible Mexican ruse, the ambush, played its part in victory; the
unsuspecting enemy were drawn on, trapped, and attacked from all
sides, many being killed or captured. The defeated rulers regaled
Ahuítzotl with huge presents, including many parrots and macaws
(quite apart from the supplies of feathers sent as tribute, many live
birds were kept in Tenochtitlan, their feathers being periodically
plucked).

The Aztec army, after a period of well-earned rest and feasting,
set out for the capital, accompanied by an endless train of prisoners.
It was the Huaxtec custom to pierce the nostrils, and this proved
convenient to their captors, who simply threaded them together by
the nose, so that they had to walk in long lines. As they went, they
sang mournful songs and emitted loud lamentations. The girl
captives and children, whose noses were not similarly perforated,
were secured by the usual wooden collars, fastened to their necks. As
the triumphant army reached Tenochtitlan, there was great rejoicing on all sides; the prisoners were distributed to the various
districts of the city, speeches of welcome were addressed to them and
they were given food and flowers, as well as special clothing, and
cacao, the beverage normally reserved for the ruling classes.

Soon after this campaign, in 1487, or one year after the ruler's
accession, the Great Temple, after its latest transformation, ordered
by Tízoc, was finally completed. This was a unique event, to be the
occasion for ceremonies on a stupendous scale. The usual invitations
were sent out, both to subject kings and to independent rulers. As
a refinement on the customary summons, subordinate princes were
themselves instructed to bring sacrificial victims, to complement the
myriads already mustered by the Mexica. From the numbers alone,
it is clear that these did not all derive from the latest campaign, just
described. Already in his brief spell as ruler, Ahuítzotl had also
conducted preliminary expeditions in other directions, to lay the
groundwork for future conquests on the Pacific coast and towards
the Guatemalan border.† These undertakings yielded their rich haul
of prisoners.

This time, Ahuítzotl was in earnest; to reject his invitation would constitute a *casus belli*.* The unfortunate ambassadors who were to convey this missive faced the usual hazards of their profession, and went their way filled with premonitions that, instead of returning safely, they might become a prey to the wild beasts.* However, after their master's initial *blitzkrieg*, his fame had already spread far and wide, as a man to be held in awe. On this occasion, none dared to refuse his bidding, and even the Tarascan ruler sent a friendly reply. The Tlaxcalans went so far as to offer profuse apologies for having rejected his previous invitation. When the envoys returned safely, bringing the acceptance of the various rulers, Ahuítzotl displayed the keenly enquiring side of his mind; he interrogated them closely on the customs of the peoples visited, their temples, houses, ceremonies, gods, and even the food and drink which they served to his messengers.*

The foreign potentates now began to arrive; all entered secretly and at night. It was never considered fitting that the common people should observe that their rulers could at times compose their differences. To their simpler way of thinking, nations were either always friends or always enemies; any contrary notions might weaken their martial ardour. To the popular mind, the cult of war was not consistent with the idea of a truce. The rulers, after this furtive entrance, were all greeted by Ahuítzotl, received their first instalment of lavish gifts, and were feasted with special foods.

> Everything was ordered and arranged with the determination to make manifest the greatness and supremacy [of Mexico] to their enemies, guests and foreign visitors – and to fill them with fear and trepidation, at the sight of how [Mexico] lorded it over this whole realm so extensive and fruitful, and with so many subject nations at its command. ... All of this [the riches to be consumed] was delivered to the royal treasurer or steward, in order that he should distribute it, in conformity with the orders given; more especially, that he should provide for the requirements of the priests, for the service of the gods and the ceremonies to be performed. And secondly, that all necessary materials should be furnished to the metal workers and stone cutters, and to the feather-workers, for the purpose of making jewels, feather ornaments, diadems and other beautiful objects, to be presented to the kings and great lords, that thereby, not only should the grandeur and sumptuousness of Mexico be made evident, but also that the great feast of the renovation and completion of the temple should be duly solemnized.*

The most elaborate preparations were made for the ceremony, including the repainting of the other temples of the city – nowadays the eye is accustomed to the sight of the stone of which the outer crust of the pyramids was built; this for restored Mexican monuments has become an accepted convention, and we are apt to forget that the temples were generally thickly coated with stucco, brightly painted on the surface. In the absence of modern mortar, the stucco helped, incidentally, to hold the temple together.†

The population of neighbouring cities was ordered to come to the capital on pain of death; no one was to miss such a ceremony and not a man, woman or child was to be found in their streets.

The poor captives themselves, duly painted and feathered, were formed into interminable queues, stretching along the three main causeways into the city, to the north, south and west, while the fourth line extended eastwards to the lagoon shore. It is traditionally related that they numbered 80,400, a figure repeated by several sources. But to slay and dispose of such a number in a city which might have numbered 300,000 is a manifest impossibility – it would be the equivalent of today killing millions in a few days in London or even Mexico City. As with the figures of enemy forces given by the Spanish conquistadors, great caution has to be exercised, even to the point of perhaps eliminating one zero; in this case, even a figure of 8400 might seem far-fetched!†

Ahuítzotl, supported by the allied rulers of Texcoco and Tacuba, as well as the Woman Snake, or Cihuacóatl, heir to the great Tlacaélel, initiated the sacrifice, accompanied by throngs of priests; both these and their victims were dressed as the different gods.* Ahuítzotl and his co-rulers first celebrated the occasion with a very good lunch, and then proceeded to the temple, gaily decorated with flowers, and mounted the steep steps.* The sacrifice lasted four whole days. When Ahuítzotl and his royal colleagues wearied of gashing open the victims' breasts, the priests took up the sacrificial cudgels in their place. Streams of blood flowed everywhere and even congealed beneath the steps of the temple.

By the fifth day, the massacre was complete and the *tlatoani* bade farewell to his guests. The 'enemies' from the independent states left secretly at night, their canoes piled with gifts. The oarsmen were forbidden to disclose the nature of their mission; the penalty for any infringement of this order would be death for themselves and destitution for their womenfolk. Ahuítzotl also richly rewarded the subject princes who had attended, as well as the various bodies of artisans who had contributed so much to the resounding success of the occasion.

There is no exercise more defeating to the contemporary mind than to seek to comprehend even dimly the ancient Mexican approach to human sacrifice. The shock suffered by our susceptibilities when faced with slaughter on this scale obstructs any objective assessment of their civilization as a whole. The Spanish conquerors were genuinely horrified at such practices, imposing a barrier between their religion and that of the Indians.

In many ways it is remarkable that higher civilizations could develop in virtual isolation from those of the Old World, and yet reproduce, albeit in varying forms, institutions and customs corresponding quite closely, such as kings, nobles, councils, knights, wars, judges, law-courts and markets – and even the practice of human sacrifice. But, despite such similarities, the approach to life in ancient Mexico was different in many respects. It is difficult enough for a European to fathom the mental processes of the modern Mexican Indian, so remote from his own, to say nothing of his forebears of antiquity. The problem is further complicated by the very nature of our information on the subject; much of our knowledge of thought and religion among the higher civilizations of the Old World derives from original documents, in the form of deciphered written texts; on the other hand, nowithstanding codices, poems and songs, ancient Mexican religion mainly reaches us projected through a Spanish lens.

The accounts of Sahagún and others, as gleaned from their informants, are admirable for their detail and insight; at the same time, however, something always appears wanting, in what the Aztecs told the friars of their former faith. To take an obvious example, a plethora of data exists as to the external manifestations of Mexican religion, including excellent descriptions of its outward show, of all its endless pomp and ceremony; in particular, accounts abound as to the different forms of human sacrifice, and the accompanying rites. But what is never exactly explained is *why* they did these things. We may know every detail of the finery worn and of the dances performed, but practically nothing of what passed through the minds of those participating. What, for instance, might have been the reaction of women and children summoned from Xochimilco to view Ahuítzotl's holocaust?

Based on certain historical sources, modern writers tend to dismiss the subject somewhat perfunctorily – insisting simply that Aztec sacrifices were prompted almost entirely by the pressing necessity of keeping the sun on its daily course, thus saving their world from destruction. Now, while partly exact, such affirmations leave much unexplained. But, before examining the actual motivation, certain other points need to be borne in mind, when approaching this most inscrutable of problems. Firstly, it must not be forgotten that, for reasons hardly more comprehensible to the modern mind, other peoples of antiquity have generally practised human sacrifice at some stage in their development, even if they later discarded it. This is true not only of Mesopotamia, where, in the early dynasties, slaves were immolated in the tombs of their royal masters, but equally of Egypt and China – not to speak of ancient Greece and republican Rome, where the occasional immolation of a slave is easily forgotten.

The offering of human life itself – the ultimate form of propitiation of the divine – is endemic to the development of our species, and any distinction between the Aztecs and other peoples is a mere question of degree. They possibly differed in their tendency to intensify the tempo of sacrifice as their civilization matured, rather than the reverse. And even this supposition incurs the risk of over-generalization: it would indeed appear that the Aztecs developed the practice of mass sacrifice on a colossal scale, but we have no certainty that in this they were the real innovators.†

It may, however, be true that with the Aztecs sacrifice grew from being an impulse to becoming an obsession. Such tendencies added a new element of insecurity to the whole situation, since ever greater offerings necessitated unceasing wars, to which the energies of the whole state were geared. Whatever may have been its origins, mass, as opposed to individual, sacrifice undoubtedly existed at the time of the Conquest; and it has to be admitted that such a practice, unlike the sacrifice of individuals, is an unusual phenomenon, even if it has also occurred in other places, such as west Africa.

Even if they accelerated the pace, the Aztecs did not, however, invent human sacrifice in Mexico, let alone elsewhere. Evidence exists from Teotihuacan of human sacrifice a thousand years before the Aztecs appeared, in the presence of sacrificial knives, the portrayal of human hearts, blood as a sacred element, as well as of the cult of the Flayed God, and the existence of the Eagle and Ocelot Knights, who performed the gladiatorial ceremony, dedicated to his cult.* The frescoes of this civilization may depict scenes of paradise, almost hedonistic in their verdant beauty – but the reality may have been grimmer. Their leading diety, the Rain God, Tlaloc, was certainly not averse to human offerings, particularly children; and of the sacrifices to mark the twenty-day months of the Aztec ritual calendar more were dedicated to this deity, than to their own god, Huitzilopochtli.†

Thus, even in the Mexican golden age indications exist that life was not so peaceful or idyllic as the fine serenity of their works of art might imply. There is evidence of human sacrifice and war, whether on the high plateau, or in the Maya lowlands; here, the cutting-out of hearts is portrayed in exquisite reliefs, frescoes show victors dragging captives by their hair, and an occasional trophy head is carried as an adornment. The notion of the Aztecs as the sole villains of the piece appeals more to the unenthusiastic amateur than to the professional investigator, obliged to seek deeper perspectives.

Moreover, to be fair, it must be recalled that, however much such proceedings shocked the Spaniards, the Aztecs in their turn were horrified by the Spanish practice of burning people alive, not as a sacrifice, but for common crimes, as well as for religious deviation – or equally by the branding of captives as slaves, a practice unknown in ancient Mexico, where they enjoyed well-established rights as human beings, not as mere chattels. The Aztecs would never have tortured one of their own rulers, as the Spaniards did Cuauhtémoc, to satisfy a lust for gold.

Such points, however, mainly relate to *our* attitude to the question. What still remains unanswered is: What was *their* attitude?

The usual explanation given – the pressing necessity to keep the sun on its course and the world in existence – is at least in part true. The legend of creation of the Fifth Sun, and of its eventual destruction by earthquakes, has already been explained (pp. 143–5). Man thus lived on borrowed time, obsessed by the need to appease the gods, to lengthen its span and to avert the day of doom. Conquest of empire was not a mere urge but a necessity – to secure enough victims that the gods might consent to keep the world in being. It was not a case of placating them in order to live better, but simply to stay alive at all!

It is also true, as such accounts suggest, that many sacrifices were dedicated to the sun, or to Huitzilopochtli, partly himself a sun-god. It must, however, constantly be borne in mind that human beings were offered not only to this deity, but also to countless others, each with its prescribed ritual and its due form of sacrifice. For instance, victims of the Fire God would be burnt, those of the Rain God often drowned, and those of the God of Hunting pierced with arrows.† Each twenty-day month had its particular fasts and sacrifices, mostly connected with very ancient gods.

It is thus clear that much sacrifice was devoted to other ends than that of simply keeping the world in being. When talking to the Spaniards of their old gods, Moctezuma and others usually refer to the necessity to appease them, not only to ensure victory in their wars, but also abundance in their harvests. Such accounts do not mention the need to save the world from destruction.

Perhaps, however, the most fundamental difficulties confront us when we examine the status and attitude of the victims themselves. It is probably not incorrect to maintain that they were offered at times *to* Huitzilopochtli as the sun, but, in the main, the victims tended themselves to *become* the god to whom they would be sacrificed. Now, it is difficult to conceive of a prisoner being offered *to* a god, if he already *was* the god concerned. In a sense, therefore, they died *as* the god, not *for* the god. The captives are frequently referred to as the 'sons of the sun', and it has already been related how on so many occasions they were fêted and honoured, and how, when sacrificed, they were dressed in the attire of the deity himself. They even in certain cases performed actions characteristic of the god, and pertaining to the legends of his life.†

This personification of the god by the victim helps to explain the apparent lack of resistance to being sacrificed.† On the one hand we know of the extraordinary ritual whereby the prisoner would address his captor as 'beloved father', while the latter would call his captive 'My beloved son'. It would seem, in fact, that the actual capture was the deciding factor; once this had taken place, the captive even considered himself as chosen by the sun or by the god, and thus specially honoured. His sacrifice then became not merely a voluntary act but almost the incidental culmination of a chain of happenings already preordained from the moment when he was originally taken prisoner. Such was the deeply imbued code of ethics, so utterly incomprehensible to ourselves. Modern war may claim its victims among civilians and soldiers alike, but the idea of a purely voluntary death is not usually present, even among those who are glad to offer themselves for the most hazardous missions, but who at least try to stay alive. But in Mexican history many examples exist, both of willing acceptance of death on the sacrificial stone, and also of actual insistence on being offered to the gods, once capture had taken place. The most striking case is that of Tlahuicole, the Tlaxcalan made prisoner in the reign of Moctezuma II. After capture, he led a successful Mexican expedition against the Tarascans. Thereupon the *tlatoani* offered him his liberty, but he asked to be sacrificed. Before succumbing, he killed eight gladiators using only the traditional pole, armed with feathers.* A further example is offered by the two young men taken at the time of Pedro Alvarado's unfortunate temple massacre, during Cortés' absence from Tenochtitlan; they indignantly rejected his offer of release, and demanded to be sacrificed.

What must surely have strengthened this attitude of abnegation and the willingness to accept death was not just the presence of a degree of oriental fatalism, absent in the Western mind; in addition, certain positive beliefs were held concerning rewards in the after-life. It was the warriors killed in battle or sacrificed after capture who went to dwell in the house of the sun, and who accompanied the morning sun, Huitzilopochtli, on the first part of his daily journey. On arriving in the west, he was greeted by another privileged group, the 'woman gods' (*cihuateteo*), the women who had died in child-birth – producing cannon fodder for the Aztec armies.

Even these fortunate warriors did not enjoy their privilege indefinitely; after four years of the joys of accompanying the sun, they returned to earth in the guise of humming birds and lived on for ever, sipping the wild honey. (Apart from the humming bird's associations with Huitzilopochtli in ancient Mexico, it is perhaps of interest that this little bird still enjoys other-worldly associations; it is not unusual for experts in the occult to advise the acquisition of a mummified humming bird – these are then usually wrapped in red thread, and candles are placed daily before them, that they may calm the evil spirits.) Victims sacrificed to the Rain God, together with those who died by drowning or of dropsy, leprosy and venereal diseases, went straight to the verdant paradise of this deity, and were thus also a privileged clan. But the remainder of mankind, whether prince or pauper, faced a dismal future; they were consigned to the ninth underworld, where they were cloistered under the grim guardianship of the God of the Nether World (the sugar-candy skulls sold all over Mexico on the Day of the Dead, 2 November, recall drawings of this god, to be found in codices). Even to reach his dark and uninviting realm, they passed four years in a kind of purgatory, and then crossed a great river with the help of a little dog, often buried with their remains; unlike the Greek dog Cerberus, its task was to facilitate entry into the underworld, not the reverse.

Important future incentives were thus offered to the victim of sacrifice. In addition, the community as a whole was impelled towards mass offerings of human life by its pessimistic philosophy: the world of the Fifth Sun was but a fleeting one, and the inescapable destiny of city and empire was to strive ever onwards and upwards, in a vain effort to keep the sun in the sky.

One factor entirely absent from such slaughter was any feeling of hate or cruelty. On no account was it held wicked to sacrifice men to the gods; on the contrary, it would have been gravely sinful not to do so; Moctezuma was constantly at pains to explain this to Cortés. While we ourselves are no more capable than the Spanish conquerors of condoning or even comprehending such practices, they must, however, be accepted as a fundamental element in Mexican civilization.

Ahuítzotl was now lusting for new lands to conquer, and he scanned the list of invited guests in search of absentees. As a result, he sent messengers to Teloloapan, now an attractive village, but then the chief city of an important province, lying to the south-west of Taxco and about half-way between Tenochtitlan and the Pacific

coast. The Mexican envoys, disguised as merchants, went to enquire why these people had not attended the inauguration of the
Great Temple. They returned to tell Ahuítzotl that the people of
Teloloapan had shut themselves up in their city, no longer desiring
to enter into relations with any neighbouring power.* The Aztec
army marched rapidly to its rendezvous, and at this point Ahuítzotl
sent instruction to his Texcocan and Tacuban colleagues concerning
preparations for the attack. To his utter fury, he was told that
neither one had accompanied his army, pleading old age as an
excuse.†

Ahuítzotl, short-tempered at the best of times, upbraided the
leaders of his Texcocan and Tacuban allies, threatening to reduce
them to the status of subject cities and to deprive the rulers of their
foibles, their roses and their perfumes.*

After a night march, Teloloapan was taken by storm, and a
massacre followed as the streets ran with blood. Although heavy
tribute-payments were imposed, the punishment had been so severe
hat the people of the city never dared to revolt.*

The vanquished enemies now served as guides for the assault on
two other cities, Alahuiztla and Oztoma. The people of the latter
bitterly upbraided those of Teleloapan, complaining that they themselves had previously enjoyed peaceful relations with the Mexica; it
was Teloloapan which had now set them at odds. Instead of peacefully trading their wares against the produce of the Mexican lagoon,
these would in future be seized as tribute; they would rather die
than comply.

This little battle of words illustrates once more the Aztec mode of
operation. They tended to make conquests in an ever-widening arc
of territory, wherever their merchants had already established
relations. As in British India, the flag often followed trade – the
latter tending to dictate the pattern of military operations. In this
particular instance, on the Aztec north-west frontier, the strategic
necessities of shoring up the defences against the Tarascans certainly
also had to be taken into consideration.

The people of Oztoma reaped a grim reward for their defiance. On
Ahuítzotl's orders, only boys and girls were spared, since they could
be carried off to the capital and serve as a reward for the Mexican
leaders. The remainder of the population was put to the sword – the

people of Alahuiztla suffering the same fate. During the battle against the latter, an enemy captain had the temerity to fight his way up to the person of Ahuítzotl; the *tlatoani*, however, fell upon his assailant with such demoniac fury that one crushing blow sufficed to split open his head in two places.*

The ruler now made his triumphal return to Tenochtitlan – being first welcomed royally by the peoples of the newly conquered region. He then made a slow progress through provinces that lay on his route; everywhere the subject rulers hastened to do homage to the proud conqueror.*

On arrival, the captives were accorded the prescribed ritual reception; on this occasion, they were even given an additional treat, consisting of a special quality of *cacao*, taken from their own province.*

On his return from the expedition, the ruler sent for his faint-hearted colleagues of Texcoco and Tacuba. His rage at their abstention from his wars had apparently subsided, and he told them that he proposed to recolonize the two frontier posts, whose population he had butchered; he planned to send 400 people to the area from each of the three allied cities, and 1200 more from neighbouring subjects, making a colonizing force of 2400 in all.

Nezahualpilli of Texcoco said that he greatly favoured the idea of repeopling such areas – a policy already put into effect on other occasions. However, to take 400 people from Tenochtitlan (and presumably he had also in mind his own Texcoco) would impose an excessive population-drain; he thought that 200 from each city would be sufficient. Moreover, he insisted on the voluntary principle, opposing Ahuítzotl's notion that people could be forced to go.*

The latter did not venture to disagree with the sagacious Nezahualpilli, and accepted his proposals. In this instance, as so often, his advice proved to be well founded: it became unnecessary to resort to conscription; those who volunteered to go actually exceeded the required total. They were lured on by the reputation enjoyed by their prospective home as an especially rich land, abounding in fruit, cotton and nuts.

The migrants were assembled in Tenochtitlan, and Ahuítzotl gave them presents of clothing. Mexican leaders then addressed to them words of consolation at leaving home and family; they were once more reminded that they would enjoy great future prosperity; moreover, it was the will of the gods that they should go forth. They were told that their first care must be to cultivate the *cacao* plantations specially set aside for the ruler of Tenochtitlan.† Furthermore, they must always be on the alert, since their land lay on the frontier between the Empire and Tarascan territory. Arrangements were made for their reception at various places on their route, and on arrival they were given lands and houses. In addition, they were presented with a ruler of their own, the choice being confirmed by Ahuítzotl.†

This colonizing episode throws a revealing light on the politics of empire; it is not so much the event itself that is significant, but its apparently exceptional nature. It is easy to appreciate the need for reliable defenders of this vital sector of the Tarascan border, and Nezahualpilli was no doubt correct in citing previous applications of the principle of colonization.† The practice was not, however, general, and in this the Empire differed fundamentally from that of the Inca; the latter frequently consolidated conquered territories by establishing groups of their own kin. It may, of course, be true that in many parts of the Empire – for instance the coastal region in the vicinity of Veracruz – there were people who spoke Nahuatl. The Mexica, however, enjoyed no monopoly of this tongue and in the great majority of cases these were not immigrants brought in as an act of policy; their presence was often the result of previous movements of population, long before this time. The sources of Aztec history, so rich in stories of wars and battles, give a careful account of this particular act of colonization, and would have surely mentioned other examples, had they existed.

The intervention of Nezahualpilli in Ahuítzotl's plans sheds an interesting light on the different characters of the two princes, the one a towering conqueror, the other an astute statesman. Ahuítzotl would lead his armies to conquests ever more remote, whilst hurling torrents of abuse at the absent Nezahualpilli for preferring the fleshpots of Texcoco to the rigours of the camp. When, however, the two rulers met, the impetuosity of the one would often yield before the wisdom of the other.

One should, nonetheless, not exaggerate the lack of martial ardour in Nezahualpilli or suggest that he was a coward. Copious accounts exist of his warlike activities, particularly in his earlier life; his main apologist even credits him with having himself killed six kings!* However, the tendency of Ahuítzotl to dominate the military operations of the Triple Alliance more absolutely than his predecessors inevitably further increased the power of Tenochtitlan, at the expense of Texcoco. In a community where martial prowess was the supreme virtue and conquest the main motivation, primacy in war was the ultimate source of power. Moreover, in view of the close connections between trade and war, economic strength tended also to derive from the latter.

Increasingly one feels that Texcoco, notwithstanding the claims of its historians, was losing its remaining physical power within the alliance, even if it retained moral influence; this was shown by the clear supremacy of Tenochtitlan when the Spaniards arrived, only some thirty years after these events. That Texcoco still enjoyed great prestige was something of a *tour de force* on the part of Nezahualpilli, like his father a man of such outstanding personality. Like a Talley-rand or even a Charles de Gaulle, he was able to maintain the status of his country at a level no longer to be accounted for by the mere yardstick of physical strength. Possibly Nezahualcóyotl, as the founder of empire, was the greater figure of the two, and was cast in a sterner mould. The father may have outmatched the son as a warrior, but in the arts of peace the latter was his equal. Both rulers, their wisdom aided by relative longevity, added nobly to the glories of Texcoco.

Moreover, Nezahualpilli succeeded in maintaining at a high level the Texcocan stock in spite of a gruesome incident which did little to enhance his popularity in Tenochtitlan. Axayácatl, when ruler, had sent his daughters to Nezahualpilli, in order that he might select from among them a legitimate queen. He chose a maiden called Chalchiuhnenetzin, and also retained other daughters of his colleague as concubines: the curious practice prevailed whereby the ruler would possess additional wives also of noble or royal birth, to ensure the succession in case the legitimate queen produced no heirs. The princess chosen as queen was assigned her own palaces and lived in great state; she was served in all by 2000 menials. The latter respected her for her feigned gravity. Appearances, however were apt to deceive, and she grew up to display a diabolical character.* Left to her own devices, she sought pleasure with any gallant youths or fine gentlemen who came her way. The brief romance once terminated, she had her suitor killed; then she would have made a kind of statue of the victim, which she adorned with rich garments and placed in her boudoir. Nezahualpilli himself commented upon the presence of so many of these human likenesses in her apartments, and was told that they were her gods; the Mexica enjoyed such a reputation for devoutness, that he believed this unlikely tale.

But such atrocity could not remain forever undetected. The female bluebeard made her great mistake when she spared the lives of three paramours; these included a prince who was a grandee of the court of Texcoco in his own right. Nezahualpilli chanced to recognize on his person a much-prized jewel which he had given to his consort. He hid his anger but, on the following night, made his way into her quarters, when she was supposedly asleep. In her bed he merely found a figure that was her living likeness; she herself was immediately discovered in compromising circumstances with her three gallants. Texcoco was a state where the rule of law prevailed, even where the sovereign was concerned. The latter accordingly referred the matter to his judges. A royal commission was set on foot, and enquiries were made of all concerned, including the palace servants and even the purveyors who, by appointment to Her Majesty the Queen, had made the statues.

Nezahualpilli informed the rulers of Tenochtitlan and Tacuba of the results of this inquisition, and of the future execution of the culprits. He then sent for all the subject rulers, with specific instructions that they should bring their wives and daughters, however young. He was determined that the lesson should be lost on none, and that the penalties of infidelity should be engraved once and for all, even on infant minds. He went so far as to declare a truce with enemies, in order that they, too, should send representatives to the ceremony: evidently the execution of a queen was equal in attraction to the best of sacrificial ceremonies, and such was the interest aroused that space was lacking in Texcoco for all the visitors. The four offenders, the princess and her lovers, were strangled, and, as befitted people of high birth, their bodies were burnt, together with

178

the statues of her previous victims. To put it mildly, the Mexica were 'rather vexed' at the slaying of their ruler's niece, but postponed their vengeance.*

Nezahualpilli, notwithstanding his intellectual pre-eminence, displayed, like his father, a marked streak of cruelty. His own eldest son and heir, among his other qualities, was gifted as a poet and philosopher, like his father and grandfather before him. However, he was rash enough to let his talents get the better of him, and composed a lampoon, making fun of the Lady of Tula, already referred to as a bluestocking of note, and as the ruler's favourite concubine. She also was something of a poetess, and a kind of war of words in verse ensued. Such conduct, however, constituted a clear case of *lèse majesté*, and the prince was subject to the death penalty, much as his father loved him. He was executed, and his palaces were closed up.*

Nezahualpilli's second legitimate son was no more fortunate. He erected palaces to which he had no right. Even the heir to the throne was not entitled to do this unless he had first taken four captives in war. He was also executed.

But the ruler was not only relentless in applying the law to his own family; he was equally insistent on the observance of correct legal procedures in more general cases. He, for instance, had a judge condemned to death for hearing a legal case in his house and not in the courts, as required by law. Another judge was killed for pronouncing an unjust sentence. Moreover, he substantially implemented the body of legislation established by his father, adding such provisions as permanent exile for soldiers who committed adultery, and the right of sons of slaves to go free. It is worth noting once more that the status of the latter was strictly regulated in ancient Mexico.

Such stories might seem to be exaggerated, were they not told by the chroniclers of Texcoco itself. Like all great rulers, he had his weak points, and doubtless found himself at times in a somewhat anomalous position, being by instinct a thinker more than a fighter, in a society where the arts of war were paramount. Nezahualpilli may have possessed the brains of the Alliance, but it was Tenochtitlan which controlled the sinews of war.

The campaign previously described was only the beginning of the drive to the Pacific. Ahuítzotl had now consolidated an important sector of the Tarascan frontier, and Oztoma in particular became a key fortified city and one of a series of bastions destined to withstand attack from this adversary. While large tracts of land had been absorbed in the process, even Ahuítzotl realized his limitations; his Tarascan policy was mainly defensive in orientation and he never resorted to all-out invasion.

Probably between 1491 and 1495, using this recently dominated region in the north-west of the modern state of Guerrero as a springboard, Ahuítzotl made a great push towards the sea.† Acapulco itself is included in the conquest lists for his reign, and he achieved the subjection of a vast stretch of coastal territory, running from Acapulco in a north-westerly direction for about 150 miles, as far as Zacatula.†

This long-range thrust along the coast was made partly for economic reasons, but was also an outflanking movement, directed against the Tarascans. As can be seen from Map 5, the border of the latter ran almost due south until a point not too far distant from the ocean; here it turned north-west, not reaching the actual coast before distant Zacatula, the farthest point attained by the forces of the Empire.†

The map also shows that the frontier of the unconquered Yopi tribes lay not far to the east, leaving a relatively narrow corridor which connected the new coastal province with the rest of the Empire; however, these Yopis were a relatively primitive people and doubtless presented little threat to the Aztec lines of communication.

The conquered coastal region hardly nowadays constitutes a leading agricultural area. However, in ancient times, its importance was great and its carefully terraced hills produced bountiful crops. It now was to become a leading supplier of cotton, providing 800 bales as its annual tribute.

One of the most alluring parts of all Mexico is the state of Oaxaca, whose capital city, of the same name, lies some 300 miles to the southeast of the city of Mexico. It is a land of rugged peaks, interspersed by fertile valleys; even on the modern road, the traveller must negotiate an infinite succession of twists and turns, before finally emerging into one of the world's most beautiful valleys, where lies the state capital. The whole region, including other neighbouring valleys, contained important centres of population ever since higher civilization had made its appearance in Mexico. The site now known as Monte Alban, on the outskirts of the city of Oaxaca, had already risen to prominence nearly 2000 years before the arrival of the Aztecs in the area.†

And, just as the region was of continuous importance in pre-hispanic times, so also it was greatly valued by the Spaniards themselves, being the main centre for the cultivation of cochineal, one of the most important products of New Spain. It was also a principal source of gold. The many beautiful churches both in the city and outside bear witness to its significance in colonial times. It had already produced these commodities in precolonial days, paying an annual tribute to the Aztecs of twenty gold discs the size of an average plate and each as thick as a man's forefinger, as well as twenty bags of cochineal.

Moctezuma I had made conquests in the north-western part of the state, and had probably penetrated yet farther. It seems, though the more descriptive sources say little, that the area immediately surrounding the city of Oaxaca was already raided and probably conquered by Ahuítzotl in the early years of his reign, in 1488 or 1489.† Like the conquest of the Pacific coast this was achieved, not by a single lightning thrust but by a series of expeditions, the first taking place in the third or fourth year of his reign – while the absorption of other centres of population, apart from Oaxaca itself, was only completed by 1495.† The region, though never fully subdued by Ahuítzotl, then became an important tributary province, providing, apart from the gold and the cochineal, 400 bundles of richly worked mantles and 800 bundles of mantles of ordinary quality.

The population of Oaxaca was predominantly Zapotec when the Aztecs arrived upon the scene, but for some time this people had been deprived of political power, following an invasion by the Mixtecs. The great centre of Monte Alban had thus been virtually abandoned for centuries, the Mixtec conquerors using it mainly as a place of burial – it was in their tombs that Dr Alfonso Caso found such exquisite examples of goldwork.

Although so many Zapotecs had remained in the area, others had sacrificed home for independence and moved farther to the south-east, towards Tehuantepec, the town at the southern extremity of the isthmus of that name, nowadays famed for the beauty of its women and for their colourful dress. Tehuantepec, so strategically situated, had become a key trading-point for the merchants of the High Plateau; from the time of Ahuítzotl's earlier conquests these had apparently enjoyed a certain degree of military protection, and the possibility of invasion from Aztec possessions in Oaxaca was ever present.

The Mexica traders were thus able to conduct their business on terms prejudicial to the customer; they foisted their unappetizing lagoon-produce on the people of the isthmus, exacting in return from the reluctant buyers their *cacao*, gold, precious stones and feathers.* By the year 1496, the latter had had enough of waterflies, lagoon worms and the like. They mobilized their forces, blocked roads and killed some of the merchants.

Their territory was even more distant than any previously conquered; Ahuítzotl nevertheless decided to take the offensive, and a large army was assembled. The soldiers were eager to participate in the campaign, directed against cities famed for their riches and ripe for plunder. While the captains prepared for war, the quarter-masters assembled large quantities of stores, indispensable for such a march. So complete was the muster that in many places only women and children remained behind; not a man was to be seen in the streets. On the fourth day after the army's departure, the women came forth in mourning clothes, plastering their hair with ashes, to mark the absence of their husbands, brothers and sons. They abstained from washing their faces, hands and clothes until the first news of victory would arrive:

> Before the morning star rose, they made fire and bore it in braziers and incense burners, also containing resin. They burned incense as an offering to the gods and goddesses, to the bones [of captives previously sacrificed] and to their husbands, making prayer to the gods of war and to various demons, that they should give victory to their spouses. Having done this, they gave food to the gods, making white tortillas and large ones called *papalotlaxcalli*, maguey worms toasted in pans that they called *xonecuillin*, and ground and toasted a little maize

called *Izquiotl*, beat it up in a new blue jar, and served it to the gods, that they might drink it.†

The army was enthusiastically received by the population of the Valley of Oaxaca, including people of Mexica stock residing there. Ahuítzotl, as usual commanding in person, summoned the local rulers, to demand of them supplies and military reinforcements. The ruler of Tehuantepec heard of this, and threatened them with dire reprisals if they dared to join the forces of aggression.

Various townships on the route were first taken and the inhabitants massacred. Finally, the main objective was reached, and the troops drawn up for battle. As on other occasions, Ahuítzotl placed trained veterans between each group of four recruits.* The army was so well drilled as to prove invincible, and the forces of Tehuantepec began to falter, after losing several of their leaders. The Mexicans pursued, again killing without mercy.*

The victors proceeded to pillage the dead, removing their rich adornments of feathers and precious stones. Ahuítzotl himself was more anxious to secure continuous supplies of such prized trophies, now being offered as tribute by the chiefs; consequently, he ordered that the fighting and robbing should cease. The Mexican captains, however, had to resort to force, holding back their own soldiers to stop the looting and slaughter. Undeterred by such attempts, they continued to break into the houses of the city, sacking as they went until eventually restrained by their leaders. The troops were incensed at this limitation of their rights – the promised reward for their exertions lay solely in pillage or in war booty; the latter was distributed officially, but probably on a more parsimonious scale, the lion's share going to the ruler and his generals. The soldiers swore that never again would they march so far, if they were not to share the fruits of victory. Ahuítzotl, however, once more won them to his side, promising that he personally would make up their losses.*

Such murmurings might at first sight appear as nothing but minor incidents. They are, however, of great moment, strongly suggesting that in undertaking far-flung conquests the Aztec Empire was faced with a law of diminishing returns. However profitable to the state, such expeditions also created problems for which no real solution lay to hand. As the journey to the scene of operations became ever more exhausting, the enthusiasm of allies and subjects diminished in proportion. Such reluctance became apparent at all levels; the ruler of Texcoco stayed away, and the common soldiers complained.

Ahuítzotl had, however, settled such differences for the present, and the rulers of Tehuantepec gave him huge presents – apart from the tribute paid. The *tlatoani*, courting the favour of the army and true to his previous promise, departed from custom, and distributed all that he received, keeping nothing back. By his action in halting the massacre, he had won over the people of Tehuantepec, who were to become firm allies in the future. Such had been the magnitude of his triumph that, on return to the capital, he was given a welcome such as no ruler had ever received before.*

Our descriptions of the campaigns of Ahuítzotl and his predecessors included details giving some idea of Aztec methods of war. In some ways these are so similar, in others so different, to those of the Old World. The Spaniards themselves provided much information on native tactics and weapons, but rather less on the organization of a campaign. Moctezuma II had taken part in many an expedition in the course of his lifetime, both before and after he succeeded to Ahuítzotl. It is perhaps a pity that he did not enlarge on this subject during the long hours spent conversing or playing parlour games with his Spanish captors.

Detailed accounts of wars and warlike preparations do, however, exist in plenty. For instance, in addition to what his informants told Padre Sahagún about the merchants' expeditions, they also supplied many details about the conduct of war:

> The ruler was known as the lord of men. His charge was war. Hence he determined, disposed and arranged how war would be made.
>
> First he commanded masters of the youths and seasoned warriors to scan the [enemy] city and to study all the roads – where they were difficult, where entry could be made through them. This done, the ruler first determined, by means of a painted plan, how was placed the city which they were to destroy. . . . Then he summoned the general and the commanding general, and the brave warriors, and he commanded them how they were to take the road, what places the warriors were to enter, for how many days they would march, and how they would arrange the battle.*

The Aztec high command thus had claim to a most adequate intelligence service; this is equally apparent from the close watch which Moctezuma II's observers were to keep on the movements of the Spanish invaders – even to the point of supplying Cortés with news of further ships reaching the coast of Mexico. Continuous streams of painted plans flowed back to Moctezuma, giving lurid details of the exotic visitors. Where long-range information was concerned, the merchants naturally played a leading role. As distinct from such strategic intelligence, tactical data on the enemy order of battle was the responsibility of scouts; descriptions of various campaigns place emphasis on their activities. At times, a full reconnaissance party would be sent forward, sufficient to penetrate the enemy defences. Surprise was, however, not usually sought in battle; we hear of night marches, but battles normally took place by day. Furthermore, with certain exceptions, war was only undertaken after a ritual declaration, involving not one, but several embassies to the enemy ruler.*

As emphasized by Sahagún's account, it was the *tlatoani* himself who made the plans, after he had consulted the leading commanders. The precise calculations as to route, timing and battle order scarcely savour of primitive warfare, recalling rather operation orders issued before a modern battle.

The account already quoted further mentions that major-domos from places as distant as the Gulf coast were included in the ruler's war council; thus a major war was an undertaking involving virtually the whole Empire:

> The ruler then consulted with all the major-domos. . . . He ordered them to take out all their goods held in storage, the tributes, costly articles – insignia of gold, and with quetzal feathers, and all the shields of great price.
> And when the major-domos had delivered all the costly devices, the ruler then adorned and presented with insignia all the princes who were already able in war, and all the brave warriors. . . .*

In view of the distances involved, the supply question was paramount. Problems of logistics were further complicated by the voluminous quantities of fancy devices and insignia required, and considered quite as indispensable as arms and ammunition – serving partly as badges of rank. To us, such adornments might appear as an absurd encumbrance; however, in Mexico war was conceived within a magico-religious framework. The gods decided, and men merely executed their will. To secure victory, one first had to make sure that the former would be favourable to the outcome. Any failure, therefore, to comply with tradition, or any attempt to discard the customary paraphernalia, would be fatal to one's chances.

But, apart from such ceremonial requirements, practical steps had to be taken regarding food and other necessities. As previously related, supplies of such standard victuals as maize and beans were taken with the army, together with cooking-vessels, being carried to the scene of battle by porters. However, it was seldom possible for an expedition to carry all that it needed, and the Aztec forces partly lived off the land. Advance arrangements were made to collect food in subject cities lying on the line of march, and a grim fate awaited any that failed to comply.* Subject peoples were often required, in addition, to provide extra levies, particularly in frontier districts.

Such arrangements probably tended to be inadequate. The Aztec Empire, unlike the Inca, had no system of supply depots placed throughout its territory, depending instead on provisions produced by local potentates. Remembering that Soconusco, Ahuítzotl's most distant objective, is nearly 800 miles by road from Mexico City, the problems involved must have been considerable.

'And the ruler forthwith called upon the rulers of Texcoco and Tlacopan [Tacuba] and the rulers in all the swamp lands, and notified them to proclaim war in order to destroy a certain city. He presented them all with costly capes, and he gave them all insignia of great price. Then he also ordered the common folk to rise to go forth to war. Before them would go marching the brave warriors, the men at arms, the lord general and the commanding general.'*

The importance of help rendered by allied and subject cities has already been stressed: Tenochtitlan could not have undertaken such conquests single-handed. Of much interest in the passage quoted is the reference to the calling-up of the common soldiers, clearly not themselves part of any standing army. In the Spanish version of this same text, words are inserted to show that it was only when mobilized that the soldiers were supplied with weapons – in other words, they were not permanently under arms. We are told on various occasions that it was on declaration of war that the young men undertook practice in the use of arms.† The same was true of Texcoco, where Pomar makes it clear that the arts of war and the cultivation of the soil went hand in hand.*

'The lords of the sun, it was said, took charge and directed in war. All the priests, the keepers of the gods, took the lead; they bore the gods upon their backs, and by the space of one day, marched ahead of all the brave warriors and the seasoned warriors. These also marched one day ahead of all the warriors of Tenochtitlan. Again these marched one day ahead of all the warriors of Tlatelolco.'*

Although the battles were short, the marches were usually long and required to be carefully ordered. Once the destination was reached, the troops were drawn up for battle:

And when the warlike lands were reached, the brave warrior generals and commanding generals then showed the others the way and arranged them in order. No one might break ranks or crowd among the others; they would there and then beat or slay whoever would bring confusion or crowding among the others. All the warriors were extended there, until the moment that Yacauitztli [god of] the night, would descend – that darkness would fall. And when they already were to rise against the city to destroy it, first was awaited tensely the moment when fire flared up – when the priests brought forth fire – and for the blowing of shell trumpets, when the priests blew them. And when the fire flared up, then as one arose all the warriors. War cries were raised; there was fighting. They shot fiery arrows into the temples.*

Sahagún's account says little of the actual battle, though other versions of such encounters abound; the Aztec forces were usually divided into squadrons, according to nationality. The army tended to attack *en masse*, reminiscent more of a horde than a phalanx. The attacking force presented a dazzling spectacle as it rushed into the fray, bedecked with feathers and jewels, amid the deafening roar of the soldiers' battle-cries, the chiefs' drums and the priests' trumpets. Bows and arrows provided a kind of artillery barrage, accompanied usually by volleys of insults; the preferred tactics, however, involved hand-to-hand fighting, using heavy clubs armed with blades of obsidian. The traditional weapon of ancient Mexico, the spear-thrower (*atlatl*), continued to be used; artistic representations of warriors usually depict this arm, rather than the bow.

Military tactics were somewhat unvaried: the inevitable stratagem was the ambush, which usually succeeded. As defensive weapons, the men carried shields and wore cotton armour, also to be adopted by the Spaniards. The defence was often conducted from prepared fortifications, surrounding cities. Many towns along the Tarascan border were thus protected, though others less vulnerably placed, such as Texcoco, lay virtually open and unprotected. Barriers were often thrown up at the last moment; one has the general impression that the defence was weaker than the attack, which normally attained its objective.

And when the city had been overcome, thereupon were counted as many captives as there were, and as many Mexicans and Tlatilulcans as had died. Then they apprised the ruler that they had been orphaned for the sake of Huitzilopochtli; that men had been taken captive and had been slain. And the ruler then commanded the high judges to go tell and inform all in the homes of those who had gone to die in war, that there might be weeping in the homes of those who had gone to war to die. And they informed those in the homes of as many as had gone to take captives in war that they had received honours there because of their valour. And they were rewarded according to their merits; the ruler accorded favours to all – costly capes, breech clouts, chocolate, food and devices, and lip rods and ear plugs. Even more did the ruler accord favours to the princes if they had taken captives. . . . And if some had done wrong in battle, they then and there slew them on the battlefield; they beat them and stoned them.*

The outstanding feature of Mexican warfare was this obsession with the capture of prisoners. It may be one thing in modern war to surround pockets of enemy men, who are then obliged to surrender as a group. For the individual soldier to capture a single prisoner and drag him from a battle still in progress is quite another; but it was for such single-handed feats that a warrior gained status, and a disputed capture served no one. To abduct individual fighting men from the field of battle must have been extraordinarily complicated. And yet

the conduct of war, if not entirely devoted to such exploits, was at
least profoundly conditioned by this aim. It was not a mere question
of honour; actual military rank was governed by such norms.

A man's progress in the Aztec hierarchy thus depended on his
success in taking prisoners: a boy of fifteen wore his hair shorn, but
with a long tuft growing from the back of his head. If he never took
a captive, thus he remained, and held no place of honour even if he
were a prince. If he took a prisoner with the help of five or six others,
as a kind of collective initiation into the art, most of his tuft of hair
was removed, only a small part remaining, which reached down to
one ear.*

At this point, he was addressed by an older warrior, referred to as
his grandfather or beloved uncle: 'Thou hast taken another face;
and thou hast gone to throw thyself against the foe. Let them take
thee if, without profit, once more thou takest a captive with the aid
of others. What wouldst thou be? Wouldst thou have a young
girl's lock of hair? Take care lest thou again take a captive with
others' help. Cast thyself against our foes.'*

In other words, only raw recruits could indulge in the initial
luxury of collective capture and gain honour for it; from that point
hence, the young man must take his prisoners unaided. Those who
were successful were named leading youths, and their faces were
stained with red ochre: 'And at that time Moctezuma granted him
favours; he gave him an orange cape with a striped border and a
scorpion design to bind on, and a carmine breech clout with long
ends, and a breech clout of many colours. And he then began to wear
capes with designs.'*

Additional honours were claimed by those who had taken three
captives. But only after a fourth capture was a man promoted to the
title of 'seasoned warrior'.† He then consorted on equal terms with
the great captains. These 'seasoned warriors', their rank depending
on personal merit, constituted a kind of 'officer class', of paramount
importance in a military state. On the other hand, the great military
commanders, or 'leading captains', tended to be related to the
ruler, and thus became eminent by virtue of heredity, as well as
merit.

Apart from such regular grades of warriors, who apparently only took up arms on declaration of war, there existed several orders of 'knights' – who possibly constituted a kind of standing force, very limited in number. The chief among these were the Eagle and Ocelot Knights, who had already existed long before the age of the Aztecs.* As with certain medieval knights, their order was religious as well as military in nature; they had special connections with certain temples, one of which can still be seen at Malinalco. The eagle and the ocelot, or jaguar, were symbols of bravery; it will be recalled how, after the creation of the Fifth Sun and Moon, they both plunged into the fire, the eagle emerging completely darkened by the flames, and the ocelot merely spotted. Apart from their leading role in the gladiatorial sacrifice, it seems that in war they fought as a separate body, or a kind of *corps d'élite*.†

For Ahuítzotl's last and most ambitious campaign, pretexts varied from the usual pattern. In 1500 the people of Tehuantepec, now loyal subjects, found their resources insufficient to meet payment of tribute.* In order to obtain extra produce, they sent their own merchants to trade with Soconusco, a province yet more distant. The people of the latter derided them for their new status as tributaries, calling them cowards and women and mere lackeys of the Mexicans.

Soconusco lies on the border of present-day Mexico and Guatemala; even taking the distance as the crow flies, it is some 600 miles distant from Mexico City. An army following the endless twists and turns of mountain paths must have covered a greater distance.

Undeterred by such problems, Ahuítzotl determined to respond to the appeals of Tehuantepec; if he ignored them, this would be taken as a pretext for default on tribute and for rebellion.* To any other ruler, such an enterprise might have seemed foolhardy.

Large supplies were assembled for the distant venture. No one was permitted to absent himself on pain of death, except for the aged, children and certain priests. Once more, Ahuítzotl had trouble with his two allied rulers; their enthusiasm for the 800-mile march was limited. In order to force their hands, Ahuítzotl sent them arms and insignia such as only a sovereign prince could don. Such forceful hints fell upon deaf ears; the ruler of Tacuba pleaded old age. In spite of certain suggestions to the contrary, it appears that Neza-hualpilli also played truant – avoiding thus not only the great trek, but also the constant irritation of having to play second fiddle on such occasions to Ahuítzotl.*

The latter naturally led his army in person. A pastmaster in the simultaneous use of stick and carrot, he inspired his troops by his stern example and his lavish prodigality; they in their turn promised not to return home before victory was achieved.

Even on the outward march, the great conqueror received an almost godlike reception in Tehuantepec. In a munificent gesture of appreciation, he seated the local ruler on his right hand; the leading Mexicans served him as they did their own master. The army rested here for a few days, Ahuítzotl remaining true to his custom of staying with his army, spurning the comforts of the city.

After a further forced march, the enemy strongholds were conquered one after the other, and finally Soconusco, from which the whole province was named.† In the attack on this city, the Aztec armies displayed signs of war-weariness. We are told that, had it not been for the support of the people of Tehuantepec, whose journey had been much shorter, they might even have suffered defeat.*

Ahuítzotl as usual came to terms with the local chiefs, and gave orders that looting and killing should cease. Once more, he encountered bitter protests. He persuaded the rulers of the province to give special gifts to his men, as compensation for the booty forgone. This, in effect, was the only reward of the common soldier. The people of Soconusco were only too ready to indicate to Ahuítzotl that further heights remained to scale. They told him of neighbouring Guatemala, with which they were continuously at war; they would gladly assist him to conquer this land. Not surprisingly, he told them that his army was too exhausted for further expeditions. Such distant ventures may appear even more remarkable when it is recalled that other military operations had to be undertaken simultaneously. During the whole reign of Ahuítzotl we hear of periodical conflicts with the near-by peoples of the Puebla–Tlaxcala Valley; though perhaps of a partly ritual nature, aimed at securing prisoners, they were none the less hard-fought.

One such encounter occurred in 1499, or just before the march to Soconusco; as in many similar cases, the adversary was Huexotzingo rather than Tlaxcala, which was only then rising to a position of predominance.* The outstanding deed of bravery on this occasion was performed by a captain of Huexotzingo; hearing of the Aztec attack, when he was playing the ball game, he rushed to the scene of battle without even having the time to don his arms. As yet unarmed, he fought with such vigour that he killed several adversaries, and fought on, using their weapons.

After the battle, now the hero of the hour, Toltécatl was acclaimed ruler in Huexotzingo. Owing to the opposition of certain priests, he was forced to abandon his throne; he fled into Aztec territory, where he was killed on the orders of Ahuítzotl, not always chivalrous towards his fallen foes.

As the Empire expanded, so also did the population of the capital and of the surrounding cities; archaeological evidence suggests a considerable increase in the Valley of Mexico during the era of the *Pax Azteca*. Notwithstanding the huge flow of tribute, it was not easy to provide food for such concentration of dwellings – almost an ancient conurbation – assuming proportions unknown before in Mexico.† It was therefore essential to increase local production and augment the yield of the *chinampa* system of cultivation in the vicinity of Tenochtitlan. For this purpose, greater quantities of sweet water were needed; present supplies were inadequate and some canals even tended to dry up at certain times of the year.*

With this end in view, it occurred to Ahuítzotl to harness the water from the abundant springs of Coyoacan, some six miles to the southwest, and bring them to Tenochtitlan. Accordingly, he sent word to the ruler of that city, telling of his plan. The latter replied that these waters were most dangerous and difficult to control; if once unleashed, they could flood Tenochtitlan, since the lagoon lacked proper outlets and its level would simply rise. He, therefore, strongly advised Ahuítzotl not to utilize the springs, adding nevertheless that, if his master insisted, he would obey.

His pet project thus criticized Ahuítzotl flew into a rage. The members of his council tried to assuage his wrath; furthermore, since the ruler of Coyoacan was much respected among them, they warned him of impending doom. However, rather than hide until the storm had passed, the latter relied for protection on the powers of the occult, in which he was greatly skilled.

To such an extent did belief in the supernatural influence events that even a cruel assassination, such as that which followed, is related in a magical context. It might be added that the chroniclers themselves would not necessarily have disbelieved in their tales of magic, presumably inspired by the devil rather than the divine.

We are told that Ahuítzotl sent his henchmen, who surrounded the palace of Coyoacan, forced an entrance, and found upon the throne, not the ruler, but a beautiful eagle. Dumbfounded, they rushed back to Tenochtitlan to report. They were ordered to return immediately in added strength, and this time were astonished to find a great serpent on the throne. It began to uncoil itself and prepared to attack them. Like a dragon, it seared them with flames, and they were forced to abandon the palace and flee to Tenochtitlan, in order to tell Ahuítzotl that they could not execute his commands.

But Ahuítzotl was not a man to accept defeat at the hands of a mere magician. He now sent word to the other leaders of Coyoacan, telling them that they must deliver up their sovereign – or else he would make war and destroy them. To save his city, the ruler now surrendered his person to the envoys, saying: 'You see me here; I place myself in your hands. But go and tell your lord, Ahuítzotl, that I prophesy that before many days pass Mexico will be submerged and destroyed, and that his will be the fault, for spurning my advice.'* He thereupon dressed himself in his royal robes, and put the rope round his own neck.†

This assassination, for such it was, caused consternation among Ahuítzotl's advisers; in particular, the ruler of Tacuba was most distressed, since the victim was a close kinsman.† It might be one thing occasionally to slay a remote provincial prince after a bitter war; it was quite another to kill the sovereign of a neighbouring city in cold blood. It virtually amounted to an offence against the gods, whom this ruler, in his own sphere, represented. And in the end even Ahuítzotl himself felt remorse, and did his best to compensate the sons of the deceased.* The ambitious project to harness the waters was now set in motion. A huge labour-force was recruited, and each city was apportioned its particular task. The workers were so numerous as to resemble ants in an antheap.

When the aqueduct was completed, the most elaborate religious ceremonies took place, dedicated to the God of Rain and to the Goddess of Water.† A veritable aquatic festival ensued, replete with every symbol of rain or water – so basic to Mexican religion, in which such deities and rites were among the most ancient.†

Practically all the participants were dressed in blue, the colour characteristic of water deities. The chief priest, dressed as the Water Goddess herself, wore a blue cloak and diadem of heron feathers, symbolic of the Rain God. His face was darkened with drops of melted rubber, another rain symbol, and his forehead was painted blue. His ears, lips and wrists were adorned with green stones, a further sacred emblem.* The other priests wore similar adornments, though their bodies were almost naked.

When the chief priest arrived, dressed as the Water Goddess, he first drank the water, and then addressed it, as if speaking to the goddess herself: 'Precious lady: you come your way in most welcome fashion. It is the path which you have to follow henceforth. Thus I, representing your likeness, come to receive and greet you, and to welcome your arrival. See, my lady, that this is the day of your coming to your city of Mexico-Tenochtitlan.'*

After this, he sprinkled coloured maize-flour on the waters, while musicians devoted to the Rain God and Water Goddess sang and danced in appropriate fashion. Old men brought earthenware jars filled with fishes, frogs, leeches and water snakes, and cast them into the flow.

The climax of the ceremony was still to come. Four specially selected children of six years of age were held in readiness. They were now dressed exactly as the attendant clergy – their faces blackened with liquid rubber, stars painted on their foreheads, and their bodies festooned with green stones. As the water reached each of four predetermined points, one of the infants was sacrificed and the blood sprinkled on the stream.

Finally Ahuítzotl himself came out and made obeisance to the oncoming current. After addressing to it a further homily, he stood at the point where the water fell from the aqueduct into the canal, and threw in golden objects and precious stones, fashioned as fishes and frogs.*

Unfortunately, however, the forebodings of the murdered ruler of Coyoacan proved all too well founded; the flow was so abundant that soon the level of the lagoon began to rise, flooding some of the cultivated *chinampas* that lay between the canals.† Other cities of the lagoon, as well as Tenochtitlan, were also inundated.* All attempts to stem the flood by means of a great dam were of no avail. Houses and cultivated plots were submerged, and the people began to flee their homes.

Ahuítzotl was mortified; the hero of so many distant triumphs had met his Waterloo on the home front. He now even feared the wrath of the populace for the havoc which he had wrought. As a confession of his failure, he sent for Nezahualpilli of Texcoco. Apart from his renown as a sage, this ruler enjoyed equal fame as a magician.

He was apparently glad of an opportunity to ingratiate himself – he had previously aroused the anger of the Mexica by the public execution of Ahuítzotl's niece;* at the same time he must have been secretly delighted that this time it was he, not Ahuítzotl, who could utter the reproofs. He spoke as follows:

Most powerful king: you have been long in seeking counsel. Earlier, the ruler of Coyoacan, Tzutzumatzin, gave you his advice. Only of late has fear and dread seized you that you yourself and this noble city might be destroyed, something that you should have foreseen and considered long before. Note well that in the present battle it is not your enemies who are pressing you, for these by your valour you are well able to confound and expel from your city; now you are fighting an element so relentless as the water. How can you resist and repair the situation?
... What had Tzutzumatzin done? In what did he err? How did he offend? Was he a traitor or did he plot against your royal crown? Was he perchance an adulterer or a thief?

Recognize, most mighty lord, that you have offended and sinned against the gods, whose likeness this good ruler represented, and upon whose shoulders they had laid the burden of the government of his realm. And for that cause, the lord of creation now permits that this city should be destroyed and depopulated. How will it appear in the eyes of the enemies which surround us, when Mexico is emptied of its citizens and you and your lords are compelled to flee, as an eternal vengeance upon you and upon them? What will they say, save that what your ancestors built with so much sweat and labour, you have destroyed in forty days?

My opinion is that the dams should be demolished and that the water should follow its previous course; at the same time, a solemn sacrifice should be offered to the Goddess of Water, to appease her wrath against you, including many jewels and feathers and numerous quails, together with incense, paper and rubber – and that simultaneously some children should be brought to be offered up. Perhaps by these means we shall calm and restrain her springs, so that they may pour forth less water.*

This revealing discourse shows that even the overweening Ahuítzotl was not absolute master in his own house; one wonders who would have dared to address the Emperor Charles V or King Philip II in like fashion. The speech well illustrates the Aztec propensity for blending the soundest common sense with the strangest superstition. The Texcocan monarch first recommends the only sensible course, namely to stop the flow of water at its source, rather than to block its later flow with ineffective dams. But such practical action – even for the sage of Texcoco – must needs be accompanied by further child-sacrifices as an indispensable part of the whole plan. In peace as in war, no solution was complete, or indeed effective, without giving the gods their due; the Rain God's favourite fare happened to be young children.

To complete his rescue operation, Nezahualpilli insisted that divers should be sought who were familiar with the springs of Coyoacan. To ensure that full atonement was made to the gods for the wrongs committed, he further suggested that, in addition to the children, a few leading Mexicans should be sacrificed, a proposal which surely sent a chill down the spine of some present at the meeting.

Fifteen divers were produced who eventually plunged into the water and found practical ways of stanching its flow. In this strictly technical undertaking, they received invaluable assistance from innumerable priests, dressed this time as the Rain God himself, not as his sister, the Goddess of Water, and with their faces and bodies duly painted blue. That the material and religious aspects of the undertaking should proceed hand in hand, the divers were also painted the same colour, to honour the god.*

Such drastic measures proved effective, and the waters subsided, but only after taking a fearful toll of the city. A great work of reconstruction was needed; vast numbers of canoes were marshalled to bring materials to the scene of action:

The which [reconstruction] was now put in hand and each province and nation rallied to the task, bringing staves, earth and stone; with this they stopped up the water in all the places where it had entered. Many old buildings remained beneath the flood, and they rebuilt Mexico with better constructions, more original and elegant in style, for the previous ones were ancient and had been built by the Mexica themselves in their time of poverty and need. And thus many were lowly and dilapidated.

However, this time the nobles and others built to suit their fancy, using imported labour, each leader having a village or two assigned to him to help rebuild his house. And thus, they painted as they wished, each one in his own style, as was their own custom. And so Mexico became very fine and spectacular, with large and unusual houses, filled with great extensions of garden and splendid patios; the canals were now well controlled and with willows and poplars, both light and dark in colour planted on their sides, with many defences and embankments provided against the water, so that even if they became filled no damage would be done.*

It may thus be observed that Ahuítzotl's character was many-sided. At times the munificent conqueror, at others the petty tyrant, venting his frustration by his treatment of the ruler of Coyoacan. But, not unlike other great campaigners, he not only conquered, but also constructed; the solid masonry, designed to perpetuate his triumphs, was soon to be wondered at, and then destroyed, by a different kind of conqueror.

Clearly much more than mere repairs were involved. The project amounted to a virtual rebuilding of the city with certain 'foreign influences', just as occurred in London after the Great Fire. Relatively few years remained before the arrival of the Spaniards, and it is, therefore, logical to suppose that most of what they were to behold existed before the death of Ahuítzotl. Under the impetus of his additions to the Empire, the metropolis probably took on its final and resplendent form. The city, as well as the Empire, had expanded at a vertiginous pace.

Though started in previous reigns, the Great Temple and the surrounding edifices had also taken final shape under Ahuítzotl. The Temple was part of a vast complex, formed of seventy-eight buildings and capable of holding 10,000 people at a time. This was surrounded by a wall, surmounted by crenellations such as we still see protecting the atrium of many a sixteenth-century monastery.

The great ceremonial centre of Tenochtitlan does not correspond exactly to the present Plaza de la Constitución, but lay slightly to the west. The skull rack occupied part of the area where the Metropolitan Cathedral is now situated, with the Temple of the Plumed Serpent lying just behind and to the west.* North of these, at the corner of the Calle de la República de Guatemala, some remains of the Great Temple have been excavated; it was surrounded by a wall of serpents (coatepantli), such as can still be seen at the site of Tenayuca. The Temple itself conformed to the typical Aztec pattern, with double stairway and two sanctuaries at the top, one for Huitzilodochtli and the other for the Rain God:

> In the principal one of these [temples], was the statue of Huitzilopochtli who was also named Ilhuicatl Xoxouhqui; in the other stood the image of the God Tlaloc. In front of each one of these was a round stone like a large block, called Techcatl, where they killed those whom they sacrificed to this god, and from the stone down to the bottom was a flow of blood of those whom they slew, and it was thus in all the towers.†

Perhaps a characteristic, if rather sombre, monument to Ahuítzotl's achievements was the new skull rack (tzompantli) which he installed. After the great sacrifice for the inauguration of the Temple, so many new heads were forthcoming that they could not be accommodated on the previous rack. He accordingly ordered this to be burnt and a new one to be constructed in its place.

Another well-known monument completed in this reign is the famous temple situated high up on the hill above the village of Tepoztlan, near Cuernavaca, and often known as the Tepozteco. It is one of the few temples which can be actually dated, displaying the glyph of the year Ten Rabbit, or 1502, the last of Ahuítzotl's reign.*

Nor should it be thought that the Mexica as a whole were nothing but rough soldiers, whose artistic achievements were confined to monumental masonry – or that the arts were the exclusive province of Texcoco. Admittedly Aztec pottery leaves much to be desired; the fastidious Moctezuma II dined off plates made of the delicate Cholula ware. On the other hand, a wealth of literature in the

Nahuatl language has survived, including historical annals, poems and sagas; at least part of these derived from Tenochtitlan and Tlatelolco. In their poignant grace, they reflect the Aztec view of creation, and the need to cherish the here and now, and its brief delights so quickly snatched away by the relentless gods.

Aztec sculpture is also most worthy of note. Not only are we impressed by the monumental figures, clearly the product of a virile civilization, but also by the smaller objects fashioned in stone; whether of man or beast these exhibit a talent that is both graceful and intimate.

The great conqueror had now enjoyed his last triumph, and was soon to be struck down by a premature death. While his armies ranged far and wide over Mexico, the Spaniards had already crossed the Atlantic to Española. At this moment, therefore, we are writing of an empire, on the one hand seemingly standing at the apex of power, but whose death-knell was shortly to sound. For, regardless of the success or failure of Cortés' expedition some seventeen years later, the triumph of Spanish arms within the next generation was inevitable.

Before, therefore, embarking on the next reign and discussing the doings of the ill-fated Moctezuma II, it may be appropriate to consider the state of the Aztec nation at this supreme moment, just before the death of Ahuítzotl. Evidence has already been quoted to suggest that the Empire was nearing a point of no return; in proportion to the remoteness of the new land conquered, the complaints grew ever louder that the game was not worth the candle. The ruler himself was forced to adopt new palliatives to reward his soldiers for the privations imposed; even his own colleagues played truant when they could. It is worth noting that the next sovereign, Moctezuma, did not extend the bounds of empire in terms of distance from the capital.

Some insistence has already been placed on the rather loose-knit nature of the whole structure. The tendency to dominate without imposing direct control persisted under Ahuítzotl. In spite of one moment of aberration, he himself had been a firm upholder of the monarchic principle, even restoring dynasties in places such as Chalco, where direct government had been formerly imposed. Thus, at the time of the Conquest, virtually the whole Empire was ruled by sub-potentates acknowledging as their supreme head the rulers of the Triple Alliance. The system was not entirely dissimilar to that employed by the British in India, in those parts that were not brought under direct control; its efficacy was, however, circumscribed by the lack of any system of communications such as the British had provided.

It must, moreover, be appreciated that, while Ahuítzotl made conquests at great distances from the capital, huge tracts of inter-mediate territory remained unsubdued. This is true not only of the officially independent states such as Tlaxcala – to be discussed in the succeeding chapter – but of countless hills and valleys lying off the line of march of the Aztec armies, and where they scarcely penetrated. The Empire was more a network of strongpoints than a composite territory; the latest acquisitions, on the Guatemalan border, were only joined to the rest by a series of bastions, rather than by a continuous band of territory.* The Empire was also somewhat ill-balanced. To the north-west, Queretaro, well within Tarascan territory, is today only a two-hour drive from Mexico City and Toluca, almost a frontier city, is little more than one hour distant; on the other hand, the limits of empire in the opposite direction would take nearer twenty hours to reach on the modern road. What Ahuítzotl left behind was a vast but almost skeletal edifice. It remained for his successor to consolidate many intermediate areas. For this reason, it is well-nigh impossible to trace any true boundary line of Aztec-dominated territory at the time of his death; Map 5 marks his main conquests but does not attempt this task. It would not be altogether accurate to draw a line round these and denominate the whole area thus defined as Aztec-dominated.*

Like the sun in its daily course, an empire cannot maintain a fixed position; it must either rise or descend. It is possible that the Aztec sun was not far from its zenith when the bearded gods appeared in the east. The Tarascans in the north-west imposed an effective limit to Aztec expansion. To the south and south-east, the Aztecs faced peoples more pliant and less united; as long as they were prepared to march up hill and down dale, there was no real obstacle to their conquering as far as their legs could carry them, in spite of the difficulties already mentioned. Fantastic though the thought may seem at first, it is unlikely, but not impossible, that the Aztec and Inca armies might have met one day, had their empires been granted a further span of life.

For, if the Spaniards had not intervened in 1519, the Aztecs would have conquered Guatemala and probably the Yucatan peninsula, at the eastern extremity of Mexico. This possibility certainly exists, but in furthering such aims the Empire would have added more to its problems than to its wealth. The temptations to conquer might have been pressing, since the traders already penetrated these areas, and military expansion tended to follow closely in the wake of the merchants. What had already been achieved represented a prodigious feat of arms; one is, however, compelled to doubt whether the rather rudimentary imperial organization was capable of absorbing yet more territory, with the limited means of transport at its disposal. Moctezuma II seems to have understood this.

Moreover, the economic advantages of further expansion could have hardly outweighed the drawbacks. The traders were already obtaining the rich stones of the Maya lands through trading-posts on the Gulf coast.† Guatemala could only offer further supplies of wares already exacted from Soconusco. To break their heads against the Tarascan wall or kick against nomad pricks to the north-east would have produced no corresponding return.

Reliance on the loyalty of local rulers was a poor substitute for a system of direct or proconsular government, and led inevitably to continuous provincial revolts. The Aztec Empire was an imposing edifice, but its foundations were somewhat fragile. On the one hand Aztec society, as M. Jacques Soustelle has rightly pointed out, was basically virile, and had shown a capacity for internal change. But on the other one is left wondering whether, in the ordering of empire, they could have demonstrated a like degree of flexibility.

In assessing the Aztecs' place in history, their motivation as well as their organization require to be considered. The will to conquer has manifested itself in many forms in human history; however, the periods during which one people dominates others tend to be limited, and the rewards reaped by the conquerors often prove illusory. Where empires are concerned, the quest for power and glory is inevitably present, and was surely a leading factor in Aztec expansionism. At the same time, the religious or doctrinal motive is less easily definable. The Mexica were the chosen people of Huitzilopochtli, and belief in their special deity was a cohesive force, spurring them to excel. But the god himself was an integral member of a large pantheon and nearly all the other Mexica gods were shared by the people whom they conquered. They might add, or impose, the cult of Huitzilopochtli, but this scarcely amounted to religious proselytising. Huitzilopochtli set the Mexica apart from other peoples, but the diffusion of his cult did not motivate their conquests.

More apparent, however, in a system of domination ostensibly devoted to the gathering of tribute, is the economic urge. This may, in part at least, have arisen from sheer necessity. After the earlier conquests, in themselves partly a kind of takeover of the previous Tepanec Empire, the capital, Tenochtitlan, began to grow, and was eventually to attain proportions never before seen in a city of ancient Mexico, and hardly known at the time in the Old World. Moreover, this was only part of the story; the network of lakeside cities, including Texcoco, housed a vigorously expanding population, already too large to be fed from the limited resources of the Valley of Mexico. Without the livestock of the Old World, the pig, the cow, the sheep and the goat, and with no pack animals, it was an uphill task to provide such an urban population with a diet sufficiently nourishing, and enormous supplies of bulky foodstuffs such as maize and beans were required; the latter at least contained some protein, but only as a limited proportion of the whole, and therefore large amounts needed to be eaten to obtain an adequate diet.† The tribute-lists contain huge quantities of these products, although they are notable for the absence of meat, which could not be stored.

But it is remarkable that in the reigns of both Ahuítzotl and Moctezuma II famines occurred, notwithstanding the tribute which poured into Tenochtitlan. Perhaps for the first time in America, urban development was generating its own problems; conquest furthered its development, and in turn ever greater quantities of tribute were needed to feed more mouths in the lakeside cities. This was the first vicious circle to confront the Aztecs.

But what is perhaps the most puzzling to our own way of thinking is that much of the economy, whether deriving from trade or tribute, seems to have been based not on the securing of necessities for the toiling masses, but ever-increasing supplies of gaudy feathers and precious gems, together with gold, jaguar skins and other purely sumptuary items. If one were to take the accounts of the chroniclers at their face value, the impression would remain that all these tremendous exertions, involving such gruelling marches and hard-fought battles, were undertaken simply to accumulate fabulous quantities of feathers and other baubles. It must, however, be appreciated that much of this apparently useless finery was in itself a necessity and formed part of the panoply of war, and however expensive was indispensable for honouring the gods, on whom success depended.

Moreover, the rewards lay largely in the hands of the ruler himself, who distributed the trophies more or less as he deemed fit. No doubt the nobles were well endowed with land and riches of all kinds; the Spaniards marvelled at their city homes. However, except among the rulers themselves, they did not encounter in Mexico that vast accumulation of individual wealth, the huge estates and the throngs of menials that would have been at the disposal, for instance, of the senatorial nobility of Rome, or the grandees of Spain itself.

One therefore sees the Empire, by the time of Ahuítzotl, caught in a second vicious circle or triangle. The gods had to be appeased and the sun had to be kept on its course by vast offerings, both in terms of human life and of ostentatious display. This necessitated endless wars of conquest. As a reward for such attentions to their requirements, Huitzilopochtli and the other gods provided yet more victories. Thus conquests ever more distant were effected, these in their turn providing for yet more lavish displays in honour of the gods. This process was a never-ending one: the gods offered victory; this in its turn provided food for the gods, who, thus assuaged, offered not peace but further conflict.

As has been continually emphasized, there was little that was new either about the gods themselves or the ceremonies in their honour. Such a situation, with conquests to provide for more ceremonies, and ceremonies to produce further conquests, may have been building up throughout the history of ancient Mexico, to reach a kind of crescendo just before the Spanish Conquest.

The Aztecs accordingly conquered both to serve their gods and to fill their stomachs. However, such aims are cherished by other nations, who never dominated their neighbours. One must needs seek an additional factor that oiled the wheels of conquest. In this respect, another impulse reveals its presence among the Mexica – the obsession with display as an object in itself.

Time and time again one reads of the relentless efforts made to attract the 'enemy' rulers and representatives to each new exhibition of wealth and might. One account after another tells of lavish gifts heaped upon free and subject sovereigns. With the Aztecs, the insistence on securing an audience for their actions, a common human weakness, seems to have become a mania.

It has been rightly suggested that in the Aztec polity is to be found a basic tendency to what, among other peoples of the North American continent, is known as *potlatch* – that is to say, the intense concentration of effort on the temporary hoarding of wealth, with the simple aim of giving it away on one single occasion. With the Aztecs, this orientation was both internal and external. An example of what might be described as internal *potlatch* was to be found in the great banquets of the merchants. External forms of the same tendency were concentrated on the 'enemies', or peoples still unconquered, within or without the bounds of empire.

Thus, with some justice, the Aztec Empire might be described as the 'Potlatch State' – a concept on the whole alien to European patterns of conduct and thought. We are told, for instance, that a whole year's tribute was given away at Ahuítzotl's coronation; thus riches were not sought in order to be stored away, or hoarded and handed on to one's heir, as in the Western world. What could not be displayed on the person of the owner was best disbursed to impress whatever outside guests could be mustered.

A problem created by the conquests themselves was the reduction in the supply of independent spectators for Aztec displays, as more and more peoples joined the ranks of the conquered. This was more true of the southern reaches of empire than of the north, where the unyielding Tarascans were to be found.

The Aztec Empire, if it had been permitted to survive, would surely have faced two continuous dangers: firstly the external threat presented by these Tarascans; and secondly the constant menace of internal revolts. As the number of subject peoples increased and the distances from the capital grew ever greater, such dangers naturally augmented.

Unless, like the Assyrians, in the later phases of empire, the Aztecs could have changed their methods and introduced a form of centralized rule – something for which one may doubt their capacity – it is quite possible that, faced with increasing resistance from within and without, the Empire would have contracted, or even eventually succumbed. Much would have depended on personalities – on whether the second Moctezuma had been succeeded by rulers of great merit, or by other Tízocs.

Aztec achievement in the decades before disaster ensued had been astonishing in scope and rapid in achievement: such sudden destruction leaves room for every form of speculation. The Empire was like a man struck down in his prime; one can only guess as to his future career. But, whatever one's uncertainties as to its future course, the Aztec eagle had already soared to spectacular heights.

CHAPTER SEVEN

A MAN IN HIS PRIME

NOT LONG AFTER the events narrated above, Ahuítzotl died, in the year 1502, at a comparatively early age.† It is suggested that his death was indirectly caused by the Great Flood, the delayed result of a blow on the head when he was escaping from the inundation.* Durán, on the other hand, attributes his death to some kind of intestinal malady contracted on his last and longest campaign, leaving him so emaciated that he appeared almost fleshless.*

The most solemn funeral rites were performed, surpassing in pomp those of former sovereigns. Notwithstanding the violence of his disposition, the late ruler had been admired for his genius and loved for his bounty. The orations were more fulsome and the offerings more lavish than ever before and, while the first were addressed to his earthly remains, the second would provide for his comforts in the hereafter.

That indefatigable orator Nezahualpilli as usual rose to the occasion: after employing all the metaphors appropriate to a great monarch, he reminded his listeners of the aura of deep sanctity surrounding the office of *tlatoani*: 'Now is filled with dust and dirt the seat of the almighty god, which you kept clean, whose likeness you represented and in whose name you governed, removing from it all tares and thorns.'* He abjured the departed ruler to rest in peace, and assured him that his own servants, as well as other slaves, would be duly dispatched to the next world to serve him there, as on earth. The ashes of Ahuítzotl were buried in an urn at the side of the great Stone of the Sun.†

When it came to choosing a successor, for the electors it was a case of *embarras de richesse*. The new generation which had grown up included a plentiful supply of sons of the previous three rulers, Ahuítzotl and his two brothers.

It was once more Nezahualpilli who spoke first, pointing to the wide range of candidates at their disposal; even if none of the sons or nephews of the last sovereign was preferred, then other princes of royal lineage abounded, already of mature age. Many had held important rank in the military and religious hierarchy, as was to be expected in a community where not only the sovereign, but the whole royal family, aspired to the highest offices of state.

The ruler of Tacuba, the other surviving head of the Alliance, also spoke, pleading in particular that they should not elect a raw youth or a dotard; the Empire required a man in his prime. Both he and Nezahualpilli laid emphasis upon the perils that beset them, both of rebellion from within and attack from without. Implicitly, they gave vent to a feeling that the Empire was becoming over-extended. It now stood at the parting of the ways; a mature statesman was needed, to control its destinies and to consolidate its gains.

The electors chose Moctezuma Xocoyotzin, son of Axayácatl, and

207

nephew of Ahuítzotl.† He was thirty-four years old.* Like his predecessor, he held when elected one of the two leading army commands. While also renowned for his political wisdom, he excelled
above all in the arts of war; he had already displayed the greatest
valour and shown an invincible spirit on the field of battle.

In spite of the many apparently suitable candidates, the choice
had been fairly simple: 'They elected Moctezuma II with so much
ease, as previously mentioned, because all eyes were turned on him
with that end in view; for, as well as being most valiant, he was grave
and temperate, so that people marvelled when they heard him speak.
And when he made a discourse in the Supreme Council, he did it
with such wisdom and aptitude that all wondered; and thus before
becoming king, he was feared and revered.'* Nezahualpilli summed
up the situation by affirming that the gods had surely shown their
love for the city in providing for the choice of a ruler of such
strength and courage.* All accounts of the new sovereign stress his
great piety, apart from his other qualities, and after his election he
was found in a temple, attending to his religious duties. He was,
however, not without faults, as will later become apparent:

> He took great care that all the temples, and more especially the Great
> Temple should be well served, cleaned and swept; however the terror
> and panic instilled by auguries and false oracles of his gods were apt to
> abate his natural vigour and valour.
> He was most zealous in the punctual enforcement of his orders and
> the observance of his laws, and inexorable in the punishment of
> offenders. On occasions he tested the probity of his judges by the
> indirect offer of gifts; any found guilty, even of the highest nobility,
> paid the corresponding penalty, without hope of remission. He was the
> irreconcilable enemy of idleness, and to banish this vice from his
> dominions, he sought to keep all his vassals well occupied. . . .
> His oppression of all his subjects, the excessive taxes which he im-
> posed, his haughtiness and pride, and his extreme severity in punish-
> ment alienated many people, although, on the other hand, he con-
> ciliated by his liberality, both in providing for the necessities of his
> peoples and in rewarding the services of his captains and ministers.*

Like his predecessors, Moctezuma now submitted himself to the
established pre-coronation ritual: the piercing of the nose, the

donning of the diadem and the royal robes, the ceremony of auto-sacrifice, and the days of penitence. The electors made speeches of unusual prolixity, reminding him of his military functions, his social obligations and his religious duties:

You must go out and watch the stars, to know their course and their signs, influences and portents. Above all, you must take note of the morning star, that, when it appears, you may perform the ceremony of washing yourself free from blemish and anointing yourself with the divine pigment. . . . You must care for the mountains and deserts where the sons of god go to do penance and to live in the solitude of caves. You must care for the divine springs and fountains.†

In reply Moctezuma, at times so proud and haughty, displayed a seemly modesty. He tried three times to begin his speech, but was overcome by tears. Finally, drawing himself up, he answered briefly:

I would indeed be blind, most noble king, if I did not perceive that you have spoken thus, simply to do me honour; notwithstanding the presence of so many fine and noble men in this kingdom, you have chosen me, the most inadequate of all for this calling. I possess few accomplishments required for such an arduous task, and know not what I may do, save to rely upon the Lord of Creation to favour me, and to beg all those present that they may give their support to these my supplications.*

But Moctezuma's modesty was in part feigned: from the words of Nezahualpilli it can be seen that, if the *tlatoani* was not, like an Egyptian pharaoh, a god in his own lifetime, his status now verged on the divine. Quite apart from the oriental ritual of his court – no one might look upon his face, he might not tread upon unswept ground, others had to wear rough garments in his presence – certain aspects of his life, such as his private obeisances to the Morning Star, placed him in a category apart from other mortals in his relation to the gods. In addition, he enjoyed a special role as a kind of supreme augur; unluckily Moctezuma's talents in this field were to be over-taxed by the horrendous events destined to overtake his realm.

To learn of the great splendour surrounding the second Mocte-zuma, we are fortunately not limited to native sources, but can draw on ample accounts by Spanish eyewitnesses. Thus, by anticipating a little order of events, it is possible to give a first-hand and graphic picture of how he lived taken from his future conquerors, already installed in Española, unbeknownst to the Mexican ruler; the *tlatoani*'s style of life is not likely to have appreciably changed in the intervening seventeen years. The availability of Spanish accounts introduces a new phase in Mexican history; the information given by chroniclers and codices on pre-hispanic Mexico is admirable for the fullness of its detail. However, these native sources tend to concentrate on the bare narrating of events and their accompanying ceremonies. On the other hand, the European cult of the individual led the Spaniards to write much more of the physical traits and private life of the main protagonists in the drama. It is perhaps fair to add that native informants could hardly be expected to describe Moctezuma's physical features, since they would have been promptly executed had they dared to look him in the eye!*

By contrast, Bernal Díaz del Castillo and Cortés waxed eloquent on such subjects, and left vivid portraits of the ruler. These hard-living intruders had never themselves moved in royal circles, or even dreamt of penetrating the court of Charles V. They were thus literally stupefied by what they saw of the great Mexican monarch, and were as surprised by him as he was by them.

Bernal Díaz says about the person of Moctezuma:

> The great Moctezuma was about forty years old, of good height, well proportioned and slender; he was not very dark, but of the colour natural for an Indian. He did not wear his hair long, but only long enough to cover his ears. He had few whiskers, dark and well set and sparse. His face was a little long, but pleasant, while his eyes were attractive, and he showed in his glance both affection and when necessary, seriousness. He was most clean, bathing every day, in the afternoon. He had many women, daughters of lords, and he had two high chieftains' daughters for wives. When he enjoyed himself with them, he did it so discreetly that no one knew about it except some of the servants. He was completely free from the practice of sodomy, and the clothing he put on one day he didn't use again until three or four days later.*

And of the deference towards his person on the part of subject rulers: 'And I noticed something else. When great lords came from

afar concerning disputes or other business, when they approached
Moctezuma's residence they had to come barefoot and poorly
dressed, and could not enter directly into the palace, they had to walk
round a little to the side of the gate, for it would have been considered
a mark of disrespect to enter at once.'*

The conquistadors were astonished by Moctezuma's daily fare:

His cooks prepared over thirty kinds of dishes for every meal, done the
way he liked them, and they placed small pottery braziers under them
so they wouldn't get cold. They prepared over three hundred plates of
the food Moctezuma was going to eat, and more than a thousand plates
for the guard. Sometimes Moctezuma would go with his chiefs and
stewards, who would point out to him which dish was best, and what
birds and things were in it. Then he would eat what they suggested;
but he didn't go to inspect the food often, and then only as a pastime.
. . . Every day they cooked chicken, turkey, pheasant, partridge, quail,
tame and wild duck, venison, wild pig, reed birds, pigeons, hares,
rabbits, and many varieties of birds and other things that grow in this
country, so many that it would take a long time to name them all.*

The preparations for serving his meals were as elaborate as the
repast itself:

He was served on a very low table, on which they spread white cloths
and large napkins. Four very beautiful women brought water for
washing the hands. When he began to eat, they placed in front of him
a wooden screen, richly gilded. Four leading nobles were in attendance,
and as a favour he would give to each a plate of what seemed particularly
good, which they ate standing up, and without looking him in the face.
He ended the meal with fruit, of which he ate little. He drank cacao
from cups of fine gold. Sometimes at mealtimes he was attended by
hunchbacks and jesters, while others sang and danced for his amusement; to these he would give what remained of the food and the cacao.*

Cortés himself in the main confirms these accounts in his second
letter to Charles V. He even adds the detail that the dwarfs and
hunchbacks had special quarters in the palace; certain servants were
exclusively dedicated to their service.* Cortés was particularly impressed by the fine gardens and above all by the aviaries. There were

ten special pools for marine birds of every kind. Those for birds native to the sea contained salt water. Each kind of fowl had its special diet; this included worms and fish. These favoured pets had 300 attendants; there was even a kind of bird hospital, with specialists in the art of curing their infirmities.*

Bernal Díaz, though writing in extreme old age, displays a fine memory and a keen eye for detail. However, in speaking of the character of Moctezuma, he gives the continuous impression of a rather mild-mannered man, and often talks of his kindness and gentleness. It will, however, be clearly seen in the course of this narrative, that, whatever the impression given to his Spanish captors, his basic qualities were of a different nature, and he was the reverse of kind or gentle in the treatment of his own people. The outward display had doubtless varied little since the outset of his reign and presumably originated before his time, but the qualities described by Bernal Díaz were not at all characteristic of the newly elected *tlatoani*, whose true character it is necessary to know, if we are to understand subsequent happenings.

These Spanish accounts are essential to an understanding of the life of Moctezuma, and perhaps of his immediate predecessors, but they do not tell the whole story. Students of the Conquest tend towards over-concentration on such versions, when assessing Moctezuma and the complexity of his relationship with Cortés. But the Spaniards only saw the end of the saga, and careful note needs to be taken of native accounts of his character and actions during the earlier part of his reign. If one only witnesses the final act of a drama, it is seldom easy to grasp the plot, let alone to assess the performance of individual protagonists. What the Spanish chroniclers could not fully understand was that the Conquest came as the disastrous conclusion of the eighteen-year reign of a ruler whose pattern of behaviour requires to be seen as a whole.

The Moctezuma whom we observe as the craven captive, shackled by Cortés, lies poles apart from the overweening prince who became the great *tlatoani* half a generation before. Spanish and native sources agree in stressing Moctezuma's gravity, piety and intellect, but such qualities can manifest themselves in different forms. Native versions, often also based on the stories of those who had seen Moctezuma and lived in his times, paint a different picture of the man, and of his earlier doings to that found in Spanish sources. Under different circumstances the pious can also be fanatical, the grave pitiless, and intellect becomes arrogance.

From these descriptions of the earlier Moctezuma, one gets the impression of a prince who was as hard on his subjects as upon himself; it should not be supposed from the ritual luxury that surrounded his person that he was a mere voluptuary. He was surely as moderate in his tastes as he was cautious in affairs of state, where his constant aim was consolidation rather than all-out expansion.

Moctezuma, though a seasoned campaigner, increasingly preferred to remain at the centre of things, imposing his iron will upon his subjects. But, if his approach to problems of state contrasted with that of his predecessor, he was his equal in his overbearing demeanour and in his ruthless treatment of his underlings – particularly if they had served Ahuítzotl. The difference between the two men lay in Ahuítzotl's ability to win affection and loyalty by a warm-hearted display of generosity. Moctezuma by contrast was colder and more calculating; in his treatment of inferiors almost a martinet, and in his religious zeal nearly a bigot. He is, in fact, depicted (though one might not think it to judge by later happenings) as the most feared of all the Mexican monarchs, literally striking terror into his subjects by his mania for precision and the severity of his punishments.

But if he was implacable he was also just. On one occasion he entered a garden when hunting. His fancy led him to pluck an ear of ripe maize; he then entered the house of the owner of the place, but such was the terror which his name inspired that he found it empty. Eventually the proprietor presented himself, making a deep obeisance. Then, to Moctezuma's astonishment, the man asked him how he came to bear stolen ears of maize; Moctezuma had thus broken his own laws. The ruler, taken aback by this reproof, insisted on giving as a present his mantle that by its richness was worth a whole village. The next day he sent for the owner of the garden; when the man entered his presence, trembling with fear, Moctezuma told his attendants that this was the man who had taken his garment. They were naturally indignant, but the ruler calmed them thus: 'This miserable fellow has more courage and strength than all those here present, because he dared to tell me that I had broken my laws, and he spoke the truth.'* So intent was Moctezuma upon securing the incorruptibility of his judges that it is told – perhaps apocryphally – that he actually disguised himself to watch their conduct; if any erred, they themselves incurred the death penalty.*

Moctezuma was not slow to show his hand as a ruler: 'As soon as this Lord was elected, and felt himself in the royal throne of Mexico, he wanted to make evident the grandeur of his notions, both as to what a king should possess and as to the esteem due to his person.'

He was determined to deprive many subordinates of their posts, because he wished everything to be as he desired it, and not simply as previously ordained by his predecessor. With this in mind, he sent for the Woman Snake, or Cihuacóatl. The office had become virtually hereditary, and its holder was still the second in the land, even after the death of the illustrious Tlacaélel. Moctezuma now decreed that all officials employed by his uncle were to be replaced, whether in the capital or in the provinces. He was determined to make a clean sweep: 'Because many of them [the former officials] were of low descent, and it was most unworthy that kings should employ such people; he wished to employ those of his own class; firstly to do honour to his person and secondly because, if the sons of the great lords, and of his cousins and brothers, were always at his side and in his presence, they would learn courtly language and behaviour and the art of government, in preparation for such time as this fell to their lot.'*

Particularly to be favoured were the distressed gentry, such as descendants of former rulers, now fallen upon hard times; in future, miserable commoners, whose merits had gained them knighthood, were no longer to take precedence over men of noble lineage, now consigned to poverty and oblivion.

The unfortunate Woman Snake demurred somewhat: 'Great Lord, you are wise and powerful, and certainly you are able to do all that you will; but to me it seems that this may be taken amiss, because people will judge that you wish to denigrate former monarchs by undoing their works.'*

Moctezuma, however, insisted, and the Woman Snake was compelled to conduct a search of the most fashionable quarters of Tenochtitlan, in pursuit of suitably blue-blooded recruits for the palace staff. The outstanding qualification was to be noble and of legitimate birth. No natural sons were to be admitted, including Moctezuma's own half-brothers. In particular, children of slave mothers were to be rigorously excluded, on the grounds that they inevitably displayed the baser characteristics of their maternal descent.*

Moctezuma appears to have been motivated by two fixed notions: firstly, he was haunted by the awareness of his predecessor's pre-eminence and popularity; his reaction was to remove all whose who might dare to make comparisons. Secondly, he held a belief of almost obsessional proportions in a kind of divine right of the nobility to supremacy in affairs of state: 'Because, just as precious stones appear out of place among poor and wretched ones, so those of royal blood seem ill-assorted among people of low extraction. And consequently, just as humble feathers do not look well alongside rich ones, so the plumes that came from great lords ill behove workers and their sons.'* In his meticulous new order, Moctezuma went so far as to insist on the purity of the language to be spoken in his presence – stipulating that only the *tlatoani*'s Nahuatl was to be employed. His royal commands must never be transmitted by coarse tongues.

To please his capricious sovereign, the Woman Snake, having secured a suitable posse of candidates, actually measured their stature himself. As a result he produced a hundred youths of identical height, to be trained in his master's service. When they were duly assembled, Moctezuma recognized among them the sons of many of his own relatives – apparently severed from the service of the state in the days of his predecessor, who judged men by qualities other than mere gentility.

The Woman Snake addressed those chosen in eloquent terms, instructing them to take good care of the ruler's clothes and shoes, as well as his hunting-weapons. They must also look after his mirrors, his medals and chains, and learn how to serve his meals – in the elaborate fashion later to be witnessed by his Spanish captors.* As a passing afterthought, Moctezuma ordained that those who had served Ahuítzotl should be immediately killed – so much for the kindly king, whose amiable conversation and bounteous gifts of gold so charmed Cortés and the Conquerors.

Such actions on the part of the new ruler surely suggest more than a mere expression of pique at the liberal ways of his predecessor in office. They amount to a definite step in the direction of an absolute monarchy, such as was little known in Mexico.† At the same time, they constitute a kind of counter-revolution. People of humbler origin who had risen through merit and martial prowess were actually to lose rank, being supplanted by impoverished nobles. Ahuítzotl, more accustomed to the camaraderie of the camp, had sought for talent where he could find it. Needing officials as well as warriors for his expanded empire, he had chosen some from the lower ranks of society – a tendency now sharply reversed by his more fastidious successor. That a ruler renowned for his wisdom should so defy common sense might be hard to believe, were the facts not vouched for by eyewitnesses or their immediate descendants.

As a general principle, communities tend to prosper when governed by an élite open to the talents. Moctezuma, however, was an able ruler and a skilled politician; there must, therefore, have been some method in his apparent madness. Whatever the opportunities that had been offered to other classes, the Mexican community, like most of the Ancient World, was generally ruled by an established hierarchy. If the powers of the latter were to become too rapidly diluted as the Empire expanded, the whole fabric of government might have been exposed to disintegration. As sometimes occurs even in modern Mexico, vitality in government may be secured by an alternation of progressive and conservative forces. Possibly the latter had favoured the election of Moctezuma, and he was perhaps further influenced by their relatives, the underemployed nobles, who reacted against the intrusion of new elements into the corridors of power. In particular, the nobility as a whole resented the inevitable and continuous rise in status and power of the merchant class. These had always been important in ancient Mexico, but the triumph of Aztec arms had vastly augmented their opportunities for aggrandizement.

Apparently, therefore, Moctezuma was motivated in part by personal idiosyncrasies and equally by a cold calculation of the odds. One wonders, however, if his conclusions were correct; his actions represented a check to the rising classes, including the merchants. His insistence on breeding as a passport to office might have produced a sharp reaction under succeeding rulers, had fate not intervened so unexpectedly. Unwittingly, Moctezuma was perhaps preparing the way for the assumption of authority by the Spaniards, themselves no egalitarians!

The second Moctezuma, inflexibly resolved to stand forth as equal in valour to his predecessor, led his first campaign in person. He sought not only glory for himself, but captives for his coronation. This expedition was directed towards Nopallan on the coast of Oaxaca. He found the enemy centres heavily defended and special scaling-ladders had to be made in order to force an entry. Such tactics proved successful, and once the principal city had fallen the remainder capitulated. Moctezuma took the lead in the operations, conducting the assault in person, in full battle array and decked in plumes so resplendent that he appeared to be flying, as he rushed forward against the enemy. After victory was secured, he issued a stern warning to the local rulers that any rebellion would entail their utter destruction.†

The ruler's actual coronation did not vary substantially from the already established pattern. The usual invitations were sent out, the ambassadors facing countless perils in the course of their mission. So great was the secrecy shrouding the presence of the 'enemy' rulers that even the lights were extinguished when they took part in the dancing, which lasted for four days; only large braziers were left alight to guide their footsteps.* The gifts were more splendid than ever, and the lords of the various peoples received presents each of a different type, to suit their fancy; for instance, the Tarascans were given arms and insignia decorated with golden butterflies, their wings painted blue.*

Moctezuma himself played the gracious host throughout, charming his guests by his attention to their wants:

> To these [the visiting princes] the great lord [Moctezuma] gave thanks, with a mien both serene and gay, and he received each lord separately with great courtesy, and made them sit beside him, in order of seniority, as they entered. After they were all assembled, he gave an eloquent address, because he was by nature an accomplished orator and possessed such a fine gift for words that he charmed and captivated all with

his mode of reasoning. And thus he left them feeling well rewarded and contented with his most amiable conversation.*

Nor were the sacrifices offered on a lesser scale as compared with previous occasions. In this respect, as in others, Moctezuma was resolved not to be outmatched by his predecessor – even if the chroniclers' figures of sacrificial victims need to be treated with a certain caution.† After the main ceremony was completed, the guests joined together to eat the sacred hallucinating mushrooms – still to be found in Mexico today, though condemned in uncompromising terms by Padre Durán:

> When the sacrifice was over, and the steps and courtyard of the temple were bathed in human blood, they all went from there to eat raw mushrooms; after consuming these, they lost their reason and were in a worse state than if they had imbibed much wine. So beside themselves and intoxicated were they, that many died by their own hand, and, driven by the potency of these mushrooms, they saw visions and revelations of the future, as the devil spoke to them in their drunken state.*

Ahuítzotl had accomplished great feats of conquest but, as we already know, these had not been fully assimilated or digested; many intervening areas remained unsubdued, endangering communications with the more remote provinces.

Not only Moctezuma's internal policy but also his outlook on imperial affairs, stood in sharp contrast with that of his predecessor. During his reign conquests continued, but in modified form. The general objective henceforth lay in the absorption of the free territories, interspersed between imperial tributaries, rather than in the subjection of more peoples yet more remote from the capital. The outer confines of empire resembling a skeleton in form, Moctezuma sought to add flesh to these elongated strands or bones by dominating at least some of the countless intermediate towns and villages that iay astride Aztec territory and still enjoyed a degree of independence.

One can compile a long list of places differently cited in various sources as subdued by Moctezuma II. Moreover, the frequency with which certain place-names recur throughout Mexico often renders difficult their exact identifications.* Equally, where conquests are concerned, the identity of the reign or ruler is not always clear; the lists of places which paid tribute to the Aztecs in the final stages are much fuller than those which define the conquests of each ruler. For this reason, it is possible to trace in moderate detail the maximum extension of the Aztec Empire at the arrival of Cortés, but without knowing in every case by which ruler a particular locality was first absorbed.*

It is also important to appreciate that, notwithstanding Moctezuma's policy of consolidation, certain important areas were never conquered at all. Quite apart from those principalities which, though surrounded by Aztec territory, retained their independence, single cities also existed, whose records suggest that they did not pay tribute. No doubt these might have lost their independence in the long run, but the process of total absorption remained to be completed by the Spaniards.*

Tlaxcala and other states of the same region will be discussed separately, since they are of prime importance both for the story of the Conquest, and throughout the whole reign of Moctezuma. Only second in significance was the independent principality of Tototepec, which still clung to an important stretch of the coastline of the state of Oaxaca.* Fairly ample data are available for tracing Tototepec's frontiers at the time of the Conquest – including the Codex Colombino, which was still in the possession of the descendants of the rulers of Tototepec in 1717, when the document was actually used in a law-suit over the possession of lands. Tototepec had already constituted a powerful Mixtec principality many centuries before the Aztecs appeared upon the scene.* At the time of Ahuítzotl, it was still independent and governed by its own ruler, but its sphere of influence had been progressively reduced by a series of Aztec conquests in the area. Under Moctezuma II the process was accelerated but not completed. Tototepec remained defiant until the arrival of the Spaniards.* It was left to Pedro Alvarado to achieve its complete subjection to the central power, obtaining in the process a rich haul of gold from the coffers of the unfortunate ruler.*

Farther up the Pacific coast, and immediately east of the port of Acapulco, lay another unconquered territory, that of the wild Yopis, known as Yopitzingo.* These tribesmen were distinguished more by their special devotion to the cult of the Flayed God than by the

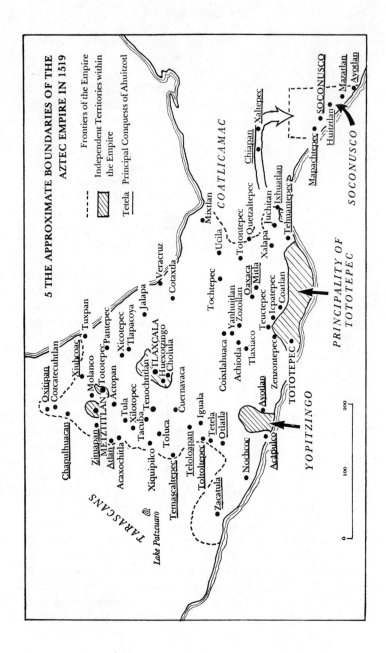

5 THE APPROXIMATE BOUNDARIES OF THE
AZTEC EMPIRE IN 1519

- - - - - Frontiers of the Empire

Independent Territories within
the Empire

Tetela Principal Conquests of Ahuitzotl

TARASCANS

Lake Patzcuaro

Chapulhuacan

Oxitlan
Cozcatecuhtlan

Xiuhcoac
Tuxpan
Molanco
Tototepec
Pantepec
Zinapan
METZTITLAN
Atlan
Acaxochitla
Actopan
Xicotepec
Tlapacoya
Jalapa
Tula
Xilotepec
Tenochtitlan
TLAXCALA
Huexozingo
Cholula
Tacuba
Veracruz
Cotaxtla
Acapulco
Xiquipilco
Toluca
Cuernavaca
Temascaltepec
Teloloapan
Iguala
Tetela
Oitlan
Tochtepec
Mixtlan
Ucila
COATLICAMAC
Totontepec
Quetzaltepec
Chiapan
Xaltepec
Toltotlepec
Zacatula
Nochco
Coixtlahuaca
Achiotla
Tlaxiaco
Yanhuitlan
Zozollan
Oaxaca
Mitla
Teuctepec
Icpatepec
Coatlan
Xalapa
Juchitan
Ishuatlan
Tehuantepec
Mapachtepec
Huitzitlan
SOCONUSCO
Mazatlan
Ayotlan
SOCONUSCO
Ayotlan
Zenzontepec
TOTOTEPEC
PRINCIPALITY OF
TOTOTEPEC
YOPITZINGO

0   100   200

cultivation of other arts.† This deity, as shown by accounts of ceremonies in his honour, was almost equally revered by the Mexica,
and the Mexican rulers even went into battle arrayed in the insignia
peculiar to him. But feelings of deference towards the Flayed God
had not deterred the Aztecs from taking the lands of his devotees.
Their free territory had been so reduced by the time of the Conquest
that they no longer constituted a serious military threat. They merely
clung to an ample stretch of rugged crags, bereft of cities, part of
which the modern traveller must cross before the road descends to
the coast at Acapulco.† These Yopis had always been a rustic race,
spurning the more civilized ways of their neighbours; the Empire
had long since absorbed such towns and cities as they had possessed,
mainly situated in the eastern part of the territory where the Yopi
tongue was spoken – and still can be heard today. Moctezuma II
had merely carried farther his predecessor's policy, actually initiated
by the first Moctezuma.†

The total number of places subdued by Moctezuma's forces was
very large; his policy, aimed at the reabsorption of the rebellious
territories and the assimilation of the free, was applied in many
directions. In the extreme north, no details survive of actual campaigns. However, in the reign of either Ahuítzotl or Moctezuma, the
frontier limits were extended, and such places as Zimapan and Oxiti-
pan were absorbed, to become themselves outposts of empire. The
Aztecs had now reached a point of no return in this northerly
direction; further conquests would have merely involved the over-
running of nomad territories, difficult to dominate and even harder
to tax. As a consequence of these new advances, the independent
principality, Metztitlan, which had held off previous Aztec assaults,
became hemmed in by imperial territory.† Metztitlan itself managed
to retain a degree of independence, though many of its former
subject pueblos now paid tribute to Moctezuma.*

Equally, towards the Gulf coast, Moctezuma pursued an active
policy of consolidation of previous gains; many cities which had
escaped the Aztec net were now added to the list of tributaries.† The
region served as a granary for Tenochtitlan and the surrounding
cities. In spite of the huge flow of tribute, there was a severe food-
shortage in the capital in 1505, and extra supplies were imported from
the Gulf coast.*

In Moctezuma's reign, however, wars were waged principally on two other fronts: firstly, the armies were locked in seemingly endless struggle with Tlaxcala and her neighbours, a conflict that will be treated separately; and, secondly, attempts were made to complete the absorption of what now constitutes the state of Oaxaca. This area, long since a favourite stamping-ground of the Mexican merchants, offered prizes more alluring than the arid north, or the implacable north-west where the Tarascans ruled.

In Oaxaca, Moctezuma's military efforts on the whole met with success, though the operation was no routine one. Hard-fought campaigns were required to subdue the proud principalities of the Mixtecs, whose historical records still survive and bear witness to many centuries of independence and greatness.

In his military undertakings against these peoples, Moctezuma did not rely mainly upon lightning incursions, often favoured by his predecessor. A process of systematic subjection was initiated in the second year of his reign, and lasted for over ten years. He first faced a rebellion threatening his lines of communication with distant Soconusco, on the Guatemalan border.† Moctezuma, himself a hardened campaigner, led the expedition in person. Apparently, on this occasion, he suffered less than his predecessor from the faint-heartedness of his imperial colleagues. On the one hand the ruler of Tacuba, newly elected, was anxious to win his spurs: Nezahualpilli of Texcoco, on the other hand, was past campaigning and efforts to secure his participation in such exertions had been abandoned.*

Moctezuma was initially accompanied by his coadjutor, the Woman Snake. On second thoughts, however, this dignitary was sent home on urgent business. He bore the rather startling instruction that he should behead all the tutors and guardians of Moctezuma's sons and the women who attended his wives. The *tlatoani* evidently feared that his *alter ego* might relent, for he dispatched additional observers to ensure that there would be no backsliding on this new domestic purge.*

As the army reached its destination, scouts were sent forward. They proceeded with great stealth, actually managing to remove kitchen utensils from the houses, and to snatch children, sleeping at their mothers' sides; these they duly delivered to Moctezuma. To teach the rebels a good lesson, the ruler – far from sparing the aged and infirm – decreed the death of all over fifty years old, on the assumption that it was they who had incited their juniors to insurrection. After returning to Tehuantepec, where he gave his daughter in marriage to the ruler, Moctezuma made a slow return to his capital that recalled the triumphs of his predecessor: 'History relates at this point that, from the time when Moctezuma left the province of Xaltepec, until he arrived at Chalco, during each day's march the princes and lords of all the neighbouring cities would come out with their people. They placed themselves on each side of the route, as in a kind of procession, and so closely packed together that nothing could pass between them.'* The crowd became so still at the passing of the great *tlatoani*, and all heads were bowed, so that it seemed that the multitude was hardly alive at all.

Moctezuma was meanwhile faced with problems involving relations with Tlatelolco, subdued by his father forty years before. He summoned the leading Tlatelolcans, and blamed them for not paying the tribute that had been imposed at that time, and for not observing the obligation to provide supplies for his wars.* They humbly complied with his demands, and as a sign of appreciation he thereupon freed them from the previous restraints, which forbade them to build their own temple; he also restored their right to fight as a separate contingent in his campaigns. The sister city of Tlatelolco was thus restored to a more equal status, though no longer enjoying the privilege of a separate reigning dynasty. A leading member of Moctezuma's council continued to act as governor.†

Moctezuma's efforts to consolidate the Aztec hold over the Oaxaca region were widely separated in distance as well as time. In 1503 he took Achiotla.* This place was one of many which had previously owed allegiance to the principality of Tototepec. It was renowned for its delicious tropical trees, and the story is told that on one occasion a small but very special tree was brought from far off to be planted in the ruler's garden. Its flowers were so exquisite and so fragrant that its fame reached the ears of Moctezuma. For him it was quite unthinkable that another ruler might own something that he did not possess, and he determined to obtain the tree, even if it perished in the colder climate of the Mexican plateau. Since the local ruler refused to hand it over, Moctezuma sent a great army against

him and killed many of his subjects; the tree also died when it was
uprooted.

But Moctezuma did not confine his ambitions in the region to the
obtaining of botanical specimens. He next proceeded to absorb
certain cities lying to the north-east of the principality of Tototepec,
the principal centre of resistance.† This campaign he again led in
person, himself directing the storming of these heavily defended
places, guarded by two rings of fortifications. To take the last of
these, Quetzaltepec, a whole battery of scaling-ladders was required.
Eventually a breach was made in the walls, through which the Aztec
forces poured; Moctezuma ordered that only women and children
should be spared.* On his return to Tenochtitlan, the pious ruler was
punctilious in performing the prescribed rituals of thanksgiving.

Further campaigns followed, directed against two important
centres, Yanhuitlan and Zozollan, where Mexican merchants had
supposedly been killed.† These places were also not far distant from
the borders of Tototepec, whose ruler lent military assistance to the
defenders, hoping thus to stem the progress of the Aztec armies
towards his own frontier. Yanhuitlan, today the site of a magnificent
sixteenth-century monastery, lies on the modern road from Mexico
City to Oaxaca, but had apparently remained unconquered by the
Aztecs up to this time. After Moctezuma's armies had taken Yanhuitlan – it appears that he himself was not present – a massacre
ensued that included old and young alike, and the devastation was
such that even the fruit trees were destroyed. The people of Zozollan,
anxious to avoid a similar fate, fled to the mountains, leaving their
city deserted.*

In 1506 yet another expedition was undertaken in the region, this
time against Teuctepec.† The city possessed excellent defences, including four lines of barricades; the inhabitants were, however,
foolish enough to emerge from the protection of their bulwarks and
to engage the Aztec armies in open combat. Not surprisingly, they
failed to deceive the latter by the device of an ambush, and suffered
a disastrous defeat, many captives being taken.

Operations, however, failed to conform to the accepted pattern;
the Mexican captains judged the actual city to be impregnable, and
retired without taking it by storm. Moctezuma, at first vexed by this
check, consoled himself when he learnt of the large number of

prisoners taken.* He arranged for their sacrifice as part of a kind of victory parade.*

Another major expedition was undertaken in 1511, when Tlaxiaco was conquered.* This place also partly derived its significance from its situation on Aztec lines of communication; the inhabitants actually had the temerity to purloin tribute sent to Tenochtitlan from distant provinces.

Moctezuma, so kindly in later years to his Spanish captors, was a man who believed that the punishment should fit the crime. He gave instructions that, if the enemy resisted strongly, half the population was to be killed; on the other hand, if they surrendered without a fight, they were to be spared, apart from the few victims that would be required for a sacrificial feast.

The Mixtecs of Tlaxiaco, guessing perhaps what lay in store, offered only token resistance, before coming to discuss details of their future liability for tribute. The prisoners met their usual fate: Moctezuma himself, after the ceremony, expressed his concern that the stone used for the gladiatorial sacrifice did not allow the prisoner sufficient room for manoeuvre in his unequal contest; accordingly, a larger platform for the purpose should be constructed.

Thus far, only the more successful military undertakings of Moctezuma have been related. Indeed, when aiming at more distant objectives, his plans were well conceived and his objectives largely achieved. There is, however, another story to be told that runs in part concurrent to the first: his reign was to be plagued by unending hostilities with the unconquered 'enemy' states of the Puebla–Tlaxcala Valley. In this direction, his efforts were dogged by failure; he provoked, but could not crush.*

This region has assumed throughout the course of Mexican history an importance almost rivalling that of the Valley of Mexico, from which it is divided by the snow-capped volcanoes of the Sierra Nevada. Any power that controlled both valleys possessed effective domination of all central Mexico. The great ceremonial centre of Teotihuacan stood astride the two; the Aztecs' immediate predecessors, the Tepanecs, were careful to maintain good relations with the realms beyond the great mountains.* In early colonial times the Spaniards founded Puebla de los Angeles, which was to play a part second only to the city of Mexico in the history of New Spain – it came to be a great cultural and religious centre, assuming the role played by neighbouring Cholula in pre-hispanic times.

As we have already insisted, Huexotzingo and not Tlaxcala had long been the leading power of this region; in addition, it of course contained other city-states, apart from Cholula, each controlling the country immediately surrounding its capital.† During the century following the foundation of Tenochtitlan, Huexotzingo, ruled in succession by three remarkable monarchs, had carved out for itself a kind of 'mini-empire', absorbing one small neighbour after another.* In the course of its period of primacy, Huexotzingo had made the fatal mistake of helping the Aztecs to crush their Tepanec masters.

Tlaxcala, owing to the part which it played in the Conquest, has achieved a more lasting fame, but it was only during the reign of Moctezuma's predecessor that this principality began to emerge as the principal power of the Puebla–Tlaxcala Valley. The Tlaxcalans had been one of the seven semi-nomad tribes who traditionally emerged from the Seven Caves, from which eastbound immigrants never ceased to flow. They passed the Sierra Nevada and established themselves in their new habitat, ostensibly at the bidding of certain fugitive Toltecs; the latter, expelled from Tula in the confusion created by the downfall of their empire, had already settled in the area.† The Tlaxcalans, like the Mexica, had followed a somewhat circuitous route to reach their promised land, and eventually established themselves on a hill situated on the opposite side of the river to the present city of Tlaxcala. From this they expelled the previous inhabitants.† The Tlaxcalans gradually multiplied and prospered, though developing on slightly different lines to the majority of their neighbours. An initial breakaway movement resulted in the foundation of a kind of sister city; later, two further centres of population were formed, and Tlaxcala became in effect not one city, but a confederation of four distinct settlements whose respective rulers formed a governing council.†

Cortés' description of the government of Tlaxcala, comparing it with the contemporary republics of Venice and Genoa, is not altogether misleading. Like the Venetian Republic, Tlaxcala was an oligarchy, and the principle of heredity was firmly entrenched among

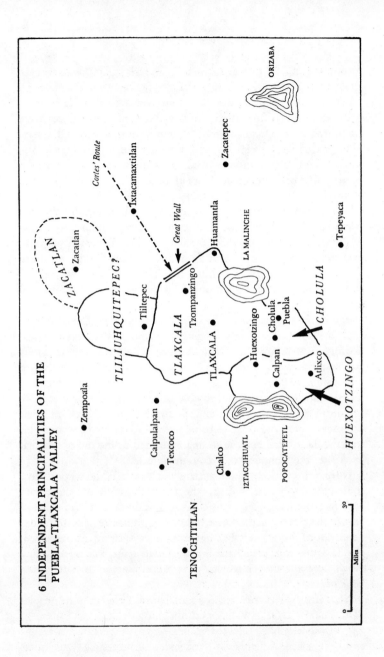

6 INDEPENDENT PRINCIPALITIES OF THE
PUEBLA-TLAXCALA VALLEY

TENOCHTITLAN

Zempoala

Calpulalpan
Texcoco

ZACATLAN
Zacatlan

TLILIUHQUITEPEC?

Cortes' Route

Ixtacamaxtitlan

Tlilepec

Great Wall

Tzompanzingo

TLAXCALA

TLAXCALA

Huamantla

LA MALINCHE

Zacatepec

ORIZABA

Chalco

IZTACCIHUATL

POPOCATEPETL

Huexotzingo

Calpan

CHOLULA

Cholula
Puebla

Atlixco

Tepeyaca

HUEXOTZINGO

0   30
Miles

its noble families.* In matters of faith, the Tlaxcalans were perhaps even less equalitarian than their foes; it was all quite simple – the nobles went to heaven and the common people to hell: 'The people of Tlaxcala believed that the souls of the lords and princes were transformed into cloud and mist, or into birds of gaudy and diverse plumage, or into precious stones of great value; on the other hand the souls of the common people became weasels, evil-smelling beetles, little beasts that emitted a fetid urine, and other low kinds of animals.'*

The Aztec drive towards the Gulf coast started under the first Moctezuma in about 1450, and caused consternation among the Tlaxcalans and their neighbours. Since time immemorial they had enjoyed trading relations with this region, on which they depended for supplies of necessities and luxuries. The principal power at this time was still Huexotzingo, though chroniclers tend to write more of Tlaxcala as if it had already taken the lead – particularly, of course, Diego Muñoz Camargo, the historian *par excellence* of Tlaxcala: 'And thus the Mexicans boldly engaged in so many encounters and skirmishes with them [the Tlaxcalans], that within a few years they were penned within their own territory. They kept them encircled for more than sixty years, lacking all human necessities, since they had no cotton for garments, no gold or silver for adornments, none of the highly prized green and multicoloured feathers for their ceremonial dress, no cacao to drink nor salt to eat.* The writer adds that the Tlaxcalans became so unaccustomed to the use of salt that even after the Conquest they consumed little.

During this period, the Tlaxcalans and their neighbours pursued a somewhat equivocal policy; they simply offered half-hearted assistance to the peoples of the coast against the Aztecs – sufficient to arouse the wrath of the latter, while inadequate to save the independence of the former. For instance, when Orizaba was attacked, the Tlaxcalans provoked the inhabitants to resist, but offered only verbal support; the Tlaxcalans were more disposed to fight to the last Orizaban.*

It has already been related how actual hostilities against the peoples of the Puebla–Tlaxcala Valley were initiated after the Great Famine of 1455. Such conflicts, directed mainly against Huexotzingo at this stage, were frequent and continued under the successive Aztec rulers who preceded Moctezuma II. According to the traditional accounts, they were of a predominantly ritual nature and were thus styled 'Wars of Flowers'. Undoubtedly this aspect was present and even paramount in such encounters at the outset, though the fighting was often bitter. The desire on both sides for a good haul of prisoners for their gods possibly at this stage outweighed ambitions to conquer.* It should be recalled that these encounters coincided with spectacular Aztec campaigns which led their armies so far afield and offered richer prizes in all other respects.

Typical of such conflicts was the war against Huexotzingo in 1499 – recounted on pages 191-2 above. It was on this occasion that the famous Toltécatl abandoned his game of pelota and, rushing virtually unarmed to the field of battle, routed the Aztecs – being rewarded for his prowess with the rulership of Huexotzingo. The War of Flowers was on the way to becoming a bed of thorns.

Whatever the previous motives of such encounters, with the accession of Moctezuma II everything changed; the flowers were cast aside and hostilities begun in earnest. Moctezuma's efforts were not to be confined to ordering the affairs of his personal staff; he was to be master in his own house in a more ample sense of the word. Defiant neighbours were no longer to be tolerated, and he would wipe from the face of the earth such recalcitrant pockets of resistance as Tlaxcala and its friends: 'His determination was to destroy Tlaxcala and lay it waste, since it was not fitting that in the government of the world the wishes and commands of more than one man should prevail; as long as Tlaxcala remained to be conquered, he could not hold himself to be Supreme Ruler of the World.'*

It was in the second year of his reign that Moctezuma resolved to conquer Tlaxcala. In 1504 war broke out in earnest and was to last intermittently until the Conquest, in which Tlaxcala itself was to play so notable a part. It began through a conflict between Tlaxcala and Huexotzingo, normally allied to each other. The latter made a deep incursion into Tlaxcalan territory, penetrating to within a few miles of Tlaxcala itself.† They were repulsed and the Tlaxcalans in their turn invaded Huexotzingo and burnt the crops. At this point Moctezuma intervened. In one of the first encounters of the ensuing struggle, the Aztec armies suffered a grave defeat. Moctezuma's wrath was now roused to its fullest extent; he assembled a vast army, but even such a force was unable to overcome the Tlaxcalan will to resist.

Not long after these events, in 1507, the Mexicans formally celebrated for the last time the New Fire ceremony, marking the commencement of a new fifty-two-year cycle. As they once again broke their pots and pans, shut in their children and pregnant women, and extinguished all fires, who would have believed that long before the new cycle ran its course they would be forced to worship new gods, and that when these events came to pass it would not be just their crockery, but the very images of their beloved deities that would be broken in pieces?

Many accounts tell of the continuation of the war against Tlaxcala, both before and after the New Fire, though it is not always easy to reconcile the different versions.* Significantly, between 1508 and 1513, on several occasions Aztec forces attacked Huexotzingo, which they had so recently rescued from Tlaxcala. Apparently, therefore, during this period, Huexotzingo again changed sides, tending to revert to its more traditional association with Tlaxcala, in opposition to the Aztec Empire.

In 1515 a new phase of the war began.* Once more Huexotzingo, again hard-pressed, and once more at war with Tlaxcala, appealed to Moctezuma for help. As a result, Aztec forces virtually occupied the territory of Huexotzingo, while many of the inhabitants, including the ruler, took refuge in Tenochtitlan. However, in various engagements with the Tlaxcalans, the Aztecs were unable to force a victory, and indecisive campaigns and even defeats followed, the news of which reduced Moctezuma to tears. In one of these hard-fought battles, the Mexicans were defeated, the majority being killed or taken prisoner, and all the leaders of the army remained in enemy hands. On the other hand, the Aztec forces succeeded in taking a mere sixty prisoners.* Moctezuma's own reaction to such a catastrophe was violent: 'How have you succumbed in this effeminate manner, that I should be shamed before all the world? To what end did so many brave lords and captains go forth, so well trained and experienced in war? Is it possible that they have forgotten how to order and reinforce their ranks, to break through any enemy? I can only believe that you have been purposely slothful, to strike a blow at myself and make fun of me.'*

But short-lived signs of royal displeasure were not enough. Strong disciplinarian that he was, Moctezuma made up his mind that his army was becoming effete. He took drastic steps to tighten discipline and to stiffen morale; he sent officials to the houses of the various captains with orders to deprive them of their insignia of rank, as well as the gifts of arms with which he had honoured them; on pain of death, they were to be forbidden to wear cotton clothing, or shoes fitting to those of high rank, and for one year they were not to enter the royal palaces. The officials, having carried out their task, returned to tell Moctezuma of the despondency caused by his orders: 'The ruler, showing no signs of regret, consigned those whom he had punished to oblivion for a whole year. And thus, they dressed like low and common people for this period, and were afflicted with great shame. At the end of the year he gave orders for hostilities against Tlaxcala, that those knights who had been penanced, if they so wished, might once more go and win back their honours.'*

The new battle proved inconclusive, but at least honour was restored, and Moctezuma himself appeared appeased. This whole episode had taken place quite shortly before the arrival of the Spaniards and served to show that Moctezuma had not yet lost his fire.

Finally, in 1518, the people of Huexotzingo were able to return to their homes; this was not due to any dazzling Aztec victory, but rather to a reconciliation between Huexotzingo and Tlaxcala. At the best of times they had been rather unwelcome guests in Tenochtitlan, owing to the commotions which they were apt to cause, including the burning of a temple.* After two disastrous flirtations with the Aztecs in the space of fifteen years, they preferred to compose their differences with the Tlaxcalans and thus were permitted to return to their homes in peace. The ruler of Huexotzingo thanked Moctezuma for his help, and went back to his own capital city.* When the Mexicans sent to invite him to a ceremony in Tenochtitlan, they found the border once more guarded.

Moctezuma's military exertions had thus served no purpose; Tlaxcala and Huexotzingo had both eluded the Aztec embrace, and the latter had now become dependent upon the former. He was, in fact, no nearer the solution of his Tlaxcalan problems than at the outset of his reign; much blood had been shed, and nothing had been achieved. Even the prisoner count had been disappointing, and the records suggest that Moctezuma lost more than he had captured.

Notwithstanding the violent nature of the battles, and the bitterness of the fighting, involving the flight of numerous refugees, the notion persists that this was perhaps after all nothing but a 'War of Flowers'. But, if native accounts were not sufficient evidence, the Spaniards, at that time ignorant of the internal politics of Mexico, bear ample witness to the hatred which the Tlaxcalans bore the Mexicans, and of their straitened circumstances, as a result of the blockade. The Aztec economic sanctions had not achieved their objective, but had reduced the Tlaxcalans to a point where, as Muñoz Camargo recalled, they lacked salt, a product most essential in the pre-hispanic economy. They were even driven to extract from their own soil a kind of synthetic salt.†

The notion that Moctezuma never seriously wanted to overthrow Tlaxcala rests upon the doubtful supposition that a great power, by the application of superior resources, can always suppress a smaller one, if it so wishes. One surely need not search far into the annals of contemporary history to find exceptions to this rule.

Admittedly Tlaxcala as a conquered province would not offer exciting prospects to the Aztec tribute-gatherer. Moreover, the inhabitants would have proved unruly subjects. It is, therefore, possible that Moctezuma was not over-anxious to annex Tlaxcala physically; by sheer weight of numbers he had sought to overcome its resistance, probably intending to reduce this enemy to the role of a satellite or subordinate.

His efforts had failed miserably. For once, as previously in the case of the Tarascans, the Aztecs encountered a people resolved to defend their independence. Faced by such valour, their big battalions achieved little. The Tlaxcalans fought all the harder for being out-numbered, having more to lose than their opponents.

Moctezuma's failure was to have a momentous effect on the future course of events. When Cortés arrived, he found the Tlaxcalans roused but not routed.

Tlatelolco, with the remains of the great pyramid which Cortés climbed, and from which the Miquihuix threw himself with his favourite dwarf. In the centre of the picture is the church of Santiago de Tlatelolco.

A close-up of part of Tízoc's stone. The stone is round, and consists of a series of portrayals of Tízoc, holding a prisoner by the hair—depicting one of his conquests.

A jaguar from the temple of the Eagle and Jaguar knights in Malinalco.

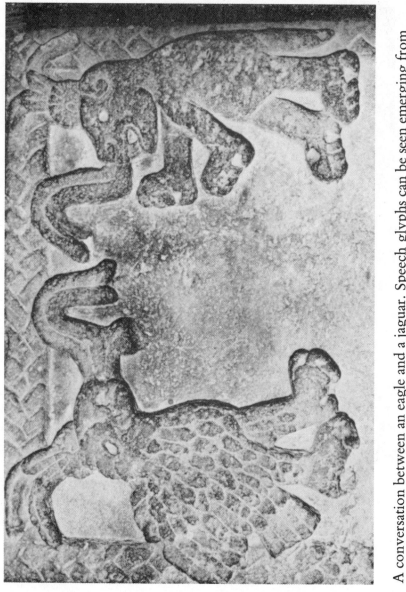

A conversation between an eagle and a jaguar. Speech glyphs can be seen emerging from their mouths.

A model of the ceremonial centre of Tenochtitlan. In the background is the Templo Mayor, surmounted by the shrines of Huitzilopochtli and Tlaloc. Immediately in front is the typical round temple of Quetzalcoatl and on the right is the tzompantli or skull-rack.

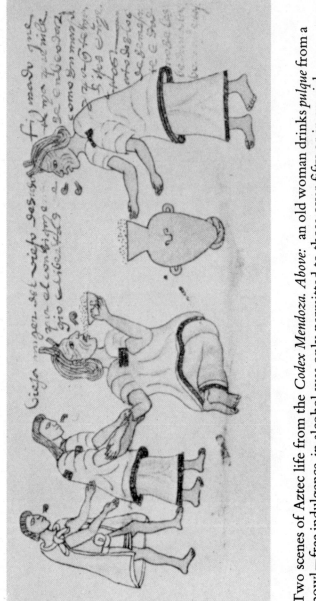

Two scenes of Aztec life from the *Codex Mendoza. Above:* an old woman drinks *pulque* from a bowl—free indulgence in alcohol was only permitted to those over fifty or in special circumstances.

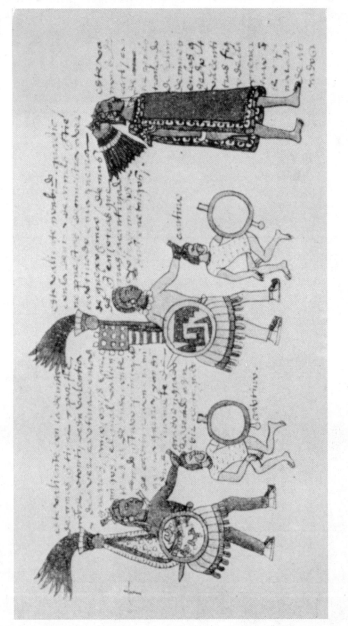

The taking of prisoners was the criterion of military success, and insignia of rank were granted according to the number of captives taken.

A view of Tenochtitlan as the Spaniards would have seen it.

The plan of Tenochtitlan traditionally attributed to
Hernan Cortés, but probably by one of his followers.
The causeways can clearly be seen.

When the Spaniards first reached the coast of Mexico it seemed to observers on the shore that 'great mountains' were moving in the sea.

The massacre of Cholula took place within the very boundaries of Quetzalcoatl's temple. Cortés' guide and translator, La Malinche, stands at the right.

The first meeting between Moctezuma II and Hernan Cortés, recorded in the *Lienzo de Tlaxcala*.

The Spaniards' retreat from Tenochtitlan, crossbows and firearms in their hands.

The 'aperriamento,' or literally 'dogging' of the Mexicans.
This codex illustration shows various forms of oppression,
from forced labour to more violent attacks.

CHAPTER EIGHT

THE SETTING SUN

MOCTEZUMA WAS A man whose faith was severe rather than serene. Long before the first Spaniards set foot in his realm, evil omens had destroyed his fragile peace of mind.

Already, ten years before Cortés' arrival, a comet was observed so bright as to turn night into day.* Moctezuma immediately summoned to his presence every available augur, astrologer and soothsayer; they merely told him that they themselves had seen no comet.

Outraged by this unhelpful attitude, he told them that they had failed in their appointed task. They were thrown into cages and allowed to die of hunger.*

Nezahualpilli of Texcoco, himself a necromancer of repute, did his best to reassure Moctezuma, telling him that there was nothing new about comets. This, however, was small consolation, particularly as he had already warned Moctezuma on a previous occasion that he would never defeat the Tlaxcalans. He now foretold worse disasters; calamities would follow which would destroy whole kingdoms.* Nezahualpilli knew he would never live to witness these happenings and he could therefore afford to take a detached attitude. Moctezuma, however, wept copiously, lamenting that such evils had to come to pass in his time:

> O Lord of all creation. O almighty gods in whose hands lies the power of life and death over mortals. How can you permit that after the passing of many powerful rulers, it should fall to my lot to witness the terrible destruction of Mexico, and that I should suffer the death of my wives and children and live to see myself dispossessed of my great kingdoms and principalities and of my vassals and of all that the Mexicans have conquered by their strong right arm and by the valour and spirit that lies within their breasts? What shall I do? Where shall I hide? Where can I seek cover? Oh, if only I could now turn to stone, or wood, or some other form of matter, before seeing that which I now await with such dread.*

Nezahualpilli's death came quite soon after this. He had of late suffered greatly from Moctezuma's arrogance, and from his determination to rule the Empire single-handed. The latter's true feelings for his allies had been demonstrated when he had permitted the flower of the Texcocan army to be slaughtered by the Tlaxcalans, as he himself watched the battle from a hilltop, like Xerxes at Salamis.*

Nezahualpilli no longer possessed either the moral or physical force with which to counter Moctezuma, and he died in 1515. It is fascinating to speculate on what might have been the reactions of this extraordinary ruler to the Spanish invasion. To judge by his later years, he would hardly have been in the vanguard of the resistance movement and would have preferred diplomacy to war.

Perhaps, however, his wise counsels might have spared Moctezuma from the deepest humiliations. He, and even Cortés, might have acted differently if Nezahualpilli had been at hand to advise and to moderate.

In the course of his varied life, he had begot no less than 145 sons and daughters. Out of all this number, however, he had named no official heir, and accordingly left his kingdom in a state of confusion. Three legitimate sons survived to claim the throne of Texcoco, and from these Moctezuma selected Cacama, the son of his own sister. So completely was Texcoco now dominated by its former partner that Moctezuma was able to impose his own choice with little difficulty.*

One of the three claimants, incensed by his rejection, offered armed resistance to his brother's election.† According to his namesake and descendant, the chronicler Ixtlilxóchitl, this prince, later to play a key role in the Conquest, as Cortés' favourite Texcocan, occupied certain of the northernmost territories controlled by Texcoco.† Possibly, however, his loyal descendant exaggerates the effectiveness of this rebellion. Nevertheless, owing to Moctezuma's intransigence, the Spanish invasion found the people of his foremost ally divided and disillusioned.

New horrors heaped themselves upon the head of Moctezuma, already hag-ridden before the first Spanish expedition reached the shores of the far-off peninsula of Yucatan. The accidental burning of the temple of the goddess Toci, owing to carelessness on the part of her priests, was taken as a fresh portent of doom; Moctezuma once more made a clean sweep of his astrologers, magicians and sorcerers. This time, he had them killed, and also decreed that their homes should be sacked and their children reduced to slavery.*

Omens now followed thick and fast. On a windless day the surface of the lagoon became as a cauldron, and waves of oceanic proportions lashed the shore, beating against the houses and shattering their foundations; women's voices wailed in the night, telling of doom and destruction. Oddest of all, hunters brought to Moctezuma a bird the size of an eagle, with a round mirror in its head; gazing into this, he could see the stars, although it was day. He also saw something more sinister: 'And, looking again at the bird's head, he saw large numbers of people, drawn up in squadrons and advancing as for war: they appeared to be half men and half deer.'* His soothsayers were able to offer no explanation and he sought consolation in the company of his dwarfs and hunchbacks.

An even stranger episode now followed. Moctezuma actually decided at this point that he wished to flee the world and take refuge with Huemac, King of the Dead. His first and second contingent of messengers entered a deep cave and reached the presence of Huemac, who dismissed them rather scathingly, remarking that Moctezuma talked of the nether regions as if life went on there just as in the world in which he lived: 'Because the inhabitants [of the underworld] are no longer as they were in the world, but different in form and manner; previously they had enjoyment, rest and contentment; now all is torment; this place is no delectable paradise, as the old refrain pretends, but a continual agony: go tell Moctezuma that if he saw this place, he would flee from sheer terror, and would even turn to stone.'†

Not surprisingly, the envoys paid for their failure with their lives. However, a third mission found Huemac in a more receptive mood. He said that Moctezuma was condemned to suffer for his pride and cruelty, and for his ruthless conduct towards his fellow men: 'Tell him [Moctezuma] that he should begin to do penance, that he should fast and give up his fine meals; and that little by little he should give up his rule and privileges: the delicate roses, flowers and carefully prepared perfumes. These things he must renounce and confine his diet to a few small loaves of meal and a spoonful of cooked beans, and that the water that he drinks must first be boiled; and that above all he must gradually separate himself from his women, and not come to them. . . .'*

Moctezuma was overjoyed and readily submitted to this rigorous and meagre diet. Eventually Huemac actually consented to a rendezvous at a place in the middle of the lagoon. But finally, instead of coming personally to console the monarch, he sent a messenger, who merely upbraided him for his cowardice.

Even if we may dismiss some of these omens as the figments of a frightened imagination, one of the strangest reports of all was based on more solid fact. A peasant came from afar on his own initiative to tell of a great mountain that he had seen moving in the sea. This seemed to Moctezuma to be the most far-fetched of all the tales he had heard, though to people accustomed only to canoes it was a natural mode of describing the first Spanish ships to be sighted. This man, too, was imprisoned for his presumption.

The report itself probably concerned the second Spanish expedition to the Mexican mainland. A previous force, led by Francisco Hernandez de Cordoba, set sail on 8 February 1517, and reached the coast of the peninsula of Yucatan at a place which they christened New Cairo (no doubt because the inhabitants were brown in colour and non-Christian). The expedition was a failure and these first Spaniards actually allowed themselves to be defeated by the inhabitants of the region of Campeche; half were killed and the rest seriously wounded. They retreated towards Florida, where Cordoba died of his wounds.

The second expedition, under Juan de Grijalva, set sail from Cuba on 1 May 1518 and reached the island of Cozumel off Yucatan in three days. When they next landed on the mainland, they found a woman who spoke the language of the natives of Jamaica; she had been one of a fishing party driven thither by the current two years before – an interesting and positive example of the possibilities of pre-Columbian navigation.* The Spaniards proceeded as far as an island that they named San Juan de Ulua, opposite the modern Veracruz, and then sailed further north as far as the River Pánuco, catching on the way their first sight of the eternal snows of the Mexican volcanoes; they now knew for sure that they were gazing at a vast country. The local inhabitants had repeated the words 'Culhua' and 'Mexico', pointing inland – hence the name Ulua, a misreading of Culhua. Lacking interpreters, they had no idea what was meant, nor were they aware that at times the people had taken them for gods.

Moctezuma's stewards or tax-gatherers of that region were quick to send back reports of such astonishing visitors.* They went to the Spanish ships in their canoes, and kissed the prow of each boat, convinced that they were greeting returning deities. They exchanged rich mantles for some glass beads, which they took to Moctezuma, saying: 'Lord, we are worthy of death, hear what we have seen and done.'* They related that they had seen gods in the midst of the sea.

Moctezuma told them to tell absolutely nothing of what had occurred. He himself informed his council and showed them the glass beads, which he described as gems. He gave instructions that they should be most carefully preserved; none were to be lost, on pain of death.

The third Spanish expedition, consisting of eleven ships under Hernán Cortés, set out on 10 February 1519, ostensibly to find Grijalva, who had not returned. The force consisted of 508 men, apart from about 100 sailors: 32 were crossbowmen and 13 musketeers, armed with the arquebus. Also included for the first time were 16 horses, as well as some bronze cannon.*

When they reached the mainland near Cape Catoche, a supreme stroke of luck befell them. A letter, accompanied by a suitable ransom of beads, was sent to Jeronimo de Aguilar and Vicente Guerrero, two Spaniards known to be living in slavery in Yucatan for some eight years, having been previously shipwrecked on that coast. Aguilar, who was overjoyed at receiving his message, managed to join Cortés, though he was in appearance and dress almost indistinguishable from an Indian. His companion Guerrero had told Aguilar that he preferred to stay where he was; he was by now looked on as a chief by his captor. Moreover, his face was tattooed and his ears were pierced – perhaps a unique example of a Spaniard virtually turned Indian.

Aguilar was invaluable, for he spoke Yucatec Maya. Moreover, soon after this, the chiefs of Tabasco, a territory situated somewhat farther to the west, were to make Cortés a present of golden diadems and masks, together with five golden ducks. As an additional item to this lavish package, twenty women were added, who were promptly baptized. One of them was to be worth far more than her weight in gold, the famous Doña Marina, known to posterity as La Malinche.† She was of royal descent, but owing to rivalries within her family had been reduced to a virtual state of slavery. She was to play an invaluable, if not commanding role, not only as Cortés' interpreter, but as his adviser on native affairs. She knew both Putun and Nahuatl; thus, by speaking in Spanish to Aguilar, who translated this into Yucatec, which Marina in turn translated into Nahuatl, Cortés would be able to communicate with Moctezuma and his subjects.

Prior to the acquisition of Doña Marina, the expedition had one of its many armed encounters with the native inhabitants of that coast. An engagement took place against a large Indian force, and a number of Spaniards were wounded.† The sight of horses and riders, at this point still taken to be one and the same animal, was enough to make the Indians turn tail; they formally submitted, after being warned that if they did not render homage to the Emperor Charles V the guns would jump out and kill them. A suitable demonstration of cannon fire was staged to show how this could be achieved.

His spies soon reported such unwonted happenings to Moctezuma; they had occurred in a region frequented by Aztec merchants, although it did not form part of the Empire. As the invasion came from the east, the ruler assumed that it was the god Quetzalcoatl who was returning, since, according to legend, he had vanished thither after the fall of Tula and the Toltec Empire. As Cortés proceeded in a north-westerly direction along the coast, more reports were received. So far no contact had been made with this expedition, but Moctezuma's observers climbed a tree and watched the Spaniards from the shore, as they fished:

Until quite late they continued to fish, and then entered a small canoe and reached the two enormous towers and climbed inside; there must have been about fifteen of them, with a kind of coloured jackets, some blue, some brown and some green and some of a dirty colour, rather ugly like our *ichtilmatl*. Some had a pinkish hue, and on their heads they had coloured pieces of cloth: these were scarlet caps, some very large and round like small maize cakes, which must have served as protection against the sun. Their flesh was very white, much more than ours, except that all wore a long beard and hair to their ears.*

Moctezuma now summoned five of his most trusted councillors and spoke as follows: 'Look, it hath been told how our Lord Quetzalcoatl has arrived; go and receive him and hear with much diligence what he may say.'* This embassy was led by a very high official.† It went provided with the most elaborate gifts; these included the traditional attire of Quetzalcoatl, and of two other gods, Tezcatlipoca and Tlaloc. Clearly Moctezuma was not altogether sure as to the true identity of Cortés. Part of the accoutrements of Quetzalcoatl consisted of a magnificent mask and shield:

> This mask was clasped into a tall and large diadem, full of rich feathers, long and beautiful, in such a way that by putting the diadem on one's head, the mask was also placed on the face: as a jewel it bore a broad round medallion of gold: it was held by nine strings of precious stones, which fell over the neck and covered the shoulders and the entire breast.
>
> They also took a large shield bordered with precious stones with golden bands from top to bottom, and with other bands of pearls that passed up and down over those of gold. And the spaces formed between these bands were like the meshes of a net, and contained little figures of toads.*

The envoys found Cortés in a place called Xicalango, to the south of the modern port of Veracruz.* They boarded the ship and kissed the deck before Cortés:

> Upon this, they adorned the Captain himself; they put upon him the turquoise mosaic serpent mask; with it went the quetzal head fan; and with it went the green stone ear plugs in the form of serpents. And they clad him in the sleeveless jacket; they put the sleeveless jacket upon him. And they put the necklace upon him: the plaited green stone neckband in the midst of which lay the golden disk. With this they bound him, on the small of his back, the mirror for the small of the back. Also with it they laid upon his back the cape named *tzitzilli*. And about the calf of the leg they placed the green stone band with the golden shells. And they gave him and placed upon his arm the shield with lines of gold and shells crossing, on whose lower rim were spread quetzal feathers and a quetzal feather flag. And before him they set obsidian sandals.†

Cortés, attired in such unusual fashion for a Spanish Hidalgo, appeared quite composed and simply asked if there was more to follow. He then caused the cannon to be fired, and the whole deputation fell to the ground as if dead. The Spaniards picked them up and tried to restore their shattered spirits with Spanish wine; the unfamiliar potion made them drunk. Cortés then defied them to individual combat with his own men. They were in no state to face such an ordeal and politely refused saying that their master had not sent them for this, and would kill them if they consented. After that, they took their leave and hurried back to Tenochtitlan, which they reached at night. Moctezuma was so ridden with anxiety that he could neither sleep nor eat, and passed the time moaning to himself, 'What will become of us?'* Captives were slain in the messengers' presence, and they were sprinkled with their blood before they told their tale: 'These ceremonies were performed because they had seen great things, and had seen the gods and spoken with them.'* Every imaginable detail was reported to Moctezuma – the Spaniards' white faces, the black countenance and curly hair of the Negroes, and even the ferocity of their dogs. Having heard all this, the monarch began to feel faint and was stricken with great anguish. The Spaniards' presents were treated with all the respect due to sacred relics. The food was put into a beautiful blue jar and taken to the main temple, where it was placed in the round stone normally used to receive human hearts (*cuauhxicalli*). Afterwards the gifts were taken to Tula and buried in the temple of Quetzalcoatl, after many quails had been sacrificed in their honour.

Moctezuma now sent a further mission to Cortés, which found him disembarked near the present-day Veracruz. The ruler was plainly in two minds about his supposedly divine visitors, since he now sent in addition sorcerers, whose spells might secure their death or departure – a treatment surely not normally to be meted out to gods. Their skills were naturally of no avail. Meanwhile Cortés had also encountered Moctezuma's stewards or tax-gatherers, stationed in this region. They actually dined with him and were treated to another exhibition of cannon fire. One of the two, called Tendile, had Cortés and his forces painted, down to the last detail, including the ships, the horses, and even the two greyhounds.*

Coincidences, sometimes almost ridiculous, continued to confound Moctezuma. Tendile had sent him a rusty Spanish helmet, rather resembling one that had reputedly been consigned by Huitzilopochtli to his chosen people – Cortés astutely took advantage of this by suggesting that the helmet be returned to him, filled with gold dust. Confronted with this relic and with news every day more alarming, Moctezuma again thought of flight to the nether regions. By now he had become totally desperate, though moments of panic were interspersed with moods of resignation: 'He did no more than simply await them [the Spaniards]. He did no more than to resolve in his heart, and to resign himself; finally he dominated his heart, withdrew into himself, and remained disposed to see and admire whatever might come to pass.'*

Tendile now returned to Cortés, bringing the helmet duly filled with gold, as well as an even more lavish assortment of gifts: 'They brought twenty ducks made of gold, very natural looking, and other beautifully cast pieces representing dogs of the kind they owned, tigers, lions and monkeys. They also brought ten necklaces of the finest workmanship, a dozen arrows with a bow and its string, and two staffs, like those of justice, five palms long, all of the finest gold.'*

At the same time Moctezuma, having seen pictures of his visitors, adopted an odd ruse. He sent with Tendile a chieftain called Quintalbor, who bore a striking resemblance to Cortés, and whom the Spaniards called 'the other Cortés'. He vainly hoped to achieve some result through magic by impersonation. He had by now received Cortés' requests to visit him; in reply he insisted that this would be highly inconvenient and begged the Spaniards to stay where they were.

Tendile, one of the first of Moctezuma's subjects to attend divine worship, expressed astonishment that the Spaniards could humble themselves before a mere piece of wood. For this he was treated to a homily by the Mercedarian friar, which probably did little but increase his bewilderment.

Moctezuma's moods were highly volatile; he tended to blow hot and cold towards the invaders, and even Cortés himself, in their voluminous exchange of messages, complained of the changing attitudes of the Mexican monarch. He simply could not make up his mind as to the identity of the Spaniards, and at one moment of doubt as to their divine nature he had the curious idea of capturing them and using them for the procreation of future sacrificial victims.*

Moctezuma had managed to impose a degree of absolutism, seldom if ever witnessed before in ancient Mexico. His conduct tended towards the capriciousness of the all-powerful; it was unheard of that any should oppose his divine will, let alone a small band of interlopers into his realm. He thus now alternated between dejection and anger. In this he was further confused by divided councils in Tenochtitlan and confounded by the opposition of the religious hierarchy to a policy of conciliation. As a result of his supreme uncertainty, the treatment accorded to the Spaniards noticeably deteriorated, as the monarch's thoughts turned from appeasement towards confrontation. One morning they awoke to find that the Indians who served them had simply disappeared.*

At this point, an entirely new factor came into play which was to have far-reaching consequences. One day on the beach, Cortés' men encountered five Indians who, though nominally subject to the Empire, were plainly hostile to its rulers. They were Totonacs, and their master was the ruler of Cempoala, a prosperous town a little farther to the north. Having now made the momentous discovery that not all Moctezuma's subjects were loyal, Cortés decided to move into the territory of his new acquaintances. On his way, he passed the present site of Veracruz. (The Villa Rica de Veracruz which he himself founded was on a small anchorage near Quiahuiztlan. This settlement did not last for long; it was first transferred to a locality a few miles to the south, still known as Villa Rica. Later it was again moved to the present site of Veracruz, opposite the island of San Juan de Ulua.)

The town of Cempoala filled the Spaniards with admiration: 'As we entered the town, and saw how much larger it was than any we had yet come across, we were stricken with admiration. The vegetation was so luxuriant and the streets were so filled with men and women who had come to see us that we thanked God for having discovered such country.'*

They were received by the ruler who, for his ample proportions, has gone down to history as the Fat Chief. He complained at length to Cortés of the treatment of his Lord and Master, Moctezuma; one of his most burning grievances being that the latter had taken away all his jewellery.* As a consolation for his loss, Cortés presented him with some Spanish clothing.* In reading of Cortés' amiable conversations with this potentate, it is worth recalling that they must have had their tedious side. Cortés' words were first put into Yucatec Maya by Aguilar; by Doña Marina they were then translated into Nahuatl, and subsequently by the Fat Chief's interpreters from Nahuatl to Totonac!

The Spaniards next proceeded to Quiahuiztlan, which they found deserted. However, on the day following their arrival, they were greeted by fifteen richly clad Indians, who begged to be excused for not having received them previously; they had been too frightened of the horses.*

Shortly thereafter, Cortés was to have his first glimpse of the Mexican imperial administration:

> While we were talking, the chiefs were informed that five Mexicans were arriving. They lost colour, trembled with fear, and hurried away to receive the newcomers. A room was decorated with branches and food was prepared, including plenty of cocoa, which is their principal drink.
>
> The five Indians passed where we were, as the houses of the chiefs were there, but they didn't speak to Cortés or to any of the rest of us and went on with an insolent and presumptuous manner. They wore richly embroidered robes and breechcloths, and their hair glistened and was so dressed that it seemed to be part of their heads. Each bore a crooked staff and carried roses. While they sniffed these, servants followed, keeping away mosquitoes. They were accompanied by the principal people of the Totonac towns, who did not leave them until the Mexicans had been shown to apartments and had eaten.*

These were the *calpixques* or tax-gatherers, who represented the imperial power in the provinces, and supervised the payment of tribute by the many peoples whom the Aztecs had subjected by conquest. To the utter astonishment of the chiefs, Cortés ordered that the five men should be seized. He actually prompted the terrified Totonacs to carry out these orders themselves. Having done so, they were then carried away by their boldness, and were eager to sacrifice the Mexicans. Cortés, exercising his customary astuteness, held them back. He went so far as to release two of the tax-gatherers, whom he sent back to Moctezuma. When the Totonacs remonstrated at his leniency, he cast the remaining three into chains and took them on board one of his ships. Thereupon they were again released and kindly treated. The imprisonment of the tax-gatherers was a fundamental step, marking the parting of the ways.

The Totonacs now became committed to a defensive alliance with the Spaniards, as the only means of saving themselves from a hideous vengeance. For the Aztecs, the Spaniards were no longer mere intruders, but hostile invaders who had suborned their subjects in an area vital to the economy of the whole Empire, which was now accordingly a victim of enemy attack.

From his handling of this and many other situations, it became clear that in Cortés the Spaniards had a leader of rare genius. It was Moctezuma's ill-luck to be confronted by a leader possessing not only the typical conquistador's virtues of physical courage and military skill, but in addition displaying a talent for diplomacy and a depth of vision and human understanding – rarely, if ever, to be encountered among the rough-hewn settlers who had poured into the islands of the Spanish Indies.

Moctezuma, his empire now faced with incipient disintegration, sent an even grander delegation, including one of his own nephews and one of his inner council of four, complaining bitterly of Cortés' attitude, and accusing him of inciting his subjects to rebellion – perhaps a rather forthright manner in which to address a god. He could not understand why Cortés remained in the house of such traitors.†

Cortés' cause had been greatly forwarded by divisions now revealing themselves within the ranks of his opponents; his ability to find friends as well as enemies among the natives of Mexico was fundamental to his success. But, just as the Spanish leader was aided by his gift for political intrigue, he was equally handicapped by an almost fanatical impetuosity in matters concerning his faith. On several occasions this tendency was to impede the successful conclusion of his venture.

At this point, a religious debate had arisen between the Spaniards and the Cempoalans. The former had meanwhile returned to Cempoala, where the Fat Chief had presented them with some women. Cortés thanked him, but insisted that they could not accept such human chattels until they became Christians, adding that it was high time that all the Cempoalans should give up their cherished idols. The leaders and priests gave the answer that the Spaniards were repeatedly to hear, until the moment when they were in a position to enforce Christianity: their own gods gave them health and sustenance, and they would therefore resist such a preposterous proposition to the last. Meanwhile, their human sacrifices continued uninterrupted.

Cortés, deeply incensed, sent fifty of his men to smash the sacred images of the Cempoalan gods: 'The words were no sooner said than fifty of us soldiers were up and smashing the idols. Some were like horrible dragons as large as calves, others were half men and half dog, of evil appearance. When they saw them this way, in pieces, the chiefs and priests wept and closed their eyes and begged for pardon, wailing that it wasn't their fault that we had broken them.'*

A church was now set up at the top of the temple, and four priests, with their matted hair now shorn, and dressed in white cloaks, were appointed to serve as acolytes! This was one of the last acts of Cortés before undertaking the arduous march inland; like the imprisonment of the stewards, it was a decisive step. From now on, not only the Aztec state, but the very church was under Spanish assault; it was from this quarter that the bitterest opposition was to be encountered. As will later be seen, a similar gesture repeated at an unfortunate moment nearly cost Cortés all his triumphs.

In many ways, he and Moctezuma were not unlike. Both were able generals and astute politicians, with a flair for ambiguous diplomatic exchanges. Both were hard-headed realists and both were religious fanatics. Cortés, however, was able to pursue a more consistent course; Moctezuma's convictions, while deep-seated, were swayed by considerations of magic and therefore liable to sudden change of direction; Cortés on the other hand, was moved by a single-minded and wholly genuine determination to win the Indians to his faith. In both protagonists, faults as well as merits were writ large. Cortés' lust for gold came second only to his zeal for the spread of Catholic Christianity; but it was his virtues rather than his vices that were to bring trouble upon his head. While one day he could have a Spanish soldier hanged for stealing two turkeys – so anxious was he to appear just to the natives – he could on other occasions go out of his way to provoke opposition by giving open vent to his horror of the Mexican gods, who for him were pure devils.

While Moctezuma vacillated, uncertain as to the very nature of his adversary, Cortés' mind was firmly made up. Come what might, he would go to Tenochtitlan and imprison Moctezuma. On 10 July, before he set out, he had already written to this effect to Charles V; at the same time he sent to the Emperor a dazzling array of gifts. As a virtual rebel from the authority of Diego Velasquez, Governor of Cuba, he could only hope to win the favour of the ever-penurious Charles by supplies of bullion. Accordingly, Cortés was resolute while Moctezuma wavered. However, on one point at least the latter's mind was also quite clear; whether human or divine, everything must be done to stop Cortés from entering his capital. With this in view, an avalanche of messengers descended upon the Spaniards as they advanced.

In the middle of August 1519, Moctezuma's intelligence service warned him that Cortés was heading inland. He had spent some five months on the coast, and now there was only one direction in which he could move – forward to Tenochtitlan and a direct confrontation with Moctezuma.

After the first day's march, he was reported to have reached Jalapa, capital of the modern state of Veracruz. The following march brought the Spaniards up to the high plateau, and from now on they were to proceed through semi-desert country, seared by freezing winds; the contrast with the fertile and balmy coastlands was extreme. Ever more alarming reports reached Tenochtitlan as the invading force gradually came nearer, greeted on their way in many towns subject to the Empire.†

At one stopping-place, Zacatlan (today Zautla), the local ruler, Olintetl, tried to impress upon Cortés the impregnability of Tenochtitlan and the might of Moctezuma. His people were even more impressed by the Spaniards, by whose appearance they were utterly astonished. On this occasion it was the greyhounds which caused the greatest sensation: one dog barked much in the night, and the inhabitants enquired of Cortés' Indian porters if they were lions or tigers. They were informed that the Spaniards took these animals along with them to kill anything that bothered them; equally the horses could run like deer, and catch anything they wished.*

The rulers of Tlaxcala were officially informed of the coming of the Spaniards by the dispatch of a letter, which they naturally were

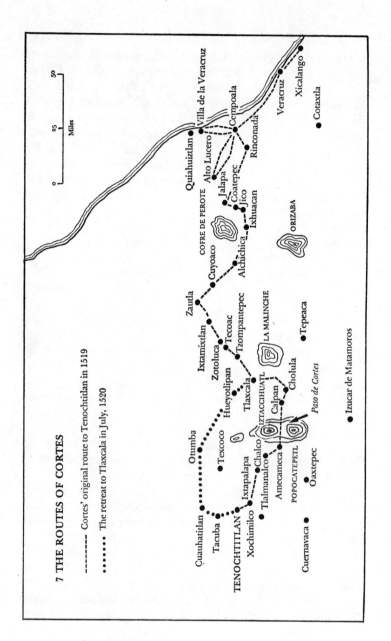

7 THE ROUTES OF CORTES

- - - - - Cortes' original route to Tenochtitlan in 1519

· · · · · · · The retreat to Tlaxcala in July, 1520

unable to read; this went accompanied with the gift of a crimson taffeta hat, a sword and a crossbow (it will be recalled that it was an ancient Mexican custom to send arms to prospective adversaries). Cortés' first sight of the frontiers of Tlaxcala was a formidable wall. The Tlaxcalan reaction was not unlike that of the Mexicans; the leaders disagreed as to how to treat the invader.* Paper charms were first tried; when they proved ineffective, armed resistance was offered and in two pitched battles the tiny Spanish force scattered a vast horde of Tlaxcalans.† One Spaniard was killed, and was buried secretly, in order not to dispel any persisting notions as to their divine nature.

After an unsuccessful night-attack – the Tlaxcalan priests had affirmed that the enemy lost all their strength in the dark – the Tlaxcalans made their peace. For the Spaniards, a relief from hostilities was most welcome; many were wounded or sick after their continuous exertions. Their erstwhile adversaries now offered a hospitality which was warm-hearted but lacking in lavish presents. They had little to give, since Moctezuma's blockade had reduced their standard of living and deprived them of luxury imports. However, they provided as best they could for Cortés' force; at first, ignorant of the fact that the horses were 'irrational beasts', they offered them the same fare as to their masters, turkeys, maize cakes and meat.*

The Aztecs now knew that a new and decisive step had been taken towards the destruction of their Empire. The new adversary from across the sea had joined forces with the old enemy from within and the continuous state of war prevailing on the high plateau between the Empire and the indomitable Tlaxcalans had proved of great assistance to Cortés.

Moctezuma was surely aghast when his spies told him of the easy Spanish triumphs over an army which had resisted his combined levies. His gifts now grew greater and his messages more frantic. He politely congratulated Cortés on his victory over his own enemies. At the same time he implored him not to come to Tenochtitlan, warning him that the way was rough and sterile; he would even pay tribute to the Spanish Emperor, if he would only agree not to proceed farther. What Moctezuma totally failed to understand was that gifts of gold only hardened the invaders' resolve to reach the founthead of such bounty. Moreover, Cortés was a man who positively thrived on opposition; the greater the obstacles placed in his way, the stronger his determination to reach his goal.* Quite apart from any political or moral consequences of victory over Tlaxcala, the military significance was immeasurable. It was now demonstrated beyond doubt that in the open field a few Spaniards could make mincemeat of any Indian host, however vast. This was to be proved time and again in many a battle, whether in Mexico or later in Peru.

At the outset, the shock caused by unfamiliar arms was clearly stunning; even in subsequent encounters, horses, guns and arquebuses were often used to good effect. It should, however, be borne in mind that later, at the very nadir of their fortunes, the Spaniards crushed the Aztecs at Otumba when they had lost all their artillery and had only twenty-three debilitated horses.* Even during part of the final operation against Tenochtitlan, cavalry could not be used.* In addition, it may be recalled that only thirteen of the original force were armed with the arquebus, at that time still a rather clumsy weapon, particularly in wet weather.*

The Spanish ability to defeat Indians was probably due more to their superiority in conventional weapons; the crossbow completely outmatched the simpler Indian bow – though it may be interesting to recall that the crossbow itself, a weapon that was slow to load, had been proved inferior to the Welsh longbow at the battle of Crécy, 173 years before the Conquest! Of even greater significance, however, was the sword, the arm of the great majority of the Spanish fighting force, which was vastly superior to the Indian weapon (*maquahuitl*), a kind of wooden club, studded with points of obsidian. The latter had to be lifted to inflict a blow, whereas the Spaniards could dispatch Indian after Indian with lightning sword-thrusts, before they could strike back with their more unwieldy arm.

Notwithstanding continuous Spanish insistence on the bravery of the Indians, their ordinary weapons appear to have been rather ineffective by European standards. One is continually struck by the high proportion of wounded among the Spaniards as compared with the relatively few who were killed in the open field. The Mexican bow and arrow seemed more able to wound than to kill the in-

vader – although he took to using native cotton armour. One is
also led to doubt of the efficacy of the Indian bow, from the constant
Spanish references to the toll taken by slings and stones – hardly a
very advanced weapon, but one which they seemed to have feared
more than Indian arrows.* Cortés himself mentions stones as among
the more effective native arms, which implies that their other weapons were not over-efficient.*

Yet another factor, decisive but hard to assess, requires to be
taken into account: Spanish superiority in tactics and morale.
Bernal Díaz, after conceding that they defeated the Tlaxcalans
principally by their swordplay (at a moment when they also had
guns and horses), relates that the Indians were often badly led; they
tended to bunch together, and their knowledge of tactics was
poor.* Initially, they were hopelessly inhibited by their obsession
with dragging away their enemies alive as sacrificial victims –
surely a most complicated manœuvre in the heat of battle. Twice
they could surely have killed Cortés himself and thus almost have
ended the war, if they had not been so intent on capturing him
alive.*

Moreover, Indian morale in battle was fragile, and depended upon
success. At the first reverse, they would lose courage, whereas the
dogged Spaniards positively thrived on adversity. The Indians were
certainly very brave fighters, but they were pitted against the greatest soldiers of the age; for a century and a half no Spanish army was
ever defeated in a pitched battle.* Moreover, they were attempting
to fight such a formidable adversary by engaging in a conflict that
was only half war, and half a process governed by ritual and magic.*
They simply did not understand the meaning of total war, as it was
conducted in sixteenth-century Europe. This is exceedingly well
illustrated in their failure to mount any truly effective resistance to
Cortés' evacuation of Tenochtitlan and later departure from Tacuba
(pages 269–70). The Spaniards, by contrast, were never to be caught
off their guard, trained as they were for a quite different kind of war.
In Tenochtitlan they were always armed and never even removed
their shoes.*

As part of their different approach to battle, the Spaniards were
more resourceful than their adversaries. Cortés' forces were able to
use the native type of lance to good effect.* The Mexicans, however,

when they captured a number of Spanish swords, would not learn to use them in the proper way. The Inca, by contrast, did try to use arquebuses in their Great Rebellion.*

The psychological superiority of the Spaniards in the battlefield was probably more decisive than any other factor, such as unknown weapons or notions of Spanish divinity. Face to face, the Indians were simply not a match for the Spaniards, however exiguous their force. It was only later, by bombarding them from the rooftops of Tenochtitlan, or from above the deep ravines in Peru, that the Indians were able to achieve a measure of success.*

Meanwhile, as Cortés cemented his alliance with the Tlaxcalans, the debate continued in Tenochtitlan as to whether to welcome the invader or fight. The leading protagonist of resistance was Cuitláhuac, Moctezuma's brother (who was later to succeed him for a brief interval as ruler). Those who favoured the admission of the Spaniards into the capital were by no means necessarily partisans of appeasement; to many it seemed easier to kill them inside the city than outside.* Such possibilities appealed particularly to the religious hierarchy.* Counsels were thus totally divided, and the poor Moctezuma could secure no firm advice.†

Cortés was by now in a most advantageous position. By his military and diplomatic successes he had the Mexicans and the Tlaxcalans competing for his favours. For once, Moctezuma instructed his messengers to beg Cortés to come to Tenochtitlan, so anxious was he to get him out of the clutches of the hated Tlaxcalans.* Moctezuma's ambassadors went so far as to indulge in a form of slanging match with the leading Tlaxcalans in Cortés' presence.*

The Spaniards had meanwhile proceeded to neighbouring Cholula, where they were well received. Cortés made one of his rather ineffective speeches, enjoining the people to renounce their gods.

But in Cholula he did not limit himself to mere exhortations. His men proceeded to massacre a great number of Cholulans in the main court of their temple.† This afforded another proof of the poor protection offered by their ancient gods. The pretext for the killing originated in an old wives' tale; an aged woman told Doña Marina of a conspiracy, instigated by Moctezuma, to surprise and kill the Spaniards. Whether such a plot ever existed remains an open question. It must, however, be admitted that it would have been consistent with Moctezuma's behaviour to instigate others, whom he could later disown, to oppose the Spaniards – just as Cortés at times urged on others into committing hostile acts against Moctezuma. He, of course, denied all complicity with the Cholulans, and exchanges between him and Cortés continued to be outwardly friendly, however much each wished to be rid of the other.

These new happenings were faithfully reported to Moctezuma, who naturally was horrorstruck that a massacre should have been perpetrated in the sacred city of Cholula in the precinct of the temple of Quetzalcoatl, the very god whom Cortés had been held to personify:

> All the road was filled with messengers, going in both directions and all the people here in Mexico and in the regions from whence the Spaniards were coming went about very alarmed and disturbed; it was as if the very earth was moving and all were filled with fear and amazement; and after the massacre in Cholula the Spaniards were coming with their Indian friends, making much clamour and throwing up clouds of dust. Their arms shone from afar and caused great fear among those who observed them: at the same time the greyhounds that they took with them inspired great terror, for they were large, with their mouths open, their tongues hanging out; as they panted, they petrified all that saw them.*

The menace drew nearer and nearer, as the Spanish force advanced, undeterred by further messengers, saying that there was no road, or no food. The tension in the Aztec capital mounted as the Spaniards proceeded between the great volcanoes (through what is still known as the Paso de Cortés). As they passed the summit, yet another large and heavily laden embassy reached them, led by a prince who resembled Moctezuma and actually pretended that he was the ruler in person. The Tlaxcalans were quick to uncover this futile ruse, and the Spaniards addressed him in rather deprecating terms: 'Do you think you can deceive us? Do you take us for imbeciles? You cannot fool us, and, whatever he may do, Moctezuma cannot hide himself, though he might be a bird, or might descend below the earth; see him we must, and hear what he has to say.'*

A further incident ensued, also verging on the ludicrous. Another deputation of sorcerers and magicians, on their way to cast spells on Cortés, met an Indian who appeared to be very drunk. By now they were ready to believe anything, and succeeded in convincing themselves that the seemingly inebriated peasant was the god Tezcatlipoca in person; to his surprise and embarrassment, they proceeded to set up an altar and prostrate themselves before him.*

The last ambassador to reach Cortés, as he drew near to Tenochtitlan, was Moctezuma's nephew, the ruler of Texcoco. 'Let us return to Moctezuma, who heard Cortés' reply and then sent a nephew named Cacamatzin, lord of Texcoco, to welcome us. He arrived in a litter embroidered with green feathers, with much silverwork and many rich stones set in the finest gold. Eight chiefs bore it, all of whom, they said, were lords of their towns.'*

The people of the thickly populated Valley of Mexico were all agog at the approach of the exotic intruders. To them, too, the scene was unfamiliar and fantastic, as they came to Ixtapalapa, guarding one of the main causeways over the lagoon leading to Tenochtitlan: 'When we saw so many cities and villages built both on the water and on dry land, and this straight, level causeway, we couldn't restrain our admiration. It was like the enchantments in the book of Amadis, because of the high towers, *cués* and other buildings, all of masonry, which rose from the water. Some of our soldiers asked if what we saw was not a dream.'*

The sheer beauty of the scene, as they surveyed the lakefront, studded with cities, did not cause the Spaniards to forget for one moment the perils which beset them. Many even feared a trap, for it was self-evident that the drawbridges which they now passed could be removed behind them.*

The climax was now to be reached, and it is Bernal Díaz who gives the best description of the scene:

When we came close to Mexico, at a place where there were other, smaller towers, Moctezuma descended from his litter while these great chiefs supported him with their arms beneath a marvellously rich canopy of green feathers, worked with gold and silver, pearls and green stones, which hung from a kind of border that was wonderful to see. He was richly dressed and wore shoes like sandals, with soles of gold covered with precious stones. The four chiefs who supported him were also richly dressed, in clothes that had apparently been held ready for them on the road, for they had not worn them when they received us. There were four other chiefs who carried the canopy and many other lords who walked before the great Moctezuma, sweeping the ground where he would pass, and putting down mats, so that he would not have to walk on the ground. None of these lords thought of looking in his face; all of them kept their eyes down, with great reverence.

When Cortés saw the great Moctezuma approaching, he jumped from his horse and they showed great respect toward each other. . . . Then Cortés gave him a necklace he had ready to hand, made of glass stones that I have already called margaritas, which have in them many designs and a variety of colours. They were strung on a golden cord and sweetly scented with musk. He placed it around Moctezuma's neck and was going to embrace him, when the princes accompanying him caught Cortés by the arm so that he could not do so, for they thought it an indignity.*

Moctezuma greeted Cortés with the following words:

Our Lord, you have wearied yourself, you have made yourself tired: now you have reached your own land. You have arrived at your city, Mexico. Here you have come to sit upon your throne and seat. Oh, for a brief span those who have already departed, your substitutes, have kept and guarded it.

The lords and kings Itzcóatl, the elder Moctezuma, Axayácatl, Tízoc, Ahuítzotl. Oh, for what a short time they protected and guarded the city of Mexico on your behalf. Beneath your frame, and under your protection the common people are now placed. . . .

No, I am not dreaming, nor am I rising heavy with sleep. I am not seeing in dreams, nor seeing visions.

I have in truth seen you and have now set eyes upon your face.

Five or ten days ago I was in anguish: my gaze was fixed towards the Region of Mystery.

And you have come between mists and clouds.

This is what was told to us by those kings, who ruled and governed your city.

That you had to install yourself in your seat and throne, that you had to come hither.

And now it has come to pass: now you have arrived, with much fatigue and toil.

Come to our land: come and repose: take possession of your royal abodes: give comfort to your body. Come to your land, O lords.*

The Spaniards were taken and settled in the spacious house that had been the palace of Moctezuma's father, Axayácatl: on their arrival they fired two cannon shots: 'And with the noise and smoke, all the Indians that were there stood as if they were mad, and walked as if drunk: they began to go in all directions in great fear, and both those present and those farther away were stricken with mortal dread.'*

Their consternation had now reached fever pitch: 'All this was as if they had eaten hallucinating mushrooms, or seen some dreadful vision. All was dominated by terror, as if all had lost heart. And when night fell, the alarm was so intense, and all were so filled with fear, that it made them unable to sleep.'*

In the end anything becomes familiar, however terrifying it may seem at first sight. Initially, no one dared to approach the Spaniards. However, at the insistence of Doña Marina, provisions were brought by tremulous Indians, who fled as soon as they had delivered their charge.*

Meeting again with Moctezuma, Cortés gave his usual homily about Christian faith and virtues, but met with an unqualified rebuff. Moctezuma's answer was unequivocal: 'Señor Malinche, I have understood what you have said to my servants about these gods and the cross, and the other things you have spoken about in the towns through which you passed. We have not answered any of it, for here we have always worshipped our own gods and hold them to be good; so must yours be. For the present do not talk about them any more.'*

Probably Cortés' words had been somewhat confused by the difficulties of interpretation, and this version of the Christian religion may not have appeared to Moctezuma as so different from his own beliefs: talk of three gods in one, of a god born by immaculate conception, and of the sacrifice of the god himself would not have seemed totally unfamiliar.† Mention of the symbolic eating of the god's flesh probably seemed suggestive of the limbs of captives, personifying Huitzilopochtli, ritually consumed at his table.

After this abortive beginning, a further exchange on the subject of religion took place. Moctezuma then took Cortés and some of the Spaniards to see the great market and temple of Tlatelolco, of which a description has already been given. After climbing to the top of the temple, Cortés again made disparaging remarks about the gods, whose images he now saw. Moctezuma once more replied that these were the deities who gave them health and good crops. He insisted that Cortés should say no more of them.* Bernal Díaz, who was present, describes the view from the lofty temple, from which all the other lakeside cities and the causeways leading to them could be seen:

> We saw the fresh water which came from Chapultepec, which supplied the city, and the bridges on the three causeways, built at certain intervals so the water could go from one part of the lake to another, and a multitude of canoes, some arriving with provisions and others leaving with merchandise. We saw that every house in this great city and in the others built on the water could be reached only by wooden drawbridges or by canoes. We saw temples built like towers and fortresses in these cities, all whitewashed. It was a sight to see. We could look down on the flat-roofed houses and other little towers and temples like fortresses along the causeways.*

The immediate course of events was to revolve around the peculiar relationship established between Cortés and Moctezuma, about which so much has already been written. Two questions have been repeatedly asked: Why did Moctezuma ever admit the Spaniards to Tenochtitlan without a fight? And, secondly, why did he then allow them to take him prisoner?

As Señor Madariaga and others have constantly and rightly emphasized, in Cortés and Moctezuma two worlds met, and two concepts totally alien one to another. In spite of certain similarities of character and a tendency on the part of both men to conceal hostile intentions beneath a mask of suavity, there were fundamental differences: Cortés' faith was not necessarily deeper or more genuine than Moctezuma's, as has been suggested, but it had the advantage of establishing an immutable goal, the conversion of the heathens at all cost. In this he never wavered. On the other hand, Moctezuma had no such clear objectives, and, as far as we know, never even tried to convert Cortés to his own beliefs.

The Mexican ruler, swayed by day-to-day prophecies and portents, was apt to act upon considerations of immediate expediency and alternated between wrath and resignation. Moctezuma's volatility of mind was made manifest in his changing views as to the identity of the Spaniards. Play has been made in innumerable accounts of Moctezuma's conviction that Cortés was the god Quetzalcoatl, as the only possible way of accounting for his seemingly cowardly and submissive attitude. Modern writers have continually placed emphasis on the suggestion that Cortés was taken for the bearded white god Quetzalcoatl, who was destined to return from the east in the year One Reed (1519).

Now, in the first place, it has to be unequivocally stated that the story of the bearded white Quetzalcoatl is a purely post-Conquest invention, and native pictorial codices give absolutely no support to such assertions. Quetzalcoatl often wears a duck-bill mask as god of the wind; when depicted without this, he either has a completely black face, or sometimes black but with a vertical yellow stripe. It is true that sometimes the deity is shown wearing a beard, but so also are many of the older Mexican gods; as a creator god, he naturally ranks among these.*

So much for the bearded white god. Even the notion of a deep-seated and ancient legend that Quetzalcoatl would return from the east in the year One Reed rests on somewhat slender foundations. This is also a story that comes to us from Hispanized chroniclers, not from earlier native accounts, and their references to the subject are moreover rather vague. Fray Motolinía, writing between 1530 and 1546, tells of a god of the wind called Quetzalcoatl, who came from Tula and who would one day return.* Fray Mendieta, writing at the end of the century, repeats the same tale, but includes the patently inaccurate detail that Quetzalcoatl was a white and bearded deity.* Alva Ixtlilxóchitl, writing even later, says much the same, but adds the refinement that he would return in the year One Reed.*

From such accounts the legend of the return of Quetzalcoatl apparently later gained substance, and finally became a commonplace, to be repeated by one commentator after another.

When, however, we turn to native sources, written in Nahuatl, we find something quite distinct. These versions are highly poetic in their language, in describing the flight of Quetzalcoatl, but quite different. In such accounts Quetzalcoatl, who in one personification was a great ruler of the Toltecs, abandoned Tula and passed by

Cholula. He then went to the 'Red and Black Land' (Tlillantlapallan) – normally taken as the Maya land, red and black being the colours of the codices, and therefore connected with learning. From thence he departed in the year One Reed, the year of his birth. According to some versions, he went away in a boat, and to others was consumed by fire and transformed into the morning star. In such form, he would have already returned frequently, long before the arrival of Cortés. But in these native accounts there is no mention of any kind of *return* of Quetzalcoatl, in the year One Reed or any other year – except for his symbolic return as the morning star.

According to a poem on the flight of Quetzalcoatl: 'It is in the Red Land, the place where you are awaited; only there is the land of your dreams. Nacxitl Topiltzin [another name for this Quetzalcoatl], never will your name perish, but for you your vassals shall weep.'*

From the Annals of Cuauhtitlan: 'They say that in the year One Reed, having arrived at the heavenly shore of the divine water [i.e. the sea], he stopped, wept, shrugged his shoulders, arranged his insignia of feathers and his green mask. Then he adorned himself, and lighted the fire and was burnt.'* The account goes on to say that he became the morning star and reappeared on the eighth day.

According to the version given to Sahagún by his native informants and transcribed in Nahuatl, after much weeping and many adventures Quetzalcoatl came to the sea-coast: 'And when he had done these things, he went to reach the sea-coast. Thereupon he fashioned a raft of serpents. When he had arranged the raft, there he placed himself, as if it were his boat. Then he set off across the sea. No one knows how he came to arrive there in Tlapallan.'*

This digression may serve to cast doubts upon the existence of any deep-seated certainty that Cortés was the returning Quetzalcoatl. It appears that what really happened is that Moctezuma, in his anguish, *deduced* that, because Quetzalcoatl had disappeared in the east, any strange being coming from that quarter must *ipso facto* be that deity. The chronicler Tezozómoc says exactly this. Moctezuma tells some of his messengers of how Quetzalcoatl had gone away to the east and adds that now 'he must have come back to enjoy what is his'.*

It must indeed be conceded that Moctezuma seems to have conceived of Cortés at certain moments as a kind of deity, even if we do not place too literal an interpretation on his welcoming address, an occasion on which it would be normal to flatter. That he was not originally sure of the nature of the returning deity is confirmed by his dispatch to Cortés, not only of the regalia of Quetzalcoatl, but also that of two other gods. Moreover, apart from doubts as to the existence of a legend of Quetzalcoatl's return in the year One Reed, it has to be remembered that the first two Spanish expeditions, of which Moctezuma was fully informed, arrived in previous years. Grijalva was also taken for Quetzalcoatl.

Although the Tlaxcalans were his enemies, Moctezuma was accurately informed of what occurred on their side of the mountains. Now, it seems highly probable that the Tlaxcalans soon became aware that Cortés and the Spaniards were only too human. The Tlaxcalan priests actually informed their leaders that the Spaniards were men, because they ate turkeys, dogs and maize cakes, and not the hearts of victims. Cortés himself went out of his way to tell them that he was a man of flesh and blood.* Equally, the Spanish gold-hunger, apparent from the moment of landing, must have helped to destroy the myth. Well before the Spaniards entered Tenochtitlan, native accounts tell of their hysterical reactions when opportunities occurred to acquire the precious metal.*

Moreover, it would have indeed been hard to explain how Cortés could have profaned the holy city of Cholula with a bloody massacre if he himself represented that deity. What occurred there was clearly regarded as a *defeat* for Quetzalcoatl, who had not protected his chosen people.* Clearly a god could not defeat himself!

If any doubts remained in Moctezuma's mind, they were surely dispelled by his first conversation with Cortés. On this occasion he actually told the latter that he could now see that they were men of bone and flesh.* It is much more feasible that he continued to think of Charles V, described to him as an all-powerful and almost legendary figure, ruling a vast realm beyond the ocean, as a kind of deity. Cortés had mentioned God and Charles V to Moctezuma almost in the same breath, asking him to offer his obedience to 'these two lords'.* Such a misconception might go far to explain Moctezuma's extreme readiness to submit his realm to Charles V at Cortés' bidding. Had Moctezuma been aware that in that very year of 1520 the seemingly godlike Charles V was in such deep trouble with his own subjects in Spain that such important cities as Toledo and Salamanca had temporarily thrown off his authority, he would have been even more greatly confused!*

The Quetzalcoatl legend is surely, therefore, in itself inadequate to explain Moctezuma's apparently pusillanimous attitude, and additional motives must be sought. Whether human or divine, he was undoubtedly afraid of the Spaniards, and might have acted as he did partly from motives of sheer fright.

It might even be worth while considering what might have occurred if the situation had been reversed and Spain had been subjected at that time to an invasion by totally unfamiliar beings using unknown weapons. Charles V was undoubtedly brave as well as astute, but one may well wonder as to his state of mind, supposing that a group of 500 men, for all he knew coming from another planet, had landed in northern Europe, equipped with, say, armoured cars and machine guns. How would he and his advisers have reacted to the news that this minute but invincible troop had obtained the submission of his subjects in the Netherlands, had totally crushed the French, whom he could defeat but never annihilate, and were now slowly advancing on Madrid, sweeping all before them?

Contrary to what is sometimes supposed, Moctezuma, like Charles V, was practical and shrewd. In his decision to admit the Spaniards to Tenochtitlan, a cool appreciation of the military situation may have carried more weight than superstitious fancy.

Already alarmed at the subversion of his important coastal provinces, he must have been shattered on learning of the ease with which the Spaniards pulverized the Tlaxcalans, who had successfully withstood the flower of his own army. If Moctezuma had demanded from his general staff a military appreciation as to whether he should admit the invaders to Tenochtitlan or fight them outside, surely on purely practical grounds the advice would have been given to lure them into the capital. The Mexican ruler was possibly less disposed than some of his critics to forget that Indian armies, however large, were no match for the Spanish force, face to face.

The Tlaxcalans, after all, had not been short of numbers, and absolutely no reason exists to suppose that the Aztecs would have fared any better in a pitched battle outside their capital than had the Tlaxcalans. This fact was later to be amply demonstrated. Moctezuma himself was aware of the limitations of his armies, when pitted against the Spaniards.* And, if prospects of victory outside the city were poor, once the enemy had entered things might be quite different. They could either be feasted into a state of heedlessness and indifference, or alternatively starved into submission. Later on, some means could surely be found to be rid of them, perhaps with the assistance of witchcraft, whose usefulness was never to be altogether discounted or divorced from practical considerations.

At this point, Moctezuma had not entirely lost his head, frightened and distraught though he was. In fact, his decision to admit the Spaniards to Tenochtitlan appears correct on purely military grounds.

On the other hand, when one considers his submission to Spanish imprisonment, it becomes impossible to argue that Moctezuma acted either rightly or wisely. The story, so often repeated, can be told briefly. The Spaniards in Tenochtitlan were naturally extremely nervous for their safety; they knew that they were now far more vulnerable than when out in the open. They had reached their goal without conquering their enemy. Thenceforth, they could not simply live in a vacuum, or admit a kind of stalemate, by remaining in the Aztec capital more as guests than victors. Some decisive move had to be made. Cortés himself pondered deeply on how to achieve this.* His captains urged him to take drastic action.* At this opportune point, events were precipitated by news of the killing of six Spaniards on the coast by subjects of Moctezuma; this gave Cortés his pretext for tackling the Mexican monarch.

Cortés and thirty Spaniards, armed to the teeth, now made their way to his palace.† The Spaniard explained that Moctezuma could only make good this injury, in supposedly ordering an attack on his men, by coming quietly to the Spanish quarters, where he would be served and honoured as in his own house. After a lengthy discussion, Moctezuma reluctantly consented, even pretending to his own followers that he was going of his own free will for a few days for his own personal amusement.† This decision was not taken before Doña Marina had issued a blunt warning that a refusal would cost Moctezuma his life.* The part which she played in the moral defeat of Moctezuma was probably very important.

Such craven compliance may seem at first sight odd, if not utterly mysterious. Again, however, one may usefully draw a reverse parallel. One wonders how Charles V would have faced up to such a group as Cortés' braves, had they entered his palace armed with modern weapons, and faced him with the alternative of death or abduction.

Comments on these strange happenings tend to harp on the suggestion that Moctezuma, with a mere nod of the head, could have had his kidnappers killed. Such an assumption is doubtful. As already emphasized, Moctezuma possessed no standing army in the strict sense of the word. Gomara tells us that the ruler had 600 lords and knights in attendance each day to guard him.* These were in essence, as in European courts at the time, retainers or attendants, not a permanent bodyguard. Now, the Spaniards had already routed great hordes of Indians in the open field, and subsequently were to take Tenochtitlan in street fighting when outnumbered by perhaps fifty to one; moreover, when Cortés later went to fight Narvaez on the coast, he felt able to leave Alvarado in the capital with only eighty men. One wonders, therefore, if it had come to a fight, just how Moctezuma's attendants could have proved a match for Spanish swords. The Spaniards could surely have stormed Moctezuma's palace, just as they later performed incredible feats of arms in taking high temples against tremendous odds. At all events, in such a skirmish, Moctezuma would have been the first to die.

His actions on this occasion appear nevertheless to have been cowardly and misguided. As an absolute monarch, he was probably nonplussed that his divine will should be so blatantly defied; what he did was to cast away his throne to save his skin. He could at least try to call the Spanish bluff. They would then have been compelled to give way, or more probably to kill the ruler and incur the immediate rage of his subjects as the assassins of a sovereign still respected and feared. Surely anything would have been better than to be peacefully abducted as a listless captive.

But only the noblest will die rather than yield, and Moctezuma was at this point too downcast to seek a hero's end; perhaps he even

failed to understand the fateful nature of his surrender. As a consequence, not he but Cortés was from now on the virtual ruler of his empire. The die was now cast, and he was committed beyond recall to the Spanish cause. Moctezuma continued to transact the business of empire from his new quarters as if nothing had happened; however, Cortés was now free to range far and wide, sending expeditions to the distant marches of the Empire in search of gold.†
Moreover, the monarch's utter subservience was soon made apparent when Cortés even had him shackled while his rebellious captains were burnt in front of his palace. Cortés himself, in a fit of generosity that he could now well afford, unlocked the fetters: 'After the burning, Cortés went with five of our captains to his quarters, and Cortés himself took off the shackles and spoke so affectionately that Moctezuma's anger quickly passed, for Cortés said that he not only regarded him as a brother, but as much dearer, and that if he could, he would make him ruler of other countries as time went on. Cortés also told him that if he wished to go to his palace, he could.'*

Needless to say, these were only fine words, and both Cortés and his captive understood perfectly well that no intention existed of releasing him. From now on a peculiar love–hate relationship was to develop between Moctezuma and Cortés and his Spaniards. The situation reached a point where some Spaniards almost came to prefer the ruler, so prodigal with his gifts, to their own commander, whose stinginess gave rise to much resentment, where the distribution of gold was concerned.*

To quote only one example of the conquistadors' affection for their prisoner, who had just offered further lavish gifts of gold: 'When we heard this, we were amazed at the goodness and liberality of Moctezuma, and with great reverence took off our helmets and expressed our thanks. With words of the greatest affection Cortés promised that he would write to His Majesty of the magnificence and freedom with which he had given us gold in his royal name.'*
The actual distribution of this munificence, however, caused further complaints among the rank-and-file Spaniards, who received little; Bernal Díaz even writes of trickery on this occasion.*

As a captive of the Spaniards, Moctezuma's subservience knew no bounds. His nephew, Cacama of Texcoco, who had actually been in favour of admitting the Spaniards to Tenochtitlan, became disgusted at the humiliation of his uncle and plotted to overthrow him, with the help of loyal elements. Moctezuma himself now betrayed his own nephew, and his henchmen kidnapped Cacama and delivered him into Cortés' hands, whence he was never to escape alive.

The Mexican ruler was now so far committed that he actually formally consented to do homage for his possessions to Charles V. He thus delivered into the hands of the invader his whole realm, without so much as firing an arrow in its defence. The ensuing ceremony was so pitiful that it even made the Spaniards weep.*

Moctezuma's courage had deserted him, but not his reason; having chosen the path of non-resistance, he pursued it to its logical conclusion. But he had not altogether given up hope, and his mood still oscillated between the sanguine and the downcast. He hoped, like Mr Micawber, that something would turn up – and, to be sure, it did!

His intelligence service was still functioning admirably and duly reported the arrival of an expedition of eighteen ships, led by Pánfilo de Narvaez, sent by the governor of Cuba to bring the rebellious Cortés to order. Narvaez actually succeeded in sending a message to Moctezuma, telling him that he had come to punish the rebel Spaniards. Moctezuma eventually told Cortés, and showed him a picture of the ships. His mood was visibly changed, and he almost recovered his spirits; he now blithely told Cortés that he could depart. The latter replied that he would have to take the Mexican monarch with him. Always mindful of his manners, Moctezuma embraced Cortés as he made his farewell, leaving Pedro Alvarado with only eighty Spaniards to guard the ruler and retain his hold on the capital.

But before he went away Cortés had made a major blunder, for which he was to pay very dearly. The Spaniards had been remarkably successful in satisfying their craving for gold, having discovered within their lodgings a vast accumulation of treasure which had belonged to Moctezuma's father, Axayácatl. The delicately wrought gold was melted down into bars, while the beautiful feathers and stones were torn off and given to the Tlaxcalans or simply cast away.

However, in achieving that other aim so dear to his heart – the conversion of Moctezuma and his subjects – progress was non-existent. He was powerless even to stop the human offerings.* He was continuously pressing Moctezuma not only to put a stop to these sacrifices, but to allow a shrine to the Virgin Mary to be placed in the main temple; one section would be quite sufficient for the purpose.* This presupposes a curious arrangement whereby the gentle Virgin and Huitzilopochtli, still avid for human sacrifice, would share the same temple!

Now Bernal Díaz tells how eventually, after warning that such a step would so incense the people as to cause an uprising, Moctezuma yielded, and the Virgin was duly installed beside the Aztec gods.† But according to nearly every account except that of Bernal Díaz, who does not mention the occurrence, Cortés went much further. Filled with genuine disgust at the practices of the ancient religion, he personally smashed certain idols. We have this firstly on his own authority: 'I cast from their thrones the principal idols, for which they have the most faith and affection.'*

Cortés, by now consumed with anger, sent for another thirty or forty men, saying he was quite ready to fight for his gods against theirs. To prove his point, he took a crowbar, and hit the image of Huitzilopochtli between the eyes, knocking off its golden mask. Eventually the other idols were taken down and handed over to Moctezuma; in their place, two altars were erected, one for the Virgin Mary and one for Saint Christopher, simply because a statue of him happened to be available. Other sources confirm these reports and suggest that it was this incident which sparked off the armed conflict.*

An eyewitness, Andrés de Tapía, confirms that Cortés hit the image of Huitzilopochtli with a crowbar: after lamenting that God should permit such devils to be honoured in Mexico, he told the assembled priests once more of the rewards of heaven and the torments of hell, and made his request that the Virgin should be given accommodation in the temple. The priests laughed, as if such a thing were inconceivable and answered: 'Not only in this city, but in all the land round about they hold these for their gods, and this is the sanctuary of Huitzilopochtli, to whom we belong; and for all the people their own parents count as nothing in comparison with him. They are ready to perish, and on seeing you come up here, they have taken up arms and wish to die for their gods.'*

However worthy the intentions of Cortés, he, too, at times could act as his own worst enemy, casting aside his accustomed political wisdom and diplomatic skill. His impetuous assault against the hated Mexican gods, just before his own departure from Tenochtitlan, created a situation from which there could be no retreat.

From henceforth the religious hierarchy, so powerful in the Aztec state and never well disposed towards the Spaniards at the best of times, became their implacable enemies; the populace, faithful to their deities, supported them. All Moctezuma's hopes of appeasement were dashed, and Cortés' own policy of bloodless conquest lay in ruins. As Moctezuma now declared, his gods were so infuriated that they wished to leave.* To prove their point, a drought ensued, and was duly attributed to the Virgin's presence in the Great Temple.*

The incident brought to a climax a problem that could no longer be ignored: the spiritual chasm dividing Spaniard and Aztec. Religion was the subject over which there could be no compromise; supple and pliant as he was in other respects, Cortés was not content to temporize, leaving conversion to be imposed after physical conquest was complete. The Aztecs on the other hand might yield their gold, their independence and even their honour, but not their gods; these they would not give up without a struggle. To seek their immediate overthrow made inevitable a war to the finish.

What was in effect a holy war was now in the making, but its mode of coming was almost incidental. Notwithstanding inferior numbers, Cortés, backing superior skill with gifts of gold, soon defeated the indolent Narvaez at Cempoala. Moctezuma's short-lived hopes of deliverance were dashed.

Far from saving Moctezuma, Narvaez' ill-starred expedition proved a godsend to his captors, whose forces were raised to a total of 1300 men.*

But, while Cortés himself now tended towards over-confidence, the impetuous Alvarado, left to his own devices in a hostile city with a mere eighty men, had grown increasingly nervous.

It was Cholula all over again. Permission had been given for the

267

celebration of an important religious festival in honour of Huit-zilopochtli. However, rightly or wrongly, an uprising was feared. Some of Sahagún's native informants must have recalled the fatal day: a great image of the god was fashioned with the dough of amaranth seed, and adorned with feathers, gold and jewels; as the worshippers danced before it, the Spaniards entered the temple court-yard: 'Then they surrounded those who danced, whereupon they went among the drums. Then they struck the arms of one who beat the drums; they severed both his hands, and afterwards struck his neck, so that his head flew off, falling far away. Then they pierced them all with iron lances, and they struck each with iron swords. Of some they slashed open the back, and then the entrails gushed out. Of some they split the head; they hacked their heads to pieces; their heads were completely cut up . . .'*

Another native source is equally graphic: 'The first whom they attacked were the old priests who played the drums, and shook the timbrels made of gourds. They cut off their hands and heads, and after that, all died. All those who sang, and those who watched, perished.'*

Certain captains had advised Cortés not to re-enter Tenochtitlan under the prevailing circumstances.* He had, however, confidently told his new recruits from Narvaez' force of his complete domina-tion over Moctezuma; he thus returned, certain that he could con-trol the situation. Moctezuma was, however, by now in quite a different frame of mind. Cortés found the markets closed and sup-plies cut off; the ruler sent a delegation of two chiefs, to whom the Spaniard gave a cutting reply: 'You dog, you won't even hold a market, or order food for us.'*

War had now begun in earnest, and in the course of a few days the Spaniards lost a total of thirty soldiers killed.* Cortés first tried to conciliate the enraged Moctezuma; he then decided that he must evacuate Tenochtitlan. His forces were by now deprived of food and drinking-water.*

The Mexicans had meanwhile cast off their renegade monarch and chosen a new *tlatoani* – Moctezuma's brother, Cuitláhuac, who had been from the outset the foremost advocate of resistance. He was a gallant prince, but after a reign of eighty days he succumbed to smallpox, now sweeping through Mexico with deadly effect, having been introduced by a Negro attached to the army of Narvaez.

The wretched Moctezuma made one last desperate attempt to stem the tide of war that he had sacrificed his honour to prevent: he stationed himself behind a battlement, and besought his former subjects to lay down their arms, promising that the Spaniards would then depart. What followed is best described by Bernal Díaz:

> . . . there was such a shower of stones and javelins that Moctezuma was hit by three stones, one on the head, another on the arm and the third on the leg, for our men who were shielding him neglected to do so for a moment. . . . They begged him to be doctored, and to eat something . . . but he wouldn't, and when we least expected it they came to say that he was dead.★

On this somewhat pathetic note ended the life of a great ruler, who at the height of his power was as highly regarded as any of his predecessors.

Bernal Díaz states that Cortés and his men wept for Moctezuma and that they ceremoniously handed the body over to the Mexicans.★ On the other hand, Sahagún's informants say that they threw out his remains, adding that, when they were ceremoniously burnt, they emitted an evil smell!★ Some sources go so far as to suggest that the Spaniards killed Moctezuma; this is less probable, for they lacked a motive.†

Having opted for flight, the Spaniards were now faced with an acute problem: how to evacuate their cherished stockpile of bullion. Finally seven wounded horses were loaded with gold and the rest was left for any man to help himself. To some, the added weight was to prove fatal. The Spaniards had previously captured four out of eight bridges leading out of the city on the Tacuba causeway. On 10 July 1519, almost exactly eight months after their entry, they left secretly at night, and reached the first of the uncaptured bridges. They found it unguarded, and crossed using a wooden contraption made for the purpose. The alert had now been given, and at the next canal crossing they met with heavy resistance, as the Mexicans attacked them from all sides: 'And when the Spaniards reached Tlaltecayoacan, there at the Tolteca canal, there they fell into what seemed a deep chasm; they filled an abyss. Those of Tlaxcala and Tliliuhquitepec tumbled in as well as the Spaniards, and the horses and some women. With them the canal was completely filled, full, clear to the banks. But those who came at the very rear, emerged and crossed over on men, on bodies.'* It was now a question of *sauve qui peut*; the minority who had escaped, including Cortés, pressed onward. There could be no going back to rescue fallen comrades.

The Mexicans had scored a magnificent success, but they had not won the war. This was their great moment of opportunity. However, they were more intent upon collecting up the booty, including every kind of Spanish weapon, than in following up the fugitives. Above all, the captured Spaniards had to be lined up for sacrifice: 'And the Spaniards they placed, each one, apart, in rows; like white reed shoots, or white maguey shoots, or white maize ears, were their bodies. And they removed each of the deer which bore men on their backs, called horses.'* They now confined themselves to following up Cortés' remnant force at a respectful distance: 'But the Mexicans harassed them, and followed, shouting war cries. They did not catch up with them, but shouted at them from afar; they only followed them at a distance.'*

Never had the Mexican inability to fight a total war, on a par with the Spaniards, been more clearly illustrated than in their moment of victory. In the first place, it was extraordinary that the enemy could make part of the journey out of Tenochtitlan (as far as the second uncaptured bridge), without so much as a sentry being posted to detect them. The alarm was finally given, not by a guard, but by a woman drawing water.* This was not the way that wars were fought and won in Europe.

Secondly, at the very time when they should have been in hot pursuit of the defeated adversary, spoils and sacrifices were paramount in their thoughts. The Spaniards had reached their lowest ebb. The survivors numbered only 440, including 12 crossbowmen, 7 musketeers and 20 horses. Their condition was deplorable, and they were all wounded. They had no guns, muskets or powder.

But, even when reduced to such straits, once allowed to rally they were invincible in the open field. In the absence of the thunder of the guns, the Indians flinched at the sight of Spanish steel, when a battle finally took place, at Otumba: 'Then the Spaniards met the people with sword thrusts. There was a great slaughter of Mexicans and Tlatelolcans.'* In this contest, Cortés and his tiny group took the offensive once more and charged straight for the point in the Aztec ranks where their resplendent chief was easily to be distinguished – none other than the incumbent of the office of Woman Snake – with his rich golden armour and huge feathered crest, worked with silver.* But glamour was no match for grit; once the leader had fallen, the attack subsided. The Mexicans had missed their great chance.

When the Tlaxcalans welcomed his weary contingent, Cortés found himself once more on friendly territory. The Tlaxcalans had, of course, awaited the outcome of the recent battle before committing themselves to the victors. It was now finally demonstrated that the divisions in Mexico ran too deep for the inhabitants to make common cause against the invader, even when he was in trouble.

Yet more significant for the final outcome was the steady flow of reinforcements which began to reach Cortés. Lured by news of his haul of gold, the first two ships arrived, each carrying a small band of armed men; a third followed shortly after, bringing a further sixty soldiers, yellow with disease. Thereafter, ships would reach Veracruz every month, each with its contingent of fortune-seekers.

A period of almost exactly nine months was now to follow, from 21 July 1520 until 21 April 1521, before the Spaniards, rested and reinforced, were ready to undertake the final siege of Tenochtitlan, which thus began over two years after Cortés had first landed in Mexico. The intervening time was occupied in mopping up the surrounding countryside, and in winning over as many as possible of the Mexicans' remaining allies. Preparations for the siege were initiated, and a beginning was made in constructing the all-important brigantines. A number of battles were fought – in all of which the capacity of an incredibly small number of Spaniards to rout uncountable hordes of Indians was repeatedly demonstrated. The welcome accorded to Cortés' contingents generally depended on the sentiments of the inhabitants towards the Aztec Empire. In certain places such as Chalco, where the Mexicans had always been hated, they were greeted as friends, and peace was soon made.* In other places, such as Coyoacan, the inhabitants preferred to avoid committing themselves to either side, and left their cities deserted. However, the suggestion, often repeated, that the Aztecs were so hated by all their subjects that they all rose at the first opportunity is inaccurate. A considerable number of places remained loyal to the Empire, and resisted the Spaniards, as Cortés himself affirms.* Detailed accounts survive of how, in the final siege, certain rulers and their subjects fought gallantly for the defenders.* Cuernavaca, for instance, the Spaniards found strongly fortified, and only with difficulty could they force an entry.* They had previously rested in the famous gardens of Oaxtepec, built by the first Moctezuma; Bernal Díaz describes them as the most beautiful that he had ever seen.* To take Xochimilco they had to fight a hard campaign, and resistance was bitter. The Spaniards burnt and destroyed the city.

Of crucial significance was the allegiance of Texcoco. It soon became clear that in seeking to subject this city to his imperious will, Moctezuma had overstrained the loyalty of his erstwhile partner. Whereas others remained true to the Aztec cause, Texcoco, which had formerly aided the Mexicans to conquer such peoples, now declared for the Spaniards. Cacama, the rebellious ruler, had lost his life in the evacuation of Tenochtitlan; his successor sought to make peace with Cortés. However, his overtures were rejected and he was blamed for the death of certain Spaniards. He fled to Tenochtitlan together with other loyal Texcocans.* Thereafter Texcoco was ruled by Don Fernando Ixtlilxóchitl, a firm partisan of Cortés.†

Spanish attitudes and tactics during such numerous expeditions underwent a marked change. In the first place, their leader had learnt his lesson; now he was apparently ready to afford temporary tolerance to native religious practices. The ritual consumption of prisoners by the Tlaxcalan allies took place almost before the Spaniards' very eyes. On one occasion, a Tlaxcalan chief playfully threw the heart of a spy into the face of a young warrior in Cortés' presence. Even if he could not conceal his distaste of such practices, Cortés had come to see the expediency of condoning them and therefore held his peace.* Secondly, now that the Spaniards were in what was often openly hostile country, their actions somewhat naturally went accompanied by a greater measure of brutality. Partly as a source of funds and partly to provide labour, they took to enslaving the population in places which resisted. The slaves were branded with a G (for *guerra*, or war); some were made to work for their captors, while others were sold at auction. Like the distribution of gold, the allotment of slaves provided a bone of contention among the conquerors. The chosen method gave rise to much grumbling; after Cortés had set aside the royal fifth, and his own fifth share, the others complained that there was not one pretty girl left; the best of them had simply disappeared.* The female slaves also had their own grievances; if they were auctioned to soldiers, who enjoyed a bad reputation for the treatment of their human chattels, they vanished and were never seen again.*

Meanwhile, in Tenochtitlan, warlike preparations, perhaps inadequate in scope, were also under way – in particular, the cutting of the causeways. Following the death of Cuitláhuac, after his reign of eighty days, Cuauhtémoc, son of the great emperor Ahuítzotl, was chosen to succeed him. Cuauhtémoc means 'descending eagle', symbolic of the setting sun. It was Cuitláhuac, rather than the youthful Cuauhtémoc, who had up to this point been the leading exponent of resistance; Cuauhtémoc had actually sought and advised the making of peace.* However, once he saw that this was unobtainable, he proved a gallant leader.

Following the Spaniards' evacuation, the initial reaction in the city had been that they had gone for good, never to return.* Certain dissensions arose in the city, and a few leaders were killed for having collaborated with the enemy. Meanwhile, a terrible smallpox epidemic inflicted its grim toll, carrying off not only the ruler but also many of his subjects. The nine months between the departure of the invader and his return proved an anxious interlude – made the more agonizing by the total inability of the Mexican forces to save the surrounding cities, some only a few miles from the capital, from being absorbed by the once-more victorious Spaniards.

On 28 April 1521, Cortés was at last ready for the siege. With the reinforcements which he had received, his force now numbered 86 horsemen, 118 musketeers and crossbowmen, and 700 soldiers armed with swords and shields, together with 15 guns. Nearly 300 of this force was required to man the brigantines.†

After equipping the brigantines, Cortés divided the remainder of his force into three roughly equal parts. The first, under Pedro de

Alvarado, was stationed at the entrance to the Tacuba causeway to Tenochtitlan; the second, commanded by Cristóbal de Olid, was posted in Coyoacan, opposite another causeway; the third, led by Gonzalo de Sandoval pitched its camp near Ixtapalapa, which guarded a third point of entry. Each contingent was supported by many thousands of native auxiliaries, mainly from Tlaxcala and Chalco.

This arrangement left the northernmost exit to the mainland open (see opposite). Very shortly, however, Olid and Sandoval, helped by the brigantines, advanced up their respective causeways and joined forces at the point where these two roads into Tenochtitlan became one. One force thus became redundant. Sandoval was relieved and sent to tackle the northern causeway, which reached the mainland at Tepeyac, where the Basilica of Guadalupe now stands.

The siege was now in its initial stage, during which the attacking force made steady progress, advancing from the causeways into the outskirts of the city. It was a ding-dong battle; the Spaniards would gain canal bridges by day, which the Mexicans occupied the following night. The attackers filled in the gaps in the causeways and the defenders promptly reopened them.

To counter this impediment, the Spaniards guarded their captured bridges at night, though such watches placed an added strain on their small force. In the forefront of the battle were the brigantines, which the Mexicans tried desperately to lure on to strategically placed stakes. They were now being used to waylay food supplies entering the city at night. However, as yet the blockade was not complete, and it must be borne in mind that a number of subject cities remained loyal.† At this point, some demolition had taken place, particularly of houses along the Tacuba causeway, but most of Tenochtitlan still stood intact.

This initial phase of the operation – so far successful – ended with a check. Cortés himself, fighting with Olid's contingent, attacking from the south, penetrated far into the city, but withdrew again, apparently considering his force insufficient to consolidate such gains; equally, the canal gaps were not adequately filled in, in spite of the presence of 10,000 allies to assist in this task, for which they were better fitted than for fighting.*

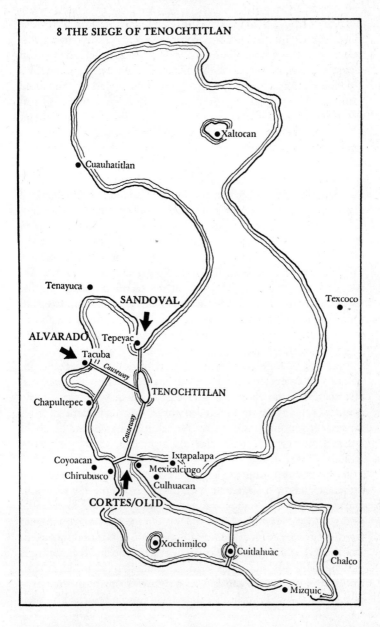

8 THE SIEGE OF TENOCHTITLAN

The ferocity of the attack was matched by the valour of the defence: 'And a number of Tlatelolcans who had quickly entered the palace which had been the home of Moctezuma then emerged in terror, and came up against the horsemen. One of them lanced a Tlatelolcan. And though he had speared him, yet he took hold firmly of the iron lance. Then his companions went to tear it from the rider's hands, threw him down upon his back and upset him. And when he had fallen tumbled to the earth, they hit him repeatedly, they struck him on the back of the head. He died there.'*

Alvarado, operating from Tacuba, now attempted the same forcing tactics, and fell into a trap. The Mexicans lured him forward and then opened a yawning gap in the causeway behind the advancing army. His small force, numbering about 180 men, was set upon from all sides and 5 men were taken alive. Had it not been for the obsession with the capture of sacrificial victims, probably far greater casualties could have been inflicted. Bernal Díaz on this occasion narrowly avoided ending his life on the sacrificial stone: 'As for myself, many Indians grappled with me, but I got my arm free, and Our Lord Jesus Christ gave me strength enough to slash with my sword so that I came out of the water safely, though I was badly wounded in one arm.'*

After this Spanish reverse, the second phase of the siege began, which was characterized by altered tactics. Cortés now realized that there was no short cut to victory and that the city simply could not be taken by a sudden thrust. He had learnt that his forces were insufficient to take Tenochtitlan by storm; he could raze it to the ground from outside, but he could not seize it from within.*

In almost any European siege operation, once the defences were breached, and the besiegers stormed the ramparts, the day was won. Such a conclusion presupposed an attacking army of comparable strength to the defenders. But, in this unique case, a great capital was besieged by a force minute in comparison with the besieged. If they forced their way into the centre, leaving behind them districts with buildings still intact, the defenders could simply surround them, bar their exit over the canals, and bombard them from the safety of their rooftops. Tenochtitlan thus could not be breached by such a force; it could only be systematically demolished. This is what now began to happen. From this point on, as the bridges were taken, the surrounding buildings were razed to the ground, with the help of native auxiliaries.* The city could thus be taken little by little by steamroller tactics, no buildings being left standing from which to assault the attackers, particularly near the causeways. Once they regained their necessary room to manœuvre, the Spaniards were again invincible.

Whatever had been their shortcomings in previous encounters, ruler, priests and people were now united to defend their city to the last. There were many feats of individual bravery: 'And when the Spaniards came, all was clear. No man of the common folk appeared. But Tzilacatzin, a great chieftain and very brave, then cast three of the stones which he carried – great, huge, round rocks: wall stones or white stones. One he had in his hand; two he bore upon his shield. Thereupon he gave chase to the Spaniards, dispersing them and scattering them in the water. Into the water they went. In truth, heavily laden on the water were the boats, as they went down into them.'* This valiant warrior further confused the enemy, as they tried every method to kill him, by adopting different disguises. On one occasion he appeared in his true guise as an Otomí warrior; on another, he would hide his identity himself by putting on a feather headdress and a wig, with a head band of two eagle-feather tufts.

So fierce was the general resistance that the Spaniards made painfully slow progress, notwithstanding the soundness of their new tactics. Cortés accordingly grew impatient, and himself fell a prey to the very rashness for which he had chided Alvarado. He actually pushed forward as far as the Great Square and sited a cannon on the stone used for the gladiatorial sacrifice.* But, once again, a fatal gap had been left in the causeway that led to safety. Well-placed stakes held off the brigantines, while squadrons of warriors and fleets of canoes fell upon the attackers, carrying off fifty-three soldiers alive.† The leader himself narrowly escaped capture:

Here is related how once again the Mexicans took captives and seized Spaniards, and, as counted, the captured Spaniards were fifty-three. . . . And when this had come to pass, then the chieftains who had been crouched, together fell upon them; they fell upon them from their ambush in the spaces among the houses. And the Spaniards, when they saw this, were as if drunk. Thereupon were captives made. . . . Truly they forced the Spaniards into the water, and indeed all the allied people. . . .

And after this, they took the captives to Yacacolco. They were urged forward; they went surrounding the captives. One went weeping; one singing; one crying war-cries while striking the mouth with the palm of the hand. And when they had been brought to Yacacolco, thereupon they were placed in rows, in files. One by one they proceeded to the small pyramid, where they were slain. First went the Spaniards.*

The Mexicans, having routed those attacking from the south, now rounded upon the Spaniards advancing from the north, who escaped with the loss of six men. Alvarado's Tacuba contingent was also subjected to heavy assault; the Mexicans threw five heads in front of his men, announcing that they had killed Cortés and would soon dispatch the remaining Spaniards.* Following this disaster, the besiegers retired to lick their wounds. To their horror, they could actually observe from the distance the sacrifice of their companions, who were driven up the temple steps, with plumes on their heads, and forced to dance before the image of Huitzilopochtli.†

Once more, the Mexicans had secured a resounding but ephemeral triumph; it was to be their last. Yet again, the fruits of victory were cast aside; at the moment when the attack might have been pressed home, more urgent matters engaged their attention – the sacrificial offerings and the victory dancing, which continued all night long.* Every evening ceremonies took place in the Great Temple, which was brilliantly lit with huge fires. But words seem to have taken precedence over action. They taunted the Spaniards, telling them that within a week none of them would be left alive; they even complained: 'To show how evil you are, even your flesh is bad to eat, for it is as bitter as gall, so bitter we can't swallow it.'*

At this moment, the outcome of the siege possibly lay in the balance; the Spaniards could not afford more losses of this nature. Many native allies, including most of the Tlaxcalans, proved to be fairweather friends, and deserted the Spaniards. Most of them left without informing Cortés. One of the faithful who remained was Don Fernando Ixtlilxóchitl of Texcoco. By an irony of history, it was an Aztec ruler who explained to Cortés how he could best defeat his own countrymen; Don Fernando told Cortés that hunger and thirst would harm the Mexicans much more than fighting.*

The siege accordingly entered its third and last phase. During the second, the policy of blockade and demolition had duly been put into effect, but had been set aside in a fit of impatience. In the third, these tactics were to be systematically applied; from this moment, the efforts of the brigantines were concentrated upon the interruption of supplies of food and water to the beleaguered city. The people were forced to eat lizards and even tanned hides; they gnawed sedum and mud bricks: 'Never had there been such suffering. It was terrifying how they were besieged; truly in great numbers they starved. And quite calmly the enemy hemmed us in and contained us.'*

Levelling operations started again, and before long the Spaniards had sufficient room to manœuvre along the streets because all the houses had been demolished.* Moreover, the causeway gaps were now being permanently filled with solid rubble, and could not be quickly reopened. A large part of the city was thus laid waste and captured. Cortés now sent to Cuauhtémoc offering peace. The messengers insisted on bearing a letter; naturally the recipients could not read such a communication, but it had become an established method of signifying that a Spanish missive was both genuine and important.

By this time the young ruler, who had fought so gallantly, was himself disposed to yield to avoid further suffering and the total destruction of the city. He summoned a council and told them that he had done all that he could; each time that he thought that the Spaniards were beaten, they turned up again, stronger than before. The Mexican allies had now finally deserted them. Only the priests, the implacable enemies of the iconoclastic Cortés, opposed surrender, and preferred to die fighting rather than submit to slavery. Their advice prevailed.*

The Mexica now stood alone. It is hard to exaggerate the forlorn courage displayed during this last stand, when the chosen of Huitzilopochtli, deserted by their friends, remained true to their god and to their traditions. One last hope remained. A famous warrior was arrayed in the quetzal-feather owl, the device of Cuauhtémoc's father, Ahuítzotl. Cuauhtémoc then spoke: 'This device was the device of my father Ahuitzotzin. Let him wear it. Let him die in it. May he gain honour before the people. May he become a portent in it. May our foes see him and marvel at him.'*

After this had been done, the second in the land, the Woman Snake, then spoke: 'O Mexicans! O Tlatelolcans! Hath Mexico been nothing – that on which Mexican rule was founded? It is said to be with the power of Huitzilopochtli, which he hurled at one. It is none other than the fire serpent, the fire drill, with which he walked, casting it at our foes – which you, O Mexicans, have held as his power of the dart. Forthwith you will aim it against our foes.'* Equipped with his hallowed weapon, armed with which the God had sprung from his mother's womb, the warrior went forth: 'And when our foes saw him, it was as if a mountain had burst. In truth all the Spaniards took fright; much did he terrify them, as if they had seen in him something inhuman.'*

But, alas, such a triumph was short-lived. The Mexican resistance was now confined to Tlatelolco, and here Alvarado's forces actually succeeded in reaching the great market-square. This was indeed the beginning of the end; Cortés, fighting a mile away, could see flames emerge from the great temple of Tlatelolco. In the last Aztec redoubt, all was anguish:

> The ways are strewn with broken lances
> Hair is scattered on all sides,
> The houses are without roofs
> Their walls are reddened.
> Worms swarm in streets and squares
> And the walls are spattered with brains.
> The waters are red, as if dyed.
> And when we drink,
> It is as if we drank liquid saltpetre.*

At last, Cuauhtémoc could hold out no more; fearful of being surrounded and captured in what remained of his capital, he made a dash for freedom. He did not get far:

It pleased our Lord God that García Holguín overtook the canoes and piraguas in which Guatemuz [Cuauhtémoc] was sailing. From the style of the man and of the awnings and the seat that he was using, he knew that it was Guatemuz, the great lord of Mexico, and signalled for them to stop. When they didn't, García Holguín pretended that he was going to fire on them with muskets and crossbows. Guatemuz was afraid and shouted, 'Don't shoot at me. I am the king of this city and they call me Guatemuz. I ask you not to disturb the things I am taking with me, or my wife or my relations; only take me to Malinche quickly.'*

The place where this event occurred can still be visited, though, needless to say, no longer by canoe. As one enters the Church of La Concepción, in the square called La Plaza de la Concepción Tequipeuca, a plaque can be seen on the wall at the right-hand side which reads as follows: 'Tequipeuhcan (the place where the slavery commenced). Here the Emperor Cuauhtemotzin was made prisoner in the afternoon of 13 August 1521.'†

Bernal Díaz gives a description of Cuauhtémoc: 'He had the appearance of a man of quality, both in features and in body. His face was somewhat large and cheerful, with eyes more grave than gay. He was twenty-six years old, and his complexion was somewhat lighter than that usual to brown Indians.'*

Cortés' initial greeting of his defeated foe was affectionate: 'When Sandoval and Holguín arrived with Guatemuz and brought him before Cortés, he embraced him with great pleasure and showed affection for him and his captains. Then Guatemuz said, "Señor Malinche, I have done what I was obliged to do in the defence of my city and my people. I can do no more. I have been brought before you by force as a prisoner. Take that dagger from your belt and kill me with it quickly." Then he wept and sobbed, and the other great lords he had brought with him wept also.'*

So ghastly was the situation in the city that Cortés gave orders that all who were able should leave: 'Let me tell you about the dead bodies. I swear that all the houses on the lake were full of heads and corpses. I have read of the destruction of Jerusalem, but I cannot believe that the massacre was greater than that of Mexico, although I cannot say for certain. The streets, squares, houses, and courts were filled with bodies so that it was almost impossible to pass. Even Cortés was sick from the stink in the nostrils.'*

The conquerors, who had themselves lived on meagre rations during the siege, could see how their adversary had suffered: 'The whole city had been dug up for roots, which they had cooked and eaten. They had even stripped the bark from some of the trees and eaten it. We found no fresh water, only salt.'*

Meanwhile the Tlaxcalan allies were permitted to exact a cruel vengeance. Cortés himself remarks in his third letter to Charles V that they dined particularly well that night on the limbs of the vanquished.* Equally to be lamented, the Tlaxcalans sacked Texcoco, burning palaces and libraries. For this they drew anguished protests from Don Fernando, the Texcocan ruler, an equally firm ally of the Spaniards.*

The victors, themselves hungry for gold, were not slow to take advantage of their triumph:

And everywhere the Spaniards were seizing and robbing the people. They sought gold; as nothing did they value the green stone, quetzal feathers, and turquoise. The gold was everywhere in the bosoms or in the skirts of the wretched women. And as for the men, it was everywhere in their breech clouts and in their mouths.

And the Spaniards seized and set apart the pretty women – those of light bodies, the fair-skinned ones. And some women, when they were about to be assaulted, covered their faces with mud and put on old, mended rags for their shifts.*

Cortés himself summoned the leaders. He demanded 200 bars of gold. They told him that most of it had gone to the bottom of the lagoon during the retreat from Tenochtitlan. They were cruelly treated for not satisfying the victors' exactions; some were even torn apart by dogs.* Acting no doubt against his better judgement, under pressure from his gold-hungry veterans, Cortés even gave orders that Cuauhtémoc's feet should be exposed to the fire, in order to extract more gold.

The struggle had been ferocious and hard-fought. At times the very issue hung in the balance: once, in the final siege, and previously when the Spaniards evacuated their capital, the Aztecs had nearly triumphed. On both occasions, true to their innate concepts of war, they had to celebrate victory when they should have been pursuing the enemy – who thus lived to fight another day.

Had the intrepid Ahuítzotl still ruled, instead of the more volatile Moctezuma, who lost his nerve at the critical moment, it is not impossible that Cortés' force might have been driven back to the coast or even into the sea. Such a victory, however, could have only proved ephemeral; it could not have altered the course of history. It might indeed have secured a few years' respite for the stricken empire, but the news of Cortés' haul of gold would have proved a magnetic attraction for ever more Spaniards, sufficient in numbers to complete the task. Nor can one suppose that the Aztecs would have profited by a temporary respite, to acquire European arms or master European tactics. During the two-year period between Cortés' first landing and the siege of Tenochtitlan, they had not learnt anything that could make them a match for the soldiers of Spain. Their resistance, however gallant, was doomed to prove futile in the end.

CHAPTER NINE

AZTEC AFTERMATH

On 13 August 1521 Tlatelolco, heroically defended by Cuauhtémoc, fell into the power of Hernán Cortés.

It was neither a triumph nor a defeat, but the painful birth of the Meztizo people that is the Mexico of today.

So reads the plaque at the side of the Great Pyramid of Tlatelolco, in the Square of the Three Cultures, where the last battles took place.

The ultimate achievement was noble, but the process long; it was to be the work of centuries.

For the present, in 1521, in the Valley of Mexico itself, the Aztec heartland, a population of about one and a half million was left face to face with 1000 Spaniards. They had little in common. Of these many Indians, perhaps the most resistant to domination were the erstwhile conquerors – who still cherished memories of former greatness, and could yet claim the proud name of Aztec, or Mexica. Later, by the end of the century, they all became simply Indians, indistinguishable one from another.

Their new master, the Conqueror, had to wait for a further year, until October 1522, before he finally learnt from the Emperor that he was legitimate ruler of New Spain, as it was now called. He bore the title of Captain-General and Governor. But official recognition, when it finally came, proved a mixed blessing. In its train came the first of a host of trusted officials of the Crown, sent to restrain the conquerors and settlers, so eager for gain and – apart from Cortés – so heedless of Indian welfare. Charles V and his predecessors, the Most Catholic Monarchs, Ferdinand and Isabella, had already learnt the bitter lesson that in the New World discovery and conquest was one thing, administration another.

Once hailed as a god, the Mexicans' new ruler was still loved as a man. His own concern for the Indians was genuine – he perhaps recalled how Moctezuma at their first meeting had greeted him as the heir to a long line of much-loved monarchs; in their turn the people accorded him their esteem. They were, however, expected to pay dearly for their conqueror's affections; later to become Marqués del Valle de Oaxaca, he carved out for himself a huge and sprawling domain, whilst some of his lesser comrades-in-arms went almost empty-handed.*

His own share of the spoils of victory was stupendous; in extensive regions of New Spain, tribute previously paid to the *tlatoani* now simply went to the 'Capitan'. Indians from the Cuernavaca province were obliged to deliver every eighty days 4800 cotton mantles, twenty rich shirts, twenty rich skirts, ten fine bedcovers, ten coarse bedcovers and ten cotton pillows; these were all listed pictorially, just as the tribute levies of the former rulers. That was only part of the payment; in addition, they had to cultivate extensive land holdings of the 'Marqués', free of charge, and supply copious livestock; they even had to provide wet nurses for his servants.*

After their downfall, the unfortunate Aztecs lived in a kind of spiritual vacuum. Without the guidance of their priests and rulers, the stern disciplines of the past collapsed; there was as yet little to take their place and men yielded to despair – or sought consolation in drink. For several years at least, no one knew for sure who ordered the universe; the old gods stood condemned, but the new had not yet made their presence felt, for want of instructors in their worship. The conquerors themselves were ill-fitted for such a task. Cortés' own homilies on the Virgin Mary had met with a stony response on the part of his audience, whether Moctezuma, the Fat Chief, or the Tlaxcalans. Where the Spaniards had destroyed temples, the Indians simply rebuilt them.*

What followed, the conversion of the Indians to the Spanish faith, though not necessarily to their way of life, may be viewed in two ways: for the Indian apologist, a unique and ancient culture was trodden under: for the Catholic evangelist, Christian civilization, thwarted by Luther in the Old World, resumed its onward march in the New.

To Cortés himself, conversion had always appeared as a solemn duty. Accordingly, he wrote to Charles V, begging that friars should be dispatched, for the purpose of saving the souls of the Indians (an argument at first arose as to whether the Indians had souls at all; this had to be settled by the Pope, who recalled the injunctions of Our Lord to the Apostles, to preach the Gospel to all the nations).

The first to arrive were three Flemish monks in 1522. Of these the leading figure was Pedro de Gante. The problems facing them were appalling: 'The common people were like animals without reason. We could not bring them into the pale or congregation of the Church, nor to the doctrine classes, nor to the sermons, without them fleeing from these things like the devil flees from the cross. For more than three years they fled like wild animals from the priests.'*

These were followed in 1524 by the famous Franciscans, the 'twelve apostles'. They walked barefooted all the way from Vera-cruz and were greeted everywhere with joy and amazement by throngs of Indians; accustomed to the proud conquerors, they were utterly baffled that Spaniards could be poor, emaciated and humble. The scene as they reached the city of Mexico was dramatic; Cortés himself was the first to kneel and seek to kiss the tattered habit of Fray Martín de Valencia: 'And when Cuauhtémoc and the other *caciques* saw Cortés kneel to kiss the friars' hands they were greatly astonished, and when they saw the friars barefoot and thin, with torn habits, and without hats, on foot and without horses, and on the other hand Cortés, whom they took for some idol or something like their gods, kneeling before them, they and all the Indians followed their example. . . .'* Seven Augustinians were to arrive in 1533, and the Dominicans, also twelve in number, in 1536.

The mendicant friars had their initial difficulties, as they vainly attempted to impart their faith by signs and gestures. Soon, however, they mastered Nahuatl, and began to win the hearts of their huge flock by their loving kindness and simple austerity. Their strict self-denial was in conformity with the stern practices and ideals of the Aztecs; the friars also believed in the mortification of the flesh, wore hair shirts, and scourged themselves.

The fallen Aztecs were fortunate that their new ruler at least cared for their welfare. However, as Governor of New Spain, he found himself in an impossible situation. He was caught between two fires: on the one hand the government of Spain or, more properly, of Castile – anxious to impose order and justice; and on the other the conquerors and settlers, out for a quick profit by the utmost exploitation of local resources, human and material. The contradictions in Cortés' own situation, and in that of New Spain, were made manifest over the pressing question of how to govern the country – and, in particular, over the system known as the *encomienda*. The term derives from the Spanish word *encomendar*, or 'to give in trust'. It had already existed in Spain as a temporary grant of rights to gather revenue. It then became, with disastrous consequences, the chosen instrument for governing Española and Cuba.

The grant of *encomienda* to a Spaniard did not in itself confer land; he was simply entrusted with the Christian welfare of a large number of Indians, from whom in return he received tribute, just as the rulers of old. Unless rigidly controlled, the system was clearly open to the grossest malpractice. It might be one thing in Spain itself, but quite another when the welfare of hordes of Indians was delivered over to a few men of alien race, apt to regard them as mere beasts of burden.*

Accordingly Charles V, determined to stop the spread of such abuses, had written to Cortés, expressly forbidding the installation in New Spain of this mode of control, already in part responsible for the decimation of his Indian subjects in Española. If Indians had been given in *encomienda*, wrote the Emperor, they were to be removed.

Now, the country had somehow to be ruled, and the Governor had no other instrument to hand for the purpose. Having initially considered that it would be fatal to introduce the *encomienda* system (except perhaps as far as he himself was concerned), he underwent a rapid conversion; when the Emperor's letter arrived, a *fait accompli* had already taken place.

Cortés simply refused to obey. He justified his failure to comply by the curious argument that the *encomienda* would protect the Indians against the very low quality of Spaniard now flocking to New Spain. The *encomenderos* had an obligation to bear arms in defence of their sovereign; if they were unable to do so royal troops would be needed. Charles V, whose finances were far less well organized than those of the late Moctezuma, could ill afford such a luxury.

Troubles now descended thick and fast upon Cortés' head. During his disastrous expedition to Honduras, intrigue was rife in the newly founded capital. To the delight of would-be successors to his honours and emoluments, he was actually reported dead, and a mass was said for his soul in the church of the Monastery of San Francisco. Cuauhtémoc was compelled to accompany his master on this ill-fated adventure, together with eight grooms, two falconers, five musicians, two jugglers and three muleteers, in addition to a herd of swine, as a living larder; things had changed since the Conquest. During the long march, on the pretext of an alleged plot, Cortés ordered Cuauhtémoc and the *cacique* of Tacuba to be hanged. According to native sources, Cuauhtémoc was the victim of mere calumny.* One wonders why Doña Marina, still acting as interpreter, could not, had she wished, have ascertained the real truth. Before the former ruler was hanged, he exclaimed: 'O Malinche, for many days I have understood that you would condemn me to this death, and have known your false words, for you kill me unjustly. . . .' Bernal

Díaz continues: 'And before they hanged them, the Franciscan friars confessed them; and truly I felt great pity for Cuauhtémoc and his cousin, having held them for great lords, and still during the march they honoured me with the things which they offered, particularly in giving me some Indians to bring grass for my horse. And their death was very unjust and made a bad impression on all present.'*

Cortés returned to the city of Mexico in 1526, to be confronted by an official, armed with full powers, known as a Juez de Residencia. This new watchdog of the Spanish government, Luis Ponce de León, died shortly thereafter. He had assigned his powers to Marcos de Aguilar, an old man who kept himself alive by sucking milk from a woman's breast; he was in such a weak state of health that power was for the present retained by Cortés.

As a next step, the Council of the Indies in Seville, stricken with an apparent fit of madness, vested the government of New Spain in the First Audience, headed by the infamous Nuño de Guzman. Two of the four members of the Audience died of pneumonia; the remaining two, together with Guzman, settled in the house of Cortés, still Captain-General, but exiled from the city of Mexico by Estrada (who had temporarily held the govenorship) before the arrival of the Audience.

Guzman's principal aim was to enrich himself and to ruin Cortés. He found a staunch adversary in Bishop Zumarraga, bishop-elect of Mexico, and officially appointed as protector of the Indians, a rather imprecise title, previously held by Bishop Las Casas. Zumarraga succeeded in smuggling a letter to Seville via Veracruz, recounting the enormities of the members of the Audience; meanwhile Cortés himself, in 1528, had left for Spain.

Once the Crown became aware of what was happening, the First Audience was replaced by the Second, composed this time of men of integrity and standing. These in their turn were followed by the first Viceroy, Don Antonio de Mendoza, former Ambassador to Hungary, and a member of one of the great families of Spain. His coming was delayed for five whole years, while he argued about his future emoluments. Finally, in November 1535, he arrived and was received with joyous celebrations.

The relations between Cortés, returned to New Spain, and Mendoza, were not slow to deteriorate. In 1542, Cortés adopted the somewhat undignified procedure of drawing up a petition against the Viceroy, summing up his numerous grievances. He retired once more to Spain, and died in 1547, after taking part in Charles V's unsuccessful siege of Algiers. His bones now lie buried in the left-hand part of the altar of the Church of the Hospital of Jesus in the city of Mexico. The title of Marqués del Valle de Oaxaca, which he bore, still survives, and belongs to a direct descendant of the Conqueror, who also holds the Sicilian Dukedom of Terranova and Monteleone.

It is of equal interest that Moctezuma can still boast of a direct descendant in Spain – though none are known in Mexico – in the person of the Fourth Duke of Moctezuma of Tultengo, who succeeded to the title in 1956; it was upgraded to a dukedom in 1864. The present ducal family is descended from Don Pedro Moctezuma, the eleventh son of the *tlatoani*.† Moctezuma II was, moreover, not the last of his name to rule; his descendant, Don José Sanmiento y Valladeros, Conde de Moctezuma y Tula, was viceroy from 1696 until 1701.

The fate of the common people depended primarily upon the institutions and laws by which they were governed – and about which a few words are therefore necessary.

In most respects Spanish rule in North and Central America came simply as the successor state of the Aztec Empire – with the major difference that policy was now determined, not in the central metropolis of Tenochtitlan but at a vast distance from Mexico and by men basically well intentioned, but often ill advised.

As we have seen, the Spanish Crown had initially been forced to yield to a *fait accompli*, and to give temporary tolerance to the *encomienda* system. In the mid-1550s, 130 *encomenderos* in the Valley of Mexico controlled some 180,000 Indians.* As Professor Gibson has pointed out, the record of the first generation of *encomenderos* was one of generalized abuse and particular atrocities.* Unlike the previous rulers, these privileged few, whose attitude to the Indian was conditioned by their experiences in Española, cared little for those with whose welfare they were charged, and in most cases received their tribute without ever seeing them.

Bishop Las Casas waxes eloquent on the abuses of this system, the chief target for his crusade on behalf of the Indians. He reports that one *encomendero*, entrusted with the Christian welfare of many souls, did not know how to sign his own name, or even how to cross himself. Another, after his Indians had delivered up their idols to the friars, secured some more from elsewhere and sold them to the same natives – proving perhaps that the trade in pre-Hispanic relics is older than one sometimes thinks!*

In the early 1530s the Spanish Government began to appoint salaried royal officials, known as *corregidores*, to reside in the principal towns and take over the duties of the *encomenderos*. The powers of the latter were definitely on the wane twenty years later, as the new system developed.* By 1570, some *encomiendas* still survived, but under stricter control, and the victory of the Crown was by then almost complete.

From the native point of view, the change to the *corregidores* was, in theory at least, for the better; however, the improvement was somewhat relative. The Indians were an easy target for abuse, and according to some reports the *corregidores* treated them even worse than the *encomenderos*; they tended to use their office for personal gain and, as royal officials, were difficult to punish for illegal acts.* Moreover, whatever the system of rule, exactions had to continue: the same methods continued in force, to provide funds for Spain's European wars.*

The Spanish Crown and the Council of the Indies, in seeking to provide for the good government of their glittering new possessions, were victims of a kind of tug-of-war between conflicting interests.

On the one hand, prodded at home by the indefatigable and formidable Bishop Las Casas, and in New Spain by the orders of Mendicant Friars, quick to attack any abuse, they issued a stream of humanitarian legislation, such as has seldom if ever been matched in the course of colonial history. And even if the effects were sometimes negligible no one could accuse the Spanish Government of any but the best intentions.

On the other hand, pressed with the necessity of obtaining money, to support the boundless dynastic ambitions of the Hapsburgs, they were often obliged to countenance the actions of those who governed on the spot, and who regarded many of these edicts as merely utopian. The settlers were certainly not prepared to work with their own hands, and could not have existed, let alone prospered, without some form of Indian forced labour, on which even the Church partly depended. Failing bounteous material rewards, the Spaniards would simply have abandoned an ailing colony – and the Conquest might as well never have taken place at all.

But if the surviving Aztecs looked on the average Spaniard as an enemy, they also possessed friends. Never before in history can an alien conqueror have produced such an array of scholars and saints to espouse the cause of the vanquished. Foremost among these, for sheer tenacity if for nothing else, was Bishop Las Casas. He had lived in Española from 1502 until 1512, and had himself held an *encomienda*; he relented and became a Dominican Friar. Henceforth, for fifty years, his life was one unceasing struggle on behalf of the Indians. For Las Casas, in accordance with the Papal Bull of 1493, the Spaniards were entitled to claim temporal dominion over the Indies for the sole and specific purpose of converting the inhabitants to Christianity.

This single-minded, fanatical advocate of their cause became a power at the court of Charles V. In his voluminous writings to his sovereign, he did not mince his words: he expounded at the greatest length his twenty reasons why the Indians should not be given to the Spaniards in *encomienda*: 'As they [the Indians] weep night and day, the thought may well occur to them that their own gods were better than our God, for under his rule they suffer such ills, while with their former deities, all went well and there was no one to harm them as the Christians do; and as a consequence, they are likely to recoil from the new faith, and abhor it. . . .'*

His sixth reason put things yet plainer: 'The sixth reason is that the Spaniards subvert, ruin and destroy the lives of the Indians, and are the capital enemies of their whole race, or *hostes*, as one says in Latin. Of this there can be no doubt, nor any necessity for proof, because all these things are perfectly manifest.'*

Las Casas emphasizes to the Emperor the lamentable impression the Indians perforce gained of Christianity by watching their Spanish masters:

And the Indians do not take the possessions of others, they do not molest, injure or attack any one; and they see the Spaniards indulging in all kinds of offence and iniquity, together with every evil that man can commit, against all reason and justice; and finally the Indians may scoff and mock at all they are told of God, and some believe nothing, and are so sceptical, that really they do not revere God, but think that he is the most iniquitous and wicked of gods, since he has such worshippers; they further believe that your Majesty must be the most cruel and unjust of kings, since you send such subjects hither and keep them here.*

In general, other leading religious concurred with these opinions. Some, however, felt that Las Casas at times went too far in stating his case. He even succeeded in provoking by his arbitrary ways the animosity of the saintly Motolinía; the latter also uses strong words in writing to Charles V: 'He [Las Casas] was restless in New Spain and did not learn any Indian tongue; nor did he humble himself to teach them. His occupation was to write charges on every hand, and of the sins that the Spaniards have committed, and in it he exaggerates a great deal. And truly this one activity ought not to take him to heaven, because what he writes is not all true or well substantiated. . . .'*

It must, indeed, have been hard for the Spanish Government to unravel such an imbroglio – when even the leading religious in New Spain could not agree among themselves.

To supplement the laws of Burgos, promulgated in 1512 in a belated attempt to save the remaining Indians of Española and neighbouring islands from extermination, the Spanish Government now formulated the New Laws. This action followed Las Casas' return to Spain; he was sent by the General Council of the Dominican order, held in the city of Mexico in 1539, in order to solicit protective legislation from the Council of the Indies. The New Laws went so far as to proscribe the *encomienda* system and provided for severe sanctions in all cases of excesses against Indians. In particular, slavery was forbidden.* Far from relying on local officers for their enforcement, special commissioners were sent for the purpose from Spain.

Needless to say, the excellent intentions of the Spanish crown, as expressed in this legislation, were very hard to put into effect. Even the friars of Las Casas' own Dominican order dismissed as impracticable the immediate abolition of the *encomienda*. However, at least a modicum of protection was being established for the inhabitants of New Spain; in the 1530s and 1540s royal officers fixed limits to the exactions of the *encomenderos*: in certain cases they were even arrested or forced to pay back excess tribute. Probably, therefore, thanks to such measures and to the men who had inspired them, the period of the cruellest abuses was passing; however, as we shall see, they had exacted a heavy toll.

Certain misdeeds of the early colonial period have given rise to the famous 'Black Legend', concerning Spanish behaviour in the Indies. It is often attributed to the invective of Protestant militants and other Spaniard-haters. But, if the truth be told, it must surely be ascribed to the great Las Casas himself; no anti-Spaniard could have been more virulent in the abuse he poured upon the heads of the settlers in Mexico, even referring to them as 'wolves, lions and tigers', preying upon the helpless natives.*

To sum up, it may be useful to quote Professor Gibson, a leading authority on the period:

> The Black Legend provides a gross but essentially accurate interpretation of relations between Spaniards and Indians. The Legend builds upon the record of deliberate sadism. It flourishes in an atmosphere of indignation, which removes the issue from the category of objective understanding. It is insufficient in its awareness of the institutions of colonial history. But the substantive content of the Black Legend asserts that Indians were exploited by Spaniards, and in empirical fact they were.*

The name Aztec, as previously explained, is little more than a convenient term to describe an empire jointly conquered by the Mexicans, the Texcocans and the Tacubans. In the stricter sense of the word the Aztecs, therefore, ceased to exist once the Empire was dissolved, and the alliance which created it.

Naturally, however, the previous conquerors lived on, as well as their former subjects. The institutions under which they were now compelled to exist have been briefly described; it remains to examine the fate of the Aztec peoples under the new régime – no longer as masters of all they surveyed, but as servants of their victors.

Not surprisingly, the rulers initially fared better than the people. The Spanish *encomenderos* were clearly not in a position to rule their charges directly. The Indian upper class accordingly served as a useful instrument for controlling the lower. The Spaniards, moreover, possessed an inherent regard for aristocratic values and respected the hereditary principle. Cortés even went so far as to recognize the authority of the second in the land after the ruler, the Woman Snake. As part of this policy, Moctezuma's own descendants received *encomiendas*, on a par with the conquistadors. Cortés, in particular, took good care of Moctezuma's daughters and married several to well-born Spaniards. The heirs of Nezahualpilli became *caciques* of Texcoco, initially fairly powerful, though their influence tended to decline (the word *cacique*, used by the Spaniards for 'Señor' or 'Ruler', did not originate in Mexico but was of Arawakian origin).

Concerning the actual dynasty of Tenochtitlan, Cortés adopted the unusual procedure, by Aztec standards, of having the Woman Snake, Don Diego Velásquez Tlacotzin, succeed Cuauhtemoc in 1525. He ruled for only one year, and the next two rulers were not of royal blood and did not become *tlatoani* in the full sense.* In 1539 the dynasty was restored in the person of Don Diego Huanitzin, a grandson of the former ruler, Axayácatl. He in turn was succeeded in 1542 by a grandson of Tízoc. The last ruler, from 1554 to 1563, was Don Luís de Santa Maria Nacatzipatzin. When he died, as the chronicler sadly remarks: 'Thus ended the rule of the sons of the much-loved kings of the Tenochca in Mexico–Tenochtitlan.'* (It may be interesting to note that whereas the title of *tlatoani* soon became extinct in Tenochtitlan it still continues to be used even today in other places in the indigenous hierarchy. For instance, the highest dignitary of his kind in Cholula is known as *tlatoani*.)

These rulers of Tenochtitlan and Texcoco forfeited all dominion over neighbouring cities, and retained some authority only over a limited territory surrounding their own capitals; moreover, Tlatelolco once more became a separate entity.

The Spanish administrative unit for controlling New Spain was the *cabecera*, or principal town. Every place that had previously possessed a local ruler of its own, acting as an Aztec vassal, now became a *cabecera*. Where cities had possessed several rulers in former times, they sometimes remained divided into separate units; more often, however, they were united under one *cacique*. These *cabeceras* constituted the centres of Indian local government, and the local nobility normally resided there. The *estancias*, or subdivisions of each *cabecera*, usually followed the somewhat irregular pre-hispanic pattern, with places owing allegiance to one centre interspersed with those belonging to another. Naturally, every place now wanted to claim the dignity of being a *cabecera*, and this led to much Indian litigation, as each pressed its claim, based on ancient territorial divisions, as defined by codices. Such a procedure was not always free from fraud and deceit.

The *caciques* were, of course, strictly subject to Spanish authority; they were merely responsible for local or municipal administration, including such matters as markets, roads, water-supply, as well as the provision of labour for Spanish projects. In particular, they had to collect the tribute for the *encomenderos*, through a system still based on Moctezuma's imperial levy. Their position was perhaps not unlike that of tribal chiefs in certain British colonies. They became pro-gressively Hispanized, wearing swords and Spanish clothing and even carrying firearms. They furnished their houses with beds, tables and chairs, previously unknown, and sometimes even owned Negro slaves.* They continued to marry among themselves. Monogamy was, of course, now obligatory; it was, however, often a thorny problem for the friars to disentangle the conflicting claims of existing wives to the new honour of sole spouse – or to know how to dis-pose of the wives rendered surplus by such provisions. Moreover, the temptation was ever present to profit by the occasion and make a clean sweep of all existing wives, grown old and ugly. The *cacique* could then start afresh with a new and pretty one, in support of whose legal claims subject witnesses would naturally produce ample and impeccable evidence.

The influence of these hereditary rulers gradually declined. In the first place the tributary system was modified, which had served to provide them, as well as the *encomenderos*, with a living. Until the middle of the sixteenth century, payment was made in produce, as under the Aztecs. This impost was then gradually converted into a kind of head tax, payable in money, not in kind.

Secondly, the authority of the rulers was superseded by elected Indian officials, based on the Spanish system of municipal govern-ment. Those so chosen were called *gobernadores*, or 'governors', and were assisted by a kind of council composed of *regidores*. It is a mark of the respect in which the former *tlatoanis* were held that in many cases the existing sovereign was chosen for the new office; the last rulers of Tenochtitlan were also governors. The electorate, it might be added, was conservative in nature and restricted in number – resembling more an English pocket borough than a modern constituency!†

While the former rulers could to some extent feather their own nests in the early years of Spanish rule, the common people were less fortunate. Even the Aztec merchant class disappeared, and was replaced by a new generation of Indian traders. The people did not merely suffer, they began to disappear. Disease, rather than ill-treatment, has now been recognized as the major cause of depopulation, and in particular the epidemics of 1545–8 and of 1576–81. They have never been clinically diagnosed, but were surely attributable to such infections as smallpox and measles, against which the natives enjoyed no immunity. The Spanish remedy of bleeding merely increased the mortality rate.

The figures speak for themselves: the population of the Valley of Mexico declined by 1570 to 325,000 from a pre-Conquest total of about one and a half millions.* Unlike their rulers, the people, or those who survived, continued to live much as before, though certain efforts were made to induce them to sleep in beds, wear clothes, and abandon drunkenness, the scourge of post-Conquest Mexico. Some Indians learned Spanish, but few gave up their own languages. Diet was largely unchanged, though by the end of the century the eating of dog was limited to ceremonial occasions and replaced by pork and other meat; according to some Indians, pork reminded them of human flesh, formerly ritually consumed on such festive occasions.* Dog, of course, also had religious connotations – and its continued sale in Acolman gave rise to the strongest expressions of disgust on the part of the distinguished chronicler, Padre Durán. He places the consumption of dog in the same category as the eating of weasels and mice.*

Under the stress of change, and faced with the dissolution of their society, the native population – literally – took to drink, so severely controlled in pre-Hispanic times and largely limited to religious ceremonies. As the population decreased, production of *pulque* actually rose, as areas previously under maize cultivation were turned over to the growing of the agave plant. Spurred by the friars' protests at excessive drinking, the Spanish administration made serious efforts to limit this addiction; their ineffectiveness well illustrates the difficulties facing the new and alien élite. The laws of the Aztecs may have been Draconian, but they were obeyed.

The Indians initially retained their communal lands. Later, owing to depopulation, many became unoccupied; this facilitated Spanish acquisition of property. These communal holdings, moreover, suffered continually from the depredations of Spanish-owned cattle, in spite of viceregal regulations for the protection of Indian property. Further lands became vacant, and available for Spanish occupation, towards the end of the century, through the policy of congregating the natives into more concentrated settlements. This was done ostensibly to facilitate supervision, to promote Christian living and to prevent drunkenness. If such worthy objectives were not fully achieved, the spread of disease was certainly facilitated.

Among the scourges listed by Fray Motolinía as afflicting the Indians was forced labour, and above all the continued tolerance of slavery, mainly to supply the growing labour-demands of the new mines.*

In fairness, it must be borne in mind that the Spaniards themselves, if taken by the Turks, were enslaved, and that this treatment was considered as the normal lot of infidel prisoners of war. Following such precepts, Columbus had gone so far as to sell Indians as slaves in Spain, until ordered to stop by an irate Queen Isabella in 1495. In spite of his lyrical descriptions of the pacific characters of the Indian, he evidently planned to establish a regular trade in Indian slaves.*

The recently developed mines needed Indian slaves, to supplement the supply of Negroes; the importation of the latter had been originally proposed by the three Jeronymite monks sent to redeem Española from the abuses of previous governors.*

Slaves could be acquired on the theory that Indians taken in rebellion, or who resisted the advance of the Spaniards, could lawfully be enslaved. Spanish legislation only gradually brought such abuses under partial control, some fifteen years after the Conquest. A law was passed stipulating that all slaves must be registered before royal officers; failing this, they were to be released. The branding iron was henceforth kept in a metal box with two keys; one of these was to be left in the custody of Bishop Zumarraga, the officially appointed protector of the Indians.*

In their travails, the Indians were offered the solace of the Cross, a blessing initially unwanted – for it is quite erroneous to suppose that they were at all eager to espouse their conquerors' faith. To quote Professor Jiménez Moreno: 'It has not been emphasized sufficiently that a considerable proportion, if not the majority, of the Indians of the ancient Mexican Empire were obliged in the first half of the sixteenth century to abandon their old religion by force.'*

This reluctance was amply illustrated when the saintly Franciscans met with the Aztec chiefs and priests, in an initial effort at conversion. The friars first made an appropriate address, outlining the Christian message. The princes or rulers replied, expressing deep appreciation that such fine gems and precious stones had been shown to them – the normal figure of speech for something significant or beautiful. They preferred that their priests, sages versed in the counting of the years and learned in the course of the stars, should give a full answer. They spoke as follows: 'You have told us that we are ignorant of him through whom we have life and being, and who is the lord of the sky and of the earth. Equally, you say that those whom we adore are not gods. This manner of speech seems to us very unfamiliar and shocking. . . . We are horrified at such words, because our ancestors, who gave us life and commanded us, never told us such things; from times long past they handed down to us the custom that we should worship our gods. . . .'

The priests went on to explain to the friars that their gods had provided the necessities of life for countless ages past; it would be an act of levity to destroy their ancient laws, and thus incur their extreme wrath. 'Sufficient let it be that the justice and the power of our kings has been taken away from us; in what concerns our gods, we would rather die than abandon their service and worship. This is our resolve; do as you will.'*

This exchange of views took place some four years after the Conquest; the coming of the friars marked the end of that strange interlude, during which the old gods, if vanquished, were still present, while the new had not yet arrived. Naturally, former practices

299

continued. The Spaniards apparently did not react strongly, as long as they did not actually *see* human sacrifices; plenty were still carried out in secret.*

The first real battle against the ancient deities was fought in 1525 in Texcoco, where pagan temples still abounded; sermons were preached and action was pursued to extirpate the old practices. Steps were then taken in other places, including the city of Mexico, and many temples were destroyed.*

A continuous struggle was now to be fought: by 1531, Bishop Zumarraga was boasting that he had destroyed 500 temples and 20,000 idols (many precious codices, alas, were added to the Bishop's bonfire). It was the Emperor Charles himself who recommended the use of the stones of the temples for building the churches.*

The coming of the twelve Franciscans had been a notable event; in spite of the unbending attitude of former priests and rulers, the impact of their presence on the common people was profound. This, indeed, was the first step towards bridging the gulf that yawned between conquerors and conquered. These were Spaniards who were as poor as they, and who lived as they did, sharing the same hardships.*

The friars certainly had work on their hands, and by the end of 1524 a million Indians had already been baptized, after somewhat hasty instruction. Language was a major difficulty. The religious were opposed to the Indians learning Spanish, and therefore they themselves had no alternative but to master the native languages. Where the population was ethnically mixed, cases would even occur of sermons being preached in several different tongues during one mass.*

Moreover, it was sometimes difficult to translate Christian notions into native languages at all. Even for the telling of the parable of the Wise and Foolish Virgins, the Spanish words for oil and lamp had to be used; certain concepts had no counterpart in some languages. When the Jesuits reached Lower California at the end of the seventeenth century, they could only make clear the meaning of resurrection to the unlettered natives of that region by immersing flies in water, taking them out before they drowned, and then letting them come to life again.

That there should be no relapse on the part of Indian converts, it was essential to instil a healthy terror of hellfire. Notions of the underworld in their own religion were less sharply defined, and the concept of hell as a punishment for sin almost absent.

To illustrate the torments of the damned, Fray Luis Caldera was obliged to adopt unorthodox methods: he arranged a kind of oven; dogs and cats were thrown into the fire, and their cries of pain vividly demonstrated the horrors awaiting those Indians who ignored the friars' teaching. The latter were so successful as to create a kind of religious fanaticism among certain of their flock; mindful of the practices of their old faith, it was not uncommon for new converts to express surprise and regret if their confessors did not order them to be scourged. After a slow start, the fight against pagan- ism was undertaken with zeal; possibly such a crusade provided an outlet for the ardour of the Aztecs, now deprived of their campaigns of conquest.*

Not unnaturally, resistance to conversion was still at times encountered. Some even parodied the mass by worshipping a maize cake.* Upper-class parents would hide their children, and send the sons of slaves to the religious schools in their place. Sorcerers and magicians, in the early years, sought to convince the Indians that the water used for baptism was really blood, that the friars were dead men and their habits winding-sheets – at night they were supposed to disappear and join their women in hell. An alternative version of such stories suggested that the religious had never been children, and that they had been born dressed in their habits.*

In order to stop pagan practices, sanctions were enforced. Indians were punished for failing to confess; idolaters from Texcoco were executed in the 1530s. The friars at times had to resort to corporal punishment, and it was not until the seventeenth century that church jails were forbidden. Problems, moreover, were caused by the use of forced labour for ecclesiastical purposes; the beautiful sixteenth- century monasteries which abound in Mexico today were not merely built of the very stones of the pyramids; they were surrounded by a similar type of crenellated wall and constructed under the same system of collective Indian labour.

However, despite any shortcomings and misunderstandings, the Indians dearly loved their friars. This is well illustrated by the anger occasioned when the Franciscan friars were taken away from San

Iuan Teotihuacán, and replaced by others. The people refused to supply the newcomers with food, and became so insubordinate that the civil authorities were forced to resort to violence and imprisonment in an attempt to restore discipline. It was all to no avail; in the end the villagers had their way and the Franciscans returned: 'When they arrived, such was their delight, that they forgot all the miseries they had suffered, and with great joy they built a holy convent and a very fine church in a few days.'*

Gradually, moreover, early tensions eased as the Mexicans, at times to the distaste of the Spanish ecclesiastics, made their own contributions to their new faith. Above all, their devotion to the Virgin of Guadalupe helped to give the Aztecs an identity of their own within the framework of New Spain. On 9 December 1531 a simple native called Juan Diego first saw a beautiful Indian lady dressed in shining garments on the Hill of Tepeyacac, where the Basilica of Guadalupe now stands. She spoke in Nahuatl and identified herself as the Mother of God. He went and related his vision to Bishop Zumarraga; in all, he saw the Virgin and the Bishop four times.

Initially, the friars displayed a fierce hostility towards the new cult. Clerical efforts at suppression, however, did not succeed, and today the Virgin of Guadalupe, the Indian Virgin *par excellence*, is hallowed not only in Mexico, but also throughout Spanish America. The early attitude of the religious is not altogether surprising; the Hill of Tepeyacac formerly housed the shrine of the goddess Tonantzin (meaning 'our mother'). This deity is even to be identified with Coatlicue, the Mother of Huitzilopochtli, with her necklace of human hearts and hands.

The coming of Christianity may have served to soften the rigours of their altered life under alien masters. The Indian conversion, however, tended towards the superficial; native attitudes and habits did not change. As Motolinía complains, they just wanted to have a hundred and one gods, instead of a hundred.* The Christian god was admitted, but not necessarily as a sole deity. Moreover, the notion died hard that a god could only exist by virtue of the sustenance and support provided by his adherents. Saints were, and often still are, not loving intermediaries, but themselves anthropomorphic deities, quick to anger and eager to punish transgressions, unless appeased by gifts of clothing, food and drink.

It remains to say something of the Aztec capital of Tenochtitlan, razed to the ground by the Conquest.

Rebuilding was a pressing task – and for the purpose Cortés charged the Woman Snake with the task of bringing back the Indian population, scattered after the siege.* Cortés himself took the decision to retain the former site. The newly built capital would thus be subject to floods and surrounded by swamp lands – for it was not the intention to build another Aztec lagoon-city, but a Spanish capital, with the finest Spanish churches, houses, streets and squares; some of these, in altered form, survive today. Following the replacement of many canals by streets, there was no way the water could flow if the rains were severe, and the danger of floods was increased.

The task of building was backbreaking, and Motolinía lists the use of forced labour for the erection of Mexico-Tenochtitlan, as the city was now called, as one of the plagues afflicting the Indians. Flood control itself over the centuries was to require armies of labourers and cost many lives. Following the critical inundation of 1555, the Viceroy summoned a force of 6000 Indians to build a dyke four miles long. He had previously asked the governors of Tenochtitlan, Texcoco and Tacuba, the heads of the former Triple Alliance, to produce ancient paintings showing how their ancestors had protected the city from flood. The organization of the labour force followed the pre-Hispanic pattern; the work, however, was of unusual severity, and many workers died.*

It was not until 1608 that a tunnel four miles long was completed, draining part of the lagoon water from the Valley of Mexico into the Tula river. This did not prevent even more devastating floods in 1629, when streets, squares and causeways stood under several feet of water; food shortage became acute, houses collapsed and trade came to a halt. It was even suggested that the city should be transferred to the mainland. Only at the end of the eighteenth century was the work finally completed of transforming the tunnel into an open canal, and the flood problem consequently reduced.

In the city of Mexico the Spaniards formed their own town, with its separate municipal authority. The Indian community of San Juan Tenochtitlan surrounded this settlement and remained divided into the four original quarters or sub-districts established at the time of its foundation.

The ruling family gradually lost its power, and its authority was assumed by elected Indian mayors, both for Tenochtitlan and for Tlatelolco. The Tlatelolco market still functioned in 1550, but by the end of the century the Indian government had lost all control over commerce and tribute collection.

In spite of a tendency to neglect the Indians, in Mexico-Tenochtitlan, much attention was paid to higher education. Special establishments were created, of which the most important were San José in Tenochtitlan and the College of Santa Cruz in Tlatelolco. The students were the sons of *caciques*; Latin, logic, philosophy and theology were taught.

The decline in population throughout the country naturally affected the capital. In pre-Hispanic times, Tenochtitlan-Tlatelolco had been larger than any European city, probably reaching a quarter of a million. By 1562, it had sunk to 75,000.*

Only in recent years has the city of Mexico regained its status as one of the great capitals of the modern world.

TENTATIVE GENEALOGY OF THE ROYAL DYNASTY OF TENOCHTITLAN

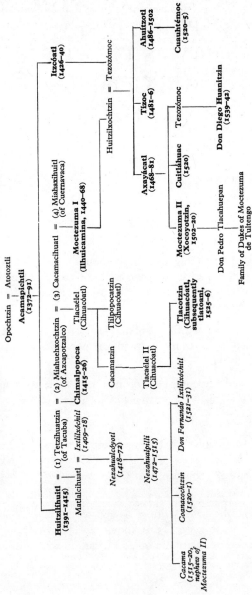

Rulers of Tenochtitlan are set in bold type, rulers of Texcoco in italic.

PRINCIPAL
DEITIES OF THE
MEXICAN
PANTHEON

GODS

Centeotl (from *centli* meaning 'maize', and *teotl* meaning 'god'). God of maize and personification of the maize plant.

Huitzilopochtli ('Humming Bird of the South'). Patron god of the Mexica. Originally perhaps more an earth- or water-god, equally to be associated with fire, he came to be principally a war-god, also linked with the sun.

Mictlantecuhtli ('Lord of the Place of the Dead'). Ruled over the nether world. Mictlan is also connected with the north. He is always depicted as a skeleton.

Mixcoatl ('Cloud Serpent'). God of hunting. Connected with Tezcatlipoca. Leading deity of the nomad Chichimecs.

Ometecuhtli ('Two Lord'). The original creator-god.

Ometochtli ('Two Rabbit'). Most important of the gods of the sacred drink *pulque*. Another principal *pulque*-god is Tepoztécatl, associated with the village of Tepoztlan, near Cuernavaca.

Quetzalcoatl ('Plumed Serpent'). As creative deity, he discovered agriculture and the art of writing. As god of the planet Venus, the morning and evening star, he is known as Tlahuizcalpantecuhtli. As god of the wind, he is also called Ehécatl. In some, but not all, respects he is the adversary of Tezcatlipoca.

Tezcatlipoca ('Smoking Mirror'). The eternally young and all-

306

powerful god of the night sky. Patron god of sorcerers and magicians. Often portrayed as a jaguar, he was identified with the constellation of the Great Bear, in which the Mexicans saw the form of this animal.

Tlaloc. The actual meaning of this god's name is rather obscure, but probably derives from the word *tlalli*, meaning 'earth', denoting that he was also originally perhaps an earth-deity. Basically, however, he is god of rain. His equivalent in the Maya area is called Chac. He is accompanied by a number of lesser gods called *tlaloques.*

Tonatiuh ('Sun'). The sun-god. Associated with the eagle and with the god Huitzilopochtli. His face appears in the centre of the famous Aztec Stone.

Xipe Totec ('Our Lord of the Flayed One'). Originally a god of vegetation and agriculture. God of spring and patron of jewellers. Also known as the Red Tezcatlipoca, he is closely to be associated with this deity.

Xochipilli ('The Prince of Flowers'). Patron of dancing and games. Associated with love and the spring.

GODDESSES

Chalchiuhtlicue ('She of the Skirt of Jade'). Goddess of water. Variously described as the wife or the sister of Tlaloc, the rain-god.

Coatlicue ('She of the Skirt of Serpents'). Earth-goddess and mother of Huitzilopochtli. Also known as Tonantzin (literally 'our mother').

Omecihuatl ('Two Lady'). The original creator-goddess, wife of Ometecuhtli.

Tlazolteotl ('Goddess of Excrement'). Apart from excrement, she was goddess of sexual pleasure, also associated with childbirth. Each person would make a confession to her towards the end of his life.

Xilonen (from *xilotl*, the young ear of maize, and *nenen* meaning 'doll'). She represented the young maize, before it ripened.

Xochiquetzal ('Precious Flower'). Personification of beauty and love, goddess of flowers, and the wife of the god Xochipilli.

NOTES AND REFERENCES

ABBREVIATIONS

Acosta	Padre Joseph de Acosta, *Historia Natural y Moral de las Indias* (1962)
Acosta Saignes	Miguel Acosta Saignes, *Los Pochteca* (1945)
Aguilar	Francisco de Aguilar, *Relación Breve de la Conquista de la Nueva España* (1954)
Anales de Cuauhtitlan	Anales de Cuauhtitlan. Published in *Codex Chimalpopoca* (1945)
Anales de Tlatelolco	'Unos Anales Históricos de la Nación Mexicana. Edited and Commented by Heinrich Berlin', *Fuentes para la Historia*, no. 2 (1948)
Anales Mexicanos	Anales Mexicanos. Published in *Anales del Museo Nacional de México*, época I, vol. 7 (1903)
Armillas	Pedro Armillas, 'Fortalezas Mexicanas', *Cuadernos Americanos*, vol. 41, no. 5 (1944)
Barlow, 'Conquistas de los Antiguos Mexicanos'	R. H. Barlow, 'Conquistas de los Antiguos Mexicanos', *Minutes of the XXVIII International Congress of Americanists* (1947)
Barlow, 'Extent of Empire'	R. H. Barlow, 'The Extent of the Empire of the Culhua Mexica', *Ibero-Americana*, no. 28 (1949)
Bernal, *Tenochtitlan*	Ignacio Bernal, *Tenochtitlan en Una Isla* (1959)
Bernal, 'Teotihuacan'	Ignacio Bernal, 'Teotihuacan, Capital de Imperio?', *Revista Mexicana de Estudios Antropológicos*, vol. xx (1966)
Beyer	Hermann Beyer, *Complete Works*, vol. I, trans. Carmen Cook de Leonard, in *El Mexico Antiguo*, vol. x (1965)
Cantares Mexicanos	MS. in National Library, Mexico City
Carrasco Pizana	Pedro Carrasco Pizana, *Los Otomíes* (1950)
Caso, *El Pueblo del Sol*	Alfonso Caso, *El Pueblo del Sol* (1953)
Caso, *Religión*	Alfonso Caso, *La Religión de los Aztecas* (1945)
Cervantes de Salazar	Francisco Cervantes de Salazar, *Crónica de Nueva España*, 3 vols (1936)
Chimalpain, *Memorial Breve*	Domingo Francisco de San Anton Muñon Cuauhtlehuantzin Chimalpain, *Das Memorial*

	Breve acerca de la Fundación de la Cuidad de Culhuacan, trans. Walter Lehmann and Gerdt Kutscher (1958)
Chimalpain, *Relaciones*	Domingo Francisco de San Anton Muñon Cuauhtlehuantzin Chimalpain, *Relaciones Originales de Chalco-Amaquemecan*, trans. Sylvia Rendon (1965)
Clavijero	Francisco Xavier Clavijero, *Historia Antigua de Mexico* (1964)
Codex Azcatitlan	*Codex Azcatitlan* (1949)
Codex Boturini	*Tira de la Peregrinación (Codex Boturini)* (1944)
Codex Mendoza	*Codex Mendoza*, ed. and trans. James Cooper Clark, 3 vols (1938)
Codex Mexicanus	Codex Mexicanus 23–4. Commentary by Ernest Mengin in *Journal de la Société des Américanistes de Paris*, vol. XLI (1952)
Codex Ramírez	*Codex Ramírez* (1944)
Codex Telleriano-Remensis	Codex Telleriano-Remensis, ed. Lord Kingsborough, in *Antiquities of Mexico* (1831) vol. III
Codex Xólotl	*Codex Xólotl*, ed. Charles Dibble (1951)
Colección de Documentos	*Colección de Documentos inéditos relativos al descubrimiento, conquista y organización de las antiguas posesiones españolas de ultramar*, 2nd series, 17 vols (1885–1925)
Cooke and Simpson	Sherburne Cooke and Lesley Byrd Simpson, *The Population of Central Mexico in the Sixteenth Century* (1948)
Cortés	Hernán Cortés, *Cartas y Documentos* (1963)
Crónica Mexicayotl	*Crónica Mexicayotl* (1949)
Davies, *Los Mexica*	Nigel Davies, *Los Mexica: Primeros Pasos hacia el Imperio* (1973)
Davies, *Los Señoríos Independientes*	Nigel Davies, *Los Señoríos Independientes del Imperio Azteca* (1968)
Trevor Davies	R. Trevor Davies, *The Golden Century of Spain, 1501–1621* (1937)
del Castillo	Cristóbal del Castillo, *Fragmentos sobre la Obra General sobre Historia de los Mexicanos* (1908)
Díaz, *Chronicles*	*The Bernal Díaz Chronicles*, trans. and ed. Albert Idell (1956)
Díaz, *Historia*	Bernal Díaz del Castillo, *Historia de la Conquista de la Nueva España* (1969)
Durán	Fray Diego Durán, *Historia de las Indias de Nueva España e Islas de la Tierra Firme*, 2 vols (1967)

Epistolario de Nueva España — *Epistolario de Nueva España, 1505–1818*, ed. Francisco del Paso y Troncoso, 16 vols (1939)

Espejo, 'Algunas Semejanzas' — Antonieta Espejo, 'Algunas Semejanzas entre Tenayuca y Tlatelolco', *Memorias de la Academia Mexicana de la Historia*, vol. III, no. 4 (1944)

Florentine Codex — *Florentine Codex. Manuscript in Nahuatl of Fray Bernardino de Sahagún*, trans. J. O. Anderson and Charles E. Dibble, 12 vols (1950)

Gante — Fray P. de Gante, *Cartas de Fray Pedro de Gante*

Garibay — Padre Angel María Garibay, *Llave del Nahuatl* (1961)

Gibson — Charles Gibson, *The Aztecs under Spanish Rule* (1964)

Gómara — Francisco Lopez de Gómara, *Historia de las Conquistas de Hernando Cortás*, 2 vols (1826)

Gorenstein — Shirley Gorenstein, 'The Differential Development of New World Empires', *Revista Mexicana de Estudios Antropológicos*, vol. XX (1966)

Gurría Lacroix — Jorge Gurría Lacroix, 'Itinerary of Hernán Cortés', *Artes de México*, año XV, no. 3 (1968)

Hemming — John Hemming, *The Conquest of the Incas* (1970)

Herrera — Antonio de Herrera, *Historia General de los Hechos de los Castellanos*, 10 vols

Historia de los Mexicanos — Historia de los Mexicanos por sus Pinturas, in *Nueva Colección de Documentos para la Historia de Mexico* (1941)

Icazbalceta — Joaquín García Icazbalceta, *Colección de Documentos para la Historia de Mexico*, 2 vols (1858–1866)

Ixtlilxóchitl — Fernando de Alva Ixtlilxóchitl, *Obras Históricas*, 2 vols (1952)

Jiménez Moreno, 'Diferentes Principios' — Wigberto Jiménez Moreno, 'Diferentes Principios del Año entre diversos Pueblos del Valle de México y sus Consecuencias para la Cronología prehispánica', *México Antiguo*, vol. IX (1961)

Jiménez Moreno, 'Indians of America and Christianity' — Wigberto Jiménez Moreno, 'The Indians of America and Christianity', *The Americas*, vol. XIV, no. 4 (1958)

Katz — Friedrich Katz, *Situación Social y económica de los Aztecas durante los Siglos XV y XVI* (1966)

Kelley and Palerm — Isabel Kelley and Angel Palerm, *The Tajin Totonac* (1952)

Kirchhoff, 'Aztlán' — Paul Kirchhoff, 'Se pueda localizar Aztlán?', *Anuario de Historia*, año 1 (1961)

Kirchhoff, 'Composición Etnica' — Paul Kirchhoff, 'Composición Etnica y Organización Política de Chalco según las Relaciones de Chimalpain', *Revista Mexicana de Estudios Antropológicos*, vol. XIV, pt. 2 (1954–5)

Kirchhoff, *Historia* — Paul Kirchhoff, Prologue to *Historia Tolteca-Chichimeca*

Las Casas — Bartolomé de Las Casas, *Tratados* (1965)

Léon Portilla, *Treces Poetas* — Miguel Léon Portilla, *Treces Poetas del Mundo Azteca* (1967)

Léon Portilla, *Vision de los Vencidos* — Miguel Léon Portilla, *Vision de los Vencidos* (1959)

Lopez Austin — Alfredo Lopez Austin, *La Constitución Real de México Tenochtitlan* (1961)

Madsen — William Madsen, 'Religious Syncretism', *Handbook of Middle American Indians*, vol. VI (1967)

Mapa Quinatzin — Mapa Quinatzin, ed. J. M. A. Aubin, in *Anales del Museo Nacional de México*, epoca I, vol. 3 (1886)

Marquina — Ignacio Marquina, *El Templo Mayor de México* (1960)

Martinez del Río — Pablo Martinez del Río, 'Resumen de Trabajos en Tlatelolco', *Memorias de la Academia Mexicana de la Historia*, vol. III, no. 4 (1944)

Mendieta — Fray Gerónimo de Mendieta, *Historia Ecclesiastica Indiana*, 4 vols (1945)

Mendizabal — Miguel O. de Mendizabal, *Influencia de la Sal en la Distribución de los Grupos Indígenas de México* (1928)

Mols — Roger Mols, *Introduction à la Démographie Historique des Villes d'Europe du XIVᵉ au XVIIIᵉ Siècle*, 3 vols (1954–6)

Motolinía, *Historia* — Fray Toribio de Benavente Motolinía, *Historia de los Indios de Nueva España* (1941)

Motolinía, *Memoriales* — Fray Toribio de Benavente Motolinía, *Memoriales* (1903)

Müller — Florencia Müller, 'La Secuencia Cerámica de Teotihuacan', *Report of Round Table Conference on Teotihuacan* (1966)

Muñoz Camargo — Diego Muñoz Camargo, *Historia de Tlaxcala* (1947)

Navarrete — Martín Fernandez de Navarrete, *Los Viajes de Colón*, 5 vols (1825–37)

Nazareo — Don Pablo Nazareo, 'Carta al Rey Don Felipe II', *Epistolario de Nueva España*, vol. X (1940)

Noguera, *La Cerámica* — Eduardo Noguera, *La Cerámica Arqueológica de Mesoamérica* (1965)

Origen de los Mexicanos — Origen de los Mexicanos, in *Nueva Colección de Documentos para la Historia de México* (1941)

Papeles de Nueva España — *Papeles de Nueva España*, ed. Francisco de Paso y Troncoso, 2nd series, 6 vols (1905–6)

Piña Chan — Roman Piña Chan, 'Estratigrafía en los Terrenos Adyacentes a la Catedral Metropolitana', *Memorias de la Academia Mexicana de la Historia*, vol. x (1950)

Pomar — Juan Bautista Pomar, 'Relación de Texcoco', *Nueva Colección de Documentos para la Historia de México* (1941)

Relación de Cempoala — Relación de Cempoala, in *Tlalocan*, vol. III (1949)

Relación de Chilapa — Relación de Chilapa, in *Papeles de Nueva España*, vol. v

Relación de Michoacán — *Relación de las Ceremonias y Ritos y Población y Gobierno de los Indios de la Provincia de Michoacán* (1956)

Relaciones Geograficas — See *Papeles de Nueva España*

Ricard — Robert Ricard, *The Spiritual Conquest of Mexico*, trans. Lesley Byrd Simpson (1966)

Sahagún, *Colloquios* — Fray Bernardino de Sahagún, *Colloquios y Doctrina Christiana* (1944)

Sahagún, *Historia General* — Fray Bernardino de Sahagún, *Historia General de Las Cosas de Nueva España*, 6 vols (1956)

Seler — Eduard Seler, *Gesammte Abhandlungen zur Amerikanischen Sprach- und Altertumskunde*, 6 vols (1960)

Simpson — Lesley Byrd Simpson, *The Encomienda in New Spain* (1966)

Soustelle — Jacques Soustelle, *La Vie Quotidienne des Aztèques* (1955)

Andrés de Tapía — Andrés de Tapía, 'Relacion Hecha por el Sr Andrés de Tapía', *Coleccion de Documentos para la Historia de México*, vol. II

Vazquez de Tapía — Bernardo Vazquez de Tapía, *Relación de Méritos y Servicios del Conquistador Bernardo Vasquez de Tapía* (1953)

Tezozómoc — Hernando Alvarado Tezozómoc, *Crónica Mexicana* (1944)

Torquemada — Fray Juan de Torquemada, *Monarquía Indiana*, 3 vols (1943–4)

Veytia	Mariano Veytia, *Historia Antigua de México*, 2 vols (1944)
Zantwijk, 'Principios Organizadores'	Rudolf van Zantwijk, 'Principios Organizadores de los Mexicas. Una Introducción al Estudio del Sistema Interno del Régimen Azteca', *Estudios de Cultura Náhuatl*, vol. IV (1963)
Zantwijk, 'Los seis Barrios Sirvientes'	Rudolf van Zantwijk, 'Los seis Barrios Sirvientes de Huitzilopochtli', *Estudios de Cultura Náhuatl*, vol. VI (1966)
Zurita	Alonso de Zurita, 'Breve y Sumaria Relación de los Señores y Maneras y diferencias que había en ellos en la Nueva España', *Nueva Colección de Documentos para la Historia de México* (1941)

CHAPTER 1 THE LONG MIGRATION

2 *pardon.* Crónica Mexicayotl, pp. 7–8.

nature. Typical of these are Veytia and Clavijero. They were already historians rather than chroniclers, but made use of certain sources which have since disappeared.

3 *Valley of Mexico.* This was particularly the view of Eduard Seler, possibly the greatest of all investigators concerned with ancient Mexico.

came. Durán, vol. II, pp. 217–18.

4 *her commands.'* Ibid. p. 220.

today. Ibid. pp. 14–18.

5 *departure.* Several sources mention the Mexica encounters with Huaxtecs, whose principal habitation is the Panuco area on the Gulf Coast. Probably, however, in those days the Huaxtecs penetrated farther westwards.

Curved Mountain (Culhuacan). The Codex Boturini, or 'Tira de la Peregrinación', gives the glyphs of Culhuacan and Chicomoztoc, but not Aztlan. The latter should be interpreted as meaning 'place of cranes' or possibly 'place of whiteness'.

boats. Chimalpain, Memorial Breve, pp. 19 and 24.

6 *was.* Crónica Mexicayotl, p. 17. Quinehuayan means literally 'the place from which one rises up or starts off'.

Seven Caves. Durán, vol. II, p. 21.

Toltec Empire. This traditional Culhuacan, as opposed to the Culhuacan in the Valley of Mexico, is often referred to as Teoculhuacan. The prefix *teo* means literally 'pertaining to the gods', but also 'authentic' or in a sense 'original'.

west. See Kirchhoff, 'Aztlán', p. 64.

Mexico City. Prof. Jiménez Moreno situates Chicomoztoc in Jilotepec, Hidalgo – to the south-west of Tula.

7 *Valley of Mexico.* The Tepanecs and Acolhua, when they arrived, were certainly 'Toltecized', even if they did not yet speak Nahuatl.

7 *afield.* See Zantwijk, 'Principios Organizadores', p. 197.

meaning 'moon'). The association of the Mexica with the moon might derive from the reflection of the moon on the lagoon which was their original home. The derivation of the name Mexica remains obscure, and is sometimes also considered to derive from *metl* (maguey cactus) and *citli* ('hare'), or alternatively from *mixtli* ('cloud').

high. Crónica Mexicayotl, pp. 22–3.

8 *settled in 1345.* On the question of early Mexica chronology, the views of Prof. Jiménez Moreno are widely accepted. He bases his calculations on the number of New Fire ceremonies, marking the end of a fifty-two-year cycle, that were held during the migration. His dates are as follows: the first New Fire ceremony was held in Coatepec in 1163; the second in Apaxco in 1215; the third in Tecpayocan (now Hill of Guadalupe) in 1267; the fourth in Chapultepec in 1319; the fifth in Tenochtitlan in 1351. Only thirty-two years occur between the fourth and fifth New Fires, owing to the probable adoption by the Mexica of a different year-count to that previously employed: see Jiménez Moreno, 'Diferentes Principios', pp. 137–52.

9 *desert.* Durán, vol. II, p. 26.

10 *Huitzilopochtli....'* Crónica Mexicayotl, p. 26.

culture. Ibid. p. 32.

maturity. Ibid. p. 27.

here. Ibid. p. 23.

snakes. Ibid. p. 18.

11 *agriculture.* Codex Xólotl gives ample illustrations of these Chichimecs.

12 *Anahuac.* Florentine Codex, bk III, ch. 12.

wander.' Codex Azcatitlan, pl. 5.

13 *differ.* The places most frequently mentioned as stopping-places before reaching Coatepec are Cuextecatl-Ichocayan ('the place where the Huaxtec wept') and Coatlicamac ('in the mouth of the serpent'). Concerning the mention of Huaxtecs, see note to p. 5 above.

migration. Codex Boturini, pl. 4.

established.' Crónica Mexicayotl, pp. 30–1.

14 *clouds....'* Durán, vol. II, p. 31.

conceived.' Florentine Codex, bk III, ch. 1.

15 *in her womb?'* Ibid.

points.' Ibid.

falling.' Ibid.

feeds. Durán, vol. II, p. 32.

16 *obey.* Ibid. p. 33.

before. Ibid. p. 34.

17 *associated.* It seems that Malinalxochitl probably came from the Chalmeca *calpulli.* On the other hand, Coyolxauhqui belonged to the Huitznahuac *calpulli,* as also did Huizilopochtli himself. See Zantwijk, 'Principios Organizadores', p. 192.

god. Chimalpain, *Memorial Breve,* p. 22. Another source, Cristóbal del

Castillo (pp. 58–9), insists that the human leader, Huitzilopochtli, was the 'servant' of the god Tetzahuitl; he took on the likeness of this god, who subsequently came to be known as Huitzilopochtli. Many sources mention Tetzahuitl as the original Mexica god.

18 *victim.* Seler, vol. IV, p. 577.

season. Opochtli was also the name of an older Fisherman's God connected, according to Seler, with *tlaloques* or rain-gods. Thus, both components of Huitzilopochtli's name have associations with water or rain.

course. Caso, *Religión*, p. 16.

south. In this role he became the opposite of Tezcatlipoca, Lord of the Night Sky.

conquer. A parallel to such a metamorphosis might perhaps be found in other parts of the world – in particular, in the Israelite god Yahweh, who started life as a kind of wind and weather deity, only later to be converted into a relentless god of war.

20 *settle.* The most comprehensive lists, which coincide only in part, are those of the Codex Azcatitlan and the Codex Boturini ('Tira de la Peregrinatión').

north-east. For Xaltocan territorial claims, see letter of Don Pablo Nazareo in *Epistolario de Nueva España*, vol. X, pp. 109–29.

22 *fall of Rome.* For detailed discussion of the dates of the Mexica stay in Chapultepec, see Davies, *Los Mexica*, app. A.

Toltec ways. These immigrant tribes are collectively known as Toltec-Chichimecs, i.e. people of barbarian antecedents who had already adopted more civilized ways.

wives. Ixtlilxóchitl, vol. II, p. 42.

23 *lagoon.* Acolhua means 'broad-shouldered' – implying connections with giants and perhaps Chichimecs. Apart from Coatlichan, Acolman and Huexotla were important Acolhua centres.

Tepanecs. The Tepanecs, like the people of Xaltocan, had Otomí connections, and revered the Otomí god Otontecuhtli. They probably came from the Matlatzinca region, in the Valley of Toluca.

more. Azcapotzalco was an important Teotihuacan site, particularly in the later (Teotihuacan IV) phase, in about A.D. 700. Churubusco (formerly Huitzilopochco), Tacubaya and Coyoacan were also Tepanec centres.

24 *wind.* As god of the wind he was known as Ehécatl; Tlahuizcalpantecuhtli, as God the Morning Star, was Quetzalcoatl under another name.

25 *rags and tatters.* Florentine Codex, bk IV, ch. 8.

agriculture. The Tepanecs probably spoke Otomí when they arrived in the Valley of Mexico, and perhaps also the Acolhua.

26 *upon us.* Codex Ramírez, p. 2.

what to do. Tezozómoc, p. 16.

origin. The Chichimecs, in particular, favoured the system of one single chief.

27 *god.* Chimalpain, *Memorial Breve*, p. 22.

himself. Anales de Cuauhtitlan, p. 15.

their own. Origen de los Mexicanos, p. 264.

27 *there.* Tezozómoc, p. 16.
could. Durán, vol. II, pp. 34-5.
28 *in about 1315.* See Davies, *Los Mexica*, app. A.
knew. Codex Ramírez, pp. 28-31.
Copil's heart.' Crónica Mexicayotl, pp. 43-4.
29 *Mexica.* The Anales de Cuauhtitlan (p. 18) speak of the attackers as Culhuacan, Azcapotzalco, Xochimilco and Coyoacan. Chimalpain's *Memorial
Breve* (p. 118) mentions Xaltocan, Azcapotzalco and Xochimilco.
cities. Anales de Tlatelolco, pp. 36-7.
posterity. The surviving records for the Valley of Mexico were written or
copied after the Conquest.
365 days. The five extra days were known as the Nemontemi and were days
of ill omen. It has never been clearly ascertained whether the Mexican calendar had any kind of leap-year or system of intercalation of extra days.
occasion. The author is indebted to Sr Madariaga, the biographer of Cortés,
for this method of explaining the Mexican system of counting the years.
copiously. Acolco, whose glyph is given to their left as the place of their last
stand, in the form of twisted water, means literally 'Place of the Twisted
Water'.
30 *foes.* According to their glyphs, those foes were the Culhua, the Tepanecs
and the Xaltocans.
31 *them.'* Crónica Mexicayotl, pp. 49-51.
priest-rulers. Anales de Tlatelolco, pp. 3 and 37; Crónica Mexicayotl, p. 60.
capital. Anales de Tlatelolco, p. 39; Historia de los Mexicanos, p. 226.
32 *kinsmen.'* Codex Ramírez, p. 33.
staves. Torquemada, vol. I, p. 90.
made. Anales de Tlatelolco, p. 41.
33 *annihilation.* Ibid. p. 42.
persons. Durán, vol. II, p. 41.
cautiously.' Crónica Mexicayotl, p. 57.
34 *seasons.* Figures of Xipe Totec are even to be found in Tlatilco, corresponding
to about 600 B.C. or even earlier.

CHAPTER 2 EARLY RULERS

36 *travails.* Durán, vol. II, p. 43.
Mexicatzinco'. Ibid.
name. According to Durán (vol. II, p. 44), the place was also called Mixiuhtlan
in his day, which means 'place of giving birth'. There is still a Calzada
Mixhuca in the vicinity.
morning.' Codex Ramírez, pp. 36-7.
Tenochtitlan.' Ibid.
37 *oratory.* Durán, vol. II, p. 49.
in A.D. 1345. The Two House date for the foundation of Tenochtitlan has
traditionally been taken as belonging to the official Mexica year-count,

according to which it would be the equivalent of A.D. 1325. The author, however, agrees with Prof. Jiménez Moreno in considering that the foundation-date belongs to the Culhua-Texcocan count, in which case it would correspond to 1345, twenty years later.

37 *capital.*' Codex Ramírez, p. 37.

38 *mainland.* In addition, Torquemada (vol. i, p. 289) writes of the site as a place called Temazcaltitlan, as if it was already inhabited.

times. These bore the names Moyotlan, Teopan, Tzacualco and Cuepopan. See Crónica Mexicayotl, pp. 74–5.

39 *districts.* The question of the *barrios* and *calpulli* of Tenochtitlan is a complicated one. See Zantwijk, 'Principios Organizadores', pp. 188–222, and 'Los seis Barrios Sirvientes', pp. 178–82.

commerce. Tlatelolco tended, as far at least as its dynasty and nobility were concerned, to be orientated more towards the Tepanecs of Azcapotzalco, whilst Tenochtitlan had greater affinities with Culhuacan.

foundation. Aztec II pottery, found in considerable quantities in the lower levels in Tlatelolco, certainly does not owe its origin to the Aztecs. It appears in considerable quantities in Tula, which is considered to have fallen nearly 200 years before Tlatelolco was founded. Noguera actually calls this pottery 'Pyramid Pottery' – referring to the Pyramid of Tenayuca, associated with the Chichimecs of Xólotl during the heyday of Tenayuca in the thirteenth century; see Noguera, *La Cerámica*, p. 113. Aztec II has also been located in Tenochtitlan, but in smaller quantities; see Piña Chan, pp. 201 and 224.

On the other hand, Müller (pp. 31–4) and others consider that Aztec III dates from the time of the foundation of Tenochtitlan.

The whole question is discussed in more detail in Davies, *Los Mexica.*

1350. Martínez del Rio, pp. 516–21; Espejo, 'Algunas Semejanzas', 522–6.

40 *greatly.*' Crónica Mexicayotl, p. 67.

place. Codex Ramírez, p. 39.

time. Codex Mendoza, f. 1; Crónica Mexicayotl, pp. 70–1 and 77; Torquemada, vol. i, p. 291.

41 *in 1372.* The astonishing variety of dates given in different sources for the accession and death of Acamapichtli are sufficient in themselves to illustrate the complications of Mexican chronology. The question is discussed in detail in Davies, *Los Mexica*, app. A, nn. 3 and 4. The author reaches the conclusion that Acamapichtli came to the throne in 1372, or one year after Tezozómoc of Azcapotzalco. Cuacuapitzahuac succeeded in Tlatelolco in the same year as Acamapichtli.

Culhuacan. Durán, vol. ii, p. 52. In point of fact Coatlichan, not Texcoco, mentioned in the text, would still have been the chief Acolhua city.

42 *ruler.* Crónica Mexicayotl, p. 84.

time. Ibid. p. 85.

son.' Durán, vol. ii, p. 57.

spouse. Historia de los Mexicanos, p. 227.

43 *Tezozómoc*. Anales de Tlatelolco, p. 48.

clan-leader. Codex Ramírez, p. 42.

condition. It should be borne in mind that the principal military leaders after the *tlatoani*, the Tlacochcálcatl and the Tlacatécatl (also members of the inner council of four), bore the names of two of the original *barrios* of Aztlan.

power. Lopez Austin, p. 61.

44 *canals*. Durán, vol. II, p. 59.

Toltecs. The 'empire' of Xólotl had been an ephemeral affair, and probably much less extensive than Alva Ixtlilxóchitl maintains.

45 *north-east*. For some definition of the boundaries of the Tepanec Empire, see Carrasco Pizana, p. 271.

relatives. Anales de Tlatelolco, p. 22; Anales de Cuauhtitlan, p. 37.

roses.' Durán, vol. II, p. 58.

ezcahuitli.' Ibid. p. 59. The *ezcahuiztli* is a water-worm of reddish colour. Because it recalled blood, it was eaten to recall certain wars. See Muñoz Camargo, p. 33.

46 *conquest*. Other conquests were Cuitláhuac and Mizquic. For details of such conquests, see Codex Mendoza, f. v; Historia de los Mexicanos, p. 229.

common. See Davies, *Los Mexica*.

role. Sources mention such places as Toluca and Xilotepec, inhabited by Matlatzinca, ethnically related to the Tepanecs.

Chalco-Amecameca. Kirchhoff, 'Composición Etnica', lists no less than thirteen entities that formed part of Chalco-Amecameca.

47 *own*. Chimalpain, *Relaciones*, no. 7, p. 184.

custom. Ibid. p. 182.

nineteen years. See note to page 41 above.

Azcapotzalco. Durán, vol. II, p. 59.

48 *courage*.' Ibid. p. 62.

overlord. Tezozómoc, pp. 20–1.

themselves.' Durán, vol. II, p. 66.

49 *towns. . . .*' Ibid. p. 66.

fashion. . . .' Ibid. pp. 64–5.

tribute. Tezozómoc, p. 22.

council. Durán, vol. II, p. 65.

clothes. Torquemada, vol. I, p. 104.

arms. The Crónica Mexicayotl (p. 95) says a war with Cuernavaca started at that time that lasted forty years.

50 *beautifully*. Crónica Mexicayotl, pp. 94–5.

emperors. Ibid. p. 95.

51 *ancestors*. Nazareo, pp. 109–29.

Tlaxcala. Many went to Metztitlan. Like Xaltocan, Metztitlan had Otomí connections.

51 *cultivate.* Ixtlilxóchitl, vol. II, p. 78.
campaign. Barlow and others have argued that the correct date for this conquest is 1430. But the more obvious interpretation of the native calendar-date of Ten Rabbit (1398) is probably the correct one. An additional proof of this is that two daughters of Cuacuapitzahuac, ruler of Tlatelolco at the time, married into the royal family of Totomihuacan, the nearest neighbour of Cuauhtinchan.

52 *setback.* Historia de los Mexicanos, p. 229.
recovery. Anales de Tlatelolco, p. 53.
Azcapotzalco. Chimalpain, *Relaciones*, no. 7, p. 187.
'*Smoking Shield*'. Cuacuapitzahuac of Tlatelolco had already died, probably in 1407, and was succeeded by Tlacoteotl.
die for it. Durán, vol. I, pp. 69–70.

53 *foul.*' Tezozómoc, p. 23.
in 1426. Ibid. p. 25.
nobility. Sahagún, *Historia General*, bk IX, ch. 1.
son. The chronology of this war is also rather complicated, owing to the use of different calendar-counts to give dates; see Davies, *Los Mexica*, app. A, table A.
Acolhua. Prof. Jiménez Moreno considers that Huexotla became the chief Acolhua city for a short time after the decline of Coatlichan and before the rise of Texcoco.
times. Ixtlilxóchitl, vol. II, p. 61.

54 *language.* Mapa Quinatzin, p. 83.
south. These were known as Tlaillotlaca, 'the returned ones'; see Ixtlilxóchitl, vol. II, pp. 69–70.
Nahuatl. Ibid. pp. 73–4.
group. Culhua, in this context, could well mean 'Mexica'. The four groups are described as Culhua, Mexica, Tepanecs and Huitznahua. There was a Huitznahua element among the Mexica who came from Aztlan.
Rain God. Pomar, pp. 34–5.
war. He had even played an equivocal part in the Tepanec war on Xaltocan, first mobilizing his armies to take part in the assault, and later taking pity on refugees from Xaltocan and giving them lands.

55 *earth.* Ixtlilxóchitl, vol. I, p. 146.
domination. Ibid. p. 146.

56 *done.* Ibid. pp. 146–7.
arms. Ibid. p. 148.
Tezozómoc. Only Huexotla and Coatlichan had remained loyal.

57 *repulsed.* See fourth note to page 53 above.
months. Ixtlilxóchitl's route can be followed on Map 3. He continued on to Xilotepec, wheeled back down to Tepotzotlan, where he fought another battle, and, after sacking Cuauhtitlan, defeated the Tepanec armies again at Tecpatepec.
repulsed. Ixtlilxóchitl, vol. I, p. 156.

58 *Tezozómoc.* Ibid. pp. 167–8.
   himself. Ibid. p. 185. Tezozómoc took Coatlichan for himself, and Huexotla was given to Tlatelolco.
   foliage. Torquemada, vol. I, p. 114.
59 *war.* The Anales de Cuauhtitlan (p. 36) and the Anales de Tlatelolco (p. 16) suggest the possibility of previous clashes between Mexica and Tepanecs before 1428.
   this war. Ixtlilxóchitl, vol. I, p. 185.
   reign. Chimalpain, *Relaciones*, no 3, p. 91; Codex Mexicanus, p. 443.
   gold. Ixtlilxóchitl, vol. I, pp. 191–2.
60 *occasions.* Ibid. pp. 193–4.
   civil war. Tezozómoc, p. 24.
   brother. Ixtlilxóchitl, vol. I, pp. 197–8.
61 *Lake of Texcoco.* Ibid. vol. II, p. 120.
   doom. Torquemada, vol. I, pp. 123–6.
   Chimalpopoca. Anales Mexicanos; Chimalpain (*Relaciones*, no. 7, p. 191) also says that it was Tepanecs from Tacuba who killed Chimalpopoca.

CHAPTER 3 THE OBSIDIAN SERPENT

63 *arrow.* In many parts of Mexico it is still possible to find ancient obsidian blades on the surface, and their sharpness goes far to explain the slow progress in the practical uses of metal. The warriors' club, the weapon with which the Aztecs are so frequently portrayed, is usually referred to as *macana* in Spanish texts. This is not, as is frequently believed, a corruption of the Nahuatl word *maquauhuitl*, but a term originating in the Antilles.
   tlatoani. Moctezuma and Tlacaélel assumed also the titles of Tlacatécatl and Tlacochcálcatl, the two main military offices, involving membership of the inner council of four.
   approaching. Durán, vol. II, p. 74. It is worth noting that we have no actual information of any conflicts at this moment between Tlatelolco and the Tepanecs. There are even certain indications that Cuauhtlatoa, the new Tlatelolcan ruler, may have been opposed to the harder line now in force in Tenochtitlan.
   you. Durán, vol. II, p. 74.
64 *lords.'* Ibid. p. 75.
   Azcapotzalco?' Ibid. p. 76.
65 *destroyed.'* Ibid. p. 78.
   subjects. Tezozómoc, p. 33.
   lords.' Durán, vol. II, pp. 79–80.
66 *Moctezuma.* Torquemada, vol. I, pp. 171–2.
   throne. Ibid. p. 132.
   ancestors. Durán, Tezozómoc and the Codex Ramírez, sometimes referred to collectively as the 'Cronica X', because they stem largely from the same

source, invariably give the Tenochtitlan version of events. Alva Ixtlilxóchitl, on the other hand, is always the advocate of Texcoco.

67 *another.* The first part of the story of Nezahualcóyotl's wanderings is taken from the Anales de Cuauhtitlan, a most valuable sixteenth-century source written originally in Nahuatl. The later events stem from the accounts of Ixtlilxóchitl – his information on this subject derives mainly from the Codex Xólotl, an earlier Texcocan source. In this instance it is therefore possible to see how the written chronicles were made up – since the earlier codex on which their version is based is also available for study.

death. Ixtlilxóchitl, vol. I, p. 187.

68 *offering.*' Anales de Cuauhtitlan, p. 40. The appellation 'Xólotl', the name of the first Chichimec 'emperor', implies that Nezahualcóyotl acknowledges Tezozómoc's right to consider himself as his successor.

power. Ixtlilxóchitl, vol. I, p. 188.

long. Ibid. p. 189.

princes? Anales de Cuauhtitlan, p. 41.

rooftop.' Ibid. p. 42.

69 *father.* Ixtlilxóchitl, vol. II, p. 108.

Texcoco. Ibid. vol. II, p. 121.

immortal. Ibid. vol. II, p. 122.

ancestors . . . .' Ibid. vol. I, p. 205.

70 *native city.* Ibid. vol. II, p. 125.

wife. Ibid. p. 127.

him. Ibid. p. 133.

cause. Ibid. p. 135.

71 *civil war.* Tezozómoc, p. 24.

72 *neighbouring cities.* Davies, *Los Señoríos Independientes*, pp. 87–91.

insignia. Anales de Cuauhtitlan, p. 45.

Conquest. Ibid. p. 45.

killed. Ibid. p. 46.

73 *war.* Ibid.

Mexica. Ibid.

population. Ixtlilxóchitl, vol. II, pp. 143–4.

subjects. The historian, Ixtlilxóchitl, always a loyal Texcocan, makes it seem as if this expedition was a quite separate undertaking on the part of Neza-hualcóyotl. In point of fact, however, the latter, recently expelled from Tex-coco, cannot have had sufficient forces to recapture it on his own. It seems almost certain that this campaign was simply the initial stage of the attack on Azcapotzalco; Tepanec forces occupying Texcoco would have constituted a severe threat to the Allied lines of communication.

caution. The version of events that follows is substantially that of Veytia, an eighteenth-century historian, but who had access to sources that have since disappeared. He tells his story basically from the Texcocan point of view, and in some ways it may represent a later reconstruction of what occurred – siege warfare was not very developed in those days. It is, however, much more

detailed than that of Ixtlilxóchitl, who normally gives the orthodox Texcocan account of events.

74 *north*. Their forces actually disembarked on the lake shore at the foot of the
Hill of Tepeyacac, where now stands the shrine of Guadalupe. From thence,
they advanced towards Azcapotzalco, leaving on their left the Hill of
Cuauhtepec, which still bears the same name.
spoil. Veytia, vol. II, p. 135.
lagoon. Ibid. p. 131.

76 *Allies*. Ibid. p. 131.
fled. Ibid. 136–7.

77 *lord*. Ixtlilxóchitl, vol. I, p. 228. It needs to be borne in mind that this
is basically a Texcocan version, which extols the actions of Nezahualcóyotl.

78 *temples*. Each *calpulli*, probably numbering twenty in all, received one *suerte* of
land for the upkeep of its temple, whereas Tlacaélel himself received ten and
the other military leaders two each; see Tezozómoc, p. 41.
soil. The precise manner of land organization in ancient Mexico is not easy
to determine, since sources give somewhat meagre information and tend to
differ on details. On this subject, Zurita is the best early informant. Among
modern authorities to be consulted are Georg Freund, Manuel Moreno, and
particularly Friedrich Katz (pp. 27–46).

79 *battle*. These distinguished life-tenants (*tetecuhtzin*) are principally mentioned
by Zurita (p. 86).

80 *chosen*. Durán, vol. II, p. 103.
Itzcóatl. Lopez Austin, p. 61.

81 *condition*. On the subject of slavery, see Katz, pp. 142–4, and Soustelle,
pp. 101–6.

82 *kingdom*. Ixtlilxóchitl, vol. II, p. 153.
thrones. Ibid. pp. 167–71.
artisans. Ibid. p. 158.

83 *Coyoacan*. Tezozómoc, p. 48. Those who participated included the rulers of
Xochimilco, Cuitláhuac and Culhuacan, places that had already at least on
one occasion been subjugated by the Mexica, when acting under the aegis
of the Tepanecs.
side. Durán, vol. II, p. 89.
mocked. Tezozómoc, pp. 50–2.
delicacies. Durán, vol. II, p. 93. For the significance of the *ezcahuite*, see note
to p. 45.

84 *Empire*. Ibid. vol. II, p. 101.
army. Ibid. p. 110.
presence. Ibid. p. 114.
purpose. Tezozómoc, p. 68.
Cuitláhuac. Today known as Tláhuac – another unimposing suburb of
Mexico City, where little now remains that might suggest that it was once
the proud seat of four royal dynasties.

85 *god.'* Durán, vol. ii, p. 118.
foot. Ibid. pp. 120–1.
cities. Chimalpain (*Relaciones*, no. 7, p. 195) states that Cuernavaca was conquered in 1439.
Pacific coast. Apart from Iguala, such places included Tepequacuilco and Zaqualpa: for full details, see Kelley and Palerm, pp. 287–9.

CHAPTER 4 MOCTEZUMA I – THE EMPIRE TAKES SHAPE

87 *won?* Codex Ramírez.
skies.' This is the rather apt translation given by Frances Gillmor in her study of Moctezuma I, *The King Danced in the Market Place.* Ilhuicamina means more literally 'he who shoots arrows to the skies'.
chosen. Durán, vol. ii, p. 125.
succession. Durán and Tezozómoc both say that Moctezuma was Itzcóatl's cousin, but are almost certainly mistaken in this as we have so many accounts to the effect that he was the son of Huitzilíhuitl, the last ruler but two, and therefore Itzcóatl's nephew.
88 *Mexica.* For a description of Moctezuma I's coronation, see Codex Ramírez, pp. 78–9. Durán and Tezozómoc give relatively little.
war. Codex Ramírez, p. 79.
victims. The Codex Ramírez implies that the war started very soon after Moctezuma's accession; however, Durán says (vol. ii, p. 133) that there were twelve to thirteen years of peace at the outset of his reign. Chimalpain, who gives more chronological details, says in his third and seventh *Relaciones* that the principal war started in 1446 and lasted for twenty years; in another context, that it ended in 1464. The seventh *Relación* also mentions an attack towards Tlalmanalco as early as 1443.
89 *Amecameca.* Its ancient name was Amaquemecan ('Place of Paper Garments').
rulers. Chimalpain, *Relaciones*, no. 7, p. 195.
friendship. Ibid. p. 199.
90 *in 1444.* See note to p. 88. Chimalpain, in his seventh *Relación*, states that Cuauhteotl, one of the rulers to whom, according to Durán, the Mexica sent messengers, was killed in this year.
bear.' Durán, vol. ii, p. 139. Most of what is told of the Chalca war is derived from Durán, vol. ii, pp. 134–43, and Tezozómoc, pp. 83–8.
91 *Camaxtli.* Camaxtli corresponds closely with the Mexica god Huitzilopochtli.
shortage. Chimalpain, *Relaciones*, no. 3, p. 97.
92 *follow.* Torquemada, vol. i, pp. 157–8.
cities. Chimalpain, *Relaciones*, no. 3, p. 99. Other sources agree that the hunger began in 1450; see Historia de los Mexicanos, p. 230, and Ixtlilxóchitl, vol. ii, p. 205.
itself. Snow is reported to fall in Mexico City about every twenty-five years, apart from isolated scuds. The last time that it fell and lay was in 1967.
collapsed. Historia de los Mexicanos, p. 230; Ixtlilxóchitl, vol. ii, p. 205.

92 *occurred.* Torquemada, vol. I, p. 158.

distance. Tezozómoc, p. 165.

93 *regions.* Durán, vol. II, p. 244.

boy. Ibid. p. 243.

received. Ibid.

94 *remedy.*' Ibid.

cycle. See p. 29 for an explanation of the fifty-two-year cycle.

95 *east.* See Florentine Codex, bk VII, chs 9–12. The translation by Anderson and Dibble into English of the Florentine Codex is one of the finest translations from the Nahuatl that has been done into any language.

96 *sacrifice.* Durán and Tezozómoc tell the story as it occurred before the famine, but the two events are undoubtedly related. Ixtlilxóchitl (vol. II, p. 206) relates the start of the War of Flowers to the anger of the gods at the Empire.

appeased. Tezozómoc, pp. 163–4.

afield. Durán, vol. II, p. 233.

97 *blood.*' Ibid. p. 236.

War of Flowers. See Chimalpain, *Relaciones*, no. 3, p. 89, and no. 6, p. 157. The Anales de Cuauhtitlan also make reference to early wars among the Chalca, and between the Chalca and the Mexica at the time of Acamapichtli as Wars of Flowers. It seems quite possible that the War of Flowers originated among the Chalca rather than the Mexica. It was in part dedicated to sacrifices connected with Xipe Totec, the flayed god, especially venerated in Chalco.

ancient Mexico. See Davies, *Los Señoríos Independientes*, p. 147. The whole question of the War of Flowers is discussed in ibid. pp. 139–50.

98 *responsible.* The Atotonilco in question is the one now known as Atotonilco el Grande. Chilapa, according to the Relación de Chilapa, was conquered in 1458. Nezahualcóyotl had already occupied a stretch of land round Tulancingo in the reign of Itzcóatl (Ixtlilxóchitl, vol. II, p. 196). We have no knowledge as to when the Xilotepec–Tula area was occupied, but it seems more logical to assume that this took place before the great drive to the east and south-east.

99 *undertaken.* The question of exactly which areas were conquered in each reign is a complex one. It was thoroughly investigated by Isabel Kelley and Angel Palerm in *The Tajin Totonac*, and is also treated by Barlow in 'Conquistas de los Antiguos Mexicanos'.

There are several lists of conquests for each reign, notably those of the Codex Mendoza, the Anales de Tlatelolco and the Anales de Cuauhtitlan. One difficulty is that they do not exactly coincide; the other is that there is a tendency to repeat the same conquest in more than one reign, indicating presumably that the place had to be conquered again, as frequently happened. The Codex Mendoza, in its tribute-lists, gives us the names of many places dominated by the Aztecs at the time of the Spanish Conquest that are not included in the conquest-lists, and we can only surmise in which reign they were conquered.

In our account of these campaigns, approximately the same order is followed as by Frances Gillmor in her study of Moctezuma I, *The King Danced in the Market Place*. Questions of chronology are amply explained in her notes.

Nearly all sources agree in that the Coixtlahuaca campaign was the first of the great expansion, and they mostly give the date of 1458. It may have lasted several years, as Torquemada mentions two campaigns. For the Cotaxtla drive, sources generally give 1461 or 1462; for the final defeat of Chalco 1465, and for that of Tepeaca 1466. There are doubts as to when the campaign against the Huaxteca took place; it seems logical that it would have followed after the Cotaxtla campaign, in, say, 1462 or 1463.

100 *territory.* See Torquemada, vol. I, p. 159. Atonal is not mentioned as ruler of Coixtlahuaca by Tezozómoc or Durán, who give the most detailed accounts of other aspects of this campaign.

101 *woes.* Pulque is still one of the principal beverages of the Mexican Indian today, and is made out of the fermented root of the agave plant. In ancient times, drinking of *pulque* was strictly controlled, and it was much used for ritual purposes. Texts often refer to it as the *chalchiuhoctli* or 'sacred *pulque*': the word *pulque* is not a native Mexican word, but was imported by the Spaniards, perhaps from the Antilles.

region. Durán, vol. II, pp. 226–39; Tezozómoc, pp. 159–62.

Moctezuma. Conquest-lists give such places as Teozapotlan (now called by its Zapotec name of Zaachila) and Mitla, in the vicinity of Oaxaca, as conquered by Ahuítzotl, two reigns later, and it would seem as if Coixtlahuaca was the limit of Moctezuma I's actual conquests.

102 *forth.* Torquemada and others suggest that it was actually Nezahualcóyotl who took these places, and there is no doubt that he played a prominent part in their conquest.

time. Durán, writing in about 1580, remarks of this behaviour: 'as is the case now with our Spaniards, unless kept well under control'.

Mexica. Where Tlaxcala is mentioned by the sources, it should always be understood that, until the last few decades before the Conquest, it was in reality Huexotzingo which was the leading state of that region, and which would undoubtedly have played a more important role than Tlaxcala in such events.

103 *alone.* Torquemada, vol. I, p. 162.

eat. Durán, vol. II, p. 198.

remain.' Ibid.

104 *gold.* The full list of tribute from the Cotaxtla province – as given in the Codex Mendoza – also includes more utilitarian items such as: 400 women's tunics and skirts; 400 small mantles, with blue and white borders; 200 loads of cacao; 400 large white mantles (of two lengths).

gods.' Durán, vol. II, p. 202.

himself. Tezozómoc, p. 149.

105 *days.* Ibid. p. 105.

105 *quails.* Ibid. p. 107.

successors. Tezozómoc and Durán make out that this was a true conquest, although remaining imprecise about the places actually conquered. However, both the Codex Mendoza and the Anales de Cuauhtitlan give Tuxpan as a conquest of Axayácatl and Xiuhcoac as conquered by Ahuítzotl.

onwards.' Durán, vol. II, p. 170.

106 *father.'* Florentine Codex, bk II, chs 52–3.

107 *south-east.* Chimalpain and the Anales de Tlatelolco place this conquest in 1466. Durán and Tezozómoc give an account of it first before others, which might seem more logical in view of its location nearer Tenochtitlan.

beasts. Durán, vol. II, p. 155.

pantheon. These towns were: Cuauhtinchan, Tecalco and Acatzinco.

peoples.' Durán, vol. II, p. 161.

109 *warrior.* Durán, vol. II, p. 212.

nobility. It is sometimes suggested that it was only the Spaniards who really prized gold, and not the Aztecs. However, the Nahuatl word for gold is *teocuitlatl,* which means literally 'excrement of the gods'.

fur. The description of these sumptuary laws is taken from Durán, vol. II, pp. 211–14. As regards the distinction between the hereditary nobility and the warrior class in general, the difference is made very clear in Sahagún, *Historia General,* bk VIII, ch. 17.

value. Durán, vol. II, p. 212.

river. Ibid. vol. II, p. 213.

executioner. Ixtlilxóchitl, vol. II, p. 189. The same law can be assumed to have applied in Tenochtitlan as Texcoco.

110 *might do.* Sahagún, *Historia General,* bk VIII, ch. 17.

remoter. For instance, Tzinacantepec was subject to the ruler of Toluca; see Tezozómoc, p. 230.

111 *Empire.* Cuernavaca made war on the Cohuixca; see Anales de Tlatelolco, p. 57. Cuitlahuac fought against Tliliuhquitepec; see Anales de Cuauhtitlan, p. 57. The Relaciones Geográficas contain innumerable references to local wars between different townships.

expedient. According to the Anales de Cuauhtitlan (p. 53), Chalco was placed under military rule after its final overthrow; Toluca was also placed under a military governor – see Chimalpain, *Relaciones,* no. 3, p. 105. Azcapotzalco had also been put under direct rule, but its dynasty was restored after sixty years; see Ixtlilxóchitl, vol. II, p. 274.

Empire. Anales de Cuauhtitlan, p. 63.

gods. The killing of the ruler of Coixtlahuaca has already been related. Also Axayácatl killed the ruler of Xiquipilco, but these were rare occurrences.

Old World. Shirley Gorenstein points out (p. 56) that the Spanish word *guarnición* has given rise to a great deal of confusion. Whereas in modern Spanish it may have approximately the same meaning in the military context as the English word 'garrison', in the seventeenth-century dictionary of Covarrubias it is defined as 'soldiers guarding or protecting a place where they were', not 'troops *stationed* at a fortification' (and sent by the central power).

Alonso de Molina's Nahuatl dictionary, published in 1571, translates *guarnición* into Nahuatl as *centlamantin yaoquizque* and retranslates this same Nahuatl phrase into Spanish simply as 'a squadron of soldiers', with no implication that they are specifically stationed in any particular place.

Bernal Díaz uses the word *guarnición* quite definitely simply to mean an expedition, and not a fixed garrison as we know it; see Díaz, *Chronicles*, ch. CL.

111 *stationed*. This was at Huaquechula, but it is clear that they had been sent specially: see Torquemada, vol. I, p. 517.

112 *merchandise*. Katz (pp. 92–4) has added up all the tribute from the lists given for each province in the Codex Mendoza.

113 *peoples*. Chalco provided soldiers – Durán, vol. II, p. 157; Tehuantepec helped the Mexica ruler Ahuítzotl – Durán, vol. II; Toluca levies were used against Teloloapan – Durán, vol. II, p. 284; to quote only a few examples.

Conquest. See Cooke and Simpson.

remainder. Torquemada, vol. I, p. 398.

colonized. Two other examples of Aztec colonization are Teloloapan and Oztoma.

marriage. Durán, vol. II, p. 421.

114 *levies*. In the typical case of Oztoma, see Armillas, 'Fortalezas Mexicanas'.

defence. The Relaciones Geográficas, reports on New Spain made to Philip II, abound in examples of such places.

115 *ruler*. Zurita, pp. 74 and 100.

subjects. Ixtlilxóchitl, vol. II, p. 158.

redistributed. Ibid. p. 198.

Tulancingo. Ibid. p. 196.

116 *Gulf of Mexico*. Anales de Cuauhtitlan, p. 64; Motolinía, p. 206; Torquemada, vol. I, p. 167. Ixtlilxóchitl also mentions places in quite a different direction, round Toluca, and in the present-day state of Morelos, as tributaries of Texcoco – but in view of the same author's claims of large 'empires' for such predecessors of Nezahualcóyotl as Techotlalatzin, whose domains probably did not stretch much beyond Texcoco itself, one doubts of the reliability of this source on such matters. Equally it is worth mentioning that the 'Memorial de los Pueblos Sujetos al Señorío de Tlacopan' gives a vast area as paying tribute to this very junior member of the alliance, but no one thereby claims that Tacuba was on a par with Tenochtitlan.

reduced. The Relación de Cempoala mentions Zempoala, Tlaquilpa, Temascalapa and Tezontepec as having passed from Texcocan to Mexica control.

command. For description of Nezahualcóyotl's palace, see Ixtlilxóchitl, vol. II, pp. 175–86.

117 *little*. Cantares Mexicanos, f. 17 r, quoted in León Portilla, *Trece Poetas*, p. 49.

animal. Ixtlilxóchitl, vol. II, pp. 209–12.

117 *foot.* The modern town of Texcoco unfortunately offers little to recall its great past.

118 *wood.* Ixtlilxóchitl, vol. II, p. 210.

increased. Tenochtitlan at the time of the Conquest may have had up to 250,000 inhabitants and was a giant among Middle American cities. For instance, Mayapan, the last Maya city ruling an 'empire' in Yucatan, is estimated to have had only 12,000 inhabitants.

119 *god.* Tezozómoc.

additions. Marquina describes the Temple complex at the time of the Conquest, and in a map opposite page 60 traces what was the probable outline of the temple built by Moctezuma I before its subsequent enlargements by later rulers.

instruments. Durán, vol. II, p. 191.

stream. The original name was Ahuehuetl, still known as Ahuehuete in Mexico today. Anderson and Dibble, in their translation of the Florentine Codex, translate as 'cypress'.

120 *near by.* Clavijero, bk VII, ch. 30.

coast. Durán, vol. II, pp. 247–8.

regions. Ibid. p. 248.

121 *continued'.* Chimalpain, *Relaciones,* no. 3, p. 100.

killed. Durán, vol. II, p. 145.

man.' Ibid. p. 146. The name given for this prince is Ezahuahuacatl, but this is really an important title, one of the four councillors, and not a proper name.

Fire God. For a fuller description, see Sahagún, *Historia General,* bk II, ch. 29.

fray. Chimalpain, *Relaciones,* no. 3, p. 101.

Chalco. Durán, vol. II, p. 148.

122 *honour.'* Ibid. p. 151.

123 *demons.* Ibid. p. 154.

CHAPTER 5   A NEW ERA

124 *in 1468.* The year 1468 is generally given for the death of Moctezuma. However, certain important sources, including Durán and the Anales de Cuauhtitlan, say that he died in 1469.

city of Mexico. Durán, vol. II, p. 248.

sons. Apparently his only legitimate son had been Iquehuac, who had already died before his father; he had in his lifetime been Tlacatécatl, or leading general; see Chimalpain, *Relaciones,* no. 3, p. 103.

125 *remain.* Durán, vol. II, p. 249.

held?' Ibid. p. 250.

old. Tezozómoc, p. 193.

predecessor. Chimalpain, *Relaciones,* no. 3, p. 103; Crónica Mexicayotl, p. 114. According to Ixtlilxóchitl (vol. II, p. 260), Tezozomoctzin, Axayácatl's father, was married to the daughter of Moctezuma I, and he was thus grandson of both Itzcóatl and Moctezuma. He is also referred to in other contexts as Moctezuma's grandson.

125 *slaves.* The Crónica Mexicayotl, generally the best source of genealogical problems, says that Axayácatl was the youngest of three brothers, of whom the other two, Tízoc and Ahuítzotl, reigned later; see Crónica Mexicayotl, p. 114. Some other sources also suggest that Tízoc was older but that Ahuítzotl was younger than Axayácatl.

generation. The Codex Ramírez (p. 86) and the Crónica Mexicayotl (p. 122) both say that Tlacaélel died in the reign of Axayácatl. The latter source, which, as emphasized in the previous note, is the best-informed on such matters, says that he was succeeded as Cihuacóatl by his son Tlilpopocatzin, who died in 1503 and was in turn succeeded by his son Tlacaélel II. The existence of the latter has probably added to the confusion; the Crónica X – that is to say, both Durán and Tezozómoc – insist that Tlacaélel lived to a legendary old age (the figure of 120 years is mentioned) and continued to be the power behind the throne well into the reign of Ahuítzotl. Apart from other improbable aspects of this story, the latter, as will be seen, was hardly a character likely to play second fiddle to a doting hero from the past.

126 *remain.* León Portilla, *Trece Poetas*, p. 50.

boy. Ixtlilxóchitl, vol. II, pp. 241-3.

127 *unpunished.* Ibid. pp. 247-50.

lords. Cantares Mexicanos, ff. 29v-30r, quoted in León Portilla, *Trece Poetas*, pp. 145-7.

128 *conquered.* Chimalpain (*Relaciones*, no. 3, p. 104), Torquemada (vol. I, p. 176) and the Anales de Cuauhtitlan (p. 55) also mention a campaign against Tlatlauhquitepec in 1469. Torquemada (vol. I, p. 172) writes of a campaign against Tehuantepec, but this would seem rather premature; possibly it was a foray by Tlatelolco merchants.

Tlatelolco. Sources generally agree on the date of 1473. Only Torquemada differs, giving 1474.

129 *war.* Tezozómoc, p. 178.

allies. Torquemada, vol. I, p. 176.

ignored. Culhuacan supported Tlatelolco and, according to Torquemada, Xochimilco and Cuitláhuac as well. Huexotzingo and Tliliuhquitepec refused aid; see Tezozómoc, p. 178.

boiled. Durán, vol. II, p. 257.

130 *flat'.* Tezozómoc, p. 194.

itself. Ibid. p. 196.

action. Chimalpain, *Relaciones*, no. 3, p. 104.

133 *not.* Díaz, *Chronicles*, p. 156.

quills. Ibid. p. 157.

134 *false.* Cortés, *Cartas*, second letter to Charles V, p. 73.

135 *era.* The Esperanza phase at Kaminaljuyu, an important archaeological site on the outskirts of Guatemala City, is closely linked with the culture of Teotihuacan, near Mexico City.

135 *ranks.* Most of this account of the activities of the merchants is taken from bk IX of the Florentine Codex, which gives a Nahuatl version of what Sahagún's informants told him and which corresponds closely but not exactly with *La Historia de las Cosas de Nueva España*, Sahagún's Spanish version of such accounts. On pages 1 and 2 of bk IX are to be found the names of the various leaders or chiefs of the merchants. They are usually referred to in Nahuatl as *pochteca*, but sometimes as *oztomeca*, translated as 'vanguard merchants'.

slain. Florentine Codex, bk IX, pp. 18–21.

maize. Ibid. p. 13.

136 *ruler.* Ibid. p. 6.

Huitzilopochtli'. Ibid.

capes. Ibid.

trade. The Florentine Codex is referring to methods of operation under Ahuítzotl, but it is to be assumed that they would not have differed greatly under Axayácatl.

137 *gold.* Florentine Codex, bk IX, chs 7–8.

slaves. For more details on such forms of trade, see Acosta Saignes. A very important trading-base was Xicalango, to which the famous Maya green stones were brought from the interior.

138 *stones.* Durán, vol. II, p. 357.

chiefs. The principal merchants'-deity was Yacatecuhtli, 'the Lord who guides' (*yacana* means 'to guide'). The merchants were well provided with gods, since Yacatecuhtli had five brothers and one sister; see Florentine Codex, bk I, ch. 19.

talented. Ibid. bk IX, ch. 46.

139 *reeds.* Ibid. ch. 67.

independent. Carrasco Pizana, p. 255.

rulers. This date is given by Torquemada (vol. I, pp. 181–2) and the Anales de Cuauhtitlan (pp. 56–7). The Anales de Tlatelolco (p. 59) give 1475.

140 *men.* Durán, vol. II, p. 270.

141 *plants.* Ibid. p. 271.

bone. The stories in Tezozómoc (p. 207) and Durán (vol. II, p. 270) differ. Tezozómoc says that Axayácatl was wounded when emerging from his own ambush, while Durán states that the wound was inflicted in the enemy ambush.

speak. Tezozómoc, p. 212.

142 *feathers.* This an almost unique example that has survived of prisoners showing reluctance to be sacrificed. As such it is important; not to perform of one's own free will the prescribed ceremonies to the god amounted to a form of sacrilege.

unappreciated. Durán, vol. II, pp. 275–6.

143 *gods.* Beyer ('Mito y Simbolismo del Mexico Antiguo', *Complete Works*, vol. I, pp. 137–49) insists that this stone was intended to be a *cuauhxicalli* ('eagle vessel') in which the hearts of sacrificial victims were placed – the

eagle being identified with the sun. The original idea was probably that it should possess cylindrical form, rather like the Stone of Tízoc; a part broke off, however, as may still be noted, and it thus assumed a more disc-like shape.

143   *Lord of the Night Sky.* For a more detailed description, see Caso, *El Pueblo del Sol*, pp. 25–8.

    pantheon. Such are the complexities of the Mexican pantheon that gods tend to merge one into another. The Flayed God, Xipe, *is*, in effect, the Red Tezcatlipoca, while Huitzilopochtli, as the blue god of the midday sky, is the Blue Tezcatlipoca.

    Stone. Tezcatlipoca, Ehécatl-Quetzalcoatl, Chalchiuhtlicue and Tlaloc.

144   *to me.'* Florentine Codex, bk VII, chs 3–4.

    Pyramid of the Moon. Ibid. ch. 5.

145   *today.'* Ibid. ch. 7.

    rabbit. Ibid. ch. 7.

    moved.' Ibid. ch. 9.

    loan. Cantares Mexicanos, f. 35 (MS. in the National Library in Mexico City).

146   *subdued.* Codex Mendoza, the Anales de Cuauhtitlan and the Anales de Tlatelolco give Tochtepec as a conquest of Axayácatl, not Moctezuma I.

    Patzcuaro. Tzintzuntzan means 'place of humming birds' and Michuacan 'place of fish'. These are Nahuatl, not Tarascan words. Many details on the Tarascans are given by the Relación de Michoacán.

    tribes. The claim may seem uncertain, since Nahuatl and Tarascan have totally different roots.

    activity. The name of the god, Curicaveri, is a Tarascan appellation and means 'The Great Burner'.

147   *in 1478.* This date is given by the Anales de Cuauhtitlan and the Codex Telleriano-Remensis. Torquemada (vol. I, p. 182) gives 1474.

    secured. Torquemada says (vol. I, p. 182) that 11,060 prisoners were taken.

    ill-advised.' Durán, vol. II, p. 283. The Matlatzinca were, of course, the people of the Toluca region.

    yolatl. Durán, vol. II, p. 283. *Yolatl*, literally meaning 'heart water', was made of maize.

    four. His name is given as Huitznahuacatl, but this is really more title than name.

148   *so let us do.'* Tezozómoc, p. 229.

    wounded. Durán, vol. II, pp. 284–5.

    gods. Tezozómoc, p. 231.

149   *throne.* Oztoma and Tlacotepec are given by the Codex Mendoza as conquests of Axayácatl as well as by the Anales de Cuauhtitlan. They also attribute Mixtlan on the Gulf Coast to this ruler. Tlapa, west of Tlacotepec, was to be conquered by his successor, Tízoc.

    death. Tezozómoc and Durán still write of Tlacaélel as playing a leading part in such events. For doubts concerning his continued existence, see note to p. 125.

331

149   *leaders.* Tezozómoc (p. 238) on this occasion gives the names of sixteen Mexican leaders forming a kind of inner council. In other contests sources given a figure for these varying between thirteen and twenty.

moved. For descriptions of Axayácatl's funeral, see Tezozómoc, pp. 238–43, and Durán, vol. II, pp. 295–9.

150   *world.*' Duran, vol. II, p. 296.

son. It is interesting to find here two opposing notions of the after-life of a ruler. It was apparently usually held that death made no class distinctions and that all were consigned to the grim ninth underworld of Mictlantecuhtli, god of the dead – apart from special groups, such as those killed in battle or sacrificed. But in this oration, after mentioning the nine months of death, it is equally suggested that a departed *tlatoani* might have enjoyed the same privileges as the slain warriors – though this is not altogether clear, like much in Mexican religious beliefs.

151   *Flayed God.* The name given by Tezozómoc for this god is Youalahuan: Eduard Seler defines this name as deriving from *yohualli* ('night') and *tlavana* ('to drink much'). Seler identified this god with Xipe Totec (vol. II, pp. 1070–4.) Tezozómoc's account tells us that when attired in this garb the figure of the dead ruler wore the *tlauhquecholtzontli*, or headdress of spoon-bill feathers, characteristic of Xipe, and carried the *chicahuaztli*, or special rattle, another indispensable part of this god's accoutrements.

drink. Tezozómoc, p. 242.

ruler. Ibid. p. 242.

him.' Ibid. p. 243.

vessel. Ibid.

152   *intelligent.*' Florentine Codex, bk VIII, ch. 18.

to 1486. These dates are generally given by the sources, though the Anales de Tlatelolco say that Tízoc ascended the throne in 1482, and the Codex Telleriano-Remensis gives the date of 1483.

war. Torquemada, vol. I, p. 185.

153   *speech.* Duran, vol. II, p. 302.

golden age. The *tlatoani* equally derived his authority from Topiltzin Quetzalcoatl, the great Toltec priest-ruler.

Metztitlan. It was by now the established custom that a kind of inaugural ceremony took place when the ruler was first elected, and this was followed at a later date by his formal coronation, after captives had been taken on his first campaign. Durán says (vol. II, p. 311) that the actual coronation was always celebrated on the day One Lizard.

conquered. For a summary of what is known of Metztitlan, see Davies, *Les Señoríos Independientes*, pp. 29–66.

154   *area.* Epistolario de Nueva España, vol. XVI, pp. 56–7.

conquered. Tezozómoc, p. 251.

battle. Ibid. p. 253.

monarch. Durán, vol. II, p. 309.

155   *blankets.* Ixtlilxóchitl, vol. II, p. 261.

mantles. Ibid. vol. II, p. 266. (The measure *fanega* given by Ixtlilxóchitl is approximately one English bushel.)

156 *wishes.* Ibid. vol. II, p. 268.

Mexica. Durán, vol. II, p. 311.

survives. This stone is in reality also a *cuauhxicalli*, or 'eagle vessel', for containing the hearts cut from victims.

157 *conversion* W. Bullock, *Six Months Residence and Travel in Mexico* (1824) pp. 333-42.

Oaxaca. Anales de Cuauhtitlan, p. 67; Anales de Tlatelolco, p. 17; Historia de los Mexicanos, p. 231. The Anales de Cuauhtitlan (p. 67) report the conquest of Tízoc of Otlappan, which Kelley and Palerm identify with Tlappan.

hastened. Durán, vol. II, p. 311.

died. Torquemada, vol. I, p. 185.

CHAPTER 6 THE LION OF ANAHUAC

158 *Anahuac.* Anahuac means literally 'on the edge of the water' or 'near by the water'. Thus, the most correct use of the name signifies the warm lands bordering either ocean – of which so many were conquered by Ahuítzotl. It also came to be used to a lesser extent to designate the Valley of Mexico – also bordering the water of the lagoon. See Seler, vol. II, pp. 49-77.

master. Sources in general give 1486 for the accession of Ahuítzotl, though Ixtlilxóchitl says that it took place in 1485.

159 *respect.'* Durán, vol. II, p. 314.

chosen. The name derives from a small semi-mythical lagoon-mammal, having a hand like that of a man at the end of its tail. When it killed, it would eat only the eyes and nails of its victim.

anew. Durán, vol. II, p. 316.

people. Ibid. p. 317.

161 *Lord of the Southern Sky.* These, including the *xiuhuitzolli*, or royal diadem, are sometimes considered to have been originally associated with the earth-god Tlaltecuhtli or the fire-god Xiuhtecuhtli.

subdued. Ixtlilxóchitl (vol. II, p. 271) mentions the conquest of Chiapas or Chiapan in 1486, but is probably confusing this with the Matlatzinca town of Chiapa.

neighbourhood. Durán (vol. II, p. 319) mentions Xiquipilco, Xocotitlan, Cuauhuacan, Cilan and Maxahuacan, all in the same vicinity.

162 *field.* Durán, vol. II, p. 320.

themselves. Ibid. p. 320.

coronation. Ibid. p. 321.

splendidly. Ibid. p. 323.

163 *mountain-tracks.* Tezozómoc, p. 289.

did?' Durán, vol. II, p. 324.

coronation.' Ibid.

163 *comfort*. Tezozómoc, p. 290.
164 *peoples*. Ibid. p. 291.
   annually. Durán, vol. II, p. 326.
   complied. Ibid. p. 327.
   encampment.' Tezozómoc, p. 294.
165 *them*. Durán simply writes of 'the city', but Tezozómoc mentions Xiuhcoac
   by name. Chimalpain (*Relaciones*, no. 7, p. 220) says that Xiuhcoac was conquered in 1487. Xiuhcoac was the principal centre of population of the
   region; unlike Tuxpan, it was not included in the conquest-lists of the reign
   of Axayácatl.
   border. Chimalpain (*Relaciones*, no. 3, p. 111) mentions, apart from the
   inhabitants of Xiuhcoac, Tlappanecs and Zapotecs being sacrificed on this
   occasion, implying thus that preliminary campaigns had already been fought
   in Guerrero and Oaxaca.
166 *casus belli*. Tezozómoc, p. 302.
   beasts. Ibid. p. 303.
   messengers. Ibid. p. 306.
   solemnized. Durán, vol. II, p. 341.
167 *together*. It has even been suggested that the great site of Teotihuacan owed
   its downfall to deforestation, all the available wood being required to make
   lime and stucco in vast quantities.
   far-fetched! The correct figure might even have been five *tzontli* (units of
   400), i.e. 2000, misread as five *xiquipilli* (units of 16,000), i.e. 80,000.
   gods. Tezozómoc, p. 318.
   steps. Ibid. p. 323.
169 *innovators*. It was in Toltec not Aztec times that war first became a principal
   theme of artistic representations, and war in Middle America went hand in
   hand with sacrifice.
170 *cult*. Bernal, 'Teotihuacan', pp. 107–8.
   Huitzilopochtli. According to Sahagún's account, if the children sacrificed to
   Tlaloc wept profusely it was a propitious sign, foretelling copious rains.
171 *arrows*. Book II of the Florentine Codex gives long descriptions of these
   ceremonies.
   life. The most striking example is that of the young man who lived as the
   personification of the god Tezcatlipoca for a whole year before being
   sacrificed at the feast of Toxcatl. See Florentine Codex, bk II, ch. 24.
   sacrificed. See page 142.
172 *feathers*. Torquemada, vol. I, pp. 219–20.
174 *power*. Tezozómoc, p. 338.
   excuse. If Ixtlilxóchitl is correct in maintaining that Nezahualpilli ascended
   the throne at the age of seven in 1472, he was now still under twenty-five!
   perfumes. Tezozómoc, p. 340.
   revolt. Durán, vol. II, p. 347.
175 *places*. Tezozómoc, p. 345.
   conqueror, Ibid. p. 345.

175 *province.* Ibid. p. 347.

to go. Durán, vol. II, p. 352.

176 *Tenochtitlan.* Ibid. p. 354. It may be interesting to note that we find few such mentions of land in such distant provinces being set aside for the ruler.

Ahuítzotl. Durán (vol. II, p. 355) says that he was elected locally, but Tezozómoc (p. 352) says that he was chosen in Tenochtitlan, which would seem more probable.

colonization. One such case was the reported colonization of Oaxaca by the Aztecs during the reign of Moctezuma I, at a time when the city does not seem to have been yet conquered. Frances Gillmor suggests that the colonizers may have been fleeing from the great famine.

177 *kings!* Ixtlilxóchitl, vol. I, p. 330.

178 *character.* Ibid. vol. II, p. 285.

179 *vengeance.* Ibid. p. 287.

closed up. Ibid. p. 294.

180 *sea.* We have practically no information on the actual dates of the conquest of the coast of Guerrero. One can only assume that the main events took place between the early wars of Ahuítzotl's reign and the conquests in Oaxaca and beyond from 1485 onwards. Durán and Tezozómoc relate these campaigns in this order.

Zacatula. Acapulco is almost certainly the port of that name on the coast of Guerrero; see Davies, *Los Señoríos Independientes*, p. 178. Ancient Zacatula was one league south of the modern site; see Barlow, 'Extent of the Empire', p. 12. For the probable location of the towns of the Cihuatlan province, see ibid. pp. 8–15.

Empire. The Tarascan frontier can be traced southwards from Alahuiztlan and Oztoma to Totoltepec, Tetela and Otlatla. We know from the Relaciones Geográficas of the first two that they lay on the frontier.

181 *area.* We have a Carbon 14 date for Monte Alban I of approximately 600 B.C. or *1489.* Coyolapan, lying near the city of Oaxaca, and which was actually the capital of the Aztec province occupying this region, was conquered in 1488 (Anales de Tlatelolco, p. 60) or 1489 (Torquemada, vol. I, p. 186).

by 1495. Chimalpain, *Relaciones*, no. 3, states that Cuauhpilollan, Mizquitlan and Tzapotlan were conquered in 1494. The Codex Telleriano-Remensis gives the date of 1495 for Mitla and Teozapotlan.

182 *feathers.* Durán, vol. II, p. 357.

183 *drink it.* Tezozómoc, p. 358. *Papalotlaxcalli* means literally 'butterfly tortilla'; *xonecuilli* is a kind of maize cake or biscuit in the form of an S to represent lightning, and usually offered to the goddess Macuilxóchitl.

recruits. Ibid. p. 361.

mercy. Durán, vol. II, p. 360.

losses. Ibid. p. 361.

184 *before.* Ibid.

battle. Florentine Codex, bk VIII, ch. 17.

185 *ruler.* Ibid. ch. 17.

185 *warriors.* . . . Ibid.
186 *comply.* Tezozómoc, p. 128.
    general.' Florentine Codex, bk VIII, ch. 17.
187 *arms.* Tezozómoc (p. 371) tells how, when war was declared, the young men
    of the *telpochcalli* (the regular school, as opposed to the *calmecac*, only for the
    upper class) practised arms: they were clearly not part of any standing army.
    hand. Pomar, p. 29.
    Tlatelolco.' Florentine Codex, bk VIII, ch. 17.
    temples. Ibid. ch. 17.
188 *them.* Ibid. ch. 17.
189 *ear.* Ibid. ch. 21.
    foes.' Ibid.
    designs. Ibid.
    '*seasoned warrior*'. Ibid. 'Seasoned warrior' is the translation given for the
    Nahuatl word *tequihua*. Pomar (p. 38) confirms that also in Texcoco the
    tequihua had the right to participate in the councils of war.
190 *Aztecs.* Bernal, 'Teotihuacan', p. 108.
    corps d'élite. Another important order of knights was the Otomí knights –
    who were not necessarily Otomís themselves (Tezozómoc, p. 393).
    tribute. Ixtlilxóchitl (vol. II, p. 289) and Chimalpain (*Relaciones*, no. 3, p. 120)
    mention the conquest of Xaltepec in 1500.
    rebellion. Durán, vol. II, p. 384.
191 *Ahuítzotl.* Ixtlilxóchitl, vol. II, p. 289.
    named. Durán, vol. II, p. 388. Durán mentions Ayotla, exactly on the present
    frontier with Guatemala, and Mazatlan, very near the border, in addition to
    Soconusco itself.
    defeat. Ibid. p. 388.
    predominance. Torquemada, vol. I, p. 191.
192 *Mexico.* Tikal, in the Maya area, as well as Teotihuacan, where incipient
    urbanism is in evidence, might have covered comparable areas – but certainly
    did not house populations as great.
    year. Durán, vol. II, p. 370.
193 *advice.*' Ibid. vol. II, p. 372. The whole story is best told in ibid. pp. 369–74,
    and Tezozómoc, pp. 379–87.
    neck. Chimalpain (*Relaciones*, no. 7, p. 227) says that Ahuítzotl also killed the
    ruler of Huitzolopochco (today Chirubusco) for advising against the use of
    the Coyoacan springs.
    kinsman. Tacuba and Coyoacan were both basically Tepanec cities.
    deceased. Durán, vol. II, p. 375.
    Goddess of Water. The sister of Tlaloc, God of Rain, was Chalchiuhtlicue ('she
    who has the skirt of green stones'). She is the goddess of all horizontal water,
    of lakes and rivers, as opposed to the rain, which falls.
194 *ancient.* Tlaloc was the principal deity of Teotihuacan.
    emblem. Durán, vol. II, p. 376.
    Mexico-Tenochtitlan.' Ibid. p. 376.

194 *frogs.* Ibid. pp. 377–8.

    canals. Both Durán and Tezozómoc make it seem as if the floods came immediately after the aqueduct was completed and as if this were the sole cause. However, the Anales de Cuauhtitlan (p. 58) state that the aqueduct was made in 1499 and that the floods came in 1500. Chimalpain (*Relaciones*, no. 3, p. 119) says that there were very heavy rains in the latter year – implying that the inundation was caused by these and not by the new aqueduct.

195 *inundated.* Anales de Cuauhtitlan, pl. 58.

    niece. Ixtlilxóchitl, vol. II, p. 292.

196 *water.* Durán, vol. II, pp. 379–80.

    god. Tezozómoc, p. 387.

197 *done.* Durán, vol. II, p. 381.

198 *west.* See Marquina, pl. 2.

    towers. Sahagún, *Historia General*, bk II, app. 2. Ilhuicatl Xoxouhqui means 'azure sky', as befitting the Lord of the Southern Sky.

    reign. Seler, vol. II, p. 209.

200 *territory.* Barlow, 'Extent of the Empire', p. 99.

    Aztec-dominated. See Davies, *Los Señoríos Independientes*, pp. 205–8 and accompanying map showing six cities in the Tototepec area which seem to have remained independent.

201 *Gulf coast.* Much of this trade was done through the port of Xicalango.

202 *diet.* One can obtain sufficient protein if one eats *enough* maize and beans: 100 grammes of Mexican beans contain 7·5 grammes of protein, and 100 grammes of maize 3·2 grammes of protein, as opposed to 19·5 grammes in 100 grammes of beef. Curiously enough, turkey, one of the only domestic forms of meat available, contains nearly double the protein of beef. Dog is not listed. See Cooke and Simpson, p. 46.

CHAPTER 7 A MAN IN HIS PRIME

206 *age.* Most sources give the year Ten Rabbit (1502) for the death of Ahuítzotl and the accession of Moctezuma. A few, such as the Anales de Cuauhtitlan, give Eleven Reed (1503).

    inundation. Torquemada, vol. I, p. 193.

    fleshless. Durán, vol. II, p. 391.

207 *thorns.'* Ibid. p. 393.

    Stone of the Sun. Ibid. p. 395. Durán here mentions the Stone of the Sun as a *cuauhxicalli*, or eagle vessel, for receiving human hearts, thus confirming other reports to that effect.

208 *Ahuítzotl.* Xocoyotzin signifies 'younger son'. It means literally 'green' or 'fresh'.

    old. Tezozómoc, p. 394.

    revered.' Codex Ramírez, p. 94.

    courage. Durán, vol. II, p. 400.

    ministers. Clavijero, pp. 130–1.

209 *fountains.* Durán, vol. II, pp. 400–1. The Morning Star was important throughout ancient Mexico. One of the great achievements of the Maya was the accuracy of their calculation of the synodal revolution of the planet Venus. *supplications.* Codex Ramírez, p. 97.

210 *eye!* Durán, vol. II, p. 407.
later. Díaz, *Chronicles*, p. 154.

211 *once.'* Ibid. p. 154.
all. Ibid. pp. 154–5.
cacao. Ibid. p. 155.
service. Cortés, p. 78.

212 *infirmities.* Ibid. pp. 78–9.

213 *truth.'* Tezozómoc, p. 402.

214 *death penalty.* Acosta, p. 359.
lot.' Durán, vol. II, p. 403.
works.' Codex Ramírez, pp. 97–8.

215 *descent.* Durán, vol. II, p. 405.
sons.' Ibid. p. 404.
captors. Tezozómoc, p. 400.

216 *Mexico.* Ixtlilxóchitl (vol. II, p. 310) also stresses Moctezuma's tendencies towards absolutism.

217 *destruction.* Kelley and Palerm, who investigated the location of all Moctezuma's conquests, place Nopallan to the north-east of Tototepec (p. 311), notwithstanding Tezozómoc's mention of the presence of Otomís. Icpatepec, another objective of the same campaign, is located to the north-west of Tototepec.
footsteps. Tezozómoc, p. 417.
blue. Ibid. p. 418.

218 *conversation.* Durán, vol. II, p. 414.
caution. Durán (vol. II, p. 415) talks of thousands of prisoners being sacrificed on each of several successive days, but, as already explained, such figures must be treated with caution.
state. Ibid. p. 416.
identifications. For a list of all place-names, see Kelley and Palerm, pp. 311–15.

219 *absorbed.* Invaluable for the study of the final frontiers of the Empire is Barlow's 'Extent of the Empire'.
Spaniards. Also of great assistance in verifying which places paid tribute to Moctezuma are the Relaciones Geográficas, reports made on Mexico to Philip II, many published by Paso y Troncoso in *Papeles de Nueva España.*
state of Oaxaca. For details of the frontiers of Tototepec, see Davies, *Los Señoríos Independientes*, pp. 181–213.
scene. Ibid. p. 192.
Spaniards. Ibid. p. 197.
ruler. Ixtlilxóchitl, vol. I, p. 384.
Yopitzingo. Davies, *Los Señoríos Independientes*, pp. 157–79.

221 *arts.* Their other name for the Yopis is the Tlappanecs, which means the 'red

people', i.e. the people of Xipe Totec, who is to be identified with the Red Tezcatlipoca.

221 *Acapulco*. The Yopi border more or less corresponded with the River Papagayo; see Davies, *Los Señoríos Independientes*, map 4 opposite p. 176.

Moctezuma. The Relación de Chilapa (p. 177) says that this place was first conquered in 1468.

territory. There were, in fact, two distinct principalities – Metztitlan and Tototepec (usually referred to as Tototepec de Hidalgo, to distinguish it from the other Tototepec in Oaxaca); see Davies, *Los Señoríos Independientes*, pp. 29–56.

Moctezuma. For places in the Metztitlan–Tototepec area that were Aztec tributaries, see ibid. pp. 58–9.

tributaries. See Kelley and Palerm, pp. 278–9. Such places as Jicotepec (now Villa Juarez), Pantepec and Pancoac were conquered by Moctezuma II.

Gulf coast. Anales de Tlatelolco, p. 61, and Anales de Cuauhtitlan, p. 59.

222 *Guatemalan border*. Durán (vol. II, p. 417) mentions the objectives of this campaign as Icpatepec and Xaltepec. The Xaltepec in question must surely be the one situated to the north of Soconusco, since Durán's account makes it clear that the campaign took place beyond Tehuantepec. Durán (p. 418) also mentions that it was directed at territories very distant from Tenochtitlan.

abandoned. Ixtlilxóchitl, vol. II, p. 322.

purge. Durán, vol. II, p. 419.

223 *them*.' Ibid. p. 422.

wars. Ibid. p. 419.

governor. Anales de Tlatelolco, p. 61. The Tlacochcálcatl Tizcuecpopocatzin acted as governor for nineteen years until his death in 1506.

Achiotla. Fray Franciso Burgoa, 'Geográfica Descripción de la Parte Septentrional del Polo Artico de la América' (1934).

224 *resistance*. The towns mentioned by Durán and Tezozómoc are Tototepec and Quetzaltepec. This has led certain investigators to imply that the capital of the independent state of Tototepec was taken. The matter is argued at some length – see Davies, *Los Señoríos Independientes*, pp. 198–201 – the conclusion being reached that the reference concerns another city of that name – so frequent in Mexico.

spared. Tezozómoc, pp. 434–5.

killed. These places are mentioned together by Durán and Tezozómoc. The Anales de Tlatelolco say the campaign took place in 1505 (p. 61); Torquemada says 1506; the Codex Telleriano-Remensis gives the date of 1509.

deserted. Tezozómoc, p. 448.

Teuctepec. Durán and Tezozómoc place this campaign just before the New Fire, and therefore a date of 1506 would seem logical. Kelley and Palerm (p. 311) identify Teuctepec as lying north-east of Tototepec.

225 *taken*. Durán, vol. II, p. 441.

parade. Ibid. p. 443.

conquered. Anales de Cuauhtitlan, p. 61; Torquemada, vol. I, pp. 196–7.

225 *crush.* See Davies, *Los Señoríos Independientes,* pp. 66–139, for more detailed discussion of the Tlaxcala question.

mountains. Muñoz Camargo, pp. 58–60.

226 *capital.* Altixco also had frequent wars with the Aztecs – it had probably already lost its independence to Huexotzingo – see Davies, *Los Señoríos Independientes,* pp. 75–8. Also the mysterious Tliliuhquitepec, situated to the north of Tlaxcala; see ibid. pp. 73–4.

another. Ibid. pp. 88–9.

area. See Kirchhoff, *Historia,* p. xxvii. The Toltecs had driven out the Olmeca Xicallanca. In turn they had troubles with their neighbours and called in the seven tribes.

inhabitants. The Tlaxcala region had also previously been occupied by the Olmeca Xicallanca.

council. The four settlements were called Tepeticpac, Ocotelolco, Tizatlan and Quiahuiztlan, in the order of their foundation. The first source to mention all four is Motolinía, *Memoriales,* pp. 188–9.

228 *families.* Herrera, vol. III, p. 181.

animals.' Mendieta, vol. I, p. 105.

eat.' Muñoz Camargo, pp. 110–11.

Orizaban. Durán, vol. II, p. 177.

229 *conquer.* Davies, *Los Señoríos Independientes,* pp. 148–9.

Supreme Ruler of the World.' Muñoz Camargo, p. 116.

itself. Torquemada says that the war started in the third year of Moctezuma's reign, but unlike most sources makes him ascend the throne in 1501, not 1502. Muñoz Camargo (p. 114) says that it started fifteen years before the arrival of Cortés, thus also implying the date to be 1504.

230 *versions.* See Davies, *Los Señoríos Independientes,* table B opposite p. 120.

began. See also ibid. Sources mainly agree on the dates of the flight of the Huexotzingans to Tenochtitlan.

prisoners. Durán, vol. II, p. 460.

231 *me.*' Ibid. p. 460.

honours.' Ibid. p. 461.

temple. Ibid. p. 464.

city. Ibid. p. 457.

232 *salt.* See Mendizabal, pp. 196–7. This form of salt, in Nahuatl *tequixquitl* (today known as *tequesquite*), is in reality sesquicarbonate of soda.

CHAPTER 8 THE SETTING SUN

233 *day.* Sahagún, *Historia General,* bk XII, ch. 1.

234 *hunger.* Durán, vol. II, p. 468.

kingdoms. Ibid. p. 458.

dread. Ibid. p. 469.

Salamis. Ixtlilxóchitl, vol. II, pp. 322–4.

235 *difficulty.* Ibid. pp. 329–30.

235 *election.* According to Ixtlilxóchitl (vol. II, p. 331), he went to Metztitlan. This place, like Texcoco itself, had Otomí affiliations.

Texcoco. Ixtlilxóchitl states that he took the Totonac territories in the north of the present state of Veracruz. However, Cortés found no Texcocans when he arrived there.

slavery. Durán, vol. II, p. 470.

236 *half deer.*' Mendieta, vol. II, p. 18.

stone.' Tezozómoc, p. 507. Normally Mictlantecuhtli is the name of the ruler of the nether world. Huemac was the last ruler of Tula.

them. . . .' Tezozómoc, p. 508.

237 *navigation.* Díaz, *Chronicles*, p. 28.

visitors. Sahagún (*Historia General*, bk XII, ch. 2) mentions the *calpixque* of Cotaxtla, called Pinotl, and that of Mictlancuauhtla, called Yaotzin.

done.' Ibid. bk XII, ch. 2.

238 *cannon.* Díaz, *Chronicles*, p. 40.

La Malinche. Malinche is a corruption of Malintzin, the Nahuatized diminutive of Marina.

239 *wounded.* Díaz (*Chronicles*, p. 47) gives the figure as seventy. Cortés (p. 17) mentions twenty.

ears. Tezozómoc, p. 518.

say.' Sahagún, *Historia General*, bk XII, ch. 4.

official. Tezozómoc (pp. 520–1) mentions Tlillancanqui, one of Moctezuma's council of four. This must be the same deputation, since Tezozómoc mentions the instruction to adorn Cortés with the god's attire.

240 *toads.* Sahagún, *Historia General*, bk XII, ch. 4.

Veracruz. This Xicalango, near Boca del Río, south of Veracruz, has now disappeared. It has nothing to do with the important pre-Columbian trading-centre further to the east, along the coast.

sandals. Florentine Codex, bk XII, ch. 5.

241 *us?*' Sahagún, *Historia General*, bk XII, ch. 6.

them.' Ibid.

greyhounds. Díaz, *Chronicles*, ch. 57.

242 *pass.*' Sahagún, *Historia General*, bk XII, ch. 9.

gold.' Díaz, *Chronicles*, p. 59.

victims. Ibid. p. 61.

243 *disappeared.* Ibid. p. 61.

country.' Ibid. p. 71.

jewellery. Ibid. p. 72.

clothing. Gómara, p. 123.

244 *horses.* Díaz, *Chronicles*, p. 73.

eaten. Ibid. pp. 73–4.

245 *traitors.* According to Durán (vol. II, p. 525), this delegation included Huitznahuacatl, another member of the Council of Four.

246 *them.*' Díaz, *Chronicles*, p. 83.

247 *Empire.* For other place-names on the route, see Lacroix, pp. 35–7. The

principal among these are Xico, corrupted into Sienchimalin or Xocochima, and Ixhuacan de los Reyes, referred to as Tejutla or Teuhuixuacan.

247 *wished.* Díaz, *Chronicles*, p. 93.

249 *invader.* Torquemada, vol. I, pp. 415–16.
Tlaxcalans. Cortés mentions a figure of 149,000. The Conquistadors' figures of their adversaries' numbers are at times patently exaggerated: it can hardly be believed that the small state of Tlaxcala could field more warriors than the combined forces of Wellington and Napoleon at the battle of Waterloo!
meat. Muñoz Camargo, p. 190.

250 *goal.* Vazquez de Tapía, p. 37.
horses. Díaz, *Chronicles*, p. 258.
used. Ibid. p. 347.
weather. Ibid. p. 40.

251 *arrows.* Ibid. pp. 99, 103.
over-efficient. Cortés, p. 92.
poor. Díaz, *Chronicles*, p. 103.
alive. Ibid. pp. 302 and 305.
battle. Trevor Davies, p. 22.
magic. Soustelle (p. 247) comments very aptly on this point.
shoes. Díaz, *Chronicles*, p. 169.

252 *effect.* Ibid. p. 220.
Great Rebellion. Hemming, p. 215.
success. Ibid. p. 206.
outside. Torquemada, vol. I, p. 429.
hierarchy. Díaz, *Chronicles*, p. 138.
advice. The Origen de los Mexicanos (p. 276) says that the majority of the council favoured resistance.
Tlaxcalans. Díaz, *Chronicles*, p. 124.
presence. Ixtlilxóchitl, vol. II, p. 364.
temple. Gómara says (p. 196) that 6000 were killed, a figure repeated by Torquemada (vol. I, p. 440).

253 *them.* Sahagún, *Historia General*, bk XII, ch. 11.
say.' Ibid. ch. 12.

254 *him.* Ibid. ch. 13.
towns.' Díaz, *Chronicles*, p. 138.
dream.' Ibid. p. 139.
them. Andres de Tapía, pp. 576–9; Aguilar, p. 35.

255 *indignity.* Díaz, *Chronicles*, p. 142.
O lords. Florentine Codex, bk XII, ch. 16. This speech is not reported by Bernal Díaz.

256 *dread.'* Sahagún, *Historia General*, bk XII, ch. 17.
sleep.' Florentine Codex, bk XII, ch. 17.
charge. Ibid. ch. 18.
more.' Díaz, *Chronicles*, p. 147.

256 *unfamiliar*. Xipe Totec is the Red Tezcatlipoca, Huitzilopochtli is the Blue
Tezcatlipoca, while the Black Tezcatlipoca is Tezcatlipoca himself, thus in
effect being three gods in one. Huitzilopochtli was born of Coatlicue after
she had swallowed a ball of feathers.

257 *no more of them*. Díaz, *Chronicles*, p. 160.

  causeways. Ibid. p. 158.

258 *these*. Beyer, p. 334; Caso, *El Pueblo del Sol*, pp. 34–6.

  return. Motolinía, *Historia*, p. 75.

  deity. Mendieta, vol. I, p. 100.

  One Reed. Ixtlilxóchitl, vol. II, pp. 23–4.

259 *weep*.' Garibay, *Llave del Nahuatl*, p. 141.

  burnt.' Anales de Cuauhtitlan, vol. II.

  Tlapallan. Sahagún, *Historia General*, bk III, ch. 13.

  his.' Tezozómoc, p. 520.

260 *blood*. Gómara, p. 167.

  metal. Florentine Codex, bk XII, ch. 12.

  people. Muñoz Camargo, pp. 209 and 213.

  flesh. Díaz, *Chronicles*, p. 148.

  '*these two lords*'. Durán, vol. II, p. 541.

261 *confused!* Trevor Davies, pp. 40–1.

262 *Spaniards*. Florentine Codex, bk XII, ch. 21.

  this. Cervantes de Salazar, vol. II, p. 56.

  action. Díaz, *Chronicles*, p. 165.

  palace. Cervantes de Salazar (vol. II, p. 58) mentions a force of thirty who
entered Moctezuma's palace. Bernal Díaz, who was present, speaks of only
five (*Chronicles*, p. 169); but it would seem most probable that more were
at hand in case of need.

  amusement. Bernal Díaz (*Chronicles*, p. 170) says the talk lasted half an hour.
Cortés (p. 62) writes of 'long talks'. Cervantes de Salazar says they argued
for three hours (vol. II, p. 60).

263 *life*. Díaz, *Chronicles*, p. 170.

  him. Gómara, p. 227.

264 *gold*. Expeditions were sent to Zacatula on the coast of Guerrero (Díaz,
Chronicles, p. 185), to Malinaltepac (Cortés, p. 64) and to Tochtepec (Cortés,
p. 65).

  could.' Díaz, *Chronicles*, p. 171.

  concerned. Ibid. p. 189.

  name.' Ibid. p. 188.

  occasion. Ibid. p. 189.

265 *weep*. Ibid. p. 184.

266 *offerings*. Ibid. p. 178; Cervantes de Salazar, vol. II, p. 70.

  purpose. Díaz, *Chronicles*, p. 194.

  gods. Clearly the idols remained *in situ* for the present. Bernal Díaz says,
'Apart from their damnable idols', the image of Our Lady was set up
(*Historia*, p. 194).

266 *affection.'* Cortés, p. 74.
267 *conflict.* See Ixtlilxóchitl, vol. I, p. 340; Gómara, vol. I, p. 253; Chimalpain, *Relaciones*, no. 3, p. 121.
    gods.' Andres de Tapía, pp. 584–5.
    leave. Díaz, *Chronicles*, p. 194.
    Great Temple. Torquemada, vol. I, p. 464.
    men. Díaz, *Chronicles*, p. 238.
268 *cut up. . . .'*: Florentine Codex, bk XII, ch. 20.
    perished.' Anales de Tlatelolco, p. 63.
    circumstances. Aguilar, p. 48.
    for us.' Díaz, *Chronicles*, p. 240.
    killed. Ibid. pp. 242 and 243.
    drinking-water. Cortés, p. 95.
269 *was.* Díaz, *Chronicles*, p. 248.
    Mexicans. Ibid. p. 249.
    smell! Sahagún, *Historia General*, bk XII, ch. 23.
    motive. Chimalpain (*Relaciones*, no. 7, p. 236) says that the Spaniards strangled Moctezuma.
270 *bodies.'* Florentine Codex, bk XII, ch. 24.
    horses.' Ibid. ch. 25.
    distance.' Ibid.
    water. Sahagún, *Historia General*, bk XII, ch. 24.
271 *Tlatelolcans.'* Florentine Codex, bk XII, ch. 27.
    silver. Díaz, *Chronicles*, p. 258.
272 *made.* Ibid. p. 292; Cortés, p. 131.
    affirms. Apart from places mentioned in native accounts, Cortés writes of Culhuacan, Xochimilco, Chirubusco, Ixtapalapa, Cuitláhuac, Mizquic as having remained loyal even *during* the final siege (Cortés, p. 157).
    defenders. Florentine Codex, bk XII, ch. 33.
    entry. Díaz, *Chronicles*, p. 319; Cortés, p. 142.
    seen. Díaz, *Chronicles*, p. 320.
    Texcocans. Ixtlilxóchitl, vol. I, p. 342.
    Cortés. Ixtlilxóchitl (vol. I, p. 343) says that Coanacochtzin was succeeded by Tecocoltzin, who died soon after and was in turn succeeded by Don Carlos Ahuaxpitzactzin. But Cortés himself says that he made Don Fernando Ixtlilxóchitl *señor* immediately after Coanacochtzin's flight to Tenochtitlan.
    peace. Cervantes de Salazar, vol. II, p. 471.
273 *disappeared.* Díaz, *Chronicles*, p. 277.
    again. Ibid. pp. 313–14.
    peace. Gómara, vol. II, p. 32.
    return. Florentine Codex, bk XII, ch. 27.
274 *brigantines.* Cortés, p. 149. Bernal Díaz (*Chronicles*, p. 338) gives slightly different figures.
    loyal. Sahagún, *Historia General*, bk XII, ch. 33, mentions Xochimilco, Cuitláhuac, Mizquic, Culhuacan, Mexicalcingo and Ixtapalapa as remaining loyal.

276 *fighting.* Cortés, p. 158.
arm.' Díaz, *Chronicles*, p. 355.
there.' Florentine Codex, bk xii, ch. 31.
within. Cortés, p. 161.
277 *auxiliaries.* Díaz, *Chronicles*, p. 360.
them.' Florentine Codex, bk xii, ch. 37.
sacrifice. Cortés, p. 161.
alive. Díaz, *Chronicles*, p. 363. He gives the figure of those captured as sixty-six, as opposed to the Sahagún estimate of fifty-three.
278 *Spaniards.* Florentine Codex, bk xii, ch. 35.
remaining Spaniards. Díaz, *Chronicles*, p. 364.
Huitzilopochtli. Ibid. pp. 368-9. Bernal Díaz says that they were sacrificed not on the small pyramid but on the great temple, which would seem probably correct.
long. Ixtlilxóchitl, vol. i, p. 369.
swallow it.' Díaz, *Chronicles*, p. 373.
279 *fighting.* Ibid. pp. 374-5.
contained us.' Florentine Codex, bk xii, ch. 35.
demolished. Díaz, *Chronicles*, p. 378.
prevailed. Ibid.
280 *him.'* Florentine Codex, bk xii, ch. 38.
foes.' Ibid.
inhuman.' Ibid.
saltpetre. León Portilla, *Vision de los Vencidos*, p. 193.
281 *quickly.'* Díaz, *Chronicles*, p. 383.
13 August 1521.' Strictly speaking, Tequipeuhcan would mean 'where the toil commenced'. *Tequitl* means 'work' or 'hard work', equally 'tribute'. The normal word for 'slave' is *tlacotli*.
Indians.' Díaz, *Chronicles*, p. 384.
also.' Ibid. p. 383.
282 *nostrils.'* Ibid. p. 385.
salt.' Ibid.
vanquished. Cortés, p. 179.
Spaniards. Ixtlilxóchitl, vol. ii, pp. 379-80.
shifts.' Florentine Codex, bk xii, ch. 40.
dogs. Anales de Tlatelolco, p. 76.

CHAPTER 9 AZTEC AFTERMATH

285 *empty-handed.* Gibson, p. 60.
286 *servants.* Colección de Documentos, vol. xiv, pp. 142-7.
them. Mendieta, vol. ii, p. 72.
priests.' Gante, pp. 42-7.
287 *example....'* Díaz, *Historia*, ch. 171. All quotations from Díaz in this chapter translated by Nigel Davies.

288 *burden.* For more information and views on this subject, see Simpson.
 calumny. Crónica Mexicoyotl, p. 165.
289 *present.*' Díaz, *Historia*, ch. 177.
290 *tlatloani.* Don Pedro Moctezuma was the son of Moctezuma II and Doña
 Maria Miahuaxochtzin. This princess was the daughter of the ruler of Tula
 named Ixtlilcuechahuac; he himself was half-Mexica, being the son of a
 marriage between the Mexican ruler Axayácatl and the daughter of the
 previous ruler of Tula (Crónica Mexicayotl, pp. 151–2). Hence it is not
 surprising that the Spanish title should bear the name of Tultengo on the
 outskirts of Tula.
 Indians. Gibson, p. 61.
 atrocities. Ibid. p. 78.
291 *thinks!* Las Casas, vol. II, p. 671.
 developed. Gibson, p. 80.
 acts. Ibid. p. 92.
 wars. Simpson, p. 114.
292 *abhor it. . . .*' Las Casas, vol. II, p. 679.
 manifest.' Ibid. p. 689.
293 *here.* Ibid. p. 671.
 substantiated. . . .' Icazbalceta, vol. I, pp. 253–77.
 forbidden. Simpson, p. 130.
294 *natives.* Las Casas, vol. II, p. 725.
 were. Gibson, p. 403.
295 *sense.* Crónica Mexicayotl, p. 166.
 Mexico-Tenochtitlan.' Ibid. p. 174.
296 *slaves.* Gibson, p. 156.
297 *constituency!* There were only thirty-four electors, for example, in Cuauhtitlan; see ibid. p. 176.
 millions. Ibid. pp. 137–8.
 occasions. Codex Magliabeci, f. 72v.
 mice. Durán, vol. I, p. 181.
298 *mines.* Motolinía, *Historia*, p. 16.
 slaves. Navarrete, vol. I, pp. 225–41.
 governors. Simpson, p. 45.
299 *Indians.* Ibid. pp. 81–2.
 force.' Jiménez Moreno, 'Indians of America and Christianity', p. 82
 will.' Sahagún, *Colloquios*, pp. 56–61.
300 *secret.* Motolinía, *Historia*, p. 28.
 destroyed. Ibid. pp. 28–9.
 churches. Ricard, p. 37.
 hardships. Ibid. p. 36.
 mass. Ibid. pp. 50–1.
301 *conquest.* Madsen, p. 375.
 maize cake. Ricard, p. 265.
 habits. Ibid. p. 271.

302 *days.'* Torquemada, vol. III, pp. 320–3.
    hundred. Motolinía, *Historia*, p. 29.
303 *siege.* Cortés, p. 229.
    died. Gibson, pp. 27 and 225.
304 *sunk to 75,000.* See Mols, vol. II, pp. 504–5 and 512–13. None of the four
    largest European cities at the beginning of the sixteenth century – Paris,
    Naples, Milan and Venice – had a population of as much as 250,000.

BIBLIOGRAPHY

Acosta, Padre Joseph de, *Historia Natural y Moral de las Indias* (Fondo de Cultura Económica, Mexico City–Buenos Aires, 1962).

Acosta Saignes, Miguel, *Los Pochteca* (Acta Antropólogica, Mexico City, 1945).

Aguilar, Francisco de, *Relación Breve de la Conquista de la Nueva España* (J. Porrúa e Hijos Sucs, Mexico City, 1954).

Anales de Cuauhtitlan. Published in the *Codex Chimalpopoca*, pp. 3–118.

Anales de Tlatelolco. 'Unos Anales Históricos de la Nación Mexicana. Edited and commented by Henrich Berlin', in *Fuentes para la Historia*, no. 2 (Antigua Librería Robredo, Mexico City, 1948).

Anales de Tula (1361–1521). Sometimes known as the Anales Aztecas. Published by Robert Barlow in *Tlalocan*, vol. III, no. 1 (La casa de Tláloc, Mexico City, 1949) pp. 2–14.

Anales Mexicanos (1426–1589). Sometimes known as Anales México-Azcapotzalco. Published in *Anales del Museo Nacional de México*, época I, vol. 7 (1903) pp. 115–32.

Archivo General de la Nación, 30 vols (Talleres Gráficos de la Nación, Mexico City, 1933–4).

Armillas, Pedro, 'Fortalezas Mexicanas', in *Cuadernos Americanos*, vol. 41, no. 5 (Mexico City, 1944) pp. 143–63.

Bandelier, A. D. F., 'On the Social Organization and Mode of Government of the Ancient Mexicans', in *Twelfth Annual Report of the Peabody Museum of Archaeology* (Salem Press, Salem, Mass., 1879) pp. 557–699.

Barlow, R. H., 'Conquistas de los Antiguos Mexicanos', in *Minutes of the XXVIII International Congress of Americanists* (Paris, 1947) pp. 559–60.

—, 'The Extent of the Empire of the Culhua Mexica', in *Ibero-Americana*, no. 28 (University of California Press, Berkeley, 1949).

—, 'La Fundación de la Triple Alianza', in *Anales del Instituto Nacional de Antropología*, vol. III (Mexico City, 1949) pp. 147–57.

—, 'Some Remarks on the Term Aztec', in *The Americas*, vol. I, no. 3 (Academy of the American Franciscan Society, Washington, D.C., 1945).

Bernal, Ignacio, *Tenochtitlan en Una Isla* (Instituto Nacional de Antropología e Historia, Mexico City, 1959).

—, 'Teotihuacan, Capital de Imperio?', in *Revista Mexicana de Estudios Antropológicos*, vol. XX (Mexico City, 1966) pp. 95–109.

Beyer, Hermann. Volume I of Beyer's *Complete Works*, translated from the German by Carmen Cook de Leonard, in *El Mexico Antiguo*, vol. X (Mexico City, 1965).

Bray, Warwick, *Everyday Life of the Aztecs* (Batsford, London, 1968).

Bullock, W., *Six Months Residence and Travel in Mexico* (John Murray, London, 1824).

Burgoa, Fray Francisco, 'Geográfica Descripción de la Parte Septentrional de Polo Artico de la América', in *Publications of the Archivo General de la Nación*, vol. xxiii (Talleres Gráficos de la Nación, Mexico City, 1934).

Cantares Mexicanos. Manuscript in the National Library, Mexico City.

Carrasco Pizana, Pedro, *Los Otomíes*, Publications of the Instituto de Historia, Mexico City, 1st series, no. 15 (1950).

Caso, Alfonso, *El Pueblo del Sol* (Fondo de Cultura Económica, Mexico City, 1953).

—, *La Religión de los Aztecas* (Secretaría de Educatión Pública, Mexico City, 1945).

—, 'La Epoca de los Señoríos Independientes', in *Revista Mexicana de Estudios Antropológicos*, vol. xx (1966) pp. 147–53.

Cervantes de Salazar, Francisco, *Crónica de Nueva España*, 3 vols (Talleres Gráficos del Museo Nacional de Arqueología, Historia y Etnografía, Mexico City, 1936).

Chapman, Anne, 'La Guerra de los Aztecas contra los Tepanecas', in *Acta Antropológica*, época 2, vol. i, no. 4 (Mexico City, 1959).

Chimalpain, Domingo Francisco de San Anton Muñon Cuauhtlehuantzin, *Das Memorial Breve acerca de la Fundación de la Ciudad de Culhuacan*, translated from Nahuatl into German by Walter Lehmann and Gerdt Kutscher (W. Kohlhammer Verlag, Stuttgart, 1958).

—, *Relaciones Originales de Chalco-Amaquemecan*, translated from Nahuatl into Spanish by Silvia Rendon (Fondo de Cultura Económica, Mexico City, 1965).

Clavijero, Francisco Xavier, *Historia Antigua de Mexico* (Editorial Porrúa S.A., Mexico City, 1964).

Codex Aubin (Oficina Tipológica de la Secretaría de Fomento, Mexico City, 1902).

Codex Azcatitlan (Société des Américanistes de Paris, Paris, 1949). Commentary by Robert Barlow published in *Journal des Américanistes de Paris*, vol. 38 (Paris, 1949) pp. 101–35.

Codex Boturini, *see Tira de la Peregrinación*

Codex Chimalpopoca (Imprenta Universitaria, Mexico City, 1945).

Codex en Cruz, ed. Charles Dibble (Mexico City, 1942).

Codex Magliabeci, ed. Duc de Loubat (Biblioteca Nazionale Centrale, Florence, 1904).

Codex Mendoza, ed. and trans. James Cooper Clark (Waterlow & Sons, London, 1938).

Codex Mexicanus 23–4. Commentary by Ernest Mengin published in *Journal de la Société des Américanistes de Paris*, vol. xli (1952) pp. 387–498.

Codex Ramírez (Editorial Leyenda, Mexico City, 1944).

Codex Telleriano-Remensis, ed. Lord Kingsborough, in *Antiquities of Mexico* (Robert Havell, London, 1831) vol. iii.

Codex Vaticano-Ríos, ed. Lord Kingsborough, in *Antiquities of Mexico* (Robert Havell, London, 1831) vol. ii.

Codex Xólotl, ed. Charles Dibble, Publicaciones del Instituto de Historia, 1st series, no. 2 (Mexico City, 1951).

Coe, Michael, *Mexico. Ancient Peoples and Places* (Ediciones Lara, Mexico City, 1962).

Colección de Documentos inéditos relativos al descubrimiento, conquista y organización de las antiguas posesiones españolas de ultramar, 2nd series, 17 vols (Madrid, 1885–1925).

Colección de Documentos para la Historia de Mexico, ed. J. García Icazbalceta, 2 vols (J. M. Andrade, Mexico City, 1858–66).

Collis, Maurice, *Cortés and Montezuma* (Faber & Faber, London, 1954).

Conquistador Anónimo, *Relación de algunas Cosas de la Nueva España y de la Gran Ciudad de Temestitlan Mexico* (J. Porrúa e Hijos Sucs, Mexico City, 1961).

Cooke, Sherburne, and Simpson, Lesley Byrd, *The Population of Central Mexico in the Sixteenth Century* (University of California, Berkeley, 1948).

Cortés, Hernán, Marqués del Valle, *Cartas y Documentos* (Editorial Porrúa S.A., Mexico City, 1963).

Crónica Mexicayotl, partly written by Alvarado Tezozómoc (Imprenta Universitaria, Mexico City, 1949).

Davies, Nigel, *Los Mexica: Primeros Pasos Hacia el Imperio* (Universidad Nacíonal Autónoma de México, 1973).

—, *Los Señoríos Independientes del Imperio Azteca* (Instituto Nacional de Antropología e Historia, Mexico City, 1968).

Davies, R. Trevor, *The Golden Century of Spain 1501–1621* (Macmillan, London, 1937).

del Castillo, Cristóbal, *Fragmentos sobre la Obra General sobre Historia de los Mexicanos* (S. Landi, Florence, 1908).

Deuel, Leo, *Conquistadors without Swords* (Macmillan, London, 1967).

Díaz del Castillo, Bernal. *The Bernal Díaz Chronicles*, trans. and ed. Albert Idell (Doubleday, New York, 1956).

—, *Historia de la Conquista de la Nueva España* (Editorial Porrúa S.A., Mexico City, 1969).

Durán, Fray Diego, *Historia de Las Indias de Nueva España e Islas de la Tierra Firme*, 2 vols (Editorial Porrúa S.A., Mexico City, 1967).

Epistolario de Nueva España, 1505–1818, ed. Francisco del Paso y Troncoso, 16 vols (Antigua Librería Robredo, Mexico City, 1939).

Espejo, Antonieta, 'Algunas Semejanzas entre Tenayuca y Tlatelolco', in *Memorias de la Academia Mexicana de la Historia*, vol. III, no. 4 (1944) pp. 522–6. *See also* Griffin, James B.

Florentine Codex. Manuscript in Nahuatl of Fray Bernardino de Sahagún, trans. J. O. Anderson and Charles E. Dibble, 12 vols (University of Utah, Santa Fé, New Mexico, 1950). Book XII of the Florentine Codex has also been translated by Angel Maria Garibay, and this translation is included in the Porrúa edition of Sahagún's *Historia*. A few of the quotations in Chapter 8 are retranslations from the Spanish version of this translation, rather than from the translation of Anderson and Dibble.

Franco, José Luis, 'Comentarios sobre la Decoración Negra en la Cerámica Azteca II', in *Revista Mexicana de Estudios Antropológicos*, vol. VII (1945) pp. 163–86.

—, *Motivos Decorativos en la Cerámica Azteca*, Serie Científica no. 5 (Museo Nacional de Antropología, Mexico City, 1957).

Freund, Georg, 'Derecho Agrario y Catastro en el Mexico Antiguo', in *Traducciones Mesoamericanas*, vol. II (Sociedad Mexicana de Antropología, Mexico City, 1946) pp. 157–79.

Gamio, Manuel, 'Restos de la Cultura Tepaneca', in *Anales del Museo de Arqueología*, época III, vol. I (Mexico City, 1912) pp. 235–53.

Gante, Fray P. de. *Cartas de Fray Pedro de Gante* (Fr Junipero Serra, Provincia del Santo Evangelio de Mexico, n.d.).

Garibay, Padre Angel María, *Llave del Nahuatl* (Editorial Porrúa S.A., Mexico City, 1961).

Gibson, Charles, *The Aztecs under Spanish Rule* (Stanford University Press, Stanford, Calif., 1964).

Gillmor, Frances, *Flute of the Smoking Mirror. A Portrait of Nezahualcóyotl, Poet-King of the Aztecs* (University of New Mexico, Albuquerque, 1949).

—, *The King Danced in the Market Place* (University of Arizona Press, Tucson, 1964).

Gómara, Francisco Lopez de, *Historia de las Conquistas de Hernando Cortás*, 2 vols (Imprenta de la Testimentaria de Ontiveros, Mexico City, 1826).

Gorenstein, Shirley, 'The Differential Development of New World Empires', in *Revista Mexicana de Estudios Antropológicos*, vol. XX (1966) pp. 41–67.

Griffin, James B., and Espejo, Antonieta, 'Alfararía cotrespondiente al último Periodo de Ocupación Nahua del Valle de Mexico', in *Memorias de la Academia Mexicana de Historia*, vol. VI (1947) pp. 131–47.

Gurría Lacroix, Jorge, 'Itinerary of Hernán Cortés', in *Artes de México*, año XV no. 3 (1968). Text in English, French and German.

Hemming, John, *The Conquest of the Incas* (Macmillan, London, 1970).

Herrera, Antonio de, *Historia General de los Hechos de los Castellanos*, 10 vols (Editorial Guarania, Asunción, Paraguay).

Historia de los Mexicanos por sus Pinturas, published in *Nueva Colección de Documentos para la Historia de Mexico* (Editorial Salvador Chavez Hayhoe, Mexico City, 1941) pp. 209–40.

Historia Tolteca-Chichimeca (also known as Anales de Cuauhtinchan), Fuentes para la Historia de Mexico no. 1 (Antigua Librería Robredo, Mexico City, 1947).

Icazbalceta, Joaquín García, *Colección de Documentos para la Historia de Mexico*, 2 vols (J. M. Andrade, Mexico City, 1858–66).

Ixtlilxóchitl, Fernando de Alva, *Obras Históricas*, 2 vols (Editora Nacional, Mexico City, 1952).

Jiménez Moreno, Wigberto, 'Diferentes Principios del Año entre diversos Pueblos del Valle de México y sus Consequencias para la Cronología prehispánica', in *México Antiguo*, vol. IX (1961) pp. 137–52.

—, 'The Indians of America and Christianity', in *The Americas*, vol. XIV, no. 4 (Academy of the American Franciscan Society, Washington, D.C., 1958).

—, 'Síntesis de la Historia Precolonial del Valle de México', in *Revista Mexicana de Estudios Antropológicos*, vol. XIV, pt 2 (1956–7) pp. 219–36.

Katz, Friedrich, *Situación Social y económica de los Aztecas durante los Siglos XV y XVI* (Instituto de Investigaciones Históricas, Universidad Nacional de México, 1966). Originally published in German.

Kelley, Isabel, and Palerm, Angel, *The Tajin Totonac* (U.S. Government Printing Office, Washington, D.C., 1952).

Kingsborough, Edward King, Viscount, *Antiquities of Mexico*, 9 vols (R. Havell, London, 1831–48).

Kirchhoff, Paul, 'Calendarios Tenochca, Tlatelolca y otros', in *Revista Mexicana de Estudios Antropológicos*, vol. XIV, pt 2 (1954–5) pp. 257–67.

—, 'Composición Etnica y Organizacion Política de Chalco según las Relaciones de Chimalpain', in *Revista Mexicana de Estudios Antropológicos*, vol. XIV, pt 2 (1954–5) pp. 297–9.

—, Prologue to *Historia Tolteca-Chichimeca*, pp. xix–lxiv.

—, 'Se puede localizar Aztlán?', in *Anuario de Historia*, año I (Facultad de Filosofía y Letras, Universidad Nacional Autónoma de Mexico, 1961).

Las Casas, Bartolomé de, *Tratados* (Fondo de Cultura Económica, Mexico City–Buenos Aires, 1965).

León Portilla, Miguel, *Aztec Thought and Culture*, trans. Jack Emory Davis (University of Oklahoma Press, Norman, 1963).

—, *Trece Poetas del Mundo Azteca* (Instituto de Investigaciones Históricas, Universidad Nacional Autónoma de Mexico City, 1967).

—, *Vision de los Vencidos* (Ediciones de la Universidad Nacional de Mexico, 1959).

Lienzo de Tlaxcala, published in *Artes de Mexico*, nos 51 and 52 (Mexico City, 1964).

Lopez Austin, Alfredo, *La Constitución Real de México Tenochtitlan* (Universidad Nacional Autónoma de México, 1961).

Madariaga, Salvador de, *Hernán Cortés. Conqueror of Mexico* (University of Miami Press, Miami, Florida, 1942).

Madsen, William, 'Religious Syncretism', in *Handbook of Middle American Indians*, vol. VI (University of Texas Press, Austin, 1967).

Mapa Quinatzin, ed. J. M. A. Aubin, published in *Anales del Museo Nacional de México*, época I, vol. 3 (1886) pp. 345–68.

Mapa Tlotzin, ed. J. M. A. Aubin, published in *Anales del Museo Nacional de México*, época I, vol. 3 (1886) pp. 304–20.

Marquina, Ignacio, *El Templo Mayor de México* (Instituto Nacional de Antropología e Historia, Mexico City, 1960).

Martinez del Río, Pablo, 'Resumen de Trabajos en Tlatelolco', in *Memorias de la Academia Mexicana de la Historia*, vol. III, no. 4 (1944) pp. 516–21.

Memorial de los Pueblos Sujetos al Señorío de Tlacopan, published in *Epistolario de Nueva España*, vol. XIV (Antigua Librería Robredo, Mexico City, 1940) pp. 118–22.

Mendieta, Fray Gerónimo de, *Historia Ecclesiastica Indiana*, 4 vols (Editorial Chavez Hayhoe, Mexico City, 1945).

Mendizabal, Miguel O. de, *Influencia de la Sal en la Distribución de los Grupos Indígenas de México* (Imprenta del Museo Nacional de Arqueología, Mexico City, 1928).

Molina, Alonso de, *Vocabulario de Lengua Castellana y Mexicana* (Ediciones Cultura Hispánica, Madrid, 1944).

Mols, Roger, *Introduction à la Démographie Historique des Villes d'Europe du XIVe au XVIIIe Siècle*, 3 vols (Université de Louvain, Louvain, 1954–6).

Moreno, Manuel, *La Organización Política y Social de los Aztecas* (Instituto Nacional de Antropología e Historia, Mexico City, 1962).

Motolinía, Fray Toribio de Benavente, *Historia de los Indios de Nueva España* (Editorial Chavez Hayhoe, Mexico City, 1941).

—, *Memoriales* (Luis García Pimentel, Mexico City, 1903).

Müller, Florencia, 'La Secuencia Cerámica de Teotihuacan', in *Report of Round Table Conference on Teotihuacan* (Sociedad Mexicana de Antropología, 1966) pp. 31–44.

Muñoz Camargo, Diego, *Historia de Tlaxcala* (Publicaciones del Ateneo de Ciencias y Artes de México, 1947).

Navarrete, Martín Fernandez de, *Los Viajes de Colón*, 5 vols (Madrid, 1825–37).

Nazareo, Don Pablo de Xaltocan, 'Carta al Rey Don Felipe II', in *Epistolario de Nueva España*, vol. x (Antigua Librería Robredo, Mexico City, 1940) pp. 109–29.

Noguera, Eduardo, *La Cerámica Arqueológica de Mesoamérica* (Universidad Nacional de México, 1965).

—, 'La Cerámica de Tenayuca y las Excavaciones Estratigráficas', in *El Estudio Arqueológico de la Pyrámide de Tenayuca* (Talleres Gráficos del Museo Nacional de Arqueología, Historia y Etnografía, Mexico City, 1935) pp. 140–201.

Origen de los Mexicanos, published in *Nueva Colección de Documentos para la Historia de México* (Editorial Salvador Chavez Hayhoe, Mexico City, 1941) pp. 256–80.

Oroczo y Berra, Manuel, *Historia Antigua y de la Conquista de Mexico*, 4 vols (Editorial Porrua S.A., Mexico City, 1960).

Papeles de Nueva España, ed. Francisco de Paso y Troncoso, 2nd series, 6 vols (Est. Tip. Sucesores de Rivadeneyra, Madrid, 1905–6).

Pereira, Carlos, *Hernán Cortés* (Editorial Porrúa, Mexico City, 1971).

Peterson, Frederick, *Ancient Mexico* (Allen & Unwin, London, 1959).

Piña Chan, Roman, 'Estratigrafía en los Terrenos Adyacentres a la Catedral Metropolitana', in *Memorias de la Academia Mexicana de la Historia*, vol. x (1950) pp. 199–244.

Pomar, Juan Bautista, 'Relación de Texcoco', in *Nueva Colección de Documentos para la Historia de México* (Editorial Chavez Hayhoe, Mexico City, 1941) pp. 1–65.

Prescott, William H., *History of the Conquest of Mexico*, 3 vols (Richard Bentley, London, 1863).

Relación de Cempoala, published in *Tlalocan*, vol. II (1949).

Relación de Chilapa, published in *Papeles de Nueva España*, ed. Francisco de Paso y Troncoso (1905–6), vol. v, pp. 174–82.

Relación de la Genealogía, published in *Nueva Colección de Documentos para la Historia de México* (Editorial Chavez Hayhoe, Mexico City, 1941) pp. 240–56.

Relación de las Ceremonias y Ritos y Población y Gobierno de los Indios de la Provincia de Michoacán (Aguilar, Madrid, 1956).

Ricard, Robert, *The Spiritual Conquest of Mexico*, trans. Lesley Byrd Simpson (University of California Press, Berkeley and Los Angeles, 1966).

Sahagún, Fray Bernardino de, *Colloquios y Doctrina Christiana* (Vargas Rea, Mexico City, 1944).

—, *Historia General de Las Cosas de Nueva España*, 6 vols (Editorial Porrúa S.A., Mexico City, 1956).

Seler, Eduard, *Gesammte Abhandlungen zur Amerikanischen Sprach- und Altertumskunde*, 6 vols (Akademische Druck und Verlagsanstalt, Graz, Austria, 1960).

Siméon, Remi, *Dictionnaire de la Langue Nahuatl ou Méxicaine* (Akademische Druck und Verlagsanstalt, Graz, Austria, 1963).

Simpson, Lesley Byrd, *The Encomienda in New Spain* (University of California Press, Berkeley and Los Angeles, 1966). See also Cooke, Sherburne.

Soustelle, Jacques, *La Vie Quotidienne des Aztèques* (Librairie Hachette, Paris, 1955). Published in English as *The Daily Life of the Aztecs* (Weidenfeld & Nicolson, London, 1961).

Tapía, Andrés de, 'Relación Hecha por el Sr Andrés de Tápia', in *Colección de Documentos para la Historia de México*, vol. II (J. M. Andrade, Mexico City, 1858–66) pp. 554–94.

Tapía, Bernardo Vazquez de. *Relación de Méritos y Servicios del Conquistador Bernardo Vasquez de Tapía* (Antigua Librería Robredo, Mexico City, 1953).

Tezozómoc, Hernando Alvarado, *Crónica Mexicana* (Editorial Leyenda, Mexico City, 1944).

Tira de la Peregrinación (Codex Boturini) (Librería Anticuaria, Mexico City, 1944).

Torquemada, Fray Juan de, *Monarquía Indiana*, 3 vols (Editorial Chavez Hayhoe, Mexico City, 1943–4).

Vaillant, George C., *The Aztecs of Mexico* (Penguin Books, Harmondsworth, 1950).

Veytia, Mariano, *Historia Antigua de México*, 2 vols (Editorial Leyenda, Mexico City, 1944).

West, Robert C., and Armillas, Pedro, 'Las Chinampas de México', in *Cuadernos Americanos*, vol. L (1950) pp. 165–92.

White, Jon Manchip, *Cortés and the Downfall of the Aztec Empire* (St Martin's Press, New York, 1971).

Wolf, Eric, *Sons of the Shaking Earth* (University of Chicago Press, Chicago, 1959).

Zantwijk, Rudolf van, 'Principios Organizadores de los Mexicas. Una Introducción al Estudio del Sistema Interno del Régimen Azteca', in *Estudios de Cultura Náhuatl*, vol. IV (1963) pp. 187–220.

—, 'Los seis Barrios Sirvientes de Huitzilopochtli', in *Estudios de Cultura Náhuatl*, vol. VI (1966) pp. 176–85.

Zurita, Alonso de, 'Breve y Sumaria Relación de los Señores y Maneras y diferencias que había en ellos en la Nueva España', in *Nueva Colección de Documentos para la Historia de México* (Editorial Chavez Hayhoe, Mexico City, 1941).

INDEX

Acamapichtli: chosen as ruler of Mexica (1372), 41-2; marriage, 43; conquests, 46; death (1391), 47
Acapulco, 35, 180, 219, 221
Acatzintlan, 35
Achiotla, 223
Achitometl, 33
Acolhua: settle in Valley of Mexico, 22-3; relations with Tepanecs, 54-5; divisions among, 55, 56
Acolman, 59, 297
Aguilar, Jeronimo de, 238
Aguilar, Marcos de, 289
Ahuítzotl: and human sacrifice, 97, 167, 169, 203; character, 98, 207; elected *tlatoani* (1486), 159, 161; first campaign, 161-2; coronation, 162-4, 204; campaign against Huaxtecs, 164-5; completion of Great Temple (1487), 165-8, 197-8; assault on Teloloapan, 173-4; and colonisation, 175-6; drive to Pacific, 180; capture of Oaxaca, 181; assault on Tehuantepec, 182-4; his last campaign, 190-2; building of aqueduct, 192-6; achievement, 199-200, 218, 221; death (1502), 206, 207
Alahuiztla, 174, 175
Alvarado, Pedro: temple massacre, 172, 267-8; subjection of Tototepec, 219; left in charge of Tenochtitlan, 263, 267-8; siege of Tenochtitlan, 274, 276, 277, 278
Amecameca, 89, 121
Anahuac, 12, 333
Atonal, 100, 101, 102
Atotonilco, 98
Atotoztli, 41
Audience, First and Second, 289
Augustinians, 287

Axayácatl: elected *tlatoani* (1468), 125-7; first major campaign (1470), 128; campaign against Tlatelolco, 129-31; attack on Toluca, 140-1; attack on Huaxtecs, 146, 164; campaign against Tarascans, 146-8; death, 148, 149, 151; provides wife for Nezahualpilli, 177
Ayotlan, 135
Azcapotzalco, 23, 40, 41, 44, 45, 49, 52, 57, 64, 69, 72, 73, 76-7, 84
Aztatlan, 6
Aztec Empire: use of term 'Aztec', xiii, 7, 82, 294; Triple Alliance (Mexica, Texcocans, Tacubans), 67, 71, 80, 82, 85, 88, 90, 102, 108-16, 127, 131, 150; Itzcóatl's attack on Coyoacan, 83-4; and Xochimilco, 84; and Cuitláhuac, 84-5; Cuernavaca reconquered, 85; Moctezuma I's campaign against Chalca, 88-91; famine, 91-4, 99; floods, 91-2; children sold for maize, 93; collapse of Empire, 94, 99; New Fire (1455), 94-6; continuing hostilities against Puebla-Tlaxcala Valley, 96-8, 225-32; Wars of Flowers, 96-8; human sacrifice, 96-8, 101, 106, 142, 166, 168-73, 218, 246; Empire begins to expand, 98-107; campaign against Coixtlahuaca, 100-1; and Orizaba, 102; tax-gatherers, 103, 237, 241, 244; campaign against Huaxtecs, 104-6; and Tepeaca, 107; organisation of Empire, 108-16; priests, 119-20, 194, 246; final campaign against Chalco, 120-2; plot against Nezahualpilli foiled, 126-7; Axayácatl's campaign against Cotaxtla, 128; dispute between Tenochtitlan and

355